The Pebble

S. Robertson

Order this book online at www.trafford.com
or email orders@trafford.com

Most Trafford titles are also available at major online book retailers.

Edited by: Bill Robertson.
Cover Design/Artwork by: Martin Waugh.
www.liquidsculpture.com

Print information available on the last page.

ISBN: 978-1-4251-8264-9 (sc)
ISBN: 978-1-4269-9165-3 (e)

Trafford rev. 11/20/2021

www.trafford.com

North America & international
toll-free: 844-688-6899 (USA & Canada)
fax: 812 355 4082

Table of Contents

Dedication

This book is dedicated to my grandmother, Bridget Ellen (Curran) O'Neill and my father, Raymond Francis Stull

---

Prologue

On a cool spring morning as the sun danced on the crisp snow, an elderly woman, dressed in a black woolen coat, stylish felt hat and rose silk scarf, stood quietly looking into the tranquil water beneath the wooden bridge. A small child stood at her side. The young girl was dressed in a matching red woolen coat, leggings and hat, with a delicate white, rabbit fur trim on her hat matching her white muff where her red-mitten hands rested. The first warm Spring sun had triggered the breakup of ice under the bridge, the black water peeked through to welcome the change of season.

Gently the elderly woman took a small white pebble from her coat pocket and dropped it into the open water. Turning, she asked the young girl , "Child, do you see the hole the pebble has left in the water?"

The young girl stared at the water and replied with a somewhat puzzled look, "Nanny, there is no hole."

Ignoring the child's reply, she asked again. "Are you sure there is no hole?"

Wishing to please her grandmother, the child, frowning, took a second look and confirmed again, "There is no hole, Nanny."

" Child, remember this well. The size of the hole marks your importance in this world." The words stopped for a moment and then continued, "Life is a learning journey. It starts when you are born and ends when you die. The most important thing is to take care of the inside" pointing to the child's heart " not the outside. Do not get too attached to the world around you for it is a fleeting thing."

The meaning of her grandmother's words were beyond the grasp of a five year old. But knowing her grandmother's stories always had purpose, she tucked the story of the pebble into her memory. Little did she realize it would take decades before the wisdom of her grandmother's advice would be fully understood.

CHAPTER 1

A Victorian Beginning

O N a cradle-shaped island one cold November morn, as the nine o'clock church bells rang, a baby girl was born, the beginning of my journey. The small island in the Gulf of St. Lawrence on the eastern coast of Canada was called Abegweit (translated as "cradled in the Waves") by the First Nations people, Ile St. Jean by the French and Prince Edward Island by the British. The smallest province of Canada was referred to as the 'Cradle of Canada', not entirely because of its geographic shape but because in 1864 it was the birthplace of the Canadian nation. The importance of this miniature Island in nation-building was captured in the prophetic words of Thomas Heath Havilandon on this auspicious occasion: "I believe from all that I can learn that the Provinces will, ere long, be one country or nation, from the Pacific to the Atlantic. Never before was there such an important meeting as this held in the history of British America; and it may yet be said that here, in little Prince Edward Island, was that Union formed which produced one of the greatest nations on the face of God's earth ["]

Nearly eighty years later on November 6, 1943, the day of my arrival, the Canadian nation had existed for decades, having made its mark in the First World War. By the fall of 1943, a Second World War was in its final throws on foreign shores and the flutter of snow signaled the arrival of winter. I was the last of three children, the only girl; one brother was fourteen years older, the second, a year and a half. I would be christened Mary Eileen Stull.

In 1943, Charlottetown was still nestled in its fading Victorian quilt. Clydesdale horses delivered vegetables, coal, ice and milk and were occasionally used to pull the black funeral hearse. Ladies attired in beautiful dresses and hats with matching gloves sipped afternoon tea. Calling cards were still in evidence on silver trays in the entrance of many homes. An open farmers market formed an important element of the Queen Street Square in the city centre. Oil lamps stood in readiness for electrical shortages which occurred frequently in winter. Party telephone lines existed to the delight of those keeping up-to-date with city gossip. Cars, a luxury, were owned by few. Country life had changed little in decades. Outside the capital city and larger towns of the Island, red clay roads greeted travelers with a jelly-like surface in spring and a dust bowl in the summer. While trains and buses were becoming the transportation of choice, horse drawn wagons were still in evidence on many town streets. Regular attendance at the various Christian churches was expected on Sundays with clear boundaries between the Roman Catholic and Protestant denominations. For all of its Victorian trappings and appearances of tranquility, Prince Edward Island by the 1940s had weathered many changes from its nineteenth century independent status with its own Governor. Prince Edward Island had been reluctant to join the new confederation because: "The Island in the 1850's and 1860's enjoyed a high degree of economic self-sufficiency. The finances of the province were satisfactory, since revenue usually exceeded expenditure, and public debt was little more than the revenue of a single year. Shipbuilding was an important and lucrative business. The products of the Island's staple industries, agriculture and fishing, were readily sold in Europe, the West Indies, and especially in the United States where the Reciprocity Treaty of 1854 had opened up a steady market [2]"

The people of the Island were partly cajoled and partly forced into the Canadian Confederation, and such hesitancy would prove to be warranted. Over the decades the citizens patiently endured a national policy which favoured other provinces and enticed their children away. Joining the Canadian Confederation brought marked social, and economic changes to the Island. The lucrative trade of former years had withered, the crowded harbour of two, three and four-masted sailing boats, described by my grandmother, had disappeared. Economic trade shifted from a north-south pattern to an east-west route, favouring Upper (Ontario) and Lower (Quebec) Canada, eventually leaving the Island as one of the 'have-not' provinces of the country. The economic slump forced Islanders who did not favour Confederation to return to Britain, or emigrate to New Zealand or Australia. In later years, many sons and daughters had to leave for jobs primarily available in Ontario and Quebec. The population was further diminished by the first World War when the Island sent a higher percentage of volunteers than all other provinces to fight under the British flag. The heavy loss of life resulted in vacated farms and/or men unable to manage their farms due to chronic respiratory diseases from lethal gas used in the war. The Depression years pushed many Island families into pooling their resources resulting in homes of multi-generational families. Then came the second World War with more men, perhaps in less numbers than in the first World War, leaving their Island families to cope with food and other forms of rationing. This was the environment of my arrival.

My first home, a gray, wooden, three-story, plain, duplex house on Dorchester Street, built as rental property in 1870 by Owen Connolly [3] was located between Great George Street and Queen Street in the center of Charlottetown. It was centrally located being across the street from the Gothic, St. Dunstan's Roman Catholic Basilica, down the street from the Bishop's residence, a block from the city market and Province House, walking distance to all downtown stores, near the city wharf and train and bus transportation systems. The Coyle's lived on the other side of the duplex and the Murphy's in an adjacent tenement house. It was a perfect location in an era of few cars, everyone could walk to all essential stores and travel connections.

My ancestors on both sides of the family came to Canada by way of the United States. My father's people (Stulls, Secords) immigrated to the United States from Germany and France, in the nineteenth and seventeenth century respectively. My mother's people (O'Neills, Currans) immigrated to the United States from Ireland in the nineteenth century, one branch from the south and the other from the north. At the time of my arrival, my maternal family were Islanders while my paternal family mainly resided in Ontario, giving my father the distinction of being referred to as an 'Upper Canadian'. In the days before easy air travel, relatives in the central part of Canada lived a long distance from the Maritimes. Having a father from Upper Canada was unusual on an Island where marriages were mainly between Island families, and the generations well known.

Such generational information even turned up in introductions, with women usually identified through the male members of the family. For example, if my mother was being introduced, she might be described as 'Mary O'Neill, the daughter of John O'Neill and the grand-daughter of John Philpot Curran', with or without the resident location of each relative. Marriage would add the extra dimension of 'the wife of ….. This form of introduction lingered well into the late twentieth century.

My early home was a predominantly Irish environment, with the matriarchal head of the family being my grandmother, Bridget Ellen (Curran) O'Neill who I called 'Nanny'. My grandmother was born on January 1, 1873 near Peakes Station and baptized at St. Theresa's Roman Catholic Church. She was the youngest girl of twelve children born to John Philpot Curran and Catherine Cuddy (or Coady). A number of her siblings must have died early in life as my grandmother only spoke of two sisters and one brother. Her two older sisters, Margaret (called 'Maggie') and Elizabeth (called 'Nellie'), left the Island in their youth to work in Boston. Nellie later moved to California. In Boston, Maggie married a McCleary and had two sons. One of her sons, Joseph (called 'Joe') McCleary and his wife Gladys often visited the Island in the 1950s. Joe McCleary had his own private investigating business in Boston, following years of being a Boston policeman. Nellie married in California and occasionally sent huge boxes of used female clothing which injected a fashionable addition to our wardrobes. Nanny's younger brother, John Thomas (called 'Johnnie'), remained at Peakes Station and never married. Periodically, Johnnie would come into town by train to spend the day with his sister filling her in on all the country news. On such visits, he wore the same dark suit and smoked the most foul-smelling pipe tobacco. By the ancient art of dousing, a skill he shared with my grandmother, he located and built wells for farmers in the Georgetown area. For a man that traveled little, in his sixties he took his fiddle, boarded the Charlottetown train and traveled to California to visit his sister Nellie. The family was certain he would never return, but months later he arrived home stating that everyone in California were 'crazy' and returned to his quiet life at Peakes Station where he passed away in his seventies.

According to the family, my grandmother's parents, John Philpot Curran (born 1830) and Catherine Coady (born 1833) were both immigrants to the Island; her father from Cork, Ireland and her mother from Philadelphia, having previously immigrated to the United States from Ireland. There is far more information on my great-grandfather than my great-grandmother. John Philpot Curran was the grandson of the renowned Irish statesman of the same name.

The elder statesman, John Philpot Curran (1750-1817) was born in Newmarket, County Cork, to James Curran, a seneschal to the manor-court, and Sarah Philpot, described as 'a woman of gentle blood', well known for her sharp wit, which John inherited. Edward MacLysaght commenting on the Irish Family name 'Curran' states: "The outstanding historical personage of the name, John Philpot Curran, orator and patriot, needs no description. He was born in Co. Cork. His daughter Sarah Curran (1781-1808), a romantic and tragic figure, was engaged to be married to Robert Emmet [4]. Further information on the elder Curran can be found in the encyclopedia which states: "He studied at Trinity College, Dublin and at the Middle Temple, London, and in 1775 was admitted to the Irish Bar. In 1783 he entered the Irish Parliament, where he joined the opposition. When the government instituted its bloody series of prosecutions against the leaders of the Irish insurrection of 1798, he appeared for the prisoners, such as Wolf Tone, in nearly every case, and conducted the defense with extraordinary boldness and ability. From 1806 to 1814 he was Master of the Rolls in Ireland with a seat in the Privy Council. He retired to London where he became one of the most brilliant members of the society which included Richard Brinsley Sheridan, Thomas Erskine, Lord Byron, Thomas Moore and William Godwin. He died at his home in Brompton on the fourteenth of October 1817 ". Another reference speaks of his character: "In his parliamentary career Curran was throughout sincere and consistent. Though not a Roman Catholic himself, he spoke vigorously on behalf of Catholic emancipation, and strenuously attacked the ministerial bribery which prevailed.....His fame rests most of all upon his speeches on behalf of the accused in the state trials that were so numerous between 1794 and 1803....." In light of the turbulent times it was not surprising that he fought five duels during his career. Although there are many sayings attributed to Curran, the following two best depict his personality:

Assassinate me you may; intimidate me you cannot.

It is the common fate of the indolent to see their rights become a prey to the active. The condition upon which God hath given liberty to man is eternal vigilance; which condition if he break, servitude is at once the consequence of his crime and the punishment of his guilt.

His Catholic sympathies earned him the nickname 'The Little Jesuit of St. Omers'. The Priory-Rathfarnham' in Newmarket was his home for twenty-seven years, the Priory name taken from 'The Monks of the Screw'- a Reform Club of which Curran was Prior. The Barrister Charles Phillips recalled: "Ostentation was a stranger to his house, so was formality of any kind ....His habits were peculiar, some of them perhaps, eccentric."

John Philpot Curran married Sarah Creagh (1755-1844), his cousin in 1774, who was the daughter of Richard Creagh, a county Cork physician. They had a number of children.

In 1842, his remains were taken from London to Dublin where a white marble bust was erected at the National Cathedral and Collegiate Church of St. Patrick and an eight foot high classical style sarcophagus, a veritable tomb, in Glasnevin Cemetery. One of his sons, W.H. Curran, wrote a book about his father called the 'Life of Curran' (1819). Two other books also exist called 'Curran and his Contemporaries (1818) by Charles Phillips and Curran's Speeches (1806). The records show that John Philpot Curran was a well-respected statesman and orator of Ireland.

Lawyers ran in the Curran family, it was said that there were three generations who entered the legal profession, the elder statesman, John Philpot Curran, one of his sons and his grandson, my great-grandfather, who was educated in Dublin and Paris. In his youth my great-grandfather somehow ran afoul of the British government and had to escape to North America. He first traveled to Philadelphia, and eventually moved on to Prince Edward Island in the mid-1800s, hoping his acquaintance with the Governor would smooth the way for his return home. His plans were dashed when a relative from Ireland, an uncle, arrived with money and word from his family that he could never return to his homeland. With all his education he would spend the rest of his life in the rural part of the Island helping farmers with their legal problems and bringing up his family.

The Island land archives shows seventy-five acres of property listed in 1861 (Lot #49 bordering on Lot #66) to J.P. Curran. One set of directions in accessing the property was 'Gauls road back of Lake Verde. To get there take Georgetown Road through Vernon River'. The property was on Brothers Road, about one mile from Peakes Station. The Georgetown area was popular in the nineteenth century as, due to its deep harbour, it was initially considered the ideal location for the Island capital. This did not happen as in time Charlottetown became the preferred site. Considering his background, my great-grandfather's knowledge of farming was likely limited but his love of books and learning would filter on to the next generations.

While the Curran's in Ireland belonged to the Church of Ireland (Anglican), my grandmother was brought up as a Roman Catholic and the records show that all the Curran children were baptized in the Catholic church. This factor may, or may not, have contributed to my grandmother's children later choosing partners from other denominations than Roman Catholic. John P. Curran died on August 10, 1906 at the age of seventy-five and was buried in the St. Cuthbert's Cemetery in St. Teresa's.

Little is known of my great-grandmother, Catherine, except a brief vignette from my mother of a well-dressed lady with lace sleeves sitting in a carriage on a rare Charlottetown visit when my mother was a little girl. There were few stories of my grandmother visiting her family home in the country and she never spoke of her mother. In the 1950s, Joe McCleary reported that he found an old Philadelphian land deed in Catherine's name, the large city block of property having been sold for non-payment of taxes. No one knew if Catherine ever had a deed to such property and even if she did, likely she never expected to return to the United States. Catherine died May 31, 1915 at eighty-three and was buried at the same cemetery as her husband.

For whatever reason, my grandmother was older than most Island women when she decided to marry. On September 11, 1900 my grandmother, then twenty-seven years of age, married, John O'Neill, a thirty-six year old train engineer from County Tyrone in Ireland. Edward MacLysaght has the following to say of the O'Neill's: "The O'Neills were the chief family of the Cinel Eighan, their territory being Tir Eoghan. Tir Eoghan (modern Tyrone) in early times comprised not only that county but most of Derry and part of Donegal. Down to the time of Brian Boru, who reigned from 1002 to 1014, the Ui Neill, i.e. descendants of Niall of the Nine Hostages, were, almost without interruption, High Kings of Ireland. The Tyrone Branch is one of the main branches of the O'Neill's. A great many were kings of Ulster and sixteen were Monarchs of Ireland. Among the many fortresses, the famous Grianan Aileach fort on the summit of Greenen Hill on the Innishowen Peninsula was one of their principle residences. The chief seat of the O'Neills of Tyrone was at Tullaghoe Palace in the Parish of Descertereight in the Barony of Dungannon. The head of the O'Neills was always titled 'The O'Neill'. O'Neill's can be found in Europe, America, Canada, Australia and New Zealand. [5]" This distinguished family history was rarely mentioned in our home, likely because we were generations removed from such lofty heights.

    John O'Neill, my grandfather, was born on January 5, 1864 and became a train engineer in Ireland. Prior to arriving in Canada, he had immigrated to the United States with a wife and three sons, traveling to Vermont, where his sister lived. Either on route or shortly after arriving in the United States, his wife died. As my grandfather searched for work in North America he discovered a new train service was about to begin in Prince Edward Island, one of the perks to entice the Islanders into Confederation. When my grandfather traveled north to accept the engineering job he decided to leave his three grown sons with his sister in the United States. His photograph, now fading with time, shows a tall (the family stated he was over six foot), heavy-set man with a large mustache. In 1929 he was President of the Island Benevolent Irish Society, my grandmother saving his top hat, sash and Irish harp and other insignia in her wooden trunk. There was little discussion of my grandfather except a few snippets noted in conversations. His sons spoke of a gentle man who loved poetry and rapidly read their college textbooks expecting an immediate discussion. He also tended to spoil his only blond child, my mother. His mother's family name was Cusack, a Norman name introduced to Ireland in 1172. The records state the name itself is derived from a place in Guienne, in France, and was first anglicized as de Cussac. and rendered de Ciomhsog in Irish [6] . According to the family my grandfather O'Neill died on May 23, 1934, at home, of a bleeding gastric ulcer. He would leave a legacy of nine sons and three daughters; three sons remaining in the New England area of the United States.

    My grandmother, who lived with us on Dorchester street, was seventy years old when I arrived. She had had a full life prior to my arrival. Irrespective of her late marriage, she produced nine children, six boys and three girls, one son, Patrick, dying at birth. All her children were born in Charlottetown. By 1943 my grandfather, John O'Neill, had been dead for some years in addition to one daughter, Eileen.

    In her marriage photograph my grandmother appears as a mature, slim woman with dainty, leather-gloved hands. In her youth she attended a one-room country school house, her education being augmented by her father at home. In her seventies, she was a strongly built woman of five feet eight inches, with a square jaw, intense, blue/gray eyes and dark-brown hair, slightly graying at the temples. Daily she brushed her hair and formed it into two long braids which she wrapped in a circular crown on the top of her head. Her formidable personality would not only govern our home in the 1940s and 1950s but indelibly mark my soul as I spent a great deal of my youth in her presence. She brought a wealth of knowledge and skills to guide the family.

For many years prior to my birth and well into her seventies, my grandmother served as a midwife to many Charlottetown women. In that era, births were mainly at home, the family getting the assistance of a trained midwife to be with the mother days before and after the delivery. My grandmother worked with a local doctor who would call her on an 'as needed' basis. As a young girl I remember her leaving home with a stack of linen knowing she would be gone for days. She lived with the family cooking the meals, cleaning the house, caring for any other children and eventually assisting in the delivery of the baby. For this she received some compensation, but likely insufficient in light of the responsibilities. With large families and women sometimes dying in childbirth this was not an easy task. My Grandmother's view on women having too many children was well known. This was tested one Sunday morning when a priest at St. Dunstan's Basilica started demanding women have more babies. Furious, my grandmother stomped out of church arriving home unexpectedly early from Mass. As she stepped into the living room to greet my father and me, she snapped "How dare this man ask women to have more babies. When priests start having babies then I may listen to such foolishness!"

In addition to her midwife skills she also knew the art of using herbs in cooking and in making herbal remedies for a variety of illnesses. Goose grease and mustard poultices were the standard therapy for chest colds while potato and other poultices were used to draw out infections. Cough medicines, mainly of honey, herbs and occasionally some liquor were winter standbys. Teas were available for a variety of conditions. In the years prior to a national health system, hospitalization was expensive and families avoided such services except for surgery or, in some cases to die. Most individuals died at home being cared for by their families. Without funeral homes, the home was also the site of the funeral wake, a large dark wreath with a purple ribbon on the front door announcing the death of a family member.

Thriftiness was essential to survival in an environment of war rationing and limited funds. Like many early settlers of the nineteenth century, ideas to extend every penny came easily to my grandmother. She had the skills to make soap, candles, braided carpets, patchwork quilts, and many knitted items, obtaining the heavy gray wool at the Queen Street woolen mill. My earliest memory was with my arms high in the air while my Grandmother coiled the wool into balls. She would knit multiple, identical socks and mitts to replace worn or lost items during the winter. Even though young children had a woolen string between their mitts to prevent loss, mitts still went missing especially in the spring.

Dreams, ghosts, the banshees, little people and 'second-sight' were accepted concepts in our home. Interpreting dreams and foreseeing the future came as second nature to my grandmother, who lived comfortably in the visible and invisible worlds. Each dream had a message, and repeated dreams were critical warnings. Following a dream, Nanny, in a matter-of-fact tone would inform the family of some future event as if she were reading from some invisible script. Visitors would come to our home seeking her advice with regard to a dream or some other strange occurrence. But such ideas were frowned upon by the Catholic Church. A confrontation occurred one day when a newly appointed priest to the Island tried to point out to my grandmother the pagan nature of such thinking. Before he had time to finish his tea, my grandmother fetched his coat and hat and ushered him abruptly out the door with a parting shot; " I'll have you know young man, that the Celts were Christians long before the Romans" and slammed the door. Needless to say, he never came back. One of her sons, a Jesuit priest, would later comment that 'it would take a brave soul indeed to confront my mother on her spiritual beliefs, perhaps it's a matter best left to her and God.' While her church attendance was meticulous, she resented being manipulated or forced down any path she did not agree with. Her belief in God seemed fathomless, but her tolerance of bureaucratic church rules had its limits. She was likely spared any serious rebuke by the church because she had two sons who became Roman Catholic priests. While my grandmother held a dominant position in our family, my immediate family unit consisted of my father, mother and two brothers.

My father, Raymond Francis Stull, (I called 'Papa' and everyone else ' Ray'), was thirty-three years old when I was born. His life would entail a number of sporting accomplishments (hockey, softball, and golf) and expertise in public and industrial transportation systems. His ancestors, originally from Germany and France, had eventually immigrated to Canada from the United States. The Stull name (variations being Stolle, Stoll, Stol, Stoller, Stole, Stolhe, Stuhl and Stahl) was first found in Switzerland, in the canton of Zurich, where the name was closely identified in early medieval times with the feudal society. The name can be found mainly in Germany and throughout the United States. My father's recollection was that the Stulls came from East Friesland, Germany and immigrated to the United States sometime in the nineteenth century. It was rumored his family's arrival in Canada was accidental. In buying farm property, thought to be in the United States, one brother discovered he was in southern Ontario when the border was clarified at the time of the First World War.

Papa was born on May 13, 1910 in St. Catherine's, Ontario, the eldest of five children; four boys and a girl. His father, John Francis Stull (1889-1922) came from Ontario, and his mother, Florence E. Secord (1889-1982), from Medina, New York State. In 1909 John and Florence were married in the town of Niagara-on-the-Lake. His father worked at various jobs as a taxi driver and as a steelworker on the Welland Canal. From the little information provided, it seemed that the Stull family had interests in both steel work and orchards, a very different background from most Maritimers. In his late thirties, John was killed in a car accident, an event which would stimulate an abiding interest in transportation safety in his oldest son. The accident left my father, then a teenager, as head of the family.

Papa's grandfather, Alfred E. Stull (1851-1915), married Sara Ann Fuller (1851-1939) in 1875. Alfred came from a family of three girls (Helen Pricella, Mary Margaret and Eliza Alberta) and six sons (Frederick, Murray, Welland, James Franklin, Howard and Alfred). Sara was from Wales. Alfred and Sara had three girls (Catherine Eliza, Florence Elizabeth and Eva Pricilla) and one son, my grandfather, John Francis. A single faded photograph of Alfred shows a somewhat weary, heavy set man with a handle-bar mustache sitting on the back of a buckboard. His farm existed in Homer, in the Grantham Township of the Niagara region of Ontario. Family members stated that Papa was much like his grandfather, Alfred. Papa's only comment on my great-grandmother Sara was that she taught him to ride a horse like the stunt riders in the circus, she was involved in the underground railway helping Blacks escape slavery in the United States and, in her later years, although partially blind, could be found high up in a tree trimming branches. A very determined lady according to Papa. Information was more plentiful on the Secords, his mother's people.

The Secord name (variations being Sicard, Seacord and Secor) is a very old name, and is evident as far back as the fifth century in Languedoc, southern France. The name is derived from Sighard. Most of the Sicards/Secords in North America are descended from the same patriarch- Ambrose Sicard (1622-1712). Ambrose was born in Mornac France, near Marennes, south of La Rochelle. He was a "saunier' (i.e. a salt worker or salt farmer). Records indicate that in 1681 he, his wife, Jane Perron, and six children fled their home in France because of the religious persecutions of Huguenots (French Protestants) by the Roman Catholic church. At that time, Ambrose and his family joined thousands of Huguenots who left France following the revocation by Louis XIV of the Edict of Nantes, which had protected them from religious persecutions. He left vineyards valued at forty livres. He sailed, it is said, in his own ship, to the Westchester County area, north of 'Nouvelle' York in United States arriving with no wife and five children. His wife and the sixth child may have died enroute or perhaps the original French listing of six children was an error. Ambrose was one of the founders of New Rochelle, New York, and is honoured by a Huguenot monument in that community. He purchased one hundred and nine acres of land in 1696 and the census shows him without a wife at sixty-seven years of age. He died at seventy. The Huguenots new home was named after La Rochelle, the French port from which they departed for North America. A monument in the Hudson Park commemorates all the names of these early Huguenot settlers.

My grandmother Secord's parents were Theodore O. Secord (1850- ?) who married Elizabeth Captolia LaFrau. Both the Captolia and LaFrau names are common to New York County. Theodore and Elizabeth had seven children; four boys [Marvin, Walter, Leroy (called 'Roy'), Lloyd] and three girls [Cora, Florence (my grandmother) and Della]. Theodore worked on the first Welland Canal and died in his sixties from kidney failure. Elizabeth also died in her sixties of liver cancer. The Secord family could trace their linage all the way back to Solomon Secord (1755-1799), a son of James (Jacque) Secord (1631-

1701), who was one of Ambrose Sicard's sons. As the years passed, Secord families could be found on both sides of the Canadian/United States border in the Niagara region.

Laura Secord, a well-known Canadian heroine, is also a descendent of Ambrose Sicard, her linage originating from another son of James, also called James (1773-1841) who married Elizabeth Laura Ingersoll . James and Elizabeth were a wealthy Massachusetts family. In 1775 their daughter, Laura Ingersoll Secord, was born. The family's financial situation declined following the American Independence, so James Secord moved his family to Upper Canada (Southern Ontario) with the offer of cheap land. Laura married James Secord and by 1812 they had five children. The 1812-1814 war between Canada and the United States was fought in the lands occupied by many Secords. In 1813, after the battle for Queenston Heights, the Americans took over James's and Laura's home. While caring for her critically injured husband, Laura overheard the American plan to attack Beaver Dams. If the Americans had taken Beaver Dams they might have taken the entire Niagara region. Laura walked thirty-two miles through swamp, brush and farmland, risking death, to get word to the British forces. Lieutenant James Fitzgibbon was amazed at the thirty-eight year old woman's tenacity and later wrote: "The weather on the 22nd day of June 1813 was very hot and Mrs. Secord, whose person was slight and delicate, appeared to have been, and no doubt was, very much exhausted by the exertion she made in coming to me, and I have ever since held myself personally indebted to her for her conduct upon that occasion [7]" All but six of the American soldiers were captured and their attempt to control the Niagara Peninsula ended. In 1860, when Laura was eighty-five, the Prince of Wales, while visiting Canada, read of Laura's trek and sent her one hundred pounds, a rather small token for saving a country. Laura died in 1868 at the age of ninety-three and is buried in the Drummond Hill Cemetery.

Grandma (Secord) Stull was a petite woman of five feet, and in her youth was a skilled roller skater, proudly showing her size four, white skates to her grandchildren whenever they visited. It was said that she was more like her father, Theodore, than her mother, who was described as a big woman. When her husband died my grandmother got a bookkeeping job with the Canadian National Railway where she worked until she was sixty-five. In the days of few perks for working mothers my grandmother faced insurmountable challenges in trying to keep her family of five children together while she worked. The children ranged from my father in his teens to a two year old. Eventually, her brother, Roy Secord, arrived from the United States to help her. His arrival brought some relief to my father. My father spoke fondly of his Uncle Roy who often took him fishing.

Whatever religious denomination the Secords and Stulls followed prior to their arrival in Canada, they were mainly Anglicans by the early twentieth century. In his teens my father taught Sunday School at St. George's Anglican church in Homer. As an adult my father's church attendance was infrequent. In later years he would attend Christmas Midnight Mass in a Roman Catholic church on my request. Yet, I knew his belief in God was firm, his 'word was his bond' and he respected the spiritual belief of all people.

Released from his family responsibilities, and perhaps thinking one less mouth to feed would help his mother, in the late 1920s, as a teenager, Papa set out in an open Model-T Ford with three friends to see the east coast of Canada. One friend was Harry Richardson, who's son would later become the Chief of Police in Victoria, British Columbia. Papa often spoke with great enthusiasm of their eastern journey across Canada, of the dirt roads, limited overnight and garage facilities, ferry ride to Prince Edward Island and his first encounter with a lobster at the Borden Hotel.

Having worked with his father on the Welland Canal, he soon got a job with a company out of Amherst as a steelworker building the Charlottetown ice rink and the first oil tanks at Borden. When the 1929 economic crash hit, he was stranded with no money to return to Ontario. With few options, he leaped at an offer of being paid to be goalie for a newly formed, Maritime, semi-pro hockey league mainly funded by the fox fur industry, then a lucrative business on the Island. This invitation resulted from his prior hockey experience with the Maple Leaf farm league in St. Catherine's. Seeking new blood for the developing sports league, several out-of province players were taken on by the Abbies hockey team. Close friends would be Johnny Squarebriggs and Jack Kane, grandfather to Laurie Kane the golfer. Arrangements were made to pay the players during the winter while they found their own summer employment. Papa's summer endeavors were on the ferries and at a service station in Bordon. During the thirties he would play hockey for the Abbies in Prince Edward Island, the Glace Bay Miners, a team in Bridgewater in Nova Scotia and the Moncton Hawks in New Brunswick. Whenever he was away in the winter my mother stayed with her family in Charlottetown. During the thirties, hockey would provide my parents with a good lifestyle, much better than most, but this picture was fading by the time of my arrival.

Papa's earlier steelwork abilities also came in handy in the early 1940s when the radio tower outside Charlottetown snapped during a winter sleet storm, disconnecting Islanders from vital war news. On behalf of the community, Sterns Webster, later the Chief of Police in Charlottetown, came to recruit my father's help. When they arrived at the scene they discovered the tower's metal frame was encased in ice. Sterns would later describe a scene of ice-covered metal and driving sleet while he and my father attempted the climb to the broken segment of the tower. Using his prior steelwork abilities, Papa was able to reach the top and reconnect the broken segments.

By 1943, Papa was manager of a satellite SMT bus company in Prince Edward Island , the head office being in Moncton, New Brunswick. The Island's three buses would become a life line for transporting essential items to the farmers (i.e. feed, seed and farm parts) during the war. Items would be bundled on top of the bus as it headed up Island. For this service the farmers would pay my father in produce (i.e. a bag of vegetables). On one occasion a large live duck arrived in a huge box. The duck was stored in our clay cellar to await my grandmother's country skills and the eventual creation of a splendid family meal.

An earlier photograph of my father as a bus driver showed him with high leather boots and a dark uniform. The boots were needed because of the Island mud. The red dust in the summer imprinted a permanent pink dye into his underwear and shirts. Bus trips could often take days because of road conditions. On one of his trips Papa spotted a German U-Boat in a lonely bay off the Island. He reported the incident to the authorities and was asked to continue observing the coast on his bus trips.

My father had an athletic five feet, ten inches build, with dark curly hair, blue eyes and a rich, deep laugh that echoed through the house or across the warm summer breezes. He had a lifetime interest in sports; having played lacrosse, softball, baseball and hockey in his youth and later being a semi-pro hockey player and golfer. In his later years he would be chosen as a Pioneer of Softball for the Island. With his father's untimely death he had to leave school in grade ten. He was a resolute, somewhat stoic man, with strong principles of honesty, integrity and commitment to his family. His strength complemented my grandmother's approach to life and together they enabled me to survive through some very difficult segments of my youth.

My mother, Mary Elizabeth (O'Neill) Stull (I called 'Mother' and everyone else 'Mary') was thirty-four when I was born. She was the fifth child, and second girl, in a family of nine children. She was born on November 11, 1909 into a Roman Catholic family. She grew up to be a strikingly beautiful women of five feet, two inches, small featured with auburn hair. Her sharp wit became razor-edged when upset. She completed grade ten at St. Joseph's Convent, later part of Rochford Square School in Charlottetown. For a brief period before her marriage she worked as a secretary. This would be the only outside work she would engage in, as it was an era when few women worked outside the home after marriage. She married my father in September 1928 at the age of nineteen (my father was eighteen), having met him at a hockey game. Life was good in the early years of their marriage which supports the stories of a fun-loving woman who enjoyed the social world of parties, teas, card games and other get-togethers. She loved to dance and was regarded as one of the top 'flappers' of the twenties. Her fine figure was complimented by her keen sense of fashion. She loved to find the most elaborate hat to match her latest outfit. This sense of style was annually updated by her older sister, Helen, who arrived home from New York to spend her summers on the Island. My earliest memory of my mother was of a fashionable lady, beautifully dressed in matching dress, hat and gloves talking happily while putting on her gloves going out the door. In the multi-generational family setting, my mother gladly let my grandmother rule the kitchen although she was a good cook. Cleanliness was important, and mother took great pains to make sure her house had a full spring cleaning each year. Her sister arrived from the States with material to regularly change the living room chair covers and drapes. In the early days I remember wooden racks in the living room with lace curtains drying, the smell of jams and pickles in the autumn and the gaiety of people visiting our home. These earlier positive memories would be brief as circumstances would result in a slow deterioration of my mother's mental outlook on life from the early 1950s. But my relationship with my mother was never on sound footing.

I believe my mother and I got off on the wrong foot from our first greeting at my birth. She was not pleased with a third pregnancy, and this was further aggravated when she looked at an infant with white hair, not typical of her Irish forebears. At first she thought I was an albino until I opened my eyes to reveal blue eyes. This estrangement between a mother and child is not uncommon. She would not be the first mother who found it difficult to accept a child of another clan. Since I looked like my father's people, I was 'different' and that difference would lie between us for the rest of our lives. She preferred her sons. For this, and may be other reasons, I would spend most of my youth with my grandmother.

My oldest brother, William Raymond Stull (called 'Sonny') was fourteen years older than me. He was born January 3, 1929, a premie, in a Borden home in the midst of a raging snow storm without the benefit of any specialized neonatal equipment common in later decades. It was a miracle he survived. Although his arrival was traumatic, he would grow up to be a healthy, blond, blue-eyed boy, the only child for many years in a home of modest financial means and doting adults. One Christmas during the Depression, my brother received two bikes. He attended St. Dunstan's, Roman Catholic Boys School, located a block from our Dorchester home, completing grade ten. My oldest brother would regard the arrival of his siblings, especially his sister, as the fundamental cause of his reduced status in the family and the contributing factor to its economic downturn. Whatever happened to my brother, he would evolve from this earlier picture of a somewhat spoiled but likeable youth to an overweight, five-foot-ten male with a dislike of females and a bullying attitude to members of his own family. How he got on with those outside the family was never known by me as my objective in life was to stay clear of him which resulted is us walking very different paths.

My second brother, John David Stull (called 'David'), was born on April 12, 1941, a year and a half before my arrival. For the first three years of our lives everyone thought we were twins as my Aunt Di sent matching skirts and pants from New York for us to wear. This soon passed. David would eventually attend the same parochial Roman Catholic Boys School as my older brother until we left Charlottetown in the 1950s. As a young boy he also had blond curly hair and blue eyes, was very outgoing, and nursed a quick temper. While he too was not entirely pleased to have a sister, as young children we would play together with neighbourhood children in the Dorchester area. He would grow up to be a sturdy five foot six man with an outgoing personality. As the middle child David would not experience the same conditions as his older brother or younger sister. He would walk his own road, with his youth spent mainly in the company of other boys and outside activities.

The interrelationships with my grandmother and immediate family would evolve over the years. From my earliest memories, I knew my father and grandmother were there for me and for this I would be eternally grateful. A multi-generational house offered a number of options to support a child growing up, options which would be lost in the social changes in the decades ahead. Our home was also enhanced with the personalities of uncles and aunts, cousins and visitors. Four of my mother's siblings, one sister and three brothers, would be frequent visitors at our home. The following is a brief snapshot of the four.

Helen Dorothy (O'Neill) Walker (called 'Di'), my mother's oldest sister, was born in 1901, almost ten years before my mother. She graduated from the same convent school as my mother. Aunt Di was a slim, five foot six , attractive lady with jet-black hair and an ivory complexion. She always traveled with a case of creams and cosmetics. Being a gifted seamstress, she not only made her own clothes but also the handbag and hat to match. In the early years she worked in large hotels dealing with the linen, one being the Canadian National Hotel in Charlottetown, then a posh accommodation, and other similar hotels in Alberta and Quebec. By 1943 she was working in New York and would arrive home each summer with stacks of fabric and pictures of the latest fashions. The hum of the sewing machine was a summer tradition as she magically redid the living-room chair covers and drapes and whipped up the latest fashions for my mother and others in the family. In her late forties she enrolled in a Licensed Practical Nursing course in New York and led the class. Shifting direction, she became a companion to wealthy ladies in New York, one being Julius LeRosa's (the pop singer's) mother. Aunt Di married Neil Walker, a Presbyterian, who's family were also Islanders. Neil, like so many Islanders, went off to the first World War at fourteen, delivering messages by bicycle through no-man's land. Once he found himself well behind enemy lines. Getting injured he spent time in a hospital in Holland. Neil had an outgoing personality, loved horse racing and struggled with alcohol. This marriage between my aunt and uncle did not sit well with my Grandmother, not because of his religious affiliation, but because Neil had been divorced. In an Island community of the 1940s and 1950s divorce was greatly frowned upon. Yet, somehow the families managed to adapt. Because of Working Visa rules, my aunt and uncle returned to the Island each summer during their years in the United States. In retirement they had a home first in Murray River and later in Charlottetown. Even though Aunt Di had rheumatic heart disease as a child , she would live to her eighty-seventh year, dying in a Pugwash Nursing Home in 1988. Her husband died in 1969.

Richard Joseph O'Neill (called 'Father Dick'), the second oldest of my mother's brothers, was born on April 16, 1904. He was a Roman Catholic priest receiving his Commerce Degree at St. Dunstan's College and his Jesuit training in Montreal. At twenty-three he was sent as a missionary to a number of rural parishes in the Viking area of Alberta. There he would welcome many Polish immigrants who were coming to Canada after the war. His accounting skills were put to use balancing the financial records of a number of parishes and building a number of churches in Alberta, including his own, the Immaculate Conception Roman Catholic Church in Edmonton. In the 1950s his church was quite unique. It was round, containing a simple wooden altar with a golden backdrop cloth, hand-crafted by his Polish congregation. Every two to three years my uncle returned to the Island, by train, for four to five weeks to visit with his family. He was a heavy set, six foot man, with dark hair, a jovial personality, who loved reading and was prepared to discuss history, literature, poetry, politics and any other topic of interest. He not only read the entire works of Dante but was delighted to think anyone would be willing to discuss the theological ramifications of the material. Father Dick died of heart disease on October 14, 1958 at fifty-four.

Frank Gregory O'Neill (called 'Huck'), my mothers younger brother, was born on February 9, 1913. Uncle Huck went to St. Dunstan's Roman Catholic Boys School and between 1929-1931 was a member of the Abegweit Rugby Team when they became the Island Senior Champions. Uncle Huck was a dapper man of five feet ten with a thin mustache and an enchanting twinkle in his eyes. He initially apprenticed in a local bank and later moved to managing a fish-packing business in Charlottetown, shipping worldwide. His warmth, wisdom and generosity were treasured features of my youth. Loving the vaudeville musical world, my uncle would appear at a community concert, a bowler hat tipped on the back of his head, launching into a favourite Irish song. This love of entertaining people followed him into the Second World War which was noted in a Charlottetown Guardian article of September 6, 1945: "Mr. O'Neill is the son of the late John O'Neill and Mrs. O'Neill, ……... He left Charlottetown in 1941 and joined the Royal Rifles at Ottawa in October. He was in the Army for one year while at Charlottetown. Late in the fall of 1941 he went with the Royal Rifles to Hong Kong as entertainment supervisor of Knights of Columbus Huts and was taken prisoner by the Japanese in December." During his three years of internment Huck spent his time designing concerts, sports events and other activities to improve prison morale. At this time, my grandmother in dreams, announced the arrival of his first letter (with blackened censored sections) and later his return home on one of the first Canadian ships sent to pick up the Hong Kong prisoners. Both events occurred exactly as she described. Uncle Huck spoke little of his prison experience, returning to his fish packing business and continuing to trade with his Asian customers. His matter-of-fact statement being; "That was war, this is peace". But the malnutrition and stress of prison life took its toll, and he died on December 26, 1971 in his late fifties of a heart condition. Uncle Huck married Margaret Newsom (called 'Mudge"), of a prominent Presbyterian Island family. They would have four children (Carol, John, Phillip and Susan), the first girl dying at birth sometime before 1941. The family would spend the years moving between their Charlottetown residence and their cottage at York Point.

Charles Henry Shakespeare O'Neill (called "Shake"), my mother's youngest brother, was born August 13, 1914. He also attended St. Dunstan's Roman Catholic Boys School graduating with the Governor General medal for mathematics. Uncle Shake seemed to wander through life. While he had a superb mathematical brain that worked faster than an electric calculator, he had little interest in life, in his appearance or much else. He enjoyed reading but I rarely heard him discussing anything he ever read. During the second World War, while in the military, he managed to get himself declared unfit for combat duty which did not endear him to his brother Huck. The situation was compounded when

Shake ended up with a veterans pension after the war and Huck spent the rest of his life, along with other Hong Kong veterans, trying to get a pension. Shake would spend his final years as a night clerk in a Halifax hotel. My uncle drifted in and out of family gatherings, appearing to enjoy the company but seeming unable or unwilling to contribute much to the event. He would die in a rundown boarding house in Halifax on July 1, 1972 in his late fifties of heart disease.

While the above four siblings of my mother's were an essential part of our family in the 1940s and 1950s, some living locally and others traveling from some distance, there were three who I knew only by name.

James Rupert O'Neill was born on April 19, 1901, Rupert was also a Roman Catholic priest, completing his Commerce Degree at St. Dunstan's College and his Jesuit training in Montreal. As a young priest he was sent to Winnipeg, Manitoba, where he ministered to a French community speaking fluent French. He and his brother Richard were close friends and frequently conferred with each other by telephone. Acquaintances described a man who could concentrate on his books in a room full of men talking, and a priest who knew the fine points of theology. He was a tall, quiet individual with an abiding delight in books. He died November 6, 1947 of a brain aneurysm, his brother Richard escorting his body home to the Island for burial. His funeral wake was held in the living room of our Dorchester Street home.

Fred O'Neill (born 1908?), was just older than my mother, like his brothers attended St. Dunstan's Roman Catholic Boys School in Charlottetown. During the Depression when jobs were scarce he joined a group of young men heading west for the 'harvest'. When the harvest ended Fred found odd jobs in the forestry industry; first in Fanny Bay, Vancouver Island and later in Burnaby, British Columbia. At some time he was badly injured, possibly breaking both his legs, in a forestry accident and spent some time in hospital. His brothers Richard and Rupert kept in touch by telephone, but to my knowledge he rarely wrote to his Island family. He eventually became an accountant with one of the forestry companies, married and settled in British Columbia. He had no children and never returned to the Island.

Margaret Eileen O'Neill (called 'Sally'), the youngest of my mother's sisters, was born November 17, 1916. I would have her middle name and, in time, would also be called 'Sally'. She received her registered nurse's training at the Charlottetown Hospital, working for a brief period at the Tuberculosis Hospital after graduating. She lived at Dorchester Street prior to leaving for the west. She traveled by train to Alberta to be with her brother Richard. Shortly after her arrival, she had a diving accident which left her partially paralyzed. After months in a wheelchair, she died of complications at the Banff Rehabilitation Hospital on February 11, 1941 in her twenty-fifth year. As I grew older, Father Dick stated that if he closed his eyes he could hear his sister's voice, but we were very different in appearance. Her nursing graduation photograph shows a beautiful woman with black hair and ivory skin.

My father had only one sibling, Uncle Ernie, living on the Island, the rest of his family were in Ontario. I would have less information on my paternal relatives.

Ernest Secord Stull was the second oldest sibling in my father's family. When he came to the Island is unclear, but by 1943 he had married Eunice Acorn, from a well-known Island family. They had three sons; Leonard, Frank and Robert Allen (called 'Bobbie'). The family stated that Ernie was a lot like his father, John. He was a quiet man of about five feet seven, a slight build and brown curly hair. In the war he was an airplane mechanic, and after the war he became a bus/car mechanic, the best on the Island, according to his brother. His hidden talent was being an artist. When I visited his home in my youth he had painted Disney cartoons and beautiful pastoral scenes on the walls of his home. They were enchanting. He remained very self-conscious of his artistic talents and, to my knowledge, never displayed his art outside the family. In the 1950s he would return to Ontario with his family.

While my grandmother and my core family were the main occupants of our Dorchester home, uncles and aunts either stayed for brief periods or were regular visitors. On rare occasions my father's relatives from Ontario visited, twice my grandmother Stull and once his sister and her family. At that time travel across Canada was a long, costly affair for many families. Our Boston relatives came more often and would stay for weeks. In addition, there were business, sports and/or other friends who would come and stay a day or even weeks, as the costly Canadian National Hotel was out of reach for most. The annual country fair in August always brought people to the city. Motels would not appear until the 1960s.

This was the world of my youth, a busy, boisterous multi-generational family setting. Being the youngest, I would experience minute threads of a fading Victorian era as the Island, like many Canadians, became enchanted with the awakening North American culture on its doorstep.

My first home was filled with rhythmic chatter and laughter, of lively conversations and dinner numbers of ten of more, a setting in which a small child could easily get lost. My early years were somewhat uneventful. My grandmother tended my baby carriage under the shade of a large maple tree in the small backyard, making sure my brother David did not tip my carriage. At ten months, I pulled myself up and hit him on the nose with my rattle to stop him shaking the carriage, thus, according to my grandmother, making a fine declaration of independence for a girl.

As a child I answered to several names. My grandmother usually called me 'Child', my brother David called me 'Baw', Papa occasionally called me 'Bridget' and the rest of the family called me 'Mary'. By three, I remember my grandmother entering my bedroom in the morning singing "Lazy Mary will you get up, will you get up." My immediate reply was always 'no' as I pulled back my bedding and landed on the floor. My negative reply was not only an extension of the negative twos, I had adopted this method to make adults repeat what they were saying. As a result, Nanny kept referring to me as a 'Little Miss, No'. From the earliest age I found the conversation of adults confusing. On occasion, I found my grandmother clapping her hands behind me (i.e. thinking I was deaf) and looking concerned. Mother, who spoke quickly, found my difficulty in understanding words a sign of stubbornness. When I failed to comprehend what she saying, she would angrily grab me by the collar and march me off to my grandmother stating; "You deal with her, she is just being difficult". Nanny, staring right into my face, would slowly repeat the instructions. Once understood, I scampered off to do what was asked. Perhaps because of these difficulties and being the youngest in a large family I became a lonely child with a tendency to wander. This was greatly enhanced when I discovered the ease of pushing open the front screen door, and taking off to 'my castle'. In the 1980s I would write the following fictional story of Katrin's Castle, which provides a picture of my early years on Dorchester Street..

The mid-afternoon sunlight fell across the bed of the sleeping child. She stretched, rubbed her eyes, and yawned. She listened to the murmur of voices coming from the kitchen below, identifying her grandmother's familiar accent happy in conversation with a cousin visiting from Boston. Afternoon-tea would be well underway, if she hurried she could have her favourite treat of hot biscuits, butter and molasses. Yet, she dreamily continued watching the sunlight dance across her bedroom and finally, rolled over to gaze out the upstairs window.

The street was deserted. Across the street nestled in the trees her majestic castle stood tall and stately.

Katrin's three year old impish appearance was crowned with a head of white-blond curls, accented with a pugged, freckled nose and blue eyes. At three, she had come to live with her grandparents in PEI, traveling from Boston when her mother died. She never remembered her father, but was told he had been killed in the war.

The castle's magic beckoned. At that very moment Katrin realized that her escape was possible as the adults were busy at the back of the house. Wiggling quickly to the side of the bed, throwing aside the quilt, she jumped to the floor. She was dressed except for her shoes which she left behind preferring the freedom of her bare feet. Sneakily, she eased herself down the winding stairs, struggled momentarily with the front door knob, and descended gleefully onto the warm pavement. From *there it was clear sailing around the wired fence to the front door of her castle.*

To Katrin's delight the heavy entrance door was ajar. She laboured ascending the steps but, momentarily she was inside. Crossing the lobby she pushed open the wooden door and entered the huge vaulted chamber. Skipping from one rainbow to the next, she meandered forward stopping to let her clothes bathe in the pinks, greens and blues created by the sunlight. The sad lady was always her first stop. She climbed the cool marble steps to get a closer look, hoping the sad lady might have a wee smile for her. But the lady was grieving over the wounded man who rested in her arms. Deep in thought, she wondered if he might die, when grandpa died Nanna, her grandmother, was sad for a very long time.

Returning to the entrance she visited her many silent friends, reserving her final farewell for the winged guardian on duty with the beautiful pink shell resting in her arms. With a glance over her shoulder, she pushed the wooden door, but it would not open. She tried again. The door gave way with such force that she bounced into the outer lobby, landing at the feet of a tall dark figure. Slowly, she raised her head following the long black gown until her eyes rested on the face of an elderly man with white hair and a small red cap on his head. His warm smile allayed her immediate fears as he began to speak to her.

"Well, well, well, look what the angels delivered. What's your name, little girl?" he said. Katrin, caught between curiosity and alarm, fumbled to answer his question.

"My name is Katrin and I live with my Nanna across the street," and breathlessly she continued, "and I am visiting "My castle". "Your castle?" the man responded somewhat surprised by the announcement. With increased courage Katrin elaborated, "Oh yes, this is my very own castle, I come often to check on my friends and watch the pretty people and listen to the music."

The man smiled gently, for this was a delightful revelation, and it would be unfair to shatter the child's dream; for her magic castle in reality belonged to the Roman Catholic Church and he was its Bishop. He was certain that St. Dunstan's never had a more diminutive worker. Intrigued to hear more of the story he inquired; "Katrin, would you be interested in learning more of your castle?"

Katrin could hardly believe her good fortune, here was someone that could give life to her silent friends. Her blue eyes danced as she answered, "Oh yes,.....could you come now and tell me about the sad lady".

There was a momentary hesitation as the Bishop tried to recall to which lady the child was referring. Not wanting any further delay, Katrin took his hand, pulling him into the vaulted chamber and towards the silent statue which stood near the front alter. "Oh, 'this' sad lady", said the Bishop; "I will be glad to tell you about her."

Katrin sat down on the marble step to listen attentively as the Bishop began; "The lady's name is Mary, and this is her son, Jesus. A long time ago in a city called Jerusalem…….." so the story went on.

This would be the beginning of many stories shared between the aging Bishop and the inquisitive child. The castle image would eventually evaporate for the child, but for those few years in the late 40s, the two spirits would meet and share the mystical beauty of an invisible world, unreachable to many people.

No matter how closely my grandmother guarded the entrances, I would find an opening and escape. My presence in 'my castle' often signaled by my brother's boats bobbing in the baptismal font. Special church events had me 'on the move'. On one such occasion, I dawdled up the center aisle in my sun suit, crawled up over the communion marble steps to tell my friend how much I liked his shiny clothes. He signaled a young nun to take me home to my grandmother. I was becoming a pint-sized problem.

Another reason for my trips to 'my castle' was to play with my imaginary friend. I described her to my grandmother as looking like me with white curly hair and a shiny dress. Nanny insisted on an introduction. On my next visit she accompanied me to meet my friend. Unruffled, she greeted my invisible friend and, settling into a nearby pew said "Child, you and your friend play while your grandmother sits here awhile". She patiently watched as her granddaughter danced in the sunlit colours created by the stain-glass windows. Soon, she announced it was time for our afternoon tea. Realizing her granddaughter needed a diversion, within days Nanny had me accompany her on trips to the market and walks to the park which was terribly exciting for a wee girl.

My first trip was to the local market, a block from our downtown home. Horse-drawn wagons and trucks were parked in rows with sales conducted directly from the side or back of each conveyance. Like a wee gnome, I followed Nanny, as she went from one vehicle to the next filling her wicker basket with vegetables, herbs or fruit. She would spend time arguing with each vendor for, in her view, a fair price. I could hear the men saying, "You are a hard lady, Mrs. O'Neill, we will make nothing this round if everyone was like you". In the end, I was granted the honour of carrying the large fish wrapped in newspaper. Proudly, I marched beside Nanny the short distance to our Dorchester home. Then I would watch her clean and stuff the fish with potato dressing, cover it with herbs and butter for baking in the oven. It was a royal meal which everyone enjoyed. For me I now had a place in the family with a special job.

My second adventure was to accompany Nanny on her regular 'constitutional' to

Victoria Park, on the south side of Brighton Road, facing the Charlottetown Harbour. This was quite a journey for a small girl but I improved with practice. My grandmother did most of the talking as I scrambled along beside her. In the winter the walking was more difficult. On these trips she expounded on a variety of topics. She spoke of the busy harbour of her youth, now silent, and the building of boats in the many Island bays, all gone. She felt that joining the rest of Canada had been a grave mistake. From her comments, I gathered it was a blessing to be on this special island as the rest of the world was somewhat uncivilized. While she admitted the Island once had pirates, they existed in some remote part, a place we would never visit. My world view would be written by a lady who was born in the nineteenth century, giving me a permanent turn-of-the-century outlook on life. Soon the topics shifted to more practical matters as I reached four.

A great sadness would come over Nanny as she talked of a lost heritage, something about 'landed gentry', and the lack of a proper 'dowry' for her only grand-daughter. This would follow with her pronouncement of who should be my future husband. Being an Island midwife and familiar with interfamily connections, she announced, "Well Child, there are three possible husbands, and none are worth waiting for. You will need to find an off-Island husband." I suppose time was running out, and she needed to get key messages indelibly implanted into her granddaughter, who found such discussions somewhat bewildering. As expected, once the marriage topic was finished she launched on about having children.

I can still hear her words echoing through time; "Child, women are not designed to just have babies" and pressing her finger on my forehead, "you have a fine brain, use it" and, stopping to catch her breath, she went on; "promise your grandmother you will do something with your brain". My response was always "yes' for I had little understanding why this was so important to her. Only in my adult years would this make sense. But the topics were not always solemn.

In and around these historic and personal lessons she intertwined tales of 'the Little People', the devil, and ghosts stories (i.e. ghost trains and ships), magic and an invisible world which she described as we walked. We talked and laughed and cherished this time together; her time running out and mine just beginning. It has often been said that children replace their grandparents, and perhaps Nanny and I shared a deep empathy of two familiar souls, in which the baton was being passed on in an ongoing chain of life. Through an invisible veil of time her words still echo "Child, are you listening ?" …..and mostly I was. My difficulties with words were never a problem with my grandmother. These occasions would leave me with a treasure of a unique Island history seasoned with her wisdom and view of life much far above a small child's comprehension.

As a further diversion Papa built a large sand box in the back yard where the neighbourhood children would gather each day to play. I now had other children to play with, including David, just older than me. We spent many enjoyable hours creating villages and roads. One day, my grandmother suddenly appeared, ordering the other children to go home immediately, roughly grabbing David and I and ushering us into the house. As the screen door snapped shut a loud crunching sound was heard at the back fence. Next the fence started to bend as male voices could be heard yelling orders. A bull had escaped from the freight yard and had been corralled on the other side of the fence just behind our sand-box. With a bit more force the bull would have crashed through on top of us children at play. My grandmother's ESP had saved us from danger.

While my visits to 'my castle' had lessened, the neighbourhood children now began weekly visits to the bishop's residence. Bishop Boyle would gather us in his office for a chat, placing me on the wide, wooden windowsill. At the end of our chat, the Bishop would give each child a nickel to go to Duffy's grocery store on Queen Street for an ice cream. One day, by the time he reached me, he had run out of nickels and handed me five pennies. Holding the pennies tightly in my hand, I refused to leave with the other children saying "You gave them the shiny money and gave me the dirty money." Nothing would convince me of the equal value of the coinage. So, much to Mr. Duffy's surprise, I entered the grocery store hand-and-hand with the Bishop and hesitantly deposited my five pennies on the counter which, to my delight, garnered me an ice cream cone. The Bishop walked me home, passing me over to my grandmother with the statement; "Mrs. O'Neill, your grand-daughter doesn't even believe the Bishop when it comes to money." My grandmother's only reply was ,"I see". When the door closed she smiled and patting me on the head said, "Well Child, you seem to be learning more then I thought."

Our playing days were short lived, as in the late forties, a Polio Epidemic hit the Island. Schools and all public gathering places were shut down as the community faced the impact of this crippling disease on their children. On both sides of our Dorchester home children were stricken with the disease, some with chest and others with limb paralysis. A quarantine marker was placed on the front door of all affected homes. While David and I came down with Polio symptoms the doctor was surprised there was no paralysis. As we were recovering, our father announced we would be moving to the other side of the city. While this was exciting news, we were sad to leave our friends.

My parents had purchased a two-storey home on Euston Street, at the top of Edward Street. Our new home had a large kitchen, connecting living and dining room, and central hall downstairs, and four bedrooms and a single bathroom upstairs. The bedroom at the top of the stairs was for Nanny, a large one for my two brothers, another large one for my parents, and my bedroom, at the back of the house, had a door opening onto a veranda. That summer, Aunt Di created a frilly pink-and-white Cinderella room. This home gave our family far more living space and room for a large vegetable garden. The back yard even had plum trees. Papa wasted no time in digging and planting a vegetable garden. When the garden was dug, I asked him if we could have a few flowers. Explaining the importance of vegetables over flowers, I accepted the inevitable. Thus, I was pleased when Papa arrived home days later with four small flower plants. For the first time I had a garden of my own, and was able to care for it with Nanny's help.

In the summer, with my verandah screen-door open, I could hear the sounds of night crickets and the morning birds. As my grandmother came to waken me in the morning

I would climb out of bed and go to the verandah door and state, "OK, I'm now up." and a carpet of starlings would fly away. Nanny's only comment was "Your feathered friends are awfully noisy". Dressing I replied; "Nanny, they keep me company until I get up. They try awfully hard to be quiet". She smiled and we headed downstairs to share a cup of tea (mine being mostly milk), porridge, toast and homemade jam while she quizzed me on my dreams. It would be some time before the rest of the house woke for the day.

One morning, this routine was abruptly interrupted when instead of standing upright I collapsed on the floor unable to move my legs. My grandmother helped me back into bed, calmed my fears, and raced to fetch warm sheets to wrap my legs. She did passive exercises for some time and then got me to stand again. This time I was all right and remained so for the rest of the day. The following morning, and for some weeks, the same pattern occurred. The doctor was called and consulted daily with my grandmother on my progress. He was certain this was a delayed polio reaction. After a month or so it was over but it left a degree of upper leg weakness for the rest of my life.

I was now five and knew I would be attending Notre Dame, Roman Catholic Girls Convent on Sydney Street in the fall. This was not the same convent school as my mother and her sisters. It was some distance from Euston Street but I knew other children would be taking the same route. I had walked long distances with my grandmother so the prospect wasn't a great concern. I was looking forward to going to school.

THOUGHTS AND/OR LEARNING:

Charlottetown in the forties offered a child immense freedom. Neighbours all knew and watched out for each other. Certainly there were the dangers of accident and bacterial illness but with care these could be avoided or ameliorated. Families respected the innocence of childhood by restricting what could or could not be said or done in front of them. One wonders what is happening to the souls of today's children who seem to be exposed to everything.

The benefits of a multi-generational family provided an array of baby-sitters, lots of people to share the ups and downs of life, and role models. As the multi-generational unit slips into history for many Canadians, it has resulted in greater isolation and stress on small family units. Since it is impossible to turn back the clock, perhaps somehow in the future we might be able to capture some of the benefits of this social structure to strengthen families.

My grandmother's wisdom and love would guide me through my youth and linger with me for life. It would take many years before I could truly appreciate the value of her gifts. Her practical ease in the visible world and acceptance of the invisible, would give me an appreciation of a world not always visible to my five senses. Love in our home was never demonstrative. The greatest sign of affection was a pat on the head and a squeeze on my shoulder. Yet, there was never any doubt of the love and protection of my grandmother and father. While my mother was always present, I would remain foreign to her, and my communication difficulties would further alienate the two of us.

Duty became an engrained part of my life, strengthened at an early age by having a role to play in the home. The little tasks my grandmother had the patience to create and guide me through were important. Ancient societies thought duty and discipline were important principles to instill at a very early age, an interesting dichotomy from today's practices. Not knowing my paternal family was more of a problem for me. Having different features than my Island relatives sometimes left me lost and lonely. This is not an unusual problem when relatives are geographically separated and when there is a mixing of cultures. My inheritance of Irish, English, Welsh, French, German and American cultures was different from most Island children, something that did not fully register until I started school.

CHAPTER 2

Early Challenges

Excited and apprehensive, dressed in a white and green pinafore dress with my hair in French braids, I set off for my first day at school. My brother, David, was to accompany me to the convent door, but reaching Hillsborough Square and seeing so many girls, he chickened out. From across the square he pointed in the direction of the door, and took off. Alone and frightened, I pressed on and soon found my classroom.

Notre Dame Convent School for girls, consisted of two red-brick buildings; one, two-story and an adjacent four-story building, located on Sydney Street across from Hillsborough Square. The top floor of the smaller building contained a beautiful chapel made from white conifer wood. The sunlight danced through the clear crystals in the chandeliers just like the stain-glass rainbows of my old castle. The school was inaugurated in 1857 by the Congregation of Notre-Dame from Montreal. In the early twentieth century, a school advertisement described the school as 'the site is one of quiet beauty, lofty trees enclose the spacious and tastefully laid out pleasure-grounds, invigorating breezes from the neighbouring Hillborough inspire both physical and mental activity, while the retired nature of the locality invites reflection and study' [1]. An appreciation of such amenities was far beyond the capabilities of a five-year old. The school had both day and boarding students, the boarding students coming mainly from the country. For me, my first grade presented a variety of exciting beginnings.

Of the fifteen grade-one girls, at least seven had the name of 'Mary', a common Roman Catholic girl's name. A number of girls even had similar second names. To resolve the dilemma, our teacher, a young nun, gave the majority of 'Marys' a new name. I was renamed 'Sally' because, according to her, I looked like Sally in our grade-one reading book, 'Sally, Dick and Jane'. Delighted, I arrived home for lunch to announce to my father, quietly reading the Guardian in our front porch, that I was now 'Sally'. Surprised, my father stated he was delighted as he wanted me to be christened "Sara' after his grandmother. The rest of the family seemed content with my name change as my Aunt Eileen had previously been called Sally, the reason never given. From that day, my unofficial name was 'Sally', while my legal name remained Mary Eileen.

Quickly the nuns had all students in uniform. Our school uniform consisted of a navy-blue a-line dress with a front zipper, and white plastic collar and cuffs. A sky-blue silk ribbon was tied in a bow beneath the white collar. Each year, Aunt Di made me new uniforms and kept me well supplied with lengths of blue ribbon for my uniform tie and braids. With the addition of a small navy beanie the uniform was complete. The beanie rested in our desks ready for any church or chapel activity, as church rules stipulated the female head had to be covered in a place of worship. I liked wearing a uniform because it reduced dress competition and simplified my wardrobe into school, play and special dress attire. With the dress code settled we turned to our studies and convent school priorities.

One of the biggest events in grade one was making my First Communion. Understanding the Confessional ritual was part of this experience, the whole concept of sin and penance being somewhat lost on five and six year olds. Weeks prior to our First Communion, on Friday mornings, grade one girls marched two-by-two from Sydney Street to St. Dunstan's Basilica to practice the Confession ritual. Having a suitable sin for these weekly trips became quite a challenge. So, to streamline the process, I devised what I thought was a rather neat solution. Each Friday morning I took three pennies, no more, from a wooden cigar box in the pantry where extra pennies were stored and, placed them in my coat pocket. In reaching the Confessional, I declared my sin and said three Hail Marys for penance. I had little understanding what 'penance' meant. After school I returned the three pennies. This system worked smoothly for several weeks until the priest, often the same one for children, confronted me.

"Are you the same girl with the same sin from last week?".

Innocently, I replied, "Yes, the nun wants us to have a sin every Friday and, I have a sin". He asked me to step out of the Confessional, cancelled my Hail Marys and proceeded to talk to the young nun. After that our weekly Confessional trips stopped and I was asked to cease being so creative in my religious observance.

Nanny when she heard the tale was shocked and tried her best to explain the whole idea of sin and the need for confession, a formidable task even for my grandmother. Without further incident I made my First Communion.

The next summer when Father Dick was on his Island vacation, having heard from his colleagues about his niece's inventiveness, he introduced a special tradition whereby we would have long walks to talk about many things, particularly my school activities. On our first walk, I informed him that; "I prefer to talk to God myself, I don't want nuns or priests". Alarmed, he inquired if I had ever made such comments at school. I assured him that I had not, as the nuns didn't like children talking in class. Relieved, he made me promise that any thoughts on God, religion, or convent school life should only be discussed with my grandmother or him. I promised, not fully understanding why it was so important. However, even at a young age I knew a promise was important, for both my father and grandmother spoke frequently of the sacredness of a person's word. Children were not exempt. Nevertheless, after that, my after-school discussions with my grandmother became more intense as she inquired about any unguarded comment on sensitive topics. My promise would hold until grade two when it was thoroughly tested.

Music, particularly piano lessons, started early in a convent school. In grade one these were simple musical selections which I enjoyed. Each springtime a music Examiner arrived from the Royal Conservatory of Music in Montreal to test all the students, even the youngest. In my first year of music, when the music Examiner was scheduled to arrive, I was in bed with the flu. Whatever the nun said to my mother on the telephone, I was bounced out of bed and dressed, Papa called to drive me to school, while my grandmother kept saying; "This is the height of foolishness, the Child is ill!". Nevertheless, I went.

Upon entering the examination room I informed the Examiner that I was sick. Undaunted, he asked if I was well enough to try a few pieces. His pleasant manner relaxed me and I proceeded with the test. Completing the basic grade one musical pieces, he asked if I could play unpracticed ones. Not knowing what to do, I asked him to play one. I memorized it as best as I could and tried to play it. Several others followed. Time passed. Soon, the music teacher, wondering why it was taking so long, entered the room. At that point the music Examiner stated the test was over. I was almost to the door when I remembering my grandmother's last instructions, "This person has come a long way, so thank him/her when you leave". I raced back and shook his hand. By then I was feeling quite ill and glad to see Papa as I emerged from school. I was trundled quickly into bed, saying the test went 'O.K.' as I drifted off to sleep. Some weeks later word came from Montreal announcing that I had received First Class Honours in Grade one music. This had little effect on me or my family, but the Notre Dame nuns thought they had a musical genius on their hands. However, this musical career would be short lived. As my first year came to a close I was more excited about our trip to Ontario. The reason for the visit being initiated the previous summer.

I remembered the trip to the country, the red dust billowing behind the car as we drove. At some farm, with the adults busily catching up on the latest news, I slipped away. When my family finally found me I was with a Dutch family enjoying cookies and milk and delightfully showing off a pair of small, yellow, wooden shoes. When asked why I disappeared, I explained that 'I found kids that looked like me' (they had hair the same colour). At that moment my father decided it was time to visit his people in Ontario.

During the winter Papa and my uncle Ernie made their plans. At the close of school, two families bundled into a black, four-door Ford sedan with running boards. Papa, David and Uncle Ernie rode in the front seat and mother, me, Aunt Eunice and Bobbie in the back seat. Uncle Ernie traveled with a large tool box in case of car trouble, as garage services were still uncertain in the late forties. Since the only places to stay overnight were small cabins, and these were not plentiful, the car was packed with food and other essentials for all contingencies. The trip was hot and uncomfortable, my car-sickness exacerbated by the long winding roads. It was a welcomed relief when Papa found clear running streams to reinforce our water supply.

When we reached St. Catherine's, my grandmother Stull was ready to teach her Maritime grandchildren how to roller skate. She had acquired a number of children's four-wheeled roller skates which we screwed onto our leather shoes. Decked out in her high white skates (much like today's ice skates) she skillfully demonstrated the fine art of roller-skating to her grandchildren, skating up and down the street in front of her house. After the demonstration. we all took to the road, stumbling and thoroughly enjoying our first roller skating experience. All the while Papa kept pleading with his mother to get off the road as vehicles could appear at any moment, but to no avail. Thankfully, it was a quiet side street. It was a day of delightful fun and learning. I can still hear my grandmother laughing with glee over the successful run of each grandchild.

On this trip I finally met family who actually looked like me. One particular cousin, Barbara Williams, a daughter of my father's sister, was practically my twin. Even though I would have few visits with my Ontario relatives, just knowing they existed was a precious gift for me.

I also met my father's sister and his other two brothers. Beatrice (called 'Bea') Lorraine Stull was my father's only sister, and amazingly, she not only had similar facial features but almost the same tone of voice as my father. Her marriage to James Douglas Williams had produced three daughters; Shirley Mae, Barbara Ann, and Susan Eileen. Shirley married Robert Mathrew Hagar, Barbara married Donald Edward Halliwell, and Susan married Dennis Wainman. They all lived in Ontario. There was less information on his other two brothers. Cecil Leroy Stull was married and had one son, Craig. John Frederick Stull, my father's youngest brother, had been a jet pilot and would, at a young age, die from a brain tumor. He was married and had three daughters and one son.

Being the only daughter of the oldest son, grandma Stull had a gold ring with a small diamond made for me from my grandfather Stull's tie clip. At a family dinner she presented the ring to me. I was delighted to have such a beautiful ring of my own and something from my Stull grandparents. Unfortunately, shortly after the meal my mother took the ring stating, "This is too expensive for a child". I would never have it.

One hot sticky afternoon Papa took us to a Laura Secord gathering at Brock's Monument at Queenston Heights. Major General Sir Isaac Brock was the provisional Lieutenant-Governor and commander of the British forces in Upper Canada at the time of the 1812 war. He lost his life during the first major battle of the war by storming Queenston Heights. His remains rest at the base of the monument in his name. The Secord gathering was a huge event, the hills dotted with many families enjoying a picnic and their inherited links. These were just some of the Niagara /New York descendants. Many children looked like me. Our return trip to the Maritimes was uneventful. Grade two lay ahead.

Our pleasant, young nun of grade-one was replaced by an aging, autocratic grade-two nun who had long ceased enjoying the company of young children. Our morning routines had overtures of an army inspection. She regularly made strong pronouncements which hung unchallenged by a class of six and seven year olds. However, one day the gauntlet was thrown down for me when she announced that 'all Protestants' were going straight to Hell'. I jumped up and declared "My father is not going to Hell!"

Her commanding voice replied "Sit down, young lady!"

"No" I relied, repeating my statement even louder.

Louder she yelled "You will sit down, at once!"

"No" I replied, stubbornly holding my position and repeating my comments.

When a few rounds of this back and forth banter failed to resolve the stalemate, she relented and replied "Very well then, with the exception of your father". With that assurance, I sat down.

I was less concerned about my actions on my school life as in breaking my promise to my grandmother and uncle. On the way home from school I prepared myself for a sound scolding from my grandmother. This did not stop me from telling her what happened. With concern and little anger she said, "I understand, Child, but you must not get into battles with the nuns, this will do you no good. Try your best to remain silent and only talk to me". Again, I promised and this time it held. That evening as I worked on my homework in the dining room, I overheard my grandmother telling Papa that 'Today your daughter got you into Heaven' as she repeated the days events. I could hear my father's deep laugh and his reply, "That's great, Nan, I have no worries now." While this incident passed, other conflicts persisted.

In grade two we progressed to the next stage of our religious training, our Confirmation. Everything was going well until, one day, much to my delight, Bishop Boyle stepped into our classroom. Recognizing my old Dorchester Street friend, I jumped up from my desk and ran forward to greet him. Just as I reached him, the nun placed her hand on my head, pushing it downward and demanding, "You must kiss the Bishop's ring". Confused by this tactic, I pushed against her hand arguing, "This is my friend!".

A gentle, tired voice above me interrupted the battle with "Yes, sister, this is an old friend. Sally does not have to kiss my ring". Reluctantly, the sister released me and I sat next to my friend while he talked to his next Confirmation class.

On the day of our Confirmation, kneeling at the marble railing in my old 'castle', I watched the Bishop approaching as he blessed each candidate, the girl kissing his ring at the close of the blessing. In reaching me, he blessed me and instead of offering his ring, tapped me on the head and proceeded on. I'm certain the nun standing behind each girl was certain I was never Confirmed. Irrespective of these incidents, I managed to get through the first two critical religious events relatively unscathed. Nevertheless, I'm sure these incidents, and my routine fainting whenever incense was used in the chapel and sliding down the convent wooden bannister, got me labeled as a 'different' (if not difficult) child. However, my religious struggles paled in comparison to my communication difficulties which fully emerged in grade two.

My earlier tactic of saying 'no' to make people repeat phrases, escalated with age. I had accepted the irritation of adults by my negative replies, as it helped me better understand what they were saying. However, helpful, even this strategy failed when there were too many adults talking. At such times, getting too frustrated in trying to understand so many words, I would escape into our Euston Street garden and sit high up in the plum tree with the starlings. Birds and animals were my dearest friends, as they seemed to sense my struggle. I can still hear my grandmother at the base of the plum tree pleading, "Child, come down out of that tree at once! Everyone has gone. You and I can have a nice cup of tea". With tears running down my face I would walk to the house beside her mumbling… ."words, words, words……..why Nanny are there so many words?". This difficulty with words would now enter the education world.

The letters in my reading book danced around causing the lines to run together. Whenever I looked at a page the letters jumbled together, making reading impossible. I began using a small six-inch ruler under each line trying to separate the words but even this provided a marginal aid. To understand each story, I got every adult in my home to read and reread the story until I had it memorized according to the pictures on each page. Thus, it was the memorized story I recited at school, my method rarely being picked up by my teacher. Numbers presented even more problems. Numbers not only danced around but threes and eights, and sevens and nines looked the same and it was harder to memorize numbers.

As a child, I assumed my classmates had similar problems and that my difficulties were just worse or perhaps I was just slow. It never crossed my mind to discuss this problem with my teacher or other adults as such discussions were unheard of in the school system of the day. Children went to school and were suppose to cope as best as they could. My problem was camouflaged by my class ranking which was usually in the top three in both grade one and two. To the adults around me my copying abilities appeared fine. For this reason, my eyesight deficiencies were not identified early, which further compounded my learning difficulties.

The health nurse, who regularly checked school children's eyesight, used a large alphabetical chart and assessed the children from A to Z. 'Stull' usually came last on the list. My desk, near the chart, enabled me to memorize the letters. The Optomotrist was amazed I was doing so well at school in light of my astigmatism and short-sightedness when I finally reached him. After my eye test, I was presented with thick glasses encased in pink plastic frames which reduced the fuzziness of my world but did not stop the dancing of letters and numbers.

Somehow in my childish thinking, I decided that reading more books would help me with my reading. This was never discussed with an adult. The idea propelled me towards the public library. Each Saturday mornings, Laddie and I would walk to the Queen Square public library, many blocks from my home. Laddie was the white/golden/brown collie of our next door neighbours, the Gallants. They were an elderly couple, he being the blacksmith to the racetrack some blocks from our home. Laddie and I became quick friends. In the winter he would protect me from the many snowballs as we walked home. As the months passed, I read stacks of children's books in addition to my regular school books.

My love of books had begun. My little ruler was my constant guide. Disappointingly, while my reading improved the letters continued to dance. However, concentrating so hard on words, I sometimes was not adept at guarding myself from other hazards, particularly at home.

The years had not improved my relationship with my older brother, Sonny. When given a chance, he belted me on the back of my head making me dizzy. I would run to my grandmother holding my head. Her reply was always "Child, stay away from him, he means you no good." Even his teasing had a mean streak. As I was beginning my schooling, Sonny was finishing his. His personality had turned more negative in his latter years at school. He became loud, sarcastic, bullying and subject to telling off-coloured jokes, something which was unheard of in our family. He was in regular conflict with Nanny, she often referring to him as 'a strutting peacock'. I continued to keep clear of him as best as one could with everyone living under one roof. So arriving home one autumn day to find only Sonny at home set off alarm bells.

Usually there was always someone at home after school. This day was an exception. As David, and I entered the hallway, Sonny lunged towards me, with anger dripping from his words, saying "Now you little bitch, I'll get you this time!". I raced to the stairs leading to the second floor, while David positioned himself at the landing yelling "Leave my sister alone!" Sonny, being eleven years older, easily brushed David aside and continued up the stairs after me. I raced to the bathroom, the only door with a lock, sliding the latch just in time. The door bent with his weight and I knew the latch wouldn't hold. Seeing only one escape route, I raised the bathroom window eyeing the two story drop to a gravel driveway below. Sonny kept yelling and pushing against the door, while David kept hitting him. I had just released one of the screen hooks when I heard my grandmother's commanding voice "What is going on here, get away from that door at once! Sonny, sheepishly replied that he was 'just kidding'. This my grandmother brushed aside with "This is not kidding ………be gone with you. I'll deal with you later." Then in a quieter voice, "Child, it is all right, open the door for your grandmother". Shaking and sobbing, I released the lock, and fell into my grandmother's arms, the screen hanging open behind me. That evening I could hear the loud voices of my grandmother and parents discussing the incident. If I had been close to my grandmother before, after this incident I was glued to her. There would be no repeat of this incident. Whatever was said to Sonny, his physical abuse ceased and his verbal abuse began. For this I had some defense, while I could ignore the words his menacing intent was always clear.

That winter, when David started hitting me with snowballs and knocking me into the snow bank, Papa took action. One afternoon when both my mother and grandmother were out, he brought from the car two pairs of small, red, boxing gloves. It was not unusual for Papa to be instructing us in some new sport or game. He tied the boxing gloves on both David and I, instructing us on the foot work and defensive positions. With that, my brother and I circled each other gently touching our boxing gloves. Knowing my brother would quickly lose interest, I waited. As he dropped his guard, my right arm shot out and I clipped him squarely on the chin. To my amazement he bounced across the kitchen and fell on the floor next to the refrigerator. With that my mother and grandmother returned, mother running to David as he yelped "My sister hit me!" and rubbing his chin. Nanny stood at the kitchen doorway, saying, almost in a whisper to Papa; "This is a fine activity for a young lady". I stared at the little red boxing gloves thinking they held some magic. Papa said nothing and proceeded to unlace the gloves. The little red boxing gloves disappeared never to be seen again. This was the beginning and ending of my boxing career. My father's objective had been achieved. David remained unsure of his sister's right hook and life between us returned to normal. After these events, my attachment to my grandmother increased.

In the pre-antibiotic world, it was not unusual for the old and the young to die in the harsh winters of Canada. Knowing this, I was not surprised when my grandmother asked me to check on some elderly people on my homeward journey from school. My assignment entailed different houses each day with precise instructions. I was to check, while consuming a small glass of milk and maybe a cookie, if anyone was coughing or sneezing, had a runny nose, had food in the icebox, and if the house was warm. There was no slacking off as Nanny would grill me when I got home. A negative report resulted in a follow-up visit from my grandmother the next day. My nursing career had begun unofficially at seven.

On holidays, I would accompany my grandmother either to these same houses or to others under the strict instructions that 'children are to be seen and not heard'. I remained silent until we were out of the house, at which point Nanny would ask "What do you think of Mrs. X" . We would then have a discussion on what made some people nice and others not. On one occasion I replied. "Mrs. Y is not a nice lady, she has two faces, one is *really* mean."

My grandmother turned to look at me asking, "Do you see two faces in many people?"

"No", I replied, "just some".

"Does you grandmother have one or two faces?".

Cautiously, I responded "Oh, Nanny, you have only one face"

"That's good" she replied with a mild chuckle.

With the arrival of Spring I accompanied Nanny every day to Lenten services at the Basilica. We rose at five to walk the many blocks from Euston Street to the Basilica for six o'clock Mass. On cold crisp mornings under the street lights I would dawdle along enchanted with the flickering snow crystals and the sound of my squeaky rubber boots. On some occasions Laddie joined us. As I did not want the dog left out in the cold Nanny let me take him quietly into the church where he lay next to a Confessional adjacent to our pew. There he waited until I gave him the homeward signal. The short, Latin service, was held in the dimly lit basement of the church, attended by a small group of faithful, mostly elderly parishioners, Nanny greeting many as we entered and left the church. We hurried home, had breakfast and I prepared for my regular school day. The next day, and for forty days, weather permitting, this routine continued. As the summer arrived, there was talk of a family wedding.

At twenty-one, my brother, Sonny, announced he was going to marry Martina (called 'Teenie') Costello, a woman six years older than him. Sonny was now a heavy set man with a dark crewcut hair style which he rigidly maintained all his life. His weight would be a lifetime problem going well over two hundred pounds by the time he reached his thirties. Teenie was a petit woman with dark hair who seemed forever stuck in her teens. She was a twin, in a family of three sets of twins (all girls) and one boy. Her family home was just blocks from ours on Euston Street. Teenie had been ill with kidney problems as a young girl and for this reason, and others, the families were not in favour of the marriage. Since, both individuals were of legal age, the families were thwarted in any efforts to stop the marriage.

On the wedding day as I waited to accompany my grandmother, I overheard my father say "Well, Nan, today we have our first family marriage", trying to make the best of the situation. Plunging a long hatpin into her hat, Nanny angrily replied, "Yes, the marriage of two empty sacks". No truer words could more aptly describe the marriage. Sonny and Teenie fought before the marriage, immediately after their honeymoon and almost continuously for the next fourteen years until their divorce. The marriage would produce three pregnancies and two live births.

The first child, Sylvia Marie, was born a year after their marriage. She was a happy baby with jet black hair and gray/blue eyes. I was thrilled to be an aunt at such a young age. Since I had already been doing some baby-sitting in the neighbourhood, it was understood that I would baby-sit my niece.

Having come from middle-class homes, the home environment of my brother and his wife was deplorable, in fact it was a slum. Whenever I arrived to baby-sit, I found dirty dishes stacked in the sink, dirty and clean clothing scattered over the floors, their bed unmade and the baby soaking in a soaked bed. I would begin with cleaning up the baby and her bed, trying to find a clean ledge in the kitchen for her bottle and rocking her to sleep. When she went to sleep, with no television, I would start to clean-up the kitchen, making a very small dent in the clutter. For this I received twenty-five cents a hour. After several rounds of this I went to my grandmother. On my next baby-sitting job she accompanied me and was shocked at what she saw. Later, I could hear her loud voice telling Sonny "The Child is not your slave……..this is not to happen again!" For a spell the situation improved but slowly returned to its former state. They seemed incapable or unwilling to rectify the situation. Equally, the families seemed helpless in getting adult children to change. Life simply moved on.

During these years my father moved from managing the SMT bus company to owning an Irving Oil service station on the corner of Fitzroy and University Avenue, his brother Ernie becoming the mechanic. Other men joined him to assist with repairing cars and in pumping gas. It was a busy and lively business. On occasion when Charlie Chamberlain fell out with Don Messer, he could be found singing at the top of his lungs washing cars at my father's garage. Periodically, Charlie would come home with Papa to sing Irish songs to my grandmother.

In the 1950s girls were never found at a service station let alone pumping gas. So, on the mornings my father needed help, I put on David's jacket and tucked my braids under his baseball cap. Suitably attired I would pump gas from six to nine o'clock in the morning, the customers yelling to Papa "That youngest boy of your is a quiet one, Ray." Once the rest of the crew arrived near nine, I slipped away with a chocolate bar. Arriving home my grandmother would mumble "Some attire for a lady. I suppose you had little breakfast, Child" and we would go to the kitchen for food, hot tea and a chat. My life was full of duty and responsibilities. Before long another school year was about to start.

I had no idea how much I was lip-reading until grade three when the teacher turned to write more information on the blackboard. The immediate consequences of the teacher's move caused me to drop to thirteenth in my class standing. Not understanding the problem, the only advice I received from my teacher and parents was to 'work harder'. I remained incapable of explaining what was happening and/or likely did not think that anyone around me would, or could, do anything about it. The only family member who suspected I had a problem was my grandmother and even she knew few details. After my initial panic subsided, I started bombarding my teacher and fellow classmates with unending questions about every aspect of schoolwork. I checked and rechecked every detail until I became a nuisance. My classroom problems were only part of a much more encompassing problem.

Conversations were difficult. My mind tended to be run well ahead of my ability to form words. I panicked in groups of people talking or in new situations, such as meeting someone for the first time. My tendency was to try and anticipate what the individual might say after the first 'hello'. For example, expecting the individual to say, "Hello Sally, how are you today?" I jumped pass the greeting and answered the 'how are you today'. Confusion reigned if the question differed from my anticipated version. In addition, I tended to speak in short sentences with few adjectives in order to control my words. As a result I stumbled through conversations not only confusing myself but leaving the recipient even more bewildered.

Continuing to believe more reading would ease my difficulties, my library trips continued. My reading taste shifted from children's books to Nancy Drew, The Hardy Boys, Horatio Hornblower and even Winston Churchill. Interest in mystery and historic literature would persist for life. While the librarian gave me some guidance, most selections were mine, a bit strange perhaps for an Island girl. To augment my reading, I also started writing to four pen pals; two in Ireland and two in Japan. This exercise rewarded me with fascinating letters from other parts of the world on how other children lived. I would continue writing to my pen pals until I went to college.

At an early age I found that getting emotionally upset or excited was detrimental to my ability to communicate. By eight, I knew I had to discipline my emotions to cope with my handicap. This was done more by instinct than plan. However, such discipline in a child resulted in a rather stoic and silent personality, sometimes earning me the distinction of being 'cold' or a 'dreamer'.

With all my efforts at trying to understand the written word my enthusiasm for music was fading. While I enjoyed playing the piano, I had difficulties reading musical notes which danced even more than letters. My need to memorize each musical piece meant that new ones were always a challenge. When the pleasant music instructor was replaced by a cantankerous nun, with little patience for struggling students, the atmosphere changed. Our music lessons involved the ability of avoiding her long wooden pointer crashing down on our fingers if the wrong note was played or the musical timing was off. Fortunately, I was quick at pulling my fingers off the keyboard before the pointer hit, others were not so lucky. Thus, when it came to a choice between music and art, I gladly left this abusive setting. The art teacher, once she discovered I had some artistic talent flew open the doors to a wondrous world of watercolour, pastel, leather and even copper work.

As grade three came to a close I had progressed to fifth place standing in class, learned new techniques in mastering my handicap, and was enchanted in my discovery of art. Thus, I thought I was ready for grade four. But a new set of challenges awaited.

Grades four and five were in the same classroom. In grade four we progressed to a larger desk with a lift-up lid, designed to accommodate more books and scribblers. Our teacher, a nun, was a thin, irritable individual with an explosive personality who took an immediate dislike to me. Within days I was defending myself as bits of chalk and blackboard brushes crashed against my raised desk lid. I was the only student receiving such attention (likely because I was the only student who's father was non-Catholic). Fortunately, being quick at raising my desk top, almost all of the missiles missed. However, it made for a very disturbing school day. For some reason this missed getting reported to my grandmother until one day, chuckling, I commented on how many objects I had successfully stopped during the day. Upon hearing the details my grandmother became furious. Whatever happened, the teacher was dismissed and an older, nicer nun arrived, one that took great pains to make sure I was all right. It was an early discrimination lesson.

That summer when I walked with Father Dick he, knowing of the incident, commented "Sally, just because someone puts on black religious clothing does not necessarily change their personality. Unfortunately, some may also use the religious community for their own aims ". He quietly encouraged me to look for the true personality behind the religious mask. In my years of studying and working in religious organizations this would be an important message.

After this incident school life settled down. As grade four came to a close Papa announced we would be taking another trip to Ontario, this time just our immediate family; my mother and father, David and myself.

—◦—❈—◦—

Very early on a warm Saturday morning we set off in a pale green Ford stationwagon for the Island ferry on route to St. Catherines. The plan was, with steady driving, we could reach St. Catherine's in three days. Mother and I slept in the back of the stationwagon on a thin mattress, while father and David stayed outside in a small tent. We were on schedule until mother insisted we attend Sunday Mass. We lost several hours with the delay. As Papa kept driving late into the night on the third day, he soon realized we could not make it and needed to stop. He turned off the main highway at a clay clearing, the area devoid of trees or lights. As I stepped out of the car I was overwhelmed with a sense of panic and fear and yelled to my father; "Papa, we must leave here, there is something terribly wrong with this place!"

Realizing the weariness of father after a long day of driving Mother objected; "Stop that, your as bad as your grandmother. Your father is too tired. We'll do the best we can until morning".

Panicking, I again appealed to my father with greater emphasis; "Please, please, Papa, we have to go! This is a very bad place." Responding to the frantic pleas of his daughter, Papa wearily told us to get back in the car. We later parked at an old country school yard for the night.

The next morning I awoke to a mild tapping on the stationwagon window. As I rolled down the window Papa was standing there with a big grin on his face. "Well Sally, thanks for saving our hides". He had been listening to a local news broadcast saying that it was a miracle an accident hadn't occurred as someone failed to block one of the entrances to the new waterway scheduled to open that morning. If we hadn't moved we would have been washed away.

On this trip Papa showed me the Welland Canal where he and his father worked on the steel many years before. He pointed out the general direction of his grandfather's farmland in Homer. It was a typical hot and sticky Ontario day, the huge threatening clouds eventually bursting open as we turned to walk back to Aunt Bea's. We began running through the pounding rain, eventually stopping after we were totally drenched. We continued casually walking and laughing as we sloshed through the puddles. It was good seeing my father so happy.

Prior to making the return trip home Papa took us to the orchards of relatives somewhere in the Niagara region. These were elderly people trying to manage a large farm with few workers after the war. Our car was loaded down with peaches, pears and grapes which we ate as we traveled. Never had I seen so much fruit.

This time on our eastern journey we detoured into the United States heading to Vermont. There, mother located one of her O'Neill step-brothers. I have a dim memory of a small elderly couple, my mother's step-brother being a diminutive man with snow white hair and a pleasant, courteous manner. Mother said her step-brother had many characteristics of her father, John O'Neill. It must have been a unique experience for her to be the only Island family member to meet this step-relative. We returned home to another month of summer holidays. During that summer, like many girls of nine, I was beginning to think of my looks.

One evening, watching my mother put on her makeup prior to going out for the evening I remarked, "When I grow up I want to paint my eyebrows and be pretty just like you." Turning slowly from her vanity table, she looked straight at me saying. "Well, you'll need more than make-up to improve your looks. Perhaps you should concentrate on your brain as you have little to work with in the beauty department".

Stunned, I went to Nanny and asked "Am I really ugly?"

"Who is feeding you with such nonsense" she replied, "You are still a young girl, there is plenty of time for such thoughts."

I made no reply but went up stairs to look in the mirror. My mother had a point. I had two-tone hair (white blond on top and strawberry blond below) giving me streaked braids, totally out of step with other girls. My large, beige, plastic rimmed thick glasses made me look like an owl. My front teeth were slightly bucked, the dentist telling my mother my teeth were too large for an Irish mouth. In addition, my skin broke down in the March winds and summer sun, and I had frequent chest colds, my grandmother saying was due to the smokers in the house. All-in-all , not a picture of beauty. That evening I vowed to concentrate on my brain, even though I knew my battle with words and numbers would make this extremely difficult. Mother would never learn of my communication difficulties, and I would never mention looks again. However, that same summer I was to receive an opposite message when my aunt arrived for her annual visit.

Aunt Di and Uncle Neil arrived home from New York accompanied by a small man, a photographer with one of the leading American magazines. Deciding I was an interesting subject, the photographer went about snapping endless photographs until, annoyed, I asked him to stop. He then asked if he could take selected photographs, all discrete, under the supervision of my aunt. Later I overheard her asking my father if I could spend my Christmas holidays with her and Neil in New York. No matter how much she tried father refused to consider the idea. In the fall after my aunt returned to New York, a magazine arrived with the layout of an older girl with long braids that looked just like me. The attention and magazine layout made me think that perhaps everyone didn't think I was ugly. Nevertheless, I decided to proceed with my plan, however difficult.

Following this event, the next time my aunt arrived home she was inspired on getting me to walk properly by placing a book on my head and providing me with endless lessons on creams and cosmetics. This coupled with my grandmother's rules to prevent a girl from broadening her hands (i.e. placing my hand on a banister or milking a cow) and dress restrictions (i.e. no shorts), my life was becoming quite complicated. I was glad for the occasional sports break provided by my father.

The hockey world of my father was gone and replaced by softball, both father and Sonny being pitchers for a local team. When in Charlottetown, my father, brothers and myself would bundle out to Victoria Park baseball diamond for a game. Wearing my brother's jacket and a baseball cap I would sit in the dugout with all the wallets and other valuables of the players. When the game was going badly or the language became too rough, father signaled me to move to the first seats in the stands. There I would remain until the end of the game, no one knowing who I was. Sporting activities dominated our early years with an ice rink in the back yard, archery, table tennis, croquet and others. It was always a delight to test my skills even if I wasn't that good. Occasionally, I would accompany my father in the early morning to golf at Green Gables, then a newly developed eighteen hole golf course at the National Park. My attention span at golfing waned easily and I would leave my father to walk barefoot through the golf course woods enjoying the rabbits and cool streams. Near the fifteenth hole I would reappear from the woods to play the final holes. One day with rain threatening, I stayed closer. Seizing the opportunity Papa decided to help me improve my swing. Listening to his voice, I swung the club. The ball whizzed into the air but, with my short-sightedness I could not tell where it landed. Next, I heard my father's deep laugh and say "Well, I'll be damned!" After he stopped laughing he said; "You landed on the green. Sal, you could be a good golfer if you tried". It was a short hole. Papa kept trying to get me interested in the sport. However, being unable to see where the ball landed seemed a real drawback, stretching the whole concept of handicap. However, any frivolity in our lives was about to come to an end, as storm clouds were forming.

The service station business was going well until my father got interested in selling cars. Not any car, the Studebaker. While his brother thought mechanically the Studebaker was an exceptional car, they were unaware of the car dealership problems occurring in the United States. When the Studebaker car company failed, the repercussions landed on every car dealer like my father. The failure would financially destroy the service station business and we would lose our Euston Street home. At the time father was forty-three and mother forty-four. Their world was collapsing around them. In his democratic way, father gathered the family around the dining room table to solemnly announce the bad news and what it would mean for all of us. The word 'bankruptcy' heralded the dark days ahead. Our family would never quite be the same. Father tried very hard to get help from business acquaintances and friends but doors, and hearts, were closed. This unexpected cloud would challenge every survival instinct, with some family members fairing better than others. It was supposed to be a time to pull together.

A deathly silence enveloped the house. Mother no longer chatted gaily on the telephone to friends, had little interest in shopping and parties ceased. This financial blow would send my mother down a depression slide from which she would never recover, the symptoms worsening with the years. Frequent migraine headaches relegated her to bed for long periods of time. When difficulties appeared, fair-weather friends, happy to share the good times, evaporated like morning mist. Few people came to visit except close friends and family, and even these visits were rare. David found a newspaper route and I increased my baby-sitting and other odd jobs in the neighbourhood. I even got a job hulling strawberries at the fair grounds, being paid by the weight of cleaned berries. The crisis hung heavy on Papa as he tried to find work on the Island without much luck. Uncle Ernie packed up his family and returned to Ontario. Eventually, Papa accepted a construction job in Labrador. This meant he would be away for six months.

The family retained our residence while the bankruptcy was being finalized. We would have a roof over out heads but little funds until father's job began in Labrador. We prepared carefully for the long winter months ahead. Papa contacted friends in the country and a farmer arrived with a load of vegetables (potatoes, carrots, parsnips, turnips, onions and beets) which were stored in wooden bins in our clay cellar. Nanny and mother bottled every possible version of pickles and jams and stored them on shelves in the cellar. Fish became our staple diet, with an occasional chicken and lots of eggs. Nanny managed to get cheap soup bones and cuts of meat from the butcher, which formed the basis of large pots of vegetable and herb soups and stews. Homemade bread and biscuits complemented every meal. Store bought items were limited to small quantities of tea, sugar, margarine and other staples like flour, shortening and milk. Our diet, however monotonous, was simple and reasonably healthy.

My grandmother, now reaching her eighties, was slowing down, and rested every afternoon. Long walks were less frequent. She still cooked most meals and tended to any ailments as they arose. Her wisdom and knowledge was essential for a family in a time of hardship. As she observed the deteriorating mental status of her daughter, my mother, she increased my responsibilities, as she needed help.

In the fall, I returned to school entering my fifth year. Fortunately, I had the same teacher as grade four and, I had achieved some method of handling my handicap, at least on the surface. The dancing letters and numbers continued, and I simply eliminated difficult words from my conversation. Spelling remained a major challenge. I memorized everything. Art was a delightful outlet where I could escape from my word problems and the stress at home, which, unfortunately was about to get worse.

Supposedly, to help the family, Papa talked Sonny into moving back into the family home for the winter while he was away. So, Sonny, Teenie and the baby moved into the large bedroom at the front of the house, relegating David to a cot in the dining-room. Sonny's addition to an already stressful environment would be a terrible mistake.

Sonny, delivered soda pop to city stores, and was supposed to contribute some of his pay to the family which he avoided whenever possible. My grandmother's explanation for such behaviour was ' when it comes time for some children to step into adulthood, they prove wanting'. I also noted his lack of interest in the baby, even resenting the attention the baby was receiving.

Teenie slept until noon, leaving the care of the baby to whatever female in the house who was willing to assume the responsibility. To the annoyance of my grandmother and father, for the first month, she walked around all day in her pyjamas sitting for hours on the kitchen couch looking at a Seventeen magazine. Finally, exasperated, Nanny ordered her to be dressed like the rest of the family whenever she was downstairs. In a huff she relented.

By profession, Teenie, was a hairdresser. However, other than cutting family members hair, I do not recall her working outside the home during these years. While her actions as a young woman might be construed as laziness, she may not have been mentally capable of assuming normal adult responsibilities, perhaps the underlying reason why both families were against the marriage. Nanny, reflecting on the situation said, "Child, not all women are mothers. Some women should never have children, others hate being pregnant and reject their child at birth. Some use pregnancy as a pawn for various reasons. In all such instances the child eventually realizes that he/she was never wanted. The true mother loves and willingly takes on the long-term commitment of bringing up the child. One of the greatest roles in life is to guide children to maturity, and God help you, if you do anything to damage the next generation". Such words would have greater meaning in later years.

The constant bickering of Sonny and Teenie compounded an already over stressed setting. They seemed to have endless arguments over trivial matters, never reaching resolution. Eventually, Teenie would get fed up and take the baby to her family home down the street. She would stay with her sisters for a while and then, in time, return to our place, resuming the same behaviour and bickering. It became an endless cycle.

Shortly after Sonny and Teenie arrived, Papa took off for Labrador, not to return until the spring. This would be our first Christmas without him. In past years, Christmas had always been a time of great happiness, with a brightly lit tree, an abundance of delicious food and many family and friends dropping in to wish us seasons greetings. Father was generous in his Christmas cheer. He would trek through the woods to bring home the largest spruce tree he could find. Lower branches were removed to create a front-door wreath. Mother pinned up numerous Christmas cards on the cloth drapes, and the tree was shimmering with electric lights (including bubble lights), glass ornaments and long strands of silver tinsel. David and I would hang our socks on the fireplace mantle, expecting fruit, candy and may be a small toy. Papa somehow found fresh oranges for the holidays.

In past Christmases, David and I were allowed one large toy, chosen from a list of three possibilities we identified in the Christmas Sears catalogue. Santa always knew which one was the most desired. Most family gifts were clothing, often handmade. Nanny providing a variety of knitted items and Aunt Di sent clothing and a coat for my teddy bear. On Christmas day, the living-room fireplace glowed with red-hot coal brickets, children played with their toys and adults ate, drank and reminisced over the past year and their expectations for the year ahead. Christmas was usually a family affair while New Year's, my grandmother's birthday, was a time for many guests. People came and went all during the season. As we limped forward to our first Christmas following the bankruptcy the whole atmosphere changed.

Well before Christmas a large parcel of food and other items was readied for Papa in Labrador. We knew from his letters that anything going to the work site was being dropped by plane. With this in mind, extra warm clothing was wrapped around breakable items and Nanny devised a method of packing a large bottle of rum into a loaf of home-made bread. Papa would later write to say that he was the only one with any liquor that Christmas, thanks to Nanny's clever packing. At home we faced a more somber holiday and few gifts. With the kindness of family a Christmas tree appeared and a large goose. There were few decorations and even fewer visitors. As the festive season ended we faced the long winter months.

One mid-winter's night as we cleared the supper dishes, Nanny turned to look at Sylvia sitting playfully in her highchair. In a matter-of-fact tone she announced, "Oh dear, the child does not have a first candle". A dish slipped from my mother's hand and broke.

Mother, trying to brush off the unhappy news said; "Surely Mother, you are mistaken, what a terrible thing to say".

Again, as if looking into some distant window, with a frown on her face, she went on; "Mary, it is true. It is best the family prepares for the inevitable," and with that the topic was closed. An atmosphere of disbelief hung in the air as we all knew Nanny's predictions were rarely wrong.

In the spring, Teenie, now in her second pregnancy, following another fight with Sonny, packed up the baby and went to stay with a sister who lived outside of Charlottetown. Within weeks we heard the baby had been admitted to hospital with pneumonia. Then came the devastating news, she was dead at nine months. Within a period of weeks, the family was trying to cope with the dual emotions of welcoming Papa back from Labrador and burying a baby. For weeks I could hear her crying, my grandmother soothing my haunting with "Child, this too will pass".

In the midst of this stress, I started my menstrual period. In panic I ran to my grandmother who quietly reassured me I wasn't going to die. The arrival of this change in my life send me into a health crisis. Unable to replace the iron in my body fast enough between cycles, I became anemic. Exhausted, I dragged myself to and from school, falling into the kitchen couch after school and going fast asleep. Such weariness interfered with my ability to focus on my schoolwork. The doctor prescribed liquid iron which had to be sucked through a glass straw. Unfortunately, as soon as it hit my stomach I immediately vomited every dose. My condition worsened. Boils developed on my right wrist and in both armpits. Sties appeared on my eyelids, and encrusted eyelids prevented me from opening my eyes in the morning. I started my day bathing my eyes with warm water to release my eyelids. My grandmother tried every remedy in her arsenal and used different poultices to draw out the boil infection. Oblivious of my appearance, I was going off to school with crusted, bloodshot eyes and heavy dressings on my boils. As my condition worsened, Nanny sought outside help.

Awaking from a sound sleep one afternoon, I discovered two elderly women talking quietly over me. The stranger was an elderly First Nations, Mikmaq woman, a herbalist, who came in answer to my grandmother's call. Ignoring me, the two consulting herbalists talked on. Eventually, Nanny picked up her market basket and the two departed out the back door into the garden. Peeking my curiosity, I went to the back porch window to watch. The Mikmaq lady filled my grandmother's basket with various types of greenery as they walked and talked. Continuing their conversation, they returned to the kitchen, filled a large pot with water and the greenery, and sat to wait until it cooked. Once ready, looking much like cooked spinach, she said "The Child, will need to take three large tablespoons of this four times a day. I will be back in a month". They then, sitting down for tea and biscuits, invited me to the table.

The herbal concoction worked. As the days passed my anaemia improved, my tiredness evaporated and the infection disappeared. By the time the Mikmaq herbalist returned I was quite well. She was very pleased and told my grandmother, "The Child, cannot handle chemical products, she must use natural foods and ingredients to stay healthy." Following this advice I was inundated with raisins in every conceivable food (bread, puddings etc.), a small jug of molasses sat ready to go with biscuits, and there were regular meals of liver, all known sources of iron. My grandmother knew I needed a strong preventative program if my anemia was to be kept at bay. Not wanting a return of the frightful tiredness and infections, I was more than willing to cooperate.

Later that summer Teenie gave birth to a second girl, Mary Rayona (1954-), another girl. When Teenie returned from the hospital she spent a great deal of time in bed. Sonny adopted his usual detached attitude to the baby. With Mother, unable to handle much more stress and Nanny getting older, the petite, wrinkled, premature baby was placed in my care when I was not in school. She was so small and fragile I was afraid to touch her. Nanny sat beside me as she instructed me on each step of the baby's care. Mother, Nanny and Teenie were there during the day while I was at school. Who took what responsibility was never clear, but Teenie's attitude to life had not changed. Slowly, as the wrinkles faded, Rayona blossomed into a beautiful, healthy, blond, blue-eyed, baby. I was an aunt again! But this brief euphoria was short-lived.

Upon his return from Labrador, Papa got a job in Summerside with a company selling John Deere farm machinery. This meant we would be leaving Charlottetown once school was over. The family now faced the realization we would be losing our family home and moving into rental accommodations in Summerside. For Mother, this was another blow. She was leaving her beloved city, the place where she had grown up and found the greatest joy, and, in addition she was losing her home. Her headaches increased and her personality continued to wilt. To give her credit, she got through each day assisting with meal preparations and doing basic cleaning, but there was little enthusiasm for life. For me, for the first time, I would have an active role in the moving.

Papa brought in a large, china, wooden barrel, instructing me on how to wrap dishes and glasses to prevent breakage. Various cardboard boxes arrived for packing other items, Papa showing me how to label each box for easy identification. While I put the household items into the barrel and boxes, mother and Nanny kept the house running, David helped Papa clear out different corners of the house (i.e. the clay cellar and backyard), and Sonny and Teenie fought. On a frightfully hot day, David, myself and Papa tackled the attic, a place where items had been stored for years. We filled a large truck with garbage, and returned to the military various clothing (hats, coats, jackets, belts etc.) left when people visited during the war. Prior to the move, it was agreed Nanny would stay with Uncle Huck and Aunt Margaret in Charlottetown until we were settled. Sonny and Teenie and the baby were to remain in Charlottetown.

On the day of the move, rain clouds threatened. Very early in the morning I went to say good-bye to my friends the starlings, and especially Laddie. I would dearly miss them. Then, I watched as the men packed the furniture, the china barrels, and numerous cardboard boxes into an open, large truck, Papa directing the placement of each item. A large beige tarp was thrown over the packed truck and tied securely. After vacuuming the empty house, we bundled into our station-wagon, filled with small items, to follow the truck to Summerside. Father was silent and Mother appeared gray and withdrawn. There was little joy in leaving Charlottetown.

Just outside the city the menacing clouds burst forth and rain bounced off the tarp on the truck and the stationwagon hood. This was followed by loud cracks of thunder and sheet lighting. At times we could barely see the road. Mid-way between Charlottetown and Summerside the truck stopped and Papa and the men consulted, both growing concerned over the increasing severity of the storm and what it was doing to our belongings. We pressed on. Crossing the railway tracks as we entered Summerside, made several turns, and finally arrived at our destination on Harvard Street, with no abatement of the driving rain, thunder and lightening. What greeted us was a shock.

The two-story brown, wooden, Victorian house, was a derelict building which had clearly not been occupied for years. The weather-beaten veranda and broken doorsteps told a tale of neglect. The front door had to be forcibly opened, the screen door barely holding together as it opened. Tall grass encircled the residence. As we opened the front door, we entered a dank, dimly lit hallway, with a broken stairway banister. In a quick walkthrough we found cobwebs everywhere, thick dust on every ledge, and missing screens on most windows. Where available, the carpets were threadbare. Bush branches hugged the back door, the beginning of a jungle which obliterated the back fence. A broken-down barn was barely visible among the brambles in the back yard.

The property was owned by Charles Dalton, a wealthy fox rancher and resident of Summerside, this being his old family home. We later discovered that Mr. Dalton had closed up the house after it had been trashed by military renters in the war. He agreed to open the house again for my father with the understanding that he would pay for any repairs. A daunting task lay before us. For Mother, this seemed to be the final straw to an already bleak day. Irrespective of the mess facing us, the inclement weather necessitated a quick move of our belongings.

The men moved the furniture as fast as possible, mother and I wiping each item with towels as it was set up. We cleared a space in the kitchen for meals, and made the beds for our first night. The lack of curtains exaggerated the lightening on the dimly-lit walls, the storm continuing through most of the night. The house creaked and groaned as if waking from a long slumber. The weather and the wretchedness of the house fitted the overall gloom of the family. Drifting off to sleep, I prayed the situation would improve in the morning light, but that was not to be.

The once expensive thick oatmeal coloured wallpaper, now covered in dust, could be found in every room. Mother took a small cloth to test the depth of dirt, and it was black with just three small rubbings. Every room would have to be thoroughly cleaned. We were facing ten foot high ceilings in the downstairs rooms, a daunting task for my mother and me, as men rarely did indoor work. Cleaners would have to be paid, money we did not have. A Dutch carpenter arrived the next morning to spend weeks fixing the woodwork and screens in the house. Father, pushing his full weight against the back door, managed to open it. He was trying to get some idea of the back yard. Leaving for work the following day, he placed a small hatchet in David's hand and a hand- sickle in mine, telling us to clear the bushes as a garden had to be planted at once. The brush was so high we couldn't see a fence, only the top of the barn. David hacked a single path through the brush to locate the back fence, giving us some idea of the extent of our task. We cut and hacked for days, aided by Papa when he got home from work. A vegetable garden was planted in time for a crop.

Cutting brush in the morning, I shifted to helping Mother in the afternoon cleaning cupboards and unpacking the boxes. We steadily moved from the kitchen and bedrooms spaces to the living-room and dining room. Once the rooms were partially livable, we made a plan to clean the ceilings and walls. Mother and I dragged a step-ladder from one room to the next, cleaning the dirt and grime. As the dust and dirt disappeared we discovered beautiful mahogany wood throughout the kitchen and dining-room with fine cut glass cupboards. This had once been a grand home. Windows were cleaned and screens repaired or made new. The house was alive with activity. It took many weeks with everyone working full out. Other than the carpenter, we did all the work ourselves. Once the house was cleaned, it was apparent it needed colour. The oatmeal wallpaper made the rooms dull and uninviting. I suggested the walls would be brighter in pastel colours. Papa approached Mr. Dalton, who agreed. Papa and I selected the paint. While Mother agreed more colour was needed, she left the painting to me as she was exhausted from the cleaning. So, at the age of eleven, with Papa's help after work and on weekends, the entire downstairs walls were christened in pale pastel colours; yellow, pink and green. After many weeks of work the house was slowly becoming livable. Before the painting started, Nanny arrived from Charlottetown. Our family was back together again.

In September, David went to a public school while I attended another Notre Dame School for girls, a poorer version of the one in Charlottetown. Students did not wear uniforms which presented me with a wardrobe problem which I resolved with a few skirts and sweaters. There were music lessons but no art, a real let down for me. Prior to our arrival the community's Roman Catholic Church had been destroyed by fire, so church services were being held in the school's auditorium, eliminating that space for most school activities. The one positive point was that the school was just a few blocks from our home.

Starting a new school presented many challenges. Although still on the Island, I was entering a different learning environment. Looking somewhat older than other girls of my age, the grade-six nun placed me at a desk between two fourteen year old girls. They, likely thinking I was the same age, poured out tales of their promiscuous lifestyle with married men in the community, a foreign topic to me. Providing little comment, all I could do was listen in amazement at what they told me. I soon learned many girls in grade six were mainly interested in getting married. This fixation on sex and marriage would have dire results. Some years later, in meeting a former classmate, I discovered only myself and another girl, who became a nun, finished school. The rest of the girls were destined for early marriages and children, some by fifteen. All this was conveyed to Nanny in our after-school chats. Upon hearing of my two promiscuous classmates and the emphasis on sex, she remarked:" Child, these children have only one string to their bow. Sex is a natural event not an national one, and they are making it a national one. When will women learn that they have so much more to contribute to society then just having babies. These girls need to know they have other talents, before it is too late". In my first year in a strange school I had little to offer in response to her concerns. I was focused on surviving.

The one positive feature was that schoolwork was easier. My problems with letters and numbers became even more camouflaged in this learning environment as I moved up again to one of the top three rankings in grades six to eight. While I continued to stumble with reading and spelling, these problems were excused because I was new.

By grade six we learned the Latin responses for Mass and singing in a small church choir. The choir teacher was an enthusiastic young nun which made such activities enjoyable. The nuns were generally kindly teachers, commendably working with limited resources. On the negative side was the parish priest, a middle aged, large man with a loud, gruff, and abrasive manner. With no Confessionals, he heard the confessions of students in the open auditorium, loudly admonishing a student over some minor sin. Witnessing this, I was determined to make my confession short and uninteresting. At one point he snapped "Is that all you have to offer?""Yes, I replied bluntly, that's it", with emphasis on 'it'. At which I received my usual three Hail Mary penance. In my three years, meetings between me and this rather unpleasant man were kept to a minimum.

Restless, by grade seven, I was ready to try and act on my grandmother's advice to create novel activities for the class. I approached the teacher with a Youth Fair idea, planned for the spring. She agreed. My classmates, when they understood the idea, were equally up to the challenge. It was the first time any such Fair had been held, the money to go for books and other educational supplies. The class of about twenty students was organized into small working groups. Those with sewing skills were in one group. Simple stuffed animal toy patterns were found, fabric and stuffing obtained, and the girls given the objective of filling a huge cardboard box with stuffed animals. Somehow, our teacher found a sewing machine. So, for months, at lunch time and after school, an assembly line of young girls cut, sewed, stuffed and embroidered facial features onto a variety of multi-coloured, hand-sized stuffed animals. The lively chatter filled the room as the box filled. Another group went door-to-door after school asking for old jewelry, books and anything else useful for a Fair, the families happy to contribute to the convent school. There were stacks of items needing to be catalogued upon their return. Another group collected old records for music and tried to find a number of record players. This left the rest designing the booths, decorations, finding small amounts of food and drink, and creating signs for the event. Everyone had a job.

In the spring, just before the big event the surrounding schools were notified. Since this was an inaugural event we had no idea if anyone would come. On the day of the Fair, much to our delight, we were inundated with young people, the event running from one to five o'clock on a holiday. Every stuffed toy was gone and most other items. To the amazement of the parish priest, the Youth Fair brought in almost as much money as the Catholic Women's Guild Fair. The biggest achievement wasn't the money, although new school supplies were important, but the increased morale of the students. The girls not only discovered they could organize and achieve such a success, they had gained respect for each other. The plan would be repeated in grade eight with similar results, the groups getting more skilled with each event. Knowing how to do it, they hardly needed me for the second round.

In grade eight, building on this team effort, the groups were approached with another idea. Getting the school's approval, I asked if the groups could decorate the school windows for Christmas. I would sketch the picture and different groups would complete the painting. Everyone agreed. Once again, the students stood outside the school in the snow admiring their efforts. With the compliments of family and friends, and acknowledgements in church, they were reminded they had 'other' talents. I had put into action my grandmother's concerns. Constantly being updated on my progress, she shared in my quiet delight at their success.

After the first year in Summerside, Mother slowly adapted and occasionally a witty statement dotted her conversation. Eventually she started bowling. She was a good bowler loving the team environment. One afternoon, I took the high score in bowling in the morning and mother duplicated the effort in the evening. We made the local newspaper. I mistakenly thought she was on the mend, but it was a brief hiatus.

Sonny and Teenie left Charlottetown and moved to Summerside, Sonny first getting a job at the Schurman Lumber Company and later working in advertisement at the Journal Pioneer newspaper. For the first time he looked well as his Schurman's job gave him lots of outdoor physical work Nothing changed in their relationship, they continued to bicker. They lived, in a nearby apartment, becoming another slum. Teenie had another sister living in Summerside to whom she escaped. For me, it was delightful to have my niece nearby. Rayona by now had become a mischievous, cheerful little girl.

Unfortunately, all the family upheaval and move to Summerside, proved to be too much for my grandmother. She started having mild strokes, leaving her with some confused days and beginning to walk with a shuffle. No longer stable on her feet, a bedroom was created for her downstairs, eliminating the family dining room. I was to share the room with her, making sure she did not get disoriented at night. My task was to help her get dressed in the morning and prepared for bed at night. No task was a burden.

Papa spent two years with the John Deere farm equipment company, then found a better job with a moving company in Truro, Nova Scotia. We all gathered again around the kitchen table as Papa informed us we would be moving to Nova Scotia at the end of our school year. In the Fall, Papa would leave for his job in Nova Scotia, coming home on weekends. In spite of our protests, he again proposed that Sonny, Teenie and the baby would move into our home during the winter. For whatever reason, perhaps hoping that his eldest son would finally mature, Papa held to his decision and Sonny moved into an upstairs bedroom. This time the situation was worse.

Sonny, now working for the Journal Pioneer newspaper, had also enlisted in the reserve air force, discovering cheap liquor at the Legion. This would begin his alcoholism, which continued for the rest of his life. Whatever his personality was outside the family, he was a mean drunk, verbally bullying any females at home. His drinking bouts increased, and his reliability at work deteriorated. Home life for me got more complex.

Rising early, I got Rayona up, dressed and fed and had Nanny dressed prior to having breakfast and going off to school. After school I played with Rayona, and after supper, I reversed the duties, helping both Rayona and Nanny prepare for bed. Only, after these duties were completed did I sit down to my homework. Mother, barely managing during the day, retired early. Teenie, to my knowledge, did little housework, barely cared for her daughter, and also retired early. She adopted her old habit of sitting around during the day in her pyjamas flipping through fashion or movie star magazines. Mother did not have the energy to make her change. Periodically, she disappeared to visit her sister, sometimes taking Rayona. I could hardly fault her going to her sister's, Sonny's drinking and mean behaviour must have been frightening for her. David spent most of his days and early evenings with his school buddies. Each evening my plan was to finish my homework and retire before Sonny arrived home. This didn't always work. On those nights, he would stagger into the kitchen, yelling at me; "Well, how is the unrighteous snob of the family?" Not answering him, as he liked an argument and got belligerent, I escaped into my bedroom. I knew, even in her eighties, Sonny would not confront Nanny.

She knew immediately what was happening and would say; "Come Child, sit awhile with your grandmother. The drunken bully will get tired with no one to fight with and go to bed." We would sit there listening while Sonny, cursing all the while, banged around the kitchen. Eventually, he went to bed and I returned to the kitchen to finish my studies. At this point, Sonny was not only using most of his own earnings for liquor, he was also stealing from mother, taking money father left for groceries. He also opened Mother's mail, hoping there might be cash from Aunt Di or Father Dick. If money was found he took this as well. He was clever enough to remain sober when Papa was home, which made any negative comments about his behaviour fall on deaf ears. As his drinking increased his reliability at the newspaper declined. He managed to hold on to his job because the newspaper owner knew my father, but eventually even this had limits.

Not knowing what to do, I wrote to Aunt Di in the United States asking her not to send cash to mother. Finally, I got my father to understand what was happening to the grocery money. Acknowledging the family situation, he left me in charge of the grocery money, leaving other funds with Mother. I hid the grocery money in my bedroom, letting Nanny know what I was doing.

Unexpectedly, Father Dick arrived on the Island early that year, and came to stay with us for a few days. He asked if I would accompany him to say his obligatory daily Mass at the school auditorium (then the local Roman Catholic church), as I, not David, knew the Latin responses. This meant I had to rise at five o'clock, accompany my uncle to church, where I knelt at the alter railing assisting him with the Mass. Girls were not allowed on the altar. The church was practically empty for the six o'clock service. Walking to and from church Father Dick questioned me on the family situation. I quietly described the deteriorating state of affairs and my brother's drunken and bullying behaviour. I could see by his sombre expression he was deeply worried. While our move to Nova Scotia would change the dynamics, it was months away. From his perspective the situation was very bad. Nevertheless, his presence in our home provided some relief, as Sonny behaved when another adult male was present. I was certain letters and telephone calls were flying back and forth among my mother's siblings, all feeling somewhat helpless in knowing what to do.

Mother's mental state was deteriorating in direct relationship to the increased stress in the home. Her migraine headaches had not only returned, she also started retreating from any decision-making. With Nanny's health deteriorating she made me responsible for many major family decisions, a role for which I was ill prepared. One example of this occurred one evening when I had an opportunity to join some other children to see television for the first time at a neighbour's house. Just as I was settling down to watch the first show the telephone rang. Mother was screaming for me to get home at once. Panicking, I raced down the street expecting my grandmother had taken a turn for the worse. When I arrived, Mother told me it was Teenie and I had to go upstairs and handle the situation. Racing over the stairs I discovered Teenie in severe pain. When I pulled back the bedclothes I froze when I saw the blood. Running back down the stairs, I raced to Nanny, praying this was her clear night. It was. Once I told her the situation, she quietly instructed me on what to do, including calling an ambulance. Mother was willing to make phone calls, so she called the ambulance, the police to find Sonny, and Papa in Nova Scotia then went to bed. In the meantime, my hands shaking, I raised Teenie's legs, used heavy towels to absorb the bleeding, wrapped her tightly in several warm blankets and, finding a suitcase, packed a number of items for the hospital. This done, the ambulance arrived and bundled her off. Shivering, I returned to the room to find blood soaked linen. Again seeking Nanny's help, I was instructed to soak the soiled linen in cold water in the tub, for proper laundering the next day. I stripped and remade the bed, grateful the mattress wasn't damaged.

All the commotion woke Rayona, who was now sobbing. I warmed some milk, wrapped her in a thick blanket, and rocked her to sleep. Exhausted, I locked up the house and fell into bed. The next morning we heard that Teenie had a miscarriage, another girl. After this there were no more pregnancies. For some weeks after this episode I had severe abdominal pains and stopped eating foods that made it worse. With so much upheaval in the house I said nothing about my health, doctors were expensive. Eventually the pain went away. Within weeks the moving process was underway again.

By Easter, the china barrel and cardboard boxes appeared, and I once again began the whole packing process. However, this time I had to wait until Rayona went to bed, as she cried and kept emptying boxes as fast as I filled them. This added activity made for late bedtimes. Somehow I got through my school exams, but I was frightfully run down and barely able to control my anaemia. By the time school closed, most of the house had been packed in boxes. This time Papa arrived with a moving van and two experienced movers from Moffatt Brothers, the company he worked for.

The move was upsetting for all of us. With her parents showing so little interest in her for years, Rayona wanted to move with us to Truro but legally this was not possible. It left all of us with a frightful dilemma not knowing what this would mean for the child. Sonny delayed finding his own apartment until the very last minute. Nanny was again sent to Uncle Huck's home in Charlottetown, creating more confusion for her, which was further compounded with her later move to Nova Scotia. Mother was now leaving her Island, and going to live with strangers, as she saw it. It would be a move from which she never totally recovered. David and I were facing another school system in another province, and the difficulties of making friends as teenagers. On this occasion, Papa, David and I carried the weight of the move. Moaning about the situation was never an option in either move.

On the moving day, the sun was shining, a more positive sign than the last move. The experienced movers efficiently loaded the small, enclosed, moving van and once again we followed in our stationwagon. Early in the morning I loaded a picnic basket with sandwiches, and thermoses of coffee and fruit drink as it would be a long day. We travelled in silence, each person with their own thoughts on the life ahead. As the Bordon ferry pulled away from the Island's red-brick shore, we stood on the upper deck, each one bidding a silent and sad farewell to our beloved Island, not knowing when we would see it again.

We arrived in Truro to a three-story, gray, tenement, building, a stone's throw from the railway tracks. Our three-bedroom apartment was at the top of the building. To access the apartment, we had to climb a fifty-step stairway, with no landings, rising straight up from the ground floor to the third floor, with an open stairwell at the top. The movers groaned and cursed the stairs as they carried each heavy piece of household furniture. There was a small kitchen and living-room, no dining-room, the largest bedroom going to my parents, a smaller one for Nanny and me, and David would have another bedroom which he would later share with a boarder. The apartment was much smaller than anything we had before, our meager furnishings overcrowding the rooms. I feared the open stairway and the instability of Nanny's walking. We worked steadily to again make our home livable and to know the community. When Nanny arrived she had a frightful time climbing the stairs. She had aged greatly over the summer.

—◆—

School was a major shock. For the first time I was attending a public school with boys and girls, and a school system very different from the convent schools of my youth. I had male teachers for the first time, a different school curriculum, one in which I had to struggle to catch up in a number of subjects. My problem with words escalated and was complicated by my Island accent, a negative mark of difference with other teenagers. Reading, spelling and mathematics became almost insurmountable, and I grew more and more silent. Adding to the complexities, for the first time I faced a physical fitness program, a lot more demanding than the gentle folk dancing classes in the convent. Making friends with teenagers who had formed their own groups, added to my adjustment problems. I was thoroughly discouraged in the first six months. Fortunately, home life had improved.

—◆—

With the absence of Sonny and Teenie a great burden had been lifted from our family, although we all worried about Rayona. Papa worked long hours. Mother's mental state once again improved as life settled into a routine. At least this time she didn't face the exhaustion of cleaning an entire house. Don Webster, an RCMP officer, and son of my father's old Island friend, Sterns Webster, then Chief of Police in Charlottetown, became our boarder. He also arrived with a trained police dog, a German Sheppard, that practically attacked anyone who suddenly opened the bedroom door. Somehow David learned from Don how to successfully navigate in and out of his bedroom. In RCMP dress uniform, I could hear Don's spurs cutting into the wooden stairs as he raced to catch a drive. Having a boarder also brought in some much-needed money.

At first the railway trains kept me awake at night. I can recall laying on my bed counting the ninety plus cars of the Canadian National and/or the Canadian Pacific freight trains rolling through Truro at night, carrying cargo from Halifax to Montreal. The shunting of the railway cars at night first startled me awake, but in time actually lulled me to sleep.

Too much stress and too many moves had taken their toll on Nanny. Her confusion increased, her mind reverting back to country life as a child. At night I would wake to find her dressing telling me she was going out to milk the cow or feed the chickens. Gently, I had to persuade her to return to bed as she was now living in a different place. Some nights she awoke more than once. I also accompanied her to the washroom, fearful she would plunge headlong down the open stairs. While this meant a disturbed night's rest for me, I knew our time together was running out.

Trying to find a study corner in a crowded apartment proved difficult. Eventually

I rigged up a small place in the unheated storage room. I must have been quite a sight, crouched under a hundred watt bulb, dressed in winter garb with mitts on trying to do my homework and study for exams. It worked. By the time I was completing grade nine my grades had improved and I was in better shape to enter grade ten. With the arrival of spring, Nanny's health took a turn for the worse.

One day she lapsed into a coma and the Victorian Order of Nurses (VON) was contacted, as there were no available beds in the hospital. The nurse came every day. The days seemed endless as we waited. In time, an intravenous was needed as Nanny was taking little oral fluids. The nurse indicated she would start the intravenous therapy but could not stay. Mother, wanting nothing to do with needles, told me to stay at home to be with my grandmother. The VON nurse instructed me on what to do. I sat, hour after hour, watching the intravenous solution and occasionally bathing my grandmother's face and hands. I knew this was the end and expected she would remain unconscious until admitted to hospital. Thus, I was startled when she suddenly awoke from her coma and firmly grabbed my wrist. Turning I looked into her face seeing the clearness of her eyes. Her voice, as strong as ever, said, " Child, you will leave your mother as soon as you can. Promise your grandmother!"

Nanny had voiced this many times over the years but never in such a commanding manner. Startled by her wakening, I hesitated. Her grip grew firmer, her head raised slightly and her voice now more urgent; "Child, promise your grandmother!"

"I promise, Nanny, I promise", I quickly replied.

"Good" she replied, relaxing, she closed her eyes and drifted back into a coma. The ambulance arrived, the attendants struggling to carry my grandmother down the steep stairs. Mother and Papa went off in their car behind the ambulance. I sat forlorn on the top step of the stairs, feeling winded, dejected and lost. My guardian, and friend was leaving me. I knew it was her time but it was still a blow. I made my way into the bedroom and fell fast asleep, my responsibilities lifting after many years. Within days we got word of her death. She was eight-five.

Her final wish was to be buried back in Prince Edward Island. So, we followed the hearse back to the Island, to attend her funeral at St. Dunstan's Basilica, my old 'castle'. I was amazed at the number of people at the funeral in addition to family. My mother stated these were the many families Nanny cared for over the years, many of the attendees being the children she helped to bring into the world. That evening as I wearily drifted off to sleep I could hear Father Dick trying to persuade my father to let me finish my schooling in Alberta. Nanny was still protecting me. My father was adamant it would not happen. So I returned to school in Truro. At the funeral, Father Dick looked weary, and by the following spring he was dead.

Shortly after Nanny's death, we were again on the move, this time to a better apartment close to the high school. I was growing weary of packing and unpacking boxes. This time we moved to a two-story, gray Victoria house, with an apartment on the ground floor and another on the second floor. We occupied the second floor. This was a spacious, bright, three-bedroom apartment with a large enclosed veranda overlooking the street and a small backyard. It had a kitchen, living-room, dining-room, a large bedroom for my parents, a small bedroom for me and a bedroom for David and a boarder. Our life was improving. This change was good for Mother, she brightened, started bowling again and even got involved in the Catholic Woman's League. Carson Ferdinand, a school friend of David's, from the country, came to board with us. Since Carson looked like David, my classmates thought I had two brothers, the difference in name was ignored.

By grade ten I was slowly adapting to the public school system. Much of my energies were still absorbed in mastering my studies, there were few outside activities. The two exceptions were badminton and volley ball. I was good at the net, even with bad eyesight. In badminton, my partner was a six-foot black male student, also new to the school. Together we made it to the semi-finals. During the summer months I worked one month with Papa at Moffatt Brothers moving company, and spent a month with my Aunt Di and Uncle Neil at their home in Murray river. There, Uncle Neil taught me how to fish and, since Aunt Di had a marvelous collection of novels, I returned to reading.

I was fifteen in grade eleven, and it was time to decide on a career. With my love of history my first choice was archaeology, which didn't sit well with my father. His reply to this suggestion was, "Sal, go and find a more practical alternative, I cannot see my only daughter digging in some jungle". Disappointed, I toyed with the three options available to women in the late fifties; secretary, teacher or nurse. The first two options were quickly eliminated as I felt my struggle with words and numbers would be too great a handicap. Thus, by default, I chose nursing. Papa agreed with the choice and proposed we look into it.

Papa, Mother and I drove to Halifax where I had an interview with a nun at the Halifax Infirmary about nurses' training. She stated I was too young to enter nursing, as I was not yet seventeen. When she saw my disappointment, she offered another option. A new nursing degree program had been initiated at Mount Saint Vincent College for which my age would likely not be a problem. Getting directions to the Mount, we pressed on. There, Mother and I talked to the Dean of Studies, a tall commanding, somewhat cold, individual. The Dean confirmed I could be admitted to the Bachelor of Science Degree in Nursing program from grade eleven, if my academic record was acceptable. I still had to complete the Provincial Grade Eleven exams, the results not posted until August. In the meantime I was to register, and somehow find the money to begin my post-secondary studies. These weighty questions lay before us as we returned to Truro. Cost would be the biggest hurdle.

The next evening, Papa sat everyone around the dining-room table in which he declared Father Dick had left a legacy of over a thousand dollars for our education. Papa's democratic nature opened access to the legacy to both David (then in grade twelve) and myself stating, whoever had the best provincial marks would get the funding. True to his word, when I presented the highest marks, he gave me the funding for my first year at the Mount.

At sixteen, I was about to embark on a new adventure, a path which would allow me to keep my promise to my grandmother. I never told my parents of my grandmother's last request, it would have opened unnecessary wounds. In addition, I was left with a mystery as to why my grandmother remained so insistent I leave my mother. I knew my mother didn't want me from birth, but there seemed to be more to it than that. The mystery would remain between my grandmother and my mother.

THOUGHTS & LEARNING

Private, religious schools for girls offered both positive and negative features. Uniforms reduced competition and gave equal status to every student. For many families it was also cheaper. An all-girl environment had a female agenda, a gentler world than that of a public school and one, at least in the forties and fifties, in which the emphasis was on being a 'lady'. Music and art were offered at a young age and quality was stressed. However, the setting also fostered a rigid, disciplinary environment where opposition was not tolerated, alternate views not encouraged, and where being 'different' produced negative reactions from both teachers and classmates. Without my family's protection, life might have been very different.

In the forties and fifties, children with learning difficulties had to survive on their own. Neither the teachers nor parents had any idea what it meant and the child was incapable of describing her/his problem. Since learning problems differ in type and severity, solutions need to be tailored to the individual. Even at a young age, I chose methods that worked for me. As issues presented themselves I adapted. Without advice, I pushed myself to read and write and to discipline my emotions. Out of this came a love of books and reading which filled my life with many wondrous thoughts and adventures.

My trips, however few, to Ontario gave me a place in the family. For children disconnected from their roots cannot see themselves within the context of their own culture. They end up comparing themselves with their immediate culture, which may or may not be to their advantage.

Difficult times confront all families and such difficulties bring out the best and worst in people. The bankruptcy taught us material possessions are fleeting, people can live with far less, the inevitable desertion of fair-weather friends, and the importance of an extended family, even with its pluses and minuses. My grandmother's skills in stretching every penny were essential to our survival. On the negative side, the stress on the family proved to be critical for some. Mother drifted in and out of depression at a time when mental health care was practically non-existent. Sonny and Teenie, unable to cope in good times, slid even further into dysfunctional behaviour with difficulties. In her eighties, Nanny's health could not sustain the financial stress and physical moves. David weathered the ride by absorbing himself in school and sports, and not getting too entangled in the internal difficulties. Papa steadfastly prevented our family ship from floundering, finding work wherever he could and slowly digging us out of the financial disaster. With his energies so focused on survival and expecting everyone to pull their own weight, it was not surprising some of the family issues got lost. Never in all these years did I hear a complaint from my father, nor a negative word about anyone. He stoically pressed on saying to us, "It is good to have challenges, we can always rebuild our lives, perhaps better than before". For me, this was a difficult segment of my life. As my guardian's health declined my Mother shifted heavy decision-making onto my young shoulders. This along with my learning handicap left me older than my own age group.

I shall be eternally grateful for the guidance of my grandmother, however brief our time together. My life would have been very different without her constant protection and wise council. Her subtle words of wisdom would be with me all my life. The role of a good grandparent in a child's life is one of the immeasurable wonders of life. Indelible principles were etched into my psyche, along with an understanding of the brief nature of this learning journey. In her dying days, she firmly placed three mementoes into my hand with no explanation; an old gold/ruby/pearl cross, a strange wooden cross with a skull and cross bones at its base, and her prayer book. Perhaps in time I would understand. With her passing I was about to embark on my own.

CHAPTER 3

Health Community Entrance

TOWERING majestically over the Bedford Basin in the village of Rockingham, sat Mount Saint Vincent College (later University). It was perched above the main railway line connecting Halifax to the rest of Canada. Known familiarly as 'The Mount', in 1960, it was a female, Roman Catholic, educational facility. A winding tree-lined road welcomed each student to an educational setting encompassing acres of land. Half way up the hill stood the rectangular, gray-stoned college building, part of a much larger campus which included, at its summit, a huge building containing a private girls school (grades 1 to 12) and the Sisters of Charity, Motherhouse. Year's before my father's old friend, Jack LeClair, managed the steel construction of this large facility, describing it as a daunting project as a nun, trained in engineering and architecture, dogged his every move, necessitating an iron stricture on his usual lusty language. The Sisters of Charity were from Massachusetts, and although known to be more lenient than the Notre Dame sisters, would prove to be still generous in their supply of rules and regulations.

The gray stone college structure (now Evaristus Hall) compactly housed the college's administrative and academic facilities, as well as a residence for both boarding students and a few nuns. My semi-private room, was on the third floor, overlooking the main college entrance. While the building had a regal appearance, it was cold in the winter when winds from the Bedford Basin crashed against its protruding walls and glass windows. The first floor had a grand chapel and library. The library was a brightly lit large room with a forty-foot ceiling and rows of books. This room would become my second home, a treasury of silence and endless books. Student residence facilities were mainly on the third and fourth floors.

Mount Saint Vincent, was founded in 1873 as a teacher's college for nuns and was opened to local girls in order to promote higher education for women. It was licensed as a normal school for nuns in 1908. An agreement signed with Dalhousie University in Halifax in 1914 expanded the academy into a junior college, enabling it to offer the first two years of a bachelors' degree program, the final two years being given at Dalhousie. In 1925 the academy was chartered as Mount Saint Vincent College, the commonwealth's only independent degree-granting woman's college. This was its status when I arrived.

My parents accompanied me to college, Papa and I carrying my navy, blue metal trunk to my room on the third floor by way of the elevator. This trunk and an old suitcase contained my entire possessions. Most of the college's clothing list was neatly packed in my trunk. With no other high school students from Truro attending the college, I was on my own. A twinge of loneliness crept over me as I watched my father's green station-wagon disappear down the winding Mount road. There was no turning back. With limited funds, I would only be able to get home on holidays even though Truro was just sixty miles away.

About one third of the two to three hundred students were boarders, most coming from the Maritimes, Newfoundland, Quebec, the United States, the Caribbean, South America and Asia. Day students mainly came from the Halifax/Dartmouth area. The religious background of most students was Roman Catholic, but there were also Protestant, Jewish, Moslem, and Confucian students, girls from families who wanted their daughters educated in a disciplined setting.

At five o'clock on the first morning (my roommate had yet to arrive) I was jolted awake by a cow bell ringing near my door. I would learn later this was the nuns morning call for Mass. Not knowing what was happening, I gingerly opened my door to greet my neighbour, Lilly Wong, a senior who was also responding to the bell ringing. Silently, I prayed this would not be my morning routine for the next year. A few days later I heard the bell clapper had mysteriously disappeared. Neither Lily nor I were suspected but certainly someone closer to the bell ringing was a possibility. Once repaired, students were pleased to hear such bell ringing was to be confined to the sister's wing of the building. My roommate, however, was a different matter.

Much to my consternation, my roommate, from the south shore of Nova Scotia, rose each morning to sing off key at the top of her lungs. I tolerated this for a few days then, as politely as I could, asked her to find another venue and time for her song burst. Reluctantly, she complied, continuing her singing whenever I wasn't in the room. Some time later, my chemistry professor, a nun from Boston, inquired how I was getting along with my roommate. Not realizing she had just encountered my roommate's operetta efforts, I mumbled something about being rarely there except to sleep. My professor, with a wide grin, gave me full marks for tolerance and dropped the subject. I would discover my roommate's singing was a minor matter compared to problems other students were encountering. My grandmother often said "it is an ill wind that blows no good" and this was true. My roommate went home every weekend, giving me peaceful weekends for study, and returned with delicious homemade treats which enhanced our tea breaks.

Thirteen students entered the Bachelor of Science in Nursing Program. This was a four year program, including summers, with the nurses training component sandwiched between two university segments. The first year and summer we were at The Mount studying science (biology, zoology, anatomy and physiology, organic and inorganic chemistry, and anatomy and physiology), English, philosophy, and theology. In the fall of the second year, we were scheduled to enter the Halifax Infirmary, joining the regular three-year registered nurses training program. By cutting off a few months of training in the senior year, we would return to The Mount to complete the remaining academic courses (in theology, psychology, history and English). We floated between two institutions, feeling like an orphan in both. The Mount had little to do with us for almost two years between our university components, and the Halifax Infirmary kept constantly referring to us as 'The Mount Students'. Only seven of the original thirteen students made it to the hospital; three boarders and four Haligonians.

My finances were sparse. While Father Dick's legacy would fund the tuition and residence expenses of my first year, there was little money for much else. Finding every means to stretch my pennies, I rented most of my textbooks as well as the black academic gown. I had to purchase a miter-board. The black academic gown and miter-board were official attire at group assemblies and chapel services. Formal occasions required the addition of white gloves, Aunt Di sending me six identical pairs for the purpose. To augment my funds, I served tables in the college dining room for $1.50 a night. 'Young ladies' were expected to know proper eating habits which necessitated a formal week-day dining experience. This also gave me access to extra goodies from the kitchen staff.

Still carrying remnants of my Island accent, I found comfort in finding a similar accent in the Newfoundland students. Joining this freshman group, we sat at the back of our classes commenting on the 'unusual' speech of the 'others'. After some weeks, it slowly dawned on us we were the ones who would have to change our way of speaking, a change that took much effort. Actually, it would take decades to change some words.

A few males were interspersed among mostly female, professors, the majority being nuns. The classes were well presented and most professors willingly gave students extra time after class. Science students spent their days either in class or lab, there was little free time. Unlike the arts students who appeared to have many hours of free time, a factor we rather envied as teenagers. I was pleased to have chosen science, and was delighted when The Mount announced we would have a Science Fair for the Halifax area school children. Most science students were asked to participate in the Fair. At the time, I was dissecting birds and small animals, so my science partner and I chose this as our exhibit. Wanting to reduce the starkness of our presentation, I volunteered to paint Disney animals (i.e. Bambi and company) as a backdrop to a staged exhibit consisting of birds at the top, small animals in the middle and swamp life (turtles etc.) at the bottom. The entire wooden structure was covered with artificial grass which I obtained, on loan, from a local funeral company, the arrival of a hearse at the college creating quite a stir.

Friday night before the Fair, two resident students, in a panic, arrived at my door asking me to come quickly to help them with their sick chicken. Why they chose me I will never know. Their exhibit was to demonstrate the staged development of a chicken with the star attraction being a live chicken, called 'Charlie'. When we reached the basement classroom, I found Charlie laying at a strange angle, not peeping, with his eyes closed. I feared the worst. Recalling Nanny's efforts in caring for sick chickens, I quickly padded Charlie's box, got a lamp for heat, obtained a loud ticking clock from one of the girls and asked if anyone had any vitamin pills. I then ground up the pills into a fine powder, mixed it with water, and using an eyedropper, gently fed Charlie. We retired, with me not expecting Charlie to live through the night.

At six o'clock the next morning I awoke to the pounding of Charlie's keepers yelling at me to come and see their patient. When we reached the basement, Charlie, full of life, was prancing about, almost frenetically. Building on our good fortune (and genius) we administered the same treatment the next night, the day before the Fair. Charlie, a true performer, was the star of the Fair!

The event was a resounding success. Many elementary school children came and we enjoyed explaining the biological details of our exhibits. The children loved the Disney art but loved Charlie more. The St. Mary University adjudicators, gave the first prize to Charlie's team and the second to us. We were all delighted as the main objective was to interest school children in science. Once the Fair was over, we were back into our regular studies.

Being an educational institution with a religious affiliation, all students were expected to take courses in theology and philosophy, non-Catholic students were exempt from theology courses. Grasping the principles of philosophy for sixteen and seventeen year old students was quite a leap. I can still see the elderly professor struggling courageously as he tried to get us to understand the classroom chair was an illusion. Extending this idea further he announced life itself was an illusion. While one might think illusion and fantasy would be easy concepts for teenagers, this was not so. We struggled with such abstract thinking and prayed we could learn enough to pass an exam.

While my skills at memorization favoured science courses, its value was somewhat useless with logic. Word games and humor would always be great hurdles for me. My first academic failure was in Logic. Only three out of twenty students passed the first mid-term test, nevertheless, for me it was a shock. I called my father to report the bad news. His sound advice was to, " Go back Sal and stick to your professor like glue until you master this". I did just that and passed the exam. However, I was a bit uncertain as to whether it was due entirely to my efforts or my professor getting tired of seeing me every day after class. Whatever the reason, I was grateful to have conquered Logic, but English was a different matter.

My English professor quickly diagnosed I was floundering. She first noted the dichotomy in the way I spoke and wrote, with me explaining this may have been due to my earlier education with French, Notre Dame nuns who concentrated on written not spoken language. This explanation fell somewhat short as it did not explain my odd way of expressing myself particularly my avoidance of certain words. I was still reluctant to discuss my learning problems fearing it would stop my education. She kindly worked with me to improve my written assignments, a gigantic uphill struggle. Deep down, I kept hoping I would outgrow my handicap by twenty-one. Having to work harder than other students had long been accepted. Concentrating so hard on my studies, I had forgotten my grandmother's advice in guarding my remarks in a religious institution.

Within weeks of my arrival, I was summoned to the Dean's office. When I entered her office the Dean, whom I initially met in applying to the College, seemed very upset and in a commanding voice asked; "Why, as a Roman Catholic student, do you not attend daily Mass in the chapel?". Every week day at eleven thirty Mass was held in the chapel which every Catholic student was expected to attend.

My immediate reply was; "I do not like having my head counted when I go to church."

Abruptly she responded, "I'll have you know young lady we don't count heads at this college".

Without thinking I replied; "Well, if you don't count heads why am I standing in front of you?" and not waiting for another response, I continued. "I go every morning to the six o'clock Mass in the village. You can call the priest if you like".

"Who do you go with?" she asked, knowing that all the Catholic students were in chapel.

Ignoring the question, I pressed on; "That's not the point, all that is required is that I attend daily Mass".

Not wishing to prolong the argument she pointed to the door saying, "If it is true you go to the village, then you are dismissed". I knew this wasn't the end of the matter, she would definitely check. I was back in the world of conformity and few organizations trust non-conformists. I knew I had to try and conform but first I had to warn my morning travelers (a Protestant from Florida, a Moslem from the Caribbean and a Confucianist from China) of my encounter with the Dean and the possible implications for them. The reason my morning companions traveled with me was to know something of the Roman Catholic religion.

Undeterred, they agreed to continue our morning walks. During our journeys up and down the mount hill, we chatted about many topics in addition to religion. As young women, we had much in common. We were quite traditional in our views. We saw our life as one which included marriage, children, a role in a community and a continuance of the religious traditions of our families. We wanted healthy, educated children, boys and girls, who would strengthen society. There was little disagreement and definitely no proselytizing. We traveled this route Monday to Friday in good weather. Whatever check was made by the Dean, I was pleased no pressure was applied to my companions. More students joined us in the spring as the weather improved. When I was summoned a second time to the Dean's office I then recalled my grandmother's words, 'watch what you say as walls have ears'.

Earlier in the day while standing with a group of girls, I agreed it would be better not to have children if you knew they would starve, to me a rather practical point. Unknown to me, my comments were immediately reported as I was the only Catholic in the group. Unsure of the reason for my summons, I waited until the Dean gradually revealed my crime was not so much my morning comment but 'how' I planned to prevent such pregnancies. Seeing a loophole, I said the conversation hadn't reached that point, trying not to reveal her question had opened a tantalizing point. Almost immediately, sister realized the summons had likely achieved the opposite result, dismissed me. After this I became more cautious and circumspect in who I chatted with or near. Discussions in the open air with close friends became the norm which reduced any further trips to the Dean's office.

The early months at college were hectic, familiarizing myself with the routines and studies, an entirely different environment from high school. Thanksgiving arrived quickly. With the majority of college/university students without cars and little money, travelling home was mainly by bus or train. Mount students, heading home for the holiday, walked down the long hill to the local, dingy, Rockingham train station to join other post-secondary students who had boarded the train in Halifax. It was a lively trip with loud voices, laughter and songs, cut off too quickly as I departed at Truro. On this holiday I was anxious to share my experiences with my family.

Much to my surprise, within hours of my arrival Mother revealed my father had not spoken to her for weeks (strange behaviour for him) after delivering me to The Mount. He blamed her for my early departure from home. My mother seemed genuinely miffed by this, saying " I don't know why you went off to college, I wanted you to stay home and take care of me."

This statement made me equally perplexed as my mother's attitude over the years left me with the distinct feeling she was ashamed of having a girl, particularly a child that looked different (whatever that meant) and one that was stubborn and silent. As I listened she continued describing recent family events while I was at college, making me feel guilty that somehow I had deserted the family in my selfish pursuit of learning. As if in exasperation she concluded her remarks with; "I never understood you. You could have asked your father for anything, and you asked for nothing. You are indeed a strange individual, very different from me".

This was genuine frustration. To my mother I would always be 'different', the disparity growing greater with the passing years. Thankfully she would never know of my handicap, which would have exaggerated my difference. As a young girl I dearly wanted a normal mother-daughter relationship but seemed helpless in achieving it. In my grandmother's words 'it was not to be'.

I was puzzled by her comment of asking for more. Why would someone ask for anything extra when it was clear the family was just surviving? My father worked long hours to keep us housed, clothed and fed, why would I burden him with a request for more? Yet, deep down I knew my mother's viewpoint was likely more common than mine. It was important for me to understand her world as well as my own. However, the fact that I was at college did not mean family problems disappeared. Mother saved as many unpleasant decisions for me to handle when I came home on holidays. A factor which haunted me each time I packed my suitcase to travel home. I was glad to be on a different path and pleased to return to my studies.

The last flicker of a 'finishing school' was still evident at The Mount in the early sixties. Students were expected to participate in dancing classes, theater productions and Sunday teas. Gunther Buchta, of CBC Don Messer Jubilee TV fame, came weekly to teach us ballroom, South American and Polka dancing. With no males on campus, I was pleased when another girl agreed to lead, preventing me from indelibly imprinting such signals on my brain. Armed with such dancing skills, we thought we were ready for any social dancing demands of the time. But our social lives were limited. There were a few student dances at other universities, as well as at The Mount, swimming at Stradacona pool, movies in the city and toboggan rides off The Motherhouse hill. I let it be known I was only interested in 'platonic' relationships, as I needed to complete my studies. Thinking this would prove disastrous, I was amazed by the number of potential dates it engendered. With limited funds, few scholarships and a single opportunity to get a degree, many boys shared my objective. They also liked my directness.

Life was perhaps simpler in the early sixties. Sexual promiscuity was shunned and getting pregnant had the worst possible stigma, and certainly destroyed any academic pursuits. While most girls accepted this conservative view, there were a few Mount students from Montreal who had a different opinion. We were told, they were involved in a call-girl network. I was never interested in the details. This was pretty flamboyant for The Mount. Yet, as the sixties unfolded our conservative views would be under attack with the arrival of the sexual revolution.

As for theatre, each year, the freshman, sophomore, and senior classes were expected to present a play for adjudication. The evaluation included how smoothly stage scenery was changed between acts. The Freshmen class decided to perform 'The Bird in Nellie's Hat', a turn-of-the-century comedy. We were all neophytes in the theatre world. The greatest fun was creating the costumes, especially the huge hats. As the Director, I found it impossible to pull the entire cast together to rehearse the whole play. Weeks slid by and still we had little practice of the complete play when the show date arrived. We pressed on in faith knowing the seniors, preparing a Shakespearian play, were the favourites anyway.

The first act had scarcely begun, when one of the actors flubbed her lines bouncing us into the third act. Stunned, we madly scrambled behind stage trying to find a solution. It seemed like an eternity, but finally, a brave individual from New York walked on stage, creating a new play line, bouncing us back to Act 1. Miraculously, we finished the play without further incident and waited expectedly for a thrashing by the adjudicator.

When the adjudicator indicated he would give his judgment starting with the freshmen, we all cringed. To our amazement he began with a chuckle, then congratulated the class for their quick ingenuity in saving the play, and gave us second prize. No one but the adjudicator noticed the flub. In fairness the seniors fully deserved the first prize with their superior performance. My Director's role would give me a deep seated respect for stage managers. While we all toasted each other with pop and were delighted in telling the tale, I knew the theatre was not my calling.

Music appreciation involved endless hours of Gregorian Chant, and my luck in attending my first symphony concerts as a companion to an elderly Mount graduate. We had little time for much else. Formal teas would be a different challenge.

Monthly teas were held to prepare young ladies for their place in society, to know how to dress and speak properly. Mount students, dressed in their best (I only had one dress), hat and gloves, mingled with Mount Alumni to sip tea, eat sweets and engage in stimulating conversations over a two hour period, a daunting expectation for teenagers. How I envied my mother's social skills at such events. At my first tea, desperately trying to carry on a conversation, I made my first social blunder by asking one of Halifax 'finest' ladies if 'I ever met her potato picking'. Shocked, her response was dripping of hurt and insult as she abruptly turned and walked away. After the tea, my Newfoundland friend replied with a mischievous grin, " Sally, that's a no, no…it's like me asking if she ever went cod fishing". After that I spoke only when asked a precise question and managed to survive the rest of the afternoon teas.

Our student days were long, starting, for me, at five in the morning when I rose to go to the village church for Mass. After this there was breakfast, classes and/or lab all morning and afternoon, serving in the dining room for the five o'clock formal dinner and evening study. Any relaxation was on weekends but this too was filled with study. The weeks melted away as we faced weekly quizzes, mid-term tests and final exams. Studying for my final exams I found a unique hide-a-way in The Mount attic, a glassed-in area above the main college entrance which housed a large statue of the Virgin Mary. Student trunks and other items were stored on either sides of the space. In total isolation with a magnificent view of Bedford Basin, I spent hours summarizing every course into a few small sheets of paper. It was a painstaking exercise, but a winning strategy at exam time. I memorized the details related to the summarized pages. The night before each exam, I retired early, awoke refreshed, quickly scanned my summarized notes and went off to write. This rather laborious method helped me successfully pass my first year of studies.

By this time, Papa had his own Safety Surveys business, working on contract for insurance companies trying to rehabilitate delinquent transportation companies to reduce their accident rates and costs. Because of poor or addicted truck drivers shipments were ending up in the rivers or in crashes along the highways. Papa had the authority to stop trucks on the main highways for spot safety checks, a process I watched numerous times. If unsafe, Papa would pull the truck to the side of the road and contact the head office. Since he was on the road a lot, he often dropped in to see me and, at times, we went out for a meal. Once he arrived unexpectedly near supper time to inform me he was heading to the Halifax docks to investigate some cargo thefts. The Halifax docks, not safe at the best of times, could be worse at night. He asked me to call the police should he not check in with me by nine-thirty that evening. Needless to say, I spent the evening anxiously waiting for his call and rehearsing what I would do if he did not call. This was not required. The phone rang right on time to say he was heading back to Truro. Nothing else was ever said between us about the event.

On another occasion, Papa picked me up to go home for a rare weekend and instead of turning towards Truro, we went to the Halifax docks. We sat silently waiting for a truck to arrive. When the eighteen-wheeler came to a stop, Papa leapt from the car, yanked open the cab door and pulled out the driver, beer bottles tumbling out behind him. Papa slammed the driver against the truck fender stating in a loud voice "Your fired!" As other truck drivers gathered around I expected trouble. My father turned defiantly telling them to 'back off'. They obeyed, seemingly aware of the situation. The driver, evidently drunk, gained some strength and started swearing at my father. Papa demanded the keys and drove the truck into a parking place, locked it, and we left, stopping briefly as he talked to some security man. We talked of other matters as we drove home, Papa pointing out trucking problems as they sped by. Papa's dream was to improve the provinces truck driving record, a dream he would realize in the years ahead.

My first year at The Mount was a time of much healing and growth. I loved learning and talking to girls from other provinces and countries. It was an environment of beauty, serenity and intellectual expansion. I felt at home and life held some hope. As my first academic year came to a close, I was pleased to have not only passed my exams, but to have high marks in a number of courses. It had been quite a struggle. Only Papa was interested in my academic record when I came home.

I had barely time to refresh and repack my belongings to return to The Mount for a summer semester in organic chemistry. For July and August the three resident nursing students joined other summer students in a brown, two-story house hugging the main highway, across from the railway tracks. The house had about fifteen students and one housemother. The summer environment was more relaxed and our days were embellished with the lush greenery and flowers of The Mount campus. Organic chemistry students had few breaks.

While inorganic chemistry had been difficult, I enjoyed organic chemistry because it was logical, the formulae were easy to memorize. It was a small class of about twelve students; a mix of pure science, nursing (seven) and dietetic students, all needing this course for their degree. Leading the class, my professor asked me to tutor several classmates which I was glad to do. Surprisingly, I enjoyed teaching, perhaps because I knew how difficult learning could be. He tried to persuade me to switch to chemistry. However enticing, with no science scholarships for girls, the idea was quickly shelved. Anyway I preferred working with people.

One of my lingering lab memories is of a wee nun, with a gentle personality, who required the course for her dietetic degree. She had the unique ability of blowing up the simplest mixtures, even skillfully turning her lab partner's pink sweater a dirty green. It was unnerving for me and my lab partner to find this team working directly behind us. Every time sister said 'oh dear!' we both ducked.

One day, experimenting with chemicals containing properties close to dynamite, the professor cautioned us to avoid letting the flask fluid turn orange, as this was a pre-explosion signal. Totally absorbed in what we were doing, I momentarily looked up to see panic in the eyes of our professor as he yelled "Everyone, turn off your burners and Get Out!". I knew where to look. Turning I saw the bright orange flask. Within seconds the professor sent the flask and lab apparatus into the deep sink at the end of the work bench, turned on the taps as we all raced into the hall. We stayed there for some time until he was certain it was safe to return to the lab. Needless to say, after this, the experiment was removed from the student's curriculum for safety reasons.

The sleeves of sister's habit were in tatters by the end of the course, her religious order refusing to replace her habit until her chemistry course was over. One wondered what the future held for sister if her lab experiments were any indication.

Passing the course, I once again returned home to reshuffle my belongings and prepare for the nursing component of my degree studies. I arrived home with a long list of inoculations needed prior to entering nursing, including Typhoid and Yellow Fever. The day I went for the inoculations, the doctor made no comment as he injected both arms and my buttock. My plan was to return home to complete the ironing I was doing for my mother. I had barely started the ironing when I collapsed to the kitchen floor. When contacted, the doctor informed my mother that in light of the number and severity of the inoculations, it might be days before I recovered. This was a wake up call that the next stage of learning may hold some unexpected hazards.

The second year of my degree program started in September 1961, Papa once again, helping me carry my trunk into a beige, four-bedroom, on the ground floor of the first-year nurses' residence. The residence was an old, three-story, building situated on the corner of Morris and Queen Street in Halifax. My bed was between two large windows with metal bars, the room being at the street level corner. Quietly standing at one of the windows I could see my father was not impressed with the run-down building nor the deteriorating neighbourhood. The only saving grace for me was that it was being run by nuns. The first year nursing students residence was located next to the hospital on the edge of what might be described as skid row, a section of the city that had seen better days. The Mount students were assigned two adjacent, front rooms. This facility was a far cry from the serenity of my first year.

The Halifax Infirmary had been a two hundred and fifty bed, acute care, private hospital providing medical, surgical, obstetric and pediatric services to the citizens of Halifax. Not all patients were Roman Catholic. The building consisted of two sections; an old, four-story brown brick building (the original two hundred and fifty beds) and a new beige brick eight-story building (an additional two hundred and fifty beds) under construction which would double the bed capacity of the hospital. The construction was nearing completion. The hospital was run by the nursing order of the Sisters of Charity, the same sisters as at The Mount. The main difference between the nursing and teaching orders, was the nursing sisters wore white habits. At the beginning of the sixties, the old concept of hospitals being a place for surgery and dying was rapidly fading with the arrival of the Canadian publicly funded national health system. As we entered the nursing ranks, the Infirmary was in transition, still retaining some of its old private hospital features as it evolved to its new status of a five hundred bed acute care teaching hospital. We would be in the vanguard of the nation's publicly run health system.

The Infirmary had three nurses residences, all old houses located on Morris Street; the first year students resided in the one adjacent to the hospital, the second year students in one mid-way between Queen Street and Barrington Street, and the seniors were in the one at the corner of Morris and Barrington Street. All buildings were on the same side of Morris Street. While students experienced a raise in status as they moved from one residence to another, in reality, all facilities were old, run down and cold. As the months passed, we became too busy and tired to protest the quality of our accommodations. However, any limitations in building quality was quickly ameliorated by the comradeship of our nursing colleagues.

The seven Mount students joined thirty-five diploma students, the biggest number ever to be admitted, to form the first year nursing class. In time we would learn why such a large class had been recruited. The diploma nursing students came mostly from the Atlantic provinces; Nova Scotia, New Brunswick, Prince Edward Island and Newfoundland. The nurses training program was an apprenticeship, with the nurses receiving a monthly stipend; five dollars the first year, ten dollars the second year, and fifteen dollars the third year. Board, food and uniforms were provided by the hospital. While these were often referred to as 'benefits', student nurses worked long hours for this meager stipend and benefits.

All student nurses, regardless of year, were identically attired in starched white uniforms consisting of several separate parts; a front-buttoned under dress, an apron with four buttons in the back band, a v-shaped bib, stiff round collar and a white, winged cap. After three months of orientation, we officially received our nurse's cap in a 'capping ceremony'. White nylons and white oxford shoes with a one inch heal completed the uniform. Curved bandage scissors slipped neatly between the four pearl buttons in the back of our apron band. Over our uniform, we wore a navy blue, woolen cape with a bright red lining, the red woolen ties crossing over the starched bib and tied at the back of our uniform. A gold, 'HI', lettering was stitched into the raised collar to identify our hospital. This woolen cap served many purposes, the chief one being as an extra blanket against the cold residences. Once I used it to cover an elderly women hit by a car on Barrington Street while waiting with the policeman for the ambulance. The policeman giving me his jacket while we waited.

The official skirt length was suppose to be four inches below our knees. This being 1961, several first-year students decided to make an independent fashion statement by shorting their dresses and aprons to their knee. This, the sisters promptly dealt with, by making them undo such frivolous efforts, and cancelled their meager passes for weeks. Conformity to dress and deportment were expectations of the nursing school.

Once the probation period was over, we reported on duty every morning crisp, clean and neat. Discipline was such that if your hair touched your starched collar or your white shoes were not properly polished, you lost the few privileges of two nine-thirty passes per week and a overnight on the weekend. In the first year many of us never saw these passes due to some small infraction of the rules. It was all put down to discipline, a characteristic nursing schools inherited from the military and religious orders.

The pattern of the three-year registered nurses program consisted of the following; the first year we were taught basic nursing procedures such as bathing, bed baths, compresses, dressings etc. and spend time on the general nursing wards caring for patients, working mostly morning and evening shifts. In the second year, we were dispersed to special service areas within the Infirmary (i.e. obstetrics, operating and emergency rooms etc) and other hospitals (pediatrics, psychiatry, tuberculosis, public health etc) mainly in Halifax and Dartmouth. By the third year, we assumed greater nursing responsibilities in the Halifax Infirmary such as managing one or more nursing wards. This is what lay before us as we began our first year.

To facilitate the scheduling and movement of groups of students, the first year class was divided into sub-groups of about fifteen students. We would progress through the different learning experiences as a member of a sub-group which meant we were more familiar with the sub-group nurses than the whole class. Our main connection with the whole class was in the nurses residence. After class or duty we gathered in the resident kitchen or lounge and chatted endlessly about the day and any problems we encountered. Like the military, there was comfort in sharing the misery of long hours of duty and the nursing challenges.

By the early sixties, the national health system, just recently introduced in Canada, was gradually affecting the front lines. The idea, introduced in 1947 in Saskatchewan, took decades for public pressure to force federal politicians to approve a cross-Canada program. The initial federal/provincial agreement provided a fifty-fifty share in the costs of hospital care. Later medical service costs were also covered. As nursing students we were on the crest of a vast change in health services. A change which meant an escalation in patient numbers in every health service.

Our first lesson as student nurses was to adjust to a different cultural environment. The military-like setting of nursing demanded strict protocols between different student classes, students and graduate staff, nurses and religious orders, and nurses and doctors. In 1961, as first year students, we were expected to step aside for all those above us (which meant everyone) before entering an elevator, which resulted in first year students always taking the stairs. Protocols also required nurses to stand whenever a religious sister or doctor entered a room or nursing station. A pecking order also existed for chapel, meals and almost every other facet of life. While we accepted these unending rules, behind the scene we griped about their absurdity, including how we addressed each other.

Every nurse was to be addressed by the formal title of 'Miss ....', in my case 'Miss Stull'. The frivolous use of first names was forbidden. As Stull was an unusual Maritime name, I got tagged as 'Miss Stool', an unfortunate name in the health field. My partner, Mary Bowles, got the tag of 'Miss Bowels'. Every time we were assigned a new ward, Mary and I clinched our teeth knowing in the first roll-call our names would come out as 'Miss Bowels and Miss Stool'. Interns and nursing students would snicker thinking it was a joke until we informed them of the proper pronunciations. We endured, needing a healthy sense of humor to survive three years of training with such identities.

The expected nursing behaviour fostered by the nuns was a 'stiff upper lip', a cool exterior, never showing emotion no matter what the circumstance which took some time for young nurses to acquire. We understood it was intended to protect the emotional health of nurses and give the patient and family the assurance we were in control. For me, this reinforced my earlier need to discipline my emotions in order to understand words. Now I could excuse such behaviour to my nurses training, a definite step forward.

Our days were full. We started about five-thirty in the morning to get dressed in our starched uniform, off to breakfast and chapel before reporting to the nursing ward by six-forty-five, in time for the morning shift report. As students we worked 'split shifts'; which meant being on duty from seven to eleven in the morning, off for lunch and classes from eleven to three, and returning to the wards again at four, supposedly to work until eight, which rarely occurred. Most nurses drifted into the nurses residence any time from nine o'clock on. Then we were supposed to study but most of us usually had just enough energy for a cup of tea and getting our uniforms ready for the next day. This schedule went on for five and a half days a week, giving us either Saturday or Sunday as a full day off, the only day for study. Escape only came with a written invite to a classmate's home for a weekend overnight, that of course only occurring if we had a pass.

Finding a place to study was a challenge in a noisy nurses residence. I eventually discovered a storage closet under the first floor stairs, a hundred-watt bulb my only lighting. Notifying the housemother of my location, I escaped whenever possible. Nursing courses were less difficult than university ones, but still required respect and thorough coverage. Such study time was curtailed not only by nursing duties but also because of my responsibilities as class president.

How I was chosen president of the class is still unclear, perhaps my incessant questions in the early days gave the other students some misconception of ability. I had little prior experience with such activities and, without thinking, accepted the post not realizing it was a three-year commitment. In the beginning my responsibilities consisted of meeting with the Nursing Director and/or the Education Director about schedules, student leave, uniforms, ill students, problems etc. which seemed manageable at first but this soon changed.

The Education Director was Miss Lillian Grady, a professional nurse of the old school. Until the sixties, most non-religious nurses employed in hospitals were not married. If a nurse married she could lose her job. Upon graduation, women who chose a nursing career, usually lived in a semi-private or single room in a nurses residences near the hospital or continued to live at home. Miss Grady, a pale, white-haired lady, was firmly committed to the concept of an autocratic, disciplined approach in training nurses.

The Nursing Director was Sister Catherine Peter. She was a tall, rather austere individual, particularly in her white habit, who loved power and equally believed in a strict training model and an autocratic (perhaps ruthless) management style. There were contradictions in Sister Catherine Peter's personality. She created 'favourites' who always did her bidding, yet, she detested 'yes' people. She wanted perfect nurses but attacked good nurses with humiliation, which eventually resulted in them leaving the organization. Father Dick's message of religious clothing not changing the individual certainly applied in this case. The majority of nurses feared Sister Catherine Peter and that was the way she liked it. These two individuals would be key players during my training years.

After completing our basic Nursing Arts classes, we were assigned five or more patients to feed, bath and/or prepare for morning diagnostic tests or other therapies. Most wards were over-crowded, the new wing had yet to open. Every room was filled and many patients could be found on stretchers in corridors. In time, our training expanded from routine bed baths and back rubs to compresses, dressings, stoops, enemas, pre-operative surgical preps, catherizations, medications, injections and intravenous treatments, our duties increasing as we passed each training step. The needles, at this time, were dull, as they had to be sharpened by hand. Because of this, nurses developed a particular wrist snap to propel the dull needle through the patient's skin. We prided ourselves on being quick and accurate.

From the outset, each student nurse carried several typed pages of lists of procedures which were to be *'signed off'* by supervisors or clinical instructors over the three year training period (2 1/3 years for Mount students). These pages were tucked into our uniform pocket, ready for every opportunity to get procedures signed off. In time, it became a rumpled, torn, and stained document, but critical to completing the training requirements.

From the moment I stepped onto my first nursing ward, I loved nursing and the feeling of being needed and serving mankind. Each of the eight-hour shifts had its own musical rhythm. The morning shift (7am to 3pm) was alive with activities as hospital staff hustled about completing morning assignments, patients getting off to diagnostic or other procedures; doctors arriving for morning rounds, students arriving to complete various assignments, and instructors conducting clinical discussions with students. The afternoon shift (3pm to 11pm) brought a different rhythm with patients returning from therapies, nurses busily carrying out treatments on patients following surgery or other activities, visitors arriving from two to four or seven to nine, and trolleys delivering evening beverages and snacks to patients. After nine a quietness enveloped the ward as visitors left, lights dimmed, patient's flowers were placed in the corridor, and the nurses prepared patients for the night. The night shift (11pm to 7am) had a hushed rhythm as nurses quietly conducted routine rounds with flashlights, checking dressings, and the vital signs of certain patients, calming those who could not sleep and whispering so as not to disturb sleeping patients. Like the rhythm of a moving ship, in time one grew accustomed to the routines and blended into its harmony, with all of its ups and downs. However, pleasant, being so young, we were rather naive to the hidden hazards in nursing which were rarely mentioned in any of our textbooks or classes.

Verbal abuse was rampant. Young nurses could receive tongue lashings from doctors, nuns, nursing supervisors, head nurses and even upper class students. Some took pleasure in their superior position while, fortunately, there were others who were genuinely helpful remembering their own difficult training years. Students eventually developed a thick skin but such abuse was never pleasant and for some, it left permanent scars. My handicap with words proved helpful in such circumstances. I stopped trying to translate the words but couldn't avoid the negative energy.

Physical abuse left more long-term wounds. While patients under anesthetic or medication could be excused, others were well aware of what they were doing. My first encounter came one evening when myself and another nurse were assigned the task of getting a two-hundred and twenty pound lady out of bed. She had been admitted with a broken wrist, having fallen on it at a party. She was perfectly healthy except for her wrist, now in a cast. The doctor's orders were to keep her mobile, fearing potential complications due to her weight. Just as my one hundred pound nursing classmate and I had her in a full upright position, she announced 'she was too tired' and fell back onto her pillow. This abrupt action lifted me off the floor, throwing me across the bed and against the wall, the crashing sound echoing through the corridor, bringing her doctor and other nurses. The patient was unperturbed. X-rays found no broken bones but I was off duty for a week, sleeping on the hard resident floor to rehabilitate damaged muscles. Even with the greatest effort, in my first year I was socked in the jaw several times, bounced over a stretcher and shoved against a wall by patients. Each encounter making me more cognizant of potential risks. However, patients were not the only problem.

Qualified doctors, unlike their television image, have 'privileges' in hospitals and spend only set times each day in the building on rounds or in surgery, whereas, residents and interns may spent longer periods in the hospital. Doctors rely on nursing staff to provide the twenty-four hour assessment and care of their patients. As a general rule, in the sixties, the majority of doctors regarded nurses in a subservient role. There were always the exceptions, those few doctors who treated nurses as intelligent colleagues and valued their judgment. Unfortunately, there was a small percentage of doctors who abused nurses, and did a great deal of damage to the doctor-nurse relationship. A couple of examples follow.

One doctor, a surly, cantankerous individual, had the habit of throwing things at nurses when he got upset. One day, I was asked to accompany him on his morning rounds. In the midst of the rounds, the reason unclear, he angrily picked up an empty metal bed pan and threw it forcefully at my shins, yelling something about the stupidity of nurses. Even my long apron could not protect me from the pain as the bedpan slammed into the front of my legs. With tears in my eyes, I instinctively reacted. Grateful for my father's athletic abilities,

I picked up the bedpan and sailed it back with the same intensity at the doctor's shins. He crumbled, cursing and shouting at me. I turned and walked out of the room. Since student nurses looked alike, he encountered a silent wall when he tried to identify me. This controlled his juvenile behaviour for a few weeks.

Another doctor, one of the chief surgeons, use to sexually fondle student nurses whenever he had a chance. One evening, I raced to the elevator to get sterile supplies, the Central Supply department being on the top floor of the new wing. I entered the elevator to see Dr. A as the only other passenger. My predicament increased when the elevator abruptly stopped between floors and the doctor lunged at me. Just as I yelled "I swear, if you lay one hand on me it will be your last!", the elevator started shaking violently and, instead of dropping to the basement (the expected route), shot abruptly to the eight floor. The door snapped open to reveal Mother Superior standing, her arms folded like an avenging angel, asking "What happened?" Dr. A, pale and somewhat disoriented, sheepishly looked at me. In an angry voice I replied; "I'm sure, Dr. A will be delighted to tell you, Sister." and rushed on to get my supplies. After this, he avoided me like the plague, the episode definitely reducing his ardor. I was simply grateful for divine intervention. There was little done to discipline these delinquent individuals in the sixties leaving young nursing students to fend for themselves. Besides this, there were other nursing hazards which came with the territory.

A more serious problem was needle pricks, a common occurrence. These occurred because patients moved or struggled just as the needle was about to be inserted. Under such conditions, an unshafted needle could easily nick a nurse on the hand or any other part of her body. It happened so fast that prevention was almost impossible. The danger of this was brought home in the early days of training when a twenty-four year old graduate nurse died within forty-eight hours from a needle prick from a patient with hepatitis. The nurse had not revealed she had had a prior episode of hepatitis, and this reinfection was fatal. Hepatitis was just one disease, there were many other diseases which we had to be aware of as we cared for patients. Another routine problem was exhaustion and illness.

The Halifax Infirmary, having three student nurses residents nearby, had a guaranteed backup with any nursing shortage. In winter, with unexpected snowstorms, students often worked extra hours and even double shifts. With long shifts, study and constant contact with disease, student nurses easily came down with the flu and other illnesses. Once, working a double shift and burning up with a fever, I was rescued when a doctor decided to take my temperature. It was 102°F. I can remember the wonderful coolness of the blowing snow as I walked back to the residence, to be invalided for a week with a streptococcal throat infection. Another time it was pneumonia. Yet, my biggest health issue was not illness, however serious, but allergies.

If the Halifax Infirmary had not been so desperate for nurses, I'm certain my allergies, would have resulted in my dismissal. My hands and arms broke out in watery welts with antiseptic soaps (particularly green soap) and disinfectants, and my skin dried and cracked with formaldehyde. The powder from certain medications produced red eyes and sometimes blurred vision. Such reactions should have signaled the presence of harmful chemicals for all nurses, an occupational hazard which was mainly ignored. In addition, whenever I returned from a home visit I came down with asthmatic-like wheezing. After a few rounds of this the doctor who attended to students informed me I was allergic to cigarette smoke. I then recalled my grandmother complaining about my breathing problems as a child. Everyone in my family smoked but my grandmother and Aunt Di. Such respiratory attacks usually lasted for about forty-eight hours. An interesting side-effect of my many years with sinusitis was that, with a poor sense of smell, I could handle cases other nurses with more sensitive noses found impossible. However, all these hazards and issues were quickly dismissed when our working conditions took a turn for the worst.

In our naivety, we did not connect the size of our class to the opening of the new hospital wing, being flattered in being told we would be the first class of nurses to work in this modern facility. What we didn't realize was the Nursing Director had decided, in order to accommodate the nursing needs of this new wing, our class would be jettisoned early into second year studies. Typical of the era, this rather critical change was communicated to few, and definitely not to students.

It all came to a head when a doctor, a gynecologist, thinking he was teaching more advanced students, sarcastically referred to us as the dumbest second year students he had ever met. His reference to second year students immediately alerted us to what was happening in a number of courses. Frustrated, tired and angry, I saw, a husky nurse from New Brunswick rise from her seat with vengeance in her eyes. Jumping between the two, I crisply stated, "First, we are first year students and because we have not had the clinical experience you are expecting, we do not know what you are talking about. This is the first we knew of this. I believe we both have a problem". Furious, he stomped out of class, striding toward the Nursing Director's office. Within minutes Miss Grady arrived.

Flustered, Miss Grady, instead of acknowledging the problem, started to harangue us about unruly behaviour. The class by this point was angry. Ignoring Miss Grady (which further infuriated her) I turned to my classmates suggesting they might go to the cafeteria and wait, which they did. Then I left with a glowering Miss Grady as we marched towards the Nursing Director's office, me some steps behind. What followed, was my first encounter with human resource management under fire.

In the office the doctor angrily argued that, not being informed, he had not been able to adapt his curriculum and had wasted valuable time. Sister Catherine Peter, ignoring the doctor's plight, kept reiterating she expected more obedience from nursing students. It took some time before there was an opening for my comments. As forcefully as possible, I described the detrimental effect of such a decision on our class; ten students were in bed with the flu, eight were facing academic failure, a number had already left nursing, and the morale of the rest of the class was disintegrating. I kept hoping that the potential decline in student numbers would give me an edge. Saying students were upset at not being informed seemed a useless move as we were at the bottom of the totem pole. My words proved futile, as Sister Catherine Peter remained focused on what was going to happen to the ringleaders of this unruly behaviour, looking straight at me. Exhausted and realizing nothing was happening, I said "Well, since no one wants to listen to the student's predicament, the first year students will remain in the cafeteria until someone does!" and walked out, the Nursing Director's words burning a hole in my back as I left. For the first time, the hospital had a rebellion on their hands. As the clock ticked, the students continued their sit-in. We used the time to get better organized, knowing life would never be the same. We wrote a list of needed changes, hoping some of the items might be addressed. I knew personally standing up to Sister Catherine Peter would have consequences.

Finally, I was paged to return to sister's office. When I arrived, I found Sister Catherine Peter, Miss Grady, Sister Catherine Gerard, our hospital administrator, and the Chief of the Medical Staff. The hospital administrator, realizing at least thirty some nurses were refusing to go on duty (however humble our skills) was ready to negotiate. I presented our demands (perhaps better classified as 'needs') to improve class and work schedules, provide better resident supplies (i.e. soup and juices) for nurses off with the flu or other illnesses, and some academic leniency (i.e. more time). The students realized that expanded skills were in our best interests getting us closer to graduation. To my amazement, most of the changes were accepted and the nurses went back on duty. I was weary after so much tense conversation but knew that Sister Catherine Peter would be gunning for me. In the following weeks, she found ever excuse to punish me. When I finally thanked her for giving me more study time, she capitulated. Such stress, however, had a price.

Shortly after, I collapsed with a bleeding ulcer and was admitted to hospital. Actually, I was rather pleased for the rest. The doctor informed me I must of had an ulcer from the age of ten or eleven. I mumbled 'perhaps' providing no details. Since I had trouble with milk as a child, cream on an ulcer diet had to be sipped slowly to control the nausea. The rest proved regenerative. After discharge I ate cheese and custard and avoided milk. Within days one of my former Mount professors, a sister, arrived for a 'wee chat'. Over a glass of milk , she inquired about recent events, passing no judgment. We agreed the hospital world was very different from the tranquil world of academia. After this, whether due to the Mount's intervention, my illness, or the fact another brood of students were arriving, Sister Catherine Peter eased up on her attacks. For awhile there was relative peace.

With few, if any, passes our social life suffered. Former university dates got tired of the uncertainties and cancellations when making a date. Yet, with youthful determination we managed to get to a few dances, movies and meals out with one or another group of young people. My dates were with a tall, red-haired, Dalhousie University student from Boston and a Tech University student from India, his father being a senior administrator in one of the Indian states.

One rainy evening, on a date with my East Indian friend, when our intended movie was cancelled we went to visit his engineering friend. During the evening his friend asked if he could read my palm. Happily, I agreed. He opened with a rather uncanny understanding of my family (information not given to my boy friend) and my academic degree program stating "I see you in a nurse's uniform on a university campus, is that correct?" Then he continued, as he gazed into the distance like my grandmother:

"You will complete your present studies in the allotted time and, after many years, will complete further studies. Your first marriage will end. In time you will remarry. There will be four children, you will have no girls, and in your 26th year, an event will occur which will completely change your life".

Expectedly, I asked further questions on what he meant by the 'end' of my first marriage, and especially what was to happen in my twenty-sixth year, but to no avail, he did not seem willing or able to provide more details.

On my next trip home I told my mother of these predictions thinking she, being Irish, would enjoy the 'spooky' nature of the predictions. Being young, I took the positives and ignored the negatives, but mother appeared uneasy. Like my grandmother's predictions, I should have paid more attention.

As our first year of nurses training drew to a close we counted the cost. About twelve students had left the program; some disliked nursing, some to illness, some could not live with the severe rules, and some to marriage. Four of the twelve who found the rules too difficult managed to get into other city nursing schools.

Gratefully, my handicap was not an issue in nursing. I developed a system of memorizing medical standing orders and procedures, checking everything four times instead of the usual three, and listening carefully to patients and fellow health workers. The regimented routines in health care were easy to follow once learned. I also established an early policy, for safety reasons, of not recording doctor's verbal orders on the run (an all too common routine in hospitals) insisting they write their own orders. I endured their anger.

With all its trials and tribulations there remained a great joy in service to others, in the comradeship of my classmates and in the family feeling of being part of the heath community. I had survived the first year of nurses training and actually looked forward to the challenges of our second year.

In the fall of 1962 my brother, David, entered the Bachelor of Commerce degree program at St. Mary's University. Papa wanted him to pursue a business career but he was overruled by a local Roman Catholic priest. David enjoyed the university social life, continued to have study problems and never finished. Over the next few years he would periodically arrive at my nursing residence thinking his sister wealthy with her monthly stipend.

My second nursing year (third year of my degree program), found us on the affiliation road, spending up to three months in different clinical settings; first in different specialties within our own hospital and then in other hospitals/facilities in the region. We were on the move, signaled by our transfer to the second-year student residence. This time, the Mount students were assigned two large rooms under the eaves at the top of the building, four in one room and three in another. The room was so cold in the winter that I asked one of my classmates if I could borrow her dead grandfather's woolen robe. I was only able to get to sleep in winter clothed in flannel polo pajamas, wool socks, a woolen robe and my nurse's cape as an extra blanket.

My first affiliation was a month in the hospital kitchen, responsible for special diets. It was good Mary Bowles, my partner, had been a baker prior to entering nursing, as I had learned little cooking in a kitchen controlled by a grandmother, mother and other women in my youth. Our task as nursing students was to make custards, soups, salads and other 'special' diet items for about a hundred patients. We had little supervision and were mostly left alone with lots of manuals. Any questions were directed at the kitchen staff who were always ready to help. Although leaving two teenagers to run this segment of the kitchen should have invoked some concerns.

Most days we managed quite well until one day a Nursing Assistant student arrived to spend the day with us. Wanting something to do, she unfortunately asked me for the custard recipe. Occupied in preparing diabetic salads, without checking the manual, I rambled off 'sixty eggs' (triple the recipe). Before I could correct my mistake, the student had put sixty eggs in a blender and the eggs were flying in all directions, splattering against the walls and floor. The young student, realizing her mistake, sat down and cried. Mary panicked, fearing we would be punished because of the waste. I burst into laughter. Counting the splattered eggs I recalculated the recipe and, the next morning prayed as I inserted the first custard trays into the oven. It was great, we had enough custards for a week. The old pastry Sister, quietly congratulated us on our ingenuity in resolving a rather sticky problem. In time this affiliation would be dropped. For me, I was left with an abiding respect for the kitchen staff who day-after-day turn out reasonable meals for both patients and staff. They are one of the unrecognized stalwarts of the health system.

Our next affiliation of three months was much more challenging, the Operating and Recovery Rooms. They were located on the eight floor of the new wing. Dressed in green tunics, pants and caps, we hesitantly reported to the charge Sister. With no orientation other than a general tour, we were set loose. Our check list stipulated we had to have hands-on experience in numbers of major and minor surgical cases; including scrub up, room set up, assisting with the operation (as first or second scrub), and clean up.

The Infirmary operating rooms were busy. Patients who had previously avoided expensive surgery were lining up under Medicare. Because of the number of cases there was a twelve hour operating schedule, crews arriving at staggered hours for major cases in the morning and minor cases latter in the day, interspersed with emergencies. We became experienced with appendectomies, tonsilectomies, gastrectomies, cholecystectomies, hysterectomies, amputations, plastic surgery, eye, ear, nose and throat surgery, orthopedic surgery, kidney surgery and the list went on.

My first day's experience was almost my last. With no orientation, I was flung into my first operation, a minor surgical Dilatation and Curettage (D & C) procedure, with little knowledge of the instruments or procedure. Nervously, I entered the operating room to find the anesthetist already in place and a Registered Nurse rapidly completing the set up, and then she left. In came Dr. B, a gynecologist. After a quick banter with the anesthetist, he sat down to begin the operation.

Responding to his first request, I handed him the speculum which he angrily threw back, the metal instrument landing abruptly on the top of my gloved hand as he cursed at my stupidity. He kept demanding different surgical instruments giving me no clue as to which one. The situation for both of us was a stalemate; I was looking at a tray of metal instruments for which I had no identification and he was growing increasingly angry. All the while he kept cursing at me. Frustrated and angry at being subjected to such behaviour, in my youthful fury, I picked up the scalpel blade from the tray and started waving it under his green mask which immediately got his attention. Trembling with anger, I slowly stated; "Stop cursing at me and stop throwing instruments. This is my first day and we've received 'no' instructions, so, politely tell me what you want."

Calmly he asked me to put down the scalpel, which I did. We then proceeded, very politely through the surgical operation pointing to each instrument he wanted. I was convinced my nursing career was over once my actions got reported. I discovered later that this was Dr. B's usual behaviour with student nurses, which often resulted in tears. My career was saved by the senior anesthetist who prevented Dr. B. from reporting the incident. This was my lowest point, the rest of this affiliation went smoothly.

Our days were filled with scrubbing into one case after another and spending time in the Central Supply area cleaning trays of instruments, packing and sterilizing surgical instruments and kits; each kit carefully designed for its specific purpose. It was fascinating to see the precision and complexity of surgical procedures, and the quality of some of the surgeons. However, I found the experience too technical, lacking the patient contact I preferred. Surgical intervention held both positive and negative outcomes, with student nurses having lingering questions over radical surgery, particularly on elderly patients.

Next we spent a month in the Recovery Room. Still dressed in operating room greens, our role was to check the vital signs of post-operative patients, change dressings, check drainage and intravenous solutions, and give intramuscular injections. Intensive care wards were in the future. When patients were sufficiently recovered, we transferred them to the nursing wards, providing ward nurses with up-to-date information on the patient's post-operative status.

The usual recovery room rhythm flowed easily except for one day. I was ordered to remove an intravenous needle from the right arm of a rather heavy-set unconscious male patient. In bending his arm the patient was in danger of breaking the needle. As I withdrew the needle, his left fist automatically rose connecting with my jaw, causing me to land in a huddle against the wall. Amazingly, the patient remained unconscious. I was bruised for some days with a very sore jaw. It was a good lesson in being more observant.

Our next affiliation was a two month stint in the Emergency department and back in a white uniform. The department was ill designed and staffed for its new role. My supervisor was an older Mount graduate, a tall, slim black nurse from the Caribbean, her even temper set the tone for the department. The atmosphere was further enhanced with the arrival of several fellow classmates from Newfoundland, their quick wit greatly easing the chaos of our daily environment.

The flood gates had opened and injured and disoriented patients with every conceivable ailment walked or stumbled through the emergency doors or were delivered by taxi, car or ambulance at the emergency entrance. Often working on weekends, we became accustomed to the Friday/Saturday night bar fight candidates, drunks delivered by police for bandaging prior to jail, or hemorrhaging female teenagers from back street abortionists, joining the rest of the walk-in patients with respiratory or cardiac emergencies, cuts or breaks and numerous other illnesses. This was an exhausting service with few breaks.

Arriving home for a rare weekend, I went to Sunday Mass with my mother only to encounter a Roman Catholic priest ranting about women and abortions, suggesting they were all going straight to hell. Thinking on the senseless death of several young girls, one fifteen year old dying in my arms at the emergency entrance, in the middle of his sermon, I got up and walked out of church. I was troubled over the lack of compassion in a Christian priest, and a society, that forced a frightened young girl to choose such drastic life-threatening steps. Priests were equally against prevention. Mother arrived home later, annoyed at me leaving church. There was little discussion for I knew mother supported the church's stand, and I was on a different path.

With any affiliation gap, student nurses were reposted to Infirmary medical or surgical wards, usually on the evening or night shifts. The exception for me was that I also got reposted to the Emergency Department, likely because of my survival abilities in the midst of chaos. Other nurses were equally favoured. In addition, having been pushed ahead in our nurses training, we now found ourselves 'in charge' on the evening or night shifts which meant at eighteen, I entered the first level of nursing management.

Working the night shift student nurses could expect a dinner prior to reporting on duty at eleven. If missed, nurses were usually starving by the three o'clock tea break. One advantage of working in the old wing of the hospital was the kitchenettes had more food, supposedly there for patients.

One night my classmate, Pat, not expecting the supervisor for hours, decided to make herself an egg sandwich because she was famished. Called away to attend a patient I was unaware the supervisor, a nursing sister, had arrived unexpectedly to our ward. When I returned to the kitchenette Pat was standing like a wooden soldier with the oddest look on her face telling me of sister's visit. Startled, I inquired if sister caught her making her sandwich. "No" she replied sheepishly, "when I heard sister's rosary beads (our early warning signal), startled, I snuck the two raw eggs into my arm pits, why I will never know. All was going well until sister asked me why I was standing so stiffly. Unthinking, I corrected my posture by tightening my arms even harder against my body. Thankfully, sister was called away on an emergency". Now Pat, raised her arms to reveal the yellow yoke dripping down her white starched uniform. Relieved at not being caught, we both burst into laughter and went to the utility room for a quick cleanup. However, days of routine duty were about to be interrupted by world events.

Halifax being a military city was familiar with war time activities. It was October 1962, and the Cuban Crisis was heating up on the Atlantic coast. As the crisis escalated, a special emergency meeting was set up for all student nurses 'just in case'. Halifax military were convinced if bombs started flying between Russia and the United States, we in Canada would not only be caught in between the two super powers, the Atlantic sea lanes would be busy.

All student nurses were asked to sign a document choosing either to be trucked out of the city in Red Cross vans with mobile patients to satellite hospitals (to be set up in regional locations) or go to the hospital basement with the nuns to care for the critically ill. I immediately stepped forward and signed up for the basement, much to everyone's astonishment. When asked why, I said that getting out of Halifax was difficult at the best of times, it would be impossible in a war time emergency. I preferred to spend my last hours caring for patients. To sister's surprise, other students agreed.

Next we were asked to upgrade our skills to a senior level within forty-eight hours in preparation for increased responsibilities and possible mobility. So, for the next few days we scrambled to not only learn new skills but to get them signed off by an appropriate supervisor or clinical instructor. Successfully completed, we were ready for whatever the war might bring.

Weeks later while on evening duty at the end of visiting hours I glanced out a Queen Street window to witness a row of Red Cross trucks silently making their way towards the emergency entrance. My heart sank. Before I could reach my colleagues, a repeated message came over the public address system "All cars on Queen Street be removed immediately." Visitors left quickly. With no indication it was a drill, nurses moved into emergency mode consolidating emergency drugs, supplies and rearranging the patient/visitors sitting room to receive the injured, all the while calming patients and visitors with the assurance that this was likely a drill. As we waited for further orders we discussed the movement of patients, being on the fourth floor we were concerned about how to evacuate the sickest. Finally the 'all clear' was given. Nerves were rattled and we had weathered the test. Thankfully, this was the closest we would come to any war. Nevertheless, the event alerted us to life's realities.

In December, on a snowy morning, I was called to Sister Catherine Peter's office expecting student issues to be the topic only to be asked to replace an ill senior nurse at Pier 21. A health team composed of members from different hospitals had been there for some days doing a medical triage on European refugees, many from Hungary, who had arrived by ship. Halifax had welcomed previous Hungarian refugees in 1956, this was another group escaping the revolution in their country.

I arrived at Pier 21 to join an already established health team and following a quick orientation took my place for the days' routine. The Pier facilities were cold and I thought somewhat unwelcoming. My heart went out to the people who had lost everything, arriving in a new country in winter. Most candidates were being redirected to temporary housing in Halifax awaiting passage on the Canadian National Railway heading to Montreal and places west. Those with relatives or friends in Canada would eventually find help adjusting to their new country when they finally got connected. Others would have to make it on their own.

The day was just about over when a sad, tired and anxious looking young mother appeared with a toddler and infant. She spoke no English. She had stayed behind to care for the baby who was cranky, possibly teething. As we rushed to clear her I noted the unease in the social worker's face. When questioned, she indicated adequate quarters for a mother and two wee children would be difficult at this late hour. After some deliberation, I proposed we try a different tack. Realizing the Jewish community would certainly understand the plight of refugees, I suggested phoning Mr. Jacobson (whom I did not know personally), a well-known clothier on Gottington Street. In phoning, I wasted no time in explaining our predicament. Without hesitation, his deep voice responded positively.

Within the hour a black chauffeured car arrived and out stepped Mr. Jacobson. He quickly assessed the situation, asked me to join him so as not to upset the mother and children. The snow continued to fall. We drove to his Gottington street store, where I proceeded to select snowsuits for the children when Mrs. Jacobson arrived with a Hungarian-speaking lady. The mother relaxed. I was told accommodations had already been found and the Jewish community would continue to assist her. No longer needed, Mr. Jacobson drove me back to my residence. On departing, I asked if he might tell me how it all turned out. Some time later, a note arrived at the hospital front desk to inform me the woman's brother had been located in Montreal and she and the children, along with her interpreter, were on the train to Quebec. I quietly thanked God as I slipped the note into my uniform pocket.

In the fall of 1962, I met Ronald William Linkert, (called Ron) on a blind date. He was a dark, handsome five foot eleven inch, quiet, polite man from Ontario, a member of the Royal Canadian Navy. Other nurses were also going out with navy men. Finding time for dates was complicated by his sea voyages and my nursing schedule. It was a simple, quiet love affair. Our dates consisted of long walks, movies, picnics, occasional dances and enjoying the many low cost activities in Halifax. In time, we journeyed to Truro to see my family. My mother's assessment was "He's quite handsome, but not a Catholic (Ron was Lutheran)". Father was pleased Ron was a good golfer, practical, a real 'Mr. Fixit' around the house, and a good cook. In all, his politeness and quiet manner seemed a welcome addition to the family. Like many nurses, I chose someone compatible with my family. Looking back, I'm sure if my grandmother had been alive, she might have voiced some predilections over the relationship. I received no such comments from my family, in fact the very opposite, everyone seemed pleased with my choice. Ron and I eventually started going steady, as steady as two difficult schedules would allow. In the early sixties this was a very platonic relationship, which took great discipline. I was still mid-way in my nurses training.

⋯⟡⋯

My next three month nursing affiliation was to the obstetric (maternity) department, on the fifth floor of the old wing of the Infirmary. In similar tunic and pant attire as in the operating room, but blue rather than green, we settled down to classroom lectures on normal and complicated pregnancies, yoga and the natural delivery of babies. Halifax had only two maternity hospitals (The Halifax Infirmary and the Grace Maternity Hospital run by the Salvation Army). Since this was the pre-contraception/abortion era, we could expect a steady stream of deliveries during this affiliation, usually fifteen or more a shift. A 'natural delivery' policy at the Infirmary meant minimum drugs, no anesthesia except Trylene inhalation gas and British trained midwives on duty. Caesarian section operations were rare, and an anesthetist coming down the obstetric corridor signaled a complicated delivery. As nursing students, we were expected to guide the mother through her labour, transport her to the delivery room, assist with the delivery, and transport the mother to the maternity ward and the infant to the nursery.

Unfortunately, our affiliation occurred at the same time a newly appointed, young nun came to the obstetric department as the supervisor. From the start, she made it clear everyone (doctors, midwives, graduate and student nurses) were incompetent and, without her constant presence the quality of service would collapse. This stance immediately solidified our working relationship; 'we' against sister.

As the days unfolded and our skills increased, we felt more and more confident in delivering babies, but, of course never adequate for sister. I felt at home in obstetrics, perhaps because it was generally a happy environment or perhaps some inheritance from my grandmother. It was a busy setting with routine and complicated deliveries. By the second month, I had assisted with delivering babies in the delivery rooms, patient bedrooms, in the corridor, on elevators, on the delivery room floor when one woman refused to get onto the delivery room table, in a quarantined bedroom when the mother arrived with measles, and in a taxi cab at the hospital entrance during a snow storm. In the latter case I could feel the icy snow blowing up my tunic and pant legs as I waited for the baby to be delivered. The outcome was successful for the mother and infant, and even the taxi cab was spared from damage, but I was ill from the cold. The next thing I knew I was being wrapped in warm blankets and given many cups of hot tea. The timing and location of baby arrivals was never a precise science. To appreciate the full maternity process, we also spent time in the nursery and post-delivery ward.

The nurseries, painted pink and blue to segregate female and male babies, created endless problems for nurses as babies did not arrive in gender specific patterns. Our duties in the nursery consisted of changing numerous diapers, checking infant vital signs, preparing formula and bundling babies back and forth to their mothers on the maternity wards. About ten infants were transported in each trolley, plastic separations keeping the bundled babies firmly in place for transportation. We prided ourselves at matching babies with their mothers, although we always checked the arm bands. Having difficulties with green soap I was allowed to use a different soap, as washing our hands was paramount. Most students assisted with circumcisions. I also volunteered to assist the Jewish Rabbi. The weeks on the maternity ward were uneventful except it brought our Infirmary affiliations to a close. We were now ready to travel outside our home hospital.

My next affiliation was with a Halifax Public Health Nurse as she made home visits providing treatments, inspecting local restaurants and conducting polio immunization clinics for school children. At this time Halifax had a city Public Health department, a Provincial Public Health Department, and the Victorian Order of Nurses, all performing similar activities. It remained unclear to us as students where the lines between the three existed. As students we were assigned to one. This was our sole community nursing contact, which, to me was regrettable for I learned a great deal from this Public Health Nurse especially where to find the cleanest restaurants in Halifax.

Next we had a one month affiliation at the Dalhousie University Public Clinic where we, for the first time, joined student nurses from other nursing schools. The public clinic, a cold gray stone rectangular building was located across the street from the Children's Hospital on University Avenue. In the majority of cases we were dealing with pre- and post-natal check-ups for women, general check-ups on infants and children and dealing with venereal disease cases, the clients coming from the poorer sections of the city. Eventually this clinic would close when all patients were absorbed into the Medicare program.

At the clinic a policy existed whenever doctors discussed contraception with patients', Infirmary nurses were asked to leave the room. The first time this happened, I insisted on staying to learn what instructions were being given to these women. I knew my action would result in a summons from Sister Catherine Peter, which occurred before the day was out. Amazingly, Sister Catherine Peter calmly accepted my explanation and asked me to try and not disgrace the hospital on my affiliations, which was never my intent. Her behaviour was so unusual I suspected other forces were absorbing her attention. I continued attending the contraceptive sessions and soon, other Infirmary students joined me. Next we travelled across the street to the Children's Hospital for a three month affiliation.

The Children's Hospital, a two- story, white, wooden building was constructed around 1909 and with expansions over the years was supposed to accommodate about two hundred children. This capacity had long been exceeded by the early sixties with cribs lining every corridor and extra cots/beds jammed into rooms. With the introduction of Medicare, children from all over the Atlantic region were being referred to this teaching centre for care. The hospital admitted children from infancy to fourteen years of age. We arrived in the spring of the year to a very out-dated facility with no air conditioning. Once again we were affiliating with nurses from other city schools.

This was a challenging experience. It was always a delight to care for children. Children had a short attention span and were either very sick or playful. The medical/surgical pediatric classes were excellent except for the Child Psychology instructor who monotonously read, line-by-line, from a textbook, putting most students to sleep. Being springtime, we had lots of children with various respiratory illnesses, the children generously sharing their germs with nurses. I acquired a bad case of laryngitis which did not respond to medications and only resolved with the summer sunshine.

Giving injections to ill infants and children was difficult, especially with dull needles. The most difficult cases were children with burns. With no special burn units, these children were in single bedrooms under strict sterile technique. If they survived the initial stage, they faced extensive hospitalizations of skin grafts and possible plastic surgery. Such illness matured these young patients, a feature we noted in children with other handicaps and long-term illnesses.

Many young children with cleft lip and cleft palate came to the hospital for corrective surgery. Our task was to provide pre- and post-operative care, with lengthy feeding routines due to their complexities of breathing and swallowing. It was such a pleasure to see the positive post-operative results and the smiles on the parents faces.

Our days on the infectious disease ward involved continuous quarantine protocols (i.e. gowning and ungowning, masks , and constant hand washing). This ward was located on the third floor of an adjacent building to the Children's Hospital, a post-war, brick structure, the lower floors occupied by the Civic Hospital, an adult extended care facility. Besides the usual infections, one particular case stood out.

A young boy, about eight, was admitted with a suspected case of meningitis, diagnostic tests seemed unable to pinpoint the organism. The medical staff were anxiously watching his progress to avoid the fatal outcome of his ten year old brother who had been admitted weeks earlier. The older parents were devastated with one death and feared a second. His temperature was soaring and medications seemed to be having little effect. So, to lower the boy's metabolism giving the medications a better chance to act, the doctors decided to place him on a cooling mattress along with an open window to the cold March weather. Every four-hour shift with this boy left the nurses practically blue. For days the young boy remained unconscious while we monitored his vital signs and intravenous fluids.

One day, while I was on duty, the weather shifted and the boy woke up. Checking for any brain damage, I quickly asked him a number of questions which he answered correctly. Not certain his temperature would hold, the charge nurse and I packed more ice around him as he slipped back into a coma. After this the doctors got us to bring him out of his coma one degree at a time. He soon recovered with no complications and was delighted in telling me "Boy, wait till I get back to school and tell the kids I was frozen like a fish." While I had cared for an adult patient using freezing for leg surgery, this was the first time it was used for the entire body.

The poison control clinic was difficult as we had to mummy screaming, fighting children in sheets so that a rubber tube could be inserted into their nose and down into their stomach to extract the poisonous material. Children seemed capable of swallowing almost anything (i.e. after shave lotion, perfume, shampoo, oils of all description, soap, polish, aspirin and all varieties of pills). One would think the pain and discomfort of such a procedure would prevent further episodes, but not so. During our short stay some children were repeat offenders. It obviously was a symptom of other problems.

With so many infants, formula preparation was a major activity. Working in operating room attire (i.e. green cotton tunics and pants, caps and masks), we melted in the intense heat of a non-air conditioned formula room with large autoclaves working full time. Most of us lost five to ten pounds. One solution, however minor, was to cut our hair very short. On my next trip home, upon seeing my sheared locks, Papa complained he had enough boys in the family.

The over-crowded, wooden hospital facility was always a safety concern. One lunch hour, the fire alarm went off with three student nurses caring for a number of very ill, premature infants, all in incubators. Realizing we could neither move the incubators nor the infants, we agreed one nurse (myself) would stay behind while the others left. Before we had to implement such a decision, we were given the 'all clear'. Fortunately, a new hospital was in the offing. Our time passed all too quickly and, with regret, we prepared for our psychiatric affiliation, across the harbour in Dartmouth.

To reach the Nova Scotia Psychiatric Hospital we daily boarded a bus, hired for nursing students, and traveled across the Angus L. MacDonald Bridge. The psychiatric hospital was a five hundred bed mental health teaching facility, caring for male and female adults and some children. The beautiful campus, overlooking the Halifax Harbour, consisted of an old brick buildings dating back to 1858 when the facility was known as the Asylum for the Insane plus several upgraded facilities and single houses. Once again we joined other hospital student nurses on affiliation.

A large ring of keys jangled in our pockets to open and lock tunnel and ward doors, a security procedure which took time to adjust to. Psychology and psychiatric lectures were provided to nursing and other students (i.e. medical students, social workers and chaplains). With the arrival of more effective psychiatric drugs there was an air of change and excitement in the treatment of mental illness. Unfortunately, electric shock therapy was still is use for many patients, a procedure which had many detractors. While our daily routines seemed easier than in the acute care environment, there was a definite tiredness at the end of a shift due to hours spent dealing with the emotional problems of individuals or groups.

It didn't take long to recognize the obvious dichotomy between acute and mental health care. Mental health staff focused mainly on mental symptoms often at the exclusion of physical symptoms, while the situation was reversed in the acute care hospitals. Both approaches provided fragmented care, a side effect of a health system structured on specialization.

Occasionally psychiatric patients were admitted under a Governor General Warrant as involuntary admissions. One such case was a fourteen year old street gang youth from

Halifax. While admitting him, I observed several episodes of mild eyelid fluttering and his inability to repeat parts of our conversation. In my notes I mentioned he might be having mild epileptic seizures. This was immediately dismissed by the psychiatric medical staff (not happy that a student nurse was making a medical diagnosis) but investigated by a visiting medical consultant from the Victoria General (VG) Hospital. His tests revealed a walnut-sized brain tumor in the boy's head. After successful surgery at the VG, the tumor being benign, the seizures ceased, and the boy was discharged, hopefully away from street gangs.

The male admission ward housed both children and adults, a bad mixture. The children had a variety of mental illnesses from autism to personality disorders. Always wanting to separate the two groups, I often took the children to a quiet part of the hospital campus on sunny afternoons. There we would spend several silent hours, my difficulty with words giving me some empathy with these disturbed children.

One day while talking to Mr. James, the Head Nurse, who checked on the children, an autistic boy quietly pushed his hand towards me saying "Bee" (a bee sting). Continuing my conversation with Mr. James, I reached down, made a wet mud pack (as I had watched my Grandmother do) using water from the open tap and earth. No words were exchanged between the child and myself as we stood for a few minutes holding hands. I then rinsed off the mud, checked his hand, and he ran off gleefully. Smiling, Mr. James stated "You didn't learn that in a nursing book." "No", I replied, "I learned it from my grandmother". We then had a grand chat about grandmothers.

An interesting case was a five year old child rescued from Pictou County woods, admitted on a diagnosis of being 'socially deprived'. Her mother had refused to speak to the child preferring to let her run free like an animal in the woods. One young nurse spent weeks trying to get the child to speak, the only response being screams, scratches and punches. Almost giving up, she was rewarded one morning when the child said; "Ann" pointing to herself. Words slowly came with her first complete sentence being, "I have two fathers, one lives in our house", likely what her mother was trying to avoid. Ann eventually went to live with foster parents and attended school.

Electro-convulsive Therapy (ECT)[1] was an unpleasant nursing experience. First, adult male and female patients were given a mild anesthesia which was followed by an electric current to produce an epileptic seizure. Our role was to assist in the administration of the treatment, and later monitor the patient until they recovered. It was the treatment of choice for depressed patients and was also used with other mental conditions. As students we questioned such a traumatic approach to care, and wondered about the long-term physical damage.

Mental health presented many questions which three months could hardly address. Questions about how to prevent such illness, the benefits of group therapy and the revolving door of addiction care. Alcoholism drew my attention in light of my brother's addiction. Nevertheless, the experience left me with an abiding interest in mental health, and I would return to this specialty a number of times in my journey. As this affiliation came to a close, we once again returned to the Infirmary wards.

Medicare had not only increased patient numbers, it had also increased the need for more professional staff. At a time of such expansion it was not surprising a medical imposter could slip through the many checkpoints. In charge on morning duty, I quietly scrutinized the arriving group of interns and, for some reason, one individual bothered me. Intuitively, I was uneasy about his manner and gave instructions to my nursing staff not to let him do any procedures, especially bloods, until I could make further inquiries. Some nurses were already trained in taking bloods (I received such training in obstetrics). My suspicions were confirmed when the intern, while annoyed at my orders, made no protest. A few days later, when the Chief of the Medical Staff, stepped off the elevator, I expected an argument about my treatment of the intern. Instead he inquired why my ward was the only one in the hospital that restricted this man's activities, as the medical staff had just learned he was an imposter. I could only thank my genetic inheritance.

Our next affiliation, and the last outside the Infirmary, was to the Tuberculosis (TB) Sanitorium in Kentville. This affiliation had been delayed as I kept failing the TB test, which would have shown whether I had any resistance to the disease. This was unsettling for the school. Eventually, I had to sign a school waver in case I contracted TB while on affiliation. I then left on an Acadian Bus with other nurses for two months in the valley of Nova Scotia.

My non-reaction to the tuberculosis organism preceded me and within twenty-four hours I was relegated, for my entire affiliation, to have lunch in the medical staff dining room, the only student. This daunting experience had the eyes of six medical doctors riveted on me for any symptoms of TB. Their concern was over losing a fellow medical colleague to TB with a similar lack of defense for the disease. This time they were taking no chances.

The Tuberculosis Sanitorium, created in 1904, was a single campus housing several brick and prefab buildings for patients and residence facilities for students. The facilities had been erected to isolate patients with this very contagious disease, some being in the hospital for years. Patients were mainly from Nova Scotia, and consisted of all ages from teenagers to elderly, male and female. There were separate nursing wards for adult male and female patients, and a separate wards for teenagers and children. There were still pockets of TB in the province and some young military men acquired the disease in their travels. Only with the arrival of antibiotics and innovative surgical procedures (just being introduced as we arrived) did these patients have much hope of returning to a normal life. Even with antibiotics, we as nurses had to take extra precautions with all sputum specimens.

The Sanitorium would be my first introduction to stainless steel needles. One morning I took a tray of antibiotic injections to male patients on a nursing ward. Using the same technique we had adopted for dull needles, I was startled when the intramuscular injection swiftly cut through the skin, so fast the patient asked if I was aiming for the other side. Gladly, we adjusted our technique. For a brief period of time we needed two techniques, the old and new, as the arrival of new needles varied by hospital.

Classes in caring for respiratory patients were excellent, the nursing responsibilities reasonable and the facilities great. Why anyone would continue smoking after these lectures confounded me. The constant, gown and mask techniques were already familiar to us from earlier affiliations. The most amazing post-surgical care was occurring with immediate physiotherapy and ambulation of patients.

Prior to the completion of this affiliation, I suddenly came down with a sniffle and slight head cold, an annoyance in the middle of summer. Immediately, the doctors had me confined to bed and ordered every conceivable diagnostic test. I wasn't feeling very ill but remained in residence being checked daily by one doctor or another. Taking no chances, they decided I had to be 'shipped' home to the Infirmary. So, I found myself bounced back to home base with more weeks of tests. My cold cleared and eventually the blood tests stopped. I understood their concern, but grew impatient with the numerous needle pricks.

In each affiliation we were expected to pass the specialty exam or exams. Those who failed or for various reasons (i.e. illness) were unable to complete the affiliation, had to either repeat a full or partial year of their nursing program because of nursing school rules and difficulties with rotation schedules. Fortunately, The Mount students cleared all the affiliation hurdles. We now faced our final year of nursing and degree program.

In the Fall of 1963 we moved to the senior nurses residence on the corner of Barrington and Morris Streets. We were now in a large dormitory for eight students, the beds separated by curtains much like patient cubicles. There was little privacy and no escape from the noise. Working different shifts, it was almost impossible to get enough rest especially for those on evening and night shifts. Thankfully this would be brief. In January, the Mount students, were scheduled to return to college. Our final nursing duties would be on the emerging specialty wards such as gynecology and urology.

Gynecology was located in the old hospital wing. In my first week I encountered the gynecology doctor I had previously battled with in the operating room. Needless to say he was startled to find me in charge of the unit and remained 'very polite' the whole time we worked together. The senior gynecologists, very pleasant men, were edging towards retirement. The younger group were focused on change and introducing new procedures and technologies, a challenge for all of us.

It was a very busy service, female patients from the Halifax/Dartmouth area were finally getting surgical attention to old gynecological complications created by bad obstetrics and/or too many pregnancies. In addition, the first radiation treatment (pellets) for cervical cancer was introduced. Breast cancer, vaginal repair and hysterectomy surgeries were common. Since the word 'abortion' in hospitals refers to all lost pregnancies, we handled many such cases and were expected, as nurses, to baptize aborted infants of Roman Catholic mothers.

The complexities of gynecological problems and family dynamics were common. In one case, I had just completed the pre-operative preparations for an emergency hysterectomy on a hemorrhaging woman, her gynecologist talking quietly as to what lay ahead. Suddenly the door burst open with her husband screaming and refusing to sign the consent form (a requirement for surgery), stating if she had the operation she would no longer be his wife. Time was critical and the doctor's rage was palpable. The doctor pulled the husband out of the room continuing a heated discussion in the hall. The consent was signed, a psychiatrist called to deal with the outraged husband, as we raced to the operating room. The woman survived, but we wondered about her marriage. Surgery was capable of answering only one of a complexity of human problems.

A shortage of nurses was a daily occurrence. Senior students were mostly in charge on the evening and night shifts, working with one to two other students caring for about thirty patients. One evening I was pleased to welcome a registered nurse to fill a vacancy, and felt blessed when she agreed to do the medications, leaving the other student and myself to handle the patients. All was going well, I thought, until I opened the bathroom door to find the registered nurse injecting herself with some medication. The shocked look on her face spoke volumes. All I could say was "Damn!" and call the supervisor who arrived instantly. After a brief chat, sister and the nurse left the ward. With no other backup I faced a daunting task in covering the evening shift with another student nurse and myself. I kept reassuring my colleague we could somehow manage, as we started dividing up the work.

To my shock, Sister Catherine Peter arrived to assist me. The workload was again reorganized, my colleague covering medications, Sister and I handling the patients. Sister immediately accepted me as being in charge, a surprise move. We worked the entire shift, side-by-side, as I witnessed the expertise and quality of care provided by a skilled nurse. There was an easiness in patient/nurse banter and an efficiency I admired. This was a very different person from the one I had often battled with. We actually laughed and had tea together. That evening I learned some people are better as clinical practitioners than managers, a situation I would encounter again in my journey. Leaving gynecology, my next assignment was in charge of a ward created for patients being transferred from Prince Edward Island, Cape Breton and Newfoundland for specialty surgery in Halifax.

My team consisted of nurses from the same Atlantic provinces. I even had permission to soften the 'stiff upper lip' protocol creating a more relaxed environment with jokes and even singing. One nurse even brought her guitar. The team blended well and had a fine routine established when, short-staffed, I welcomed a somewhat austere British trained nurse to the team. Before lunch she demanded a meeting.

In a firm voice she stated, "I have never witnessed such frivolous behaviour from nurses in all my life, surely you don't condone this?"

My efforts at describing the objective of the ward proved futile so I finally gave her an option, "See if you can manage the rest of the week, and by Friday if you can tell me the nursing care is poor, then I will definitely listen." She agreed. As the days passed I observed a fine nurse but remained skeptical whether she could tolerate the environment. On Friday we met.

Before I could ask the first question she blurted out; "I take it all back. These nurses are giving the best care I've ever seen and the patients are definitely happy. I may not fully understand the jokes or songs, but I can certainly appreciate what you are trying to do". "Fine", I said, still unsure " do you want to stay, or would you still prefer a transfer?"

"I'd like to stay" she said, and in no time she blended beautifully into the team. Later one of the supervisors stated; "Well, it didn't take you long to contaminate a good nurse." I just laughed. It was good to see the innovative approach was benefiting the patients. Knowing the ward was in capable hands, I was transferred to urology.

Urology, another thirty bed surgical ward was in the old wing. The chief of staff had decided senior student nurses would be given advanced training in various urological procedures including abdominal dialysis. The workload was heavy with about six to eight surgical cases a day Monday to Friday. The sheer number and complexity of care was greater than on most other surgical services.

Not surprisingly, the ward reeked of urine. Nurses carried a small hemostat under their aprons to temporarily shut off the rubber drainage tubes to carry out certain nursing procedures, measure urinary flow or gather specimens. Soft brown rubber tubing was connected to indwelling catheters, linked to glass bottles taped to the floor under the bed. These bottles were frequently knocked over, the urine spilling onto the floor. With limited housekeeping staff, urology nurses cleaned up the mess with mop and bucket. The doctors laughed at the nurses' unscientific (in their eyes) approach of getting patients to drink lots of cranberry juice to reduce the urinary smell. In time the nurses approach would be proven correct.

Finding replacement staff for urology was a real problem, as the nurses needed to know many special protocols and procedures. Shortages were common on the evening shift. One evening there were three of us on duty; myself, another Mount senior student and a frightened Nursing Assistant student, just beginning her training. My Mount colleague agreed to handle medications, leaving the rest of the workload to me, as the Nursing Assistant could not be expected to handle complex cases. Seeing little alternative, I went looking for recruits.

I found two elderly female visitors who after some guidance agreed to prepare and serve routine evening snacks (tea, juice, toast, crackers and/or cookies). Those on special diets were being handled by the Nursing Assistant. Next, I asked a retired military officer, ready for discharge, to keep an eye on the male ward, ringing me if anything critical occurred. Then, I visited every patient explaining the staffing situation and informing them, for this one evening, they would be classified as 'A' or 'B'; 'A' patients, mainly fresh surgical patients would receive my undivided attention, while 'B' patients would buzz me on urgent matters. Everyone seemed pleased at being informed and agreed to participate in the rather unorthodox arrangement. However, one of my 'B' patients, a dear elderly religious sister, cheerfully shared the plan with the evening nursing supervisor, another sister, when she dropped in for a visit. Needlessly to say, I was immediately called on the mat for my inventive management system. Explaining, no matter how unusual, priorities were being addressed, patients and visitors seemed content and I would gladly revert back to old routines if sister could produce one urology nurse. Silence followed. Then sister rose and left the ward stating she would frequently check on our progress, which she did. The new recruits and system worked amazingly well but my innovative system was not encouraged. December had arrived and we Mount students were heading back to the academic world we left behind many months before.

My torn and fingered check list was almost completely signed off except for one item. Throughout my two and a half years, no patient had died on my shift. For some unknown reason, whenever I arrived on a ward even if the patient was close to death, the nurses would state, "Look who's here, Mr. X will not die on this shift", and he didn't. Every student had this item signed off but me. Nevertheless, Miss Grady approved my list regardless of this omission saying it would be most unusual if I continued in nursing without encountering a death. The clinical hurdles of my nurses training were completed.

At Christmas, Ron and I were engaged, Ron promising my father we would not marry until I was twenty-one and my nurses degree completed. Many of my nursing classmates were also engaged. Marriage was now feasible for nurses as more and more hospitals were opening their doors to married nurses, all except the Infirmary.

In January of 1964, I returned to The Mount penniless with no conceivable means of paying my tuition or residence accommodation. Prior to leaving the hospital I made arrangements to work at least one or more shifts a week, at a graduate nurses salary, the number dependent on my class schedule. But this money would only cover personal expenses. I was facing a major crisis. My parents didn't have the money and there was little special funding for the education of women.

Senior students were housed in a small white two story house located between the Motherhouse and the main College building. This gave us some degree of exclusiveness and a homey environment. The college was now moving towards university status which would be realized by the time we graduated. In our absence the campus had changed. Most under-graduates were better dressed than us seniors, many even had their own cars. Our years in the clinical field had changed us, we were older with little interest in college gossip or social activities.

I quickly settled into my academic and residence life but knew a decision was urgently needed regarding my bill. Gambling, I decided to negotiate with the college President, one of the college founders. My chances, I felt, were slim. So, after dinner one evening I sat on the corridor floor outside the President's office and waited for sister who usually returned to her office following evening prayers. Sister Francis Assisi was a well respected, middle aged woman, with a warm and open personality, characteristics which I prayed would now come to my aid.

Sister invited me into her office, and not wanting to waste time I dove headlong into my prepared speech. I argued the university needed two types of students; those with money and those with brains, trying desperately to classify myself in the latter category by listing some of my best marks. Then, I honestly described my financial dilemma including my hospital shifts. I declared a willingness to work anywhere on campus, but was unsure how I could add much more to my schedule. Completing my speech, I waited uneasily as she pondered my argument. Saying nothing, she rose, asking me to accompany her to the Registrar's office. The Registrar, another sister, was surprisingly on duty.

Sister Francis Assisi requested my file, and taking her pen signed a slip stating she would take responsibility for 'Sally'. I gasped, realizing my prayers were answered. The arrangement was that I would repay The Mount after graduating and in the meantime assume the role of senior student nurse. I even got the luxury of a private room. I gladly agreed to the terms and thanked her profusely for her generosity and faith in me. The contract terms would be met.

As the student nurse, my responsibilities were quite reasonable. There were the usual menstrual problems and occasional colds and flu. My biggest task was to listen to relationship problems. Often returning from class or hospital duty, I would find a student, sometimes in tears, needing to talk to someone. Placing pillows at my back, I would brace myself up in bed to listen. I soon got a reputation as the perfect listener, when in fact I was usually dead beat and kept praying the student would find her own solution on the premise there was healing in sharing thoughts. A few cases required many sessions and advice, my psychology and psychiatric training being useful.

This was mid-winter, so traveling back and forth from The Mount to the Infirmary presented some challenges. Dressed in a starched white uniform and wrapped in my navy cape, I walked down The Mount hill to the main highway to catch a bus. One Saturday I reached the bottom of the hill before realizing the snow storm had not only wiped out my footprints behind me, there was no cars or bus in sight. Thankfully, I was rescued by the telephone linesmen who seemed to be the only vehicle navigating that morning. The storm cleared while I was on duty and buses were back on for my return trip.

Returning to the academic world was a great shock as we once again faced more courses in philosophy, theology, and English (Milton). Wading through Paradise Lost and Paradise Regained was mountain climbing, aided only by Coles Notes. From January to May tests and exams seem to be coming at us from all directions. In addition to the regular college semester tests/exams we faced hospital senior exams, the provincial registered nursing exams, and the national registered nursing exams (i.e. the USA multiple choice nursing exams). We were stumbling under the pressure. In addition to these exam challenges, hospital work, and being the senior student nurse there were ongoing issues to face as the president of the nursing class.

I received an urgent call from my nursing classmates that Sister Catherine Peter was about to expel six senior students for smoking in residence. Irrespective of all our health information and training, many nurses smoked. While smoking in any of the old residences was dangerous, sister's punishment seemed severe. Heavy-hearted, I returned to the hospital to find sister in a foul mood. Nothing I said would deter her from expelling the nurses. Frustrated and mad I concluded my arguments with, "Sister, God is going to strike you dead for your callous disregard for decency and compassion for these nurses! They have served this organization faithfully for three years, and this is how you thank them." Slamming her office door, the glass reverberating behind me, I left desperately trying to find the words to convey the terrible news to the nurses waiting in the senior residence. At that moment sister called me back ending her statement with ".......before God's lightening bolt strikes me down."

The terms were not pleasant. Sister agreed to let the nurses graduate but for the next six months they would have 'no' leave, and certainly there would be no repeat of the smoking incident. Such punishment would be unthinkable in future nursing programs. At the residence I greeted many off-duty senior nurses waiting with the six candidates. Relieved to graduate, the group stood together assuring their classmates of support during the six month sentence. To improve morale and bring events to the confined students we decided to have a Valentine's dance in the residence.

On behalf of the class, I went back to Sister Catherine Peter to request refreshments for the event. She knew precisely what we were up to and gave me a resounding; "No, nothing will be provided by the hospital." Undeterred, the different groups went into action phoning city merchants for old valentine decorations and any other donations for the 'poor' Infirmary student nurses. The response was overwhelming. It likely was my call to the two breweries that brought the Bishop into the fray. I was immediately summoned to Sister's office to be informed the hospital would now provide the refreshments, if we immediately ceased community solicitations. The party was a huge success, the event giving the other nurses strength to plan additional events. The atmosphere was downright cheerful. With the situation in good hands, I returned to The Mount for my final academic push.

By May, only three of the original seven Mount nursing students were still managing to stay on schedule. The others would graduate shortly after us. The final hurdle for the three remaining nursing students was a summer course in Middle East History. Since I enjoyed history, I looked forward to these studies. At the completion of this course we were heading to our graduation.

On a beautiful afternoon in August 1964, dressed in black gown and a gold velvet hood, I received my Bachelor of Science Degree in Nursing at twenty years of age. Nanny's presence was palpable as I reached for my scroll. My success was witnessed by a number of family members; my parents, Sonny, Teenie, Rayona, David, Grandma Stull, Aunt Di, Uncle Huck, and Uncle Shake. Ron was away at sea. Papa's glee was evident in his frequent jigs and a delightful glint in his eyes. Grandma Stull was present at the graduation of her first grandchild. My gift was a gold and sapphire Mount ring. We celebrated with a gala dinner at one of the local restaurants. It was a truly happy occasion. In the sixties only two percent of nurses had a degree.

However, this graduation was only partial completion of our ceremonies, the Infirmary graduation lay ahead in September. Following a two week break, I would find summer lodging and return to the Infirmary for evening and night duty until the hospital graduation.

For the first time in years I had a two week holiday. Ron and I planned to visit his parents in Ontario. We traveled by train accompanied by Grandma Stull; Ron and I in coach while Grandma had a berth. By nine o'clock Grandma retired for the evening. Planning to stretch out and sleep on the train seats, I noticed a very weary mother in the adjacent seats coping with an infant and toddler, one train sick and the other fussing. Informing her I was a nurse, I offered to help. Ron dozed off. As the night progressed, the young woman and I took turns settling the children and stealing a few winks. In Montreal, her husband appeared, picked up the toddler and, thanking me, the family stepped out of my life.

Making sure Grandma was on the St. Catherine's train, Ron and I headed on to Toronto, giving me a change to catch a few winks. We were greeted at the railway station by Ron's mother and father, the first meeting of my future in-laws.

Lea (Lilah Elizabeth Shultz) was a robust, energetic heavy-set woman, the oldest of ten children who grew up in Saskatchewan. Lea's own mother, Bertha Dorothy Caroline (Cords) Shultz, was a smaller woman who, at the age of two, immigrated with her family from Germany. Bertha's father, Karl Johann Friedrick Cords, was born at Ruest, Mecklenburg-Schwerin. He married Marie Krueger and they immigrated to Francesville, Indiana in 1888. Karl Cords and his wife had ten children, the second oldest being Bertha. Karl Cords died at fifty-two of Tuberculosis, Marie went on to seventy-nine and died in Indiana where most of her children continued to reside.

Bertha, Lea's mother, married Henry John Karl Shultz, whose family also lived in Indiana, Henry's father coming from Germany as a young man. In 1913, Henry and Bertha immigrated to Saskatchewan with three children, one being Lea, moving to the drier climate because Henry had malaria. Being a well-off farmer, he transported his cattle by train and spent the early years developing his farm. The Shultz family would lose all their money in the 1929 depression and struggled to survive on their farm during the thirties. Lea being the oldest was sent to Regina in her teens to work as a domestic, experiencing some very difficult situations as a young woman. She would always regret not getting her education. Lea warmly welcomed me, her table bending with food which she had prepared for our visit.

Ron's father, Jacob Carl, was a tall, dark, quiet man who was also brought up in Saskatchewan. Jacob's father, also called Jacob, was born in Austria and moved to Minnesota when he was about a year old. Jacob's mother, Emelia Jackle, was also born in Austria, and moved to Regina at the age of fifteen. When I met her she could speak several languages including Yiddish. Jacob Linkert senior, was in the construction business in Saskatchewan, a business in which his sons were also skilled. There were two daughters and three sons in this family. Jacob senior, losing his money in the Depression, in 1936 moved to Ontario, finally residing in Kitchener.

Jacob, Ron's father, dearest love was building houses. One afternoon while out getting groceries, he turned the car unexpectedly into a strange driveway. Beckoning me to follow, he strode up to the garage door, touched it gently with his fingers and the door quickly opened, alerting the owner. Jacob introduced himself as the man who had built the house many years before. The owner warmly welcomed us into his house complementing Jacob on the superior quality of the building. He then demonstrated using, one finger, the ease of opening the windows.

Ron's only sibling was his older brother, Carl, who shared many of Ron's physical features. By the way they joked and tussled each other it was clear they were very close. In the sixties, Carl was already married to Marion and had a beautiful, dark, curly-haired daughter, Cindy, about two years old, a joy to her grandparents.

Jacob and Lea met in Saskatchewan, and following the depression joined the senior Linkerts in Ontario. They both worked very hard, having difficult years with little money when Jacob fell ill with rheumatic heart disease. Lea found work, from picking fruit and vegetables and eventually working in factories in the expanding industrial environment of Ontario. In the sixties, they were living in a modest high-rise apartment. It was a short and welcoming visit. As we traveled back to the Maritimes on the train I felt good about my upcoming marriage, I would be joining a well established, large family with links in both Canada and the United States. My marriage was still a year away.

Back at the Infirmary, awaiting my hospital graduation, I agreed to fill in for the evening surgical supervisor. On this shift many pre-operative forms had to be signed. However, the law in Nova Scotia at that time stipulated a nurse had to be twenty-one years of age to sign such forms. On most shifts, an older nurse could be found on one of the surgical wards but one evening only students were on duty. Thus, I had to take the stack of surgical charts to the Hospital Administrator's office. Prior to signing the forms Sister Catherine Gerard required a brief review of the patients due for surgery the following day. After she signed the forms she enquired about my age. She seemed surprised at twenty I was considered capable of supervising several surgical wards but not old enough to sign the surgical forms. I did not realize this discussion would have a bearing on the next stage of my nursing career.

Our hospital graduation finally arrived. The outcome of three years of difficult training was evident in the statistics. Out of an initial class of forty-two (35 Infirmary and 7 Mount) nursing students, only twenty-three graduated (fifty-five percent). The toll would have been worse if the six seniors had been expelled. We fully appreciated our successful completion of a very difficult program. As I stepped forward to accept my nursing diploma I could imagine my grandmother and my two aunts (Aunt Sally and Aunt Di) nodding their approval as another generation made a commitment to service.

Every graduate had a job, some at other hospitals. In 1964 change was already in the air. The ongoing need for nurses with the arrival of a publicly funded health system meant many more nurses would be needed. How these nurses were being educated would be a subject of intense scrutiny in the years ahead. For the twenty-three nursing graduates, we were now on our way, our personal and professional lives stretched out before us. This was a day of triumph!

THOUGHTS & LEARNING

In 1960, our freshman class at The Mount may have marked the dividing line between women who accepted a traditional role in society and the next generations, who would challenge almost every concept of this idea. The lingering finishing school features of dancing, theatre, Gregorian chant, symphony music and afternoon teas would disappear as academic programs demanded more and more of the student's time. Yet, these activities greatly enhanced our lives and learning. The Mount's female atmosphere gave me space to reflect on my future, to grow and to find hope. Being a small campus, students and faculty knew each other, a feature often lost in larger post-secondary educational institutions. Looking back in later years, I truly appreciated this special setting as the beginning of my professional life, I would not find it again. In addition, I would be grateful to my family, especially my father, who's democratic decision gave me an equal chance to further my education, and to Sister Francis Assisi, who's support helped me finish my senior year. One never does anything in life without help.

Our traditional nurses training program allowed me to care for hundreds of patients and many babies. The repetition, however routine, indelibly honed our skills and increased our confidence. At the end of such training we were capable of managing any type of nursing situation, and had even learned many advanced procedures usually relegated to doctors. We survived the discipline and autocratic rules and within this environment I found a spiritual focus in caring for patients, a deep love of nursing, an abiding compassion for the sick, a respect for front-line nurses and fellow health care workers, and a respect for the resiliency of my classmates. I also learned that caregivers (nurses) also need to be cared for and that good management skills are vital to the healing process.

The battles with Sister Catherine Peter taught me a great deal. I learned some negotiating skills as well as an appreciation of managers who use power humanely. The role of class president was difficult. It was good to get better study and working conditions for my classmates but it came with a great deal of stress. For a teenager, this was a difficult learning environment. Fortunately, Sister never learned of my handicap, otherwise I would likely have had an abbreviated nursing career.

The positive encounters of my nurses training far outweigh the negatives. Some negatives have been noted to explain the learning challenges of the experience. All had their purpose. I believe people and events are there for our learning, even the unpleasant. Perhaps it is the unpleasant ones that provide the greatest learning. In time, I became better able to anticipate some, but not all, potential problems.

In the early sixties we entered the health system as the effects of Medicare rolled onto the front lines creating massive increases in patient numbers. It was a time of growth; the need for new facilities and more professional workers. It was a great time to graduate as every nurse had a choice of a number of jobs.

It is hard to know whether our reduced social life as teenagers and the strict discipline of society in our generation regarding sex made us better or worse off when it came to marriage. We thought there were adequate social occasions, but compared to later generations our lives may have appeared rather restrictive. Perhaps we measured social relationships differently. We valued every opportunity our busy schedules provided to connect with other young people. Our lives were full. We had immense responsibility and knew, upon graduation, we had to get a job to support ourselves. Yet, we knew the world around us was changing. Immersed in work and studies, we quietly wondered how other teenagers had the freedom and financial resources we did not have. While we enjoyed the folk songs in local coffee houses we knew we were walking a different path. The unknown question was what this would mean for us as the years passed.

CHAPTER 4

Beginnings and Endings

L IFE had changed! I shed my starched multi-layered student's attire for regular cotton/ nylon white uniforms, the oxfords being replaced with softer leather, rubber- soled shoes. Even though I was back again on the same urology ward of my senior student days, there was a difference, I was now a registered nurse with a degree. I alternated between being a staff nurse on the morning shift and being in charge on evenings. It was invigorating to be caring for patients, and getting paid for something I loved to do. Enjoying my new status, I was unprepared for a summons to Sister Catherine Peter's office. Since I was no longer the class president, the purpose of the summons was puzzling. I arrived to find Miss Grady and Sister Catherine Gerard also in attendance. Contrary to many under-graduate meetings, the purpose of this summons was positive.

I discovered the Infirmary was about to launch a pilot nursing education project in September 1965 to test whether registered nurses could be trained in a shorter period of time due to the need for more registered nurses. Some were advocating a two year period, while others endorsed a two plus one pattern, the final year being an internship. Clearly the innumerable repetitions could be reduced but which ones and by how much. The Infirmary pilot study would focus on three specialties; paediatrics, obstetrics, and psychiatry, reducing each affiliation from three to two months. I was being offered the paediatric instructor's position, other nurses would be approached for the other two areas. However, the teaching position came with a slight catch.

In order to assume the position, I would have to go to Dalhousie University for a one year Teaching in Nursing Diploma, this being one of three post-RN diploma programs created to assist nurses specializing in teaching, administration, or community nursing. Knowing my limited finances, the offer came with a bursary which would cover the costs of my studies and some basic living. I needed to sign an agreement to work ten months at the Infirmary following graduation. During the ten months I would be paid at a first level faculty rate. The offer was sweetened by Sister Catherine Peter who agreed to place me on the private duty registry, giving me access to extra money. True to her word, I was regularly employed. Since I had already begun paying back The Mount, I was once again into the financial restraints of my university years. I suspected the secondary reason for this offer was to keep me occupied as I was officially too young to use my degree or RN status. So, I was off for additional university studies, this time in teaching.

No longer in nurses residence, I found accommodations with three other individuals in an apartment close to the hospital. Besides myself, there were two registered nurses (from New Brunswick and Newfoundland) and a Mount graduate, a teacher, (from Cape Breton). The older registered nurse was my urology head nurse who had anchored the apartment. The two bedroom flat was on the third floor of a rather ordinary apartment building, which housed other health professionals and some university students. Its strongest feature was that it was within walking distance to the Halifax Infirmary and major universities. My accommodations offered pleasant, compatible company but, for me, a much too lively setting for study. My only option was to do most of my academic work at the university during the day. Each morning I packed a small gray case with books and a hearty sandwich, and disappeared until supper time.

Twenty nurses registered for the Teaching in Nursing diploma program, most were experienced nurses who, for various reasons, needed a teaching credential. Teaching was prevalent in all aspects of nursing; hospitals, community and particularly in training programs. Being a relatively new program, this was the first time two degree nurses had been accepted, myself and another Mount graduate who had graduated a year before me.

Dalhousie University's sprawling campus consisted of a number of academic programs being administered from a series of old houses in the surrounding neighbourhood, which was where the nursing diploma program was located. For the next eight months this is where the nursing courses (i.e. curriculum development, teaching methods, audio-visual aids) would be held. The diploma program also required courses in psychology and anatomy and physiology, to be provided in the main university facilities. For the two Mount students these were repeat courses but Dalhousie, like most post-secondary institutions of the sixties, would not recognize courses from other institutions, even though the Mount was supposed to be an affiliate. As registered nurses we joined freshmen students in a psychology course of about three hundred students. The first semester focused on the sex life of the rat and the second the sex life of the monkey. For multiple reasons the failure rate in psychology was in the ninety percent range. Having had previous psychology courses was of some help. The anatomy and physiology classes, with young medical students, was provided in a dilapidated building, the snow blowing through the cracks in the windows during the winter. Note-taking wearing mitts was definitely a first. These two courses were the most negative aspects of the entire academic year.

Early in the program I discovered the age of graduating nurses was a rather touchy subject. In the first days, a heavy-set Public Health nurse stood up loudly protesting the trend of nurses being able to get their registration before their twenty-first birthday. According to her, this practice was dangerous and detrimental to patient care. The instructor uneasily glanced in my direction. I was sitting there with a degree and my nurses registration at twenty. In light of her rather angry protest, I thought it best to remain quiet. Anyway, Nova Scotia was about to lower the legal age to nineteen. Later this Public Health nurse and I became good friends, both laughing over the many changes in the health industry, age being just one.

The class schedule was a mixture of lectures and enjoyable discussions (at least for me) on how best to train nurses, with the latest teaching techniques being tested and evaluated by us students. The academic workload was reasonable. In addition, Sister Catherine Peter was generous in providing me with lots of private duty nursing shifts, letting me choose the cases that best fit my studies. Occasionally, she even allowed me to take my books if it was a quiet case. One evening she even sought my opinion on the hiring of married nurses.

With patient numbers continuing to rise and other city hospitals scooping up well-trained Infirmary married nurses, it was not surprising that sister was under pressure to reconsider the Infirmary's hiring policy. I expect the real push came from the hospital's Board. I argued strongly against her view of married nurses not being as committed to the hospital as single nurses, in my opinion there was no difference. It was a hard sell. Finally, she relented asking me to call five married nurses from our class as a test. I informed the five of their pioneer status in opening the Infirmary doors for other nurses. The Infirmary never looked back. The out-dated policy was scrapped.

With studies, work and my life in general humming along splendidly the days skipped by, Christmas came and went, with me returning to my second semester of studies. In February, I thought I was coming down with the flu, not uncommon at that time of year, but became concerned when the symptoms worsened. The illness began with blinding headaches and steadily progressed to encompass other symptoms; nausea, extreme tiredness, joint pain, difficulty in swallowing, a reddish skin rash over my nose, arms and legs, and a rapid weight loss. When the symptoms started interfering with my studies and work I sought medical help, first a neurologist and then an allergy specialist.

To relieve the headaches the neurologist prescribed a medication which hampered my ability to think, and I stopped it. Suspecting I had a brain tumor, he next proposed explorative neurological surgery. Instinctively, I knew my body was in no shape to sustain surgical intervention, so I went to my allergy specialist, an elderly British doctor. He suspected I had an immune disease, one of many being described in the medical journals. He prescribed a month of complete bed rest, not at my Halifax apartment, but at my parents home in Truro. My father was shocked at my appearance. From the healthy graduate of a few months earlier, I now appeared gray, weary and extremely ill. Inwardly, I suspected the years of stress had finally caught up with me.

For the first three weeks I left my bed only for meals, my body soaking up the healing energies of rest. Other than treating the symptoms (i.e. headaches and nausea) I took little medication. Slowly the headaches eased, my weight loss and other symptoms slightly stabilized, but my menstrual periods ceased, not to return for years. Some women might think this positive. It wasn't. As my health improved I knew something was wrong as the symptoms quickly reappeared whenever I tried to push.

I returned to my studies and a reduced number of hospital shifts as I still needed to pay my bills. I became a regular patient at the allergy clinic and the gynecologist's office, both monitoring my progress but, thankfully, not recommending any aggressive treatment. Both doctors suspected something more serious, but nothing was turning up in the diagnostic tests. Irrespective of a specific diagnosis, I knew my immune system had been compromised, and I probably was facing some kind of long-term illness. This brought to mind an old doctor's comments, 'the human race would benefit if more people had some long-term illness because it usually forces the individual to adopt a more disciplined lifestyle'. I knew if I was to survive and keep the symptoms at bay a changed lifestyle was needed. Nursing had provided plenty of examples. For the rest of my life I would adopt a semi-vegetarian diet supported by daily multivitamins, increased sleep, reduced stress (as best as one could) and avoidance of infectious diseases or harmful pollutants. Fortunately, I was assuming a teaching position, which offered me a Monday to Friday work schedule. An angel had been walking ahead of me.

I pressed on with my studies and work, eventually passing my courses and graduated in the spring of 1965. There was a momentary stir at the graduation when my Mount colleague and I arrived with our gold trimmed hoods, gold only worn by Dalhousie law students.

My diploma studies and illness had overshadowed my twenty-first birthday and my dream of a magical end to my struggle with words. Disappointed that nothing happened, I faced a second reality, my handicap would likely be another lifetime companion. By my twenties I had skilfully created an array of masks in order to appear 'normal'. Thinking my disguise was well crafted I was startled when a deaf patient inquired, "I didn't know there were deaf nurses, you are the best lip reader I've ever met". Momentarily confused, I denied being deaf and quickly found an excuse to leave the room, fearing he had unmasked my secret. The sixties was still a time when such a handicap would likely have ended my career, something I could not risk.

My illness placed a shadow over our wedding plans set for August of 1965. Ron and I even discussed cancelling or delaying our wedding, but by this time the event had taken on a life of its own. Aunt Di had returned from New York with beautiful fabric to make my wedding dress. Together we sought a local milliner to design a special crown for my veil. Ron had become a Roman Catholic, much to my amazement (I did not ask him to do this), stating quietly he did not want his own family divided on religion. We had saved money to pay for a quiet wedding and reception of about forty guests, mainly family and friends. Father agreed to pay for the reception wine and any additional entertainment costs at our family home after the reception. Everyone was busily preparing for the big event. I had mixed feelings, happiness in getting married but worried my health might become a negative factor in our marriage.

Finally the big day arrived. We were married at the Immaculate Conception Roman Catholic Church in Truro, a small, white wooden building with a reception at a local restaurant. Ron's parents and his brother, Carl, arrived from Ontario to join the celebrations. We honeymooned in Cape Cod, and, en route home, stopped in Boston to visit my relatives, Joe and Margaret McCleary. While there, Joe tried to interest me in working for his detective agency as an undercover agent in large hospitals. I declined as I already had a job.

Ron and I returned to a one bedroom apartment, the upstairs suite in an average white, wooden house near the Halifax Arm. It was sparsely furnished as we believed in only purchasing items when money was available. After years of residence living having my own home was an unimaginable luxury. Life was full and simple. We had regular get-togethers with a small group of university, hospital and navy friends. Unfortunately, shortly after our return, Ron was off on a three month Caribbean naval tour of duty. Disappointed, I was pleased to have the daunting task of designing a pilot paediatric program to fill my loneliness.

The paediatric department at the Infirmary was located on the seventh floor of the recently constructed wing of the hospital. It was a poor location for paediatrics making emergency evacuation practically impossible. My entire educational facilities consisted of a large wooden desk in a small classroom near the elevators, with a seating capacity for about twelve students.

Prior to my arrival I was informed the residing Paediatric Supervisor was not impressed in having a 'young upstart with a degree' in her department. Knowing this did not bode well for me, on my first day, I gently knocked on her office door, and opening it, with a broad smile introduced myself "Good morning, I am the young upstart, paediatric instructor, who would sincerely like to work with you. I'm sure you know more than what is found in textbooks which would be most helpful to my pilot project." Smiling, she looked up saying. "I like people with guts, welcome!' She would become an essential mentor to my first teaching position, her views on so many aspects of paediatric nursing were invaluable.

My two other colleagues were a nurse from Prince Edward Island who would be teaching obstetric nursing and a religious sister responsible for psychiatric nursing. We jelled immediately, sharing many of the same ideas even though our nurses' training had been different. We chose to have our offices on the specialty ward, making us immediately available to students. Other nursing faculty usually had offices in a separate part of the hospital, traveling back and forth to the clinical wards on an as needed basis. Ten students volunteered for the project bringing a random mixture of talents.

The three of us collaborated on the overall project design and principles (i.e. curriculum structure, streamlining process, teaching methods, etc), giving some freedom to the individual faculty member as to the lectures, textbooks and handouts. Even here we collaborated, as we had copies of each other's teaching materials to assure consistency. For me, it was quite a struggle to thoroughly cover both child psychology and paediatric clinical nursing topics in time for the start up. As I worked on my lectures, children peddled their tricycles in and out of my office/classroom, using the blackboard and telling me they liked a teacher on their ward.

The ten students were scheduled to rotate through obstetrics first, then paediatrics and finally psychiatric nursing. Eventually, I welcomed the students to paediatrics. I had deliberately chosen a textbook which forced the students to explore other textbooks and materials. My objective was to make them think and expand their learning of paediatrics under my guidance. In light of the limited two months time period the course was designed to teach child psychology and clinical paediatric material in tandem, the students blending the two components as they explored each age group.

Following introductions and an orientation, I presented the students with my brief child psychology philosophy which went something like;

> *All children need love and trust in their lives. If these essential ingredients do not exist or have been damaged, it will be difficult to heal such scars in later years.*

As the days passed the students quickly grasped the paediatric material, entwining the child psychology and clinical information around the key principles of love and trust. Walking a new path I daily monitored the students' progress which was being confirmed in the positive comments of graduate nursing staff and doctors who were impressed with the students' enthusiasm and interest in paediatrics. Of course, the children loved all the attention.

In the weekly nursing rounds each Friday, students presented a detailed profile of a child in their care, giving a graphical demonstration of the child's psychological growth pattern compared to normal, a picture of the child's current diagnosis noting how he/she differed from the textbook, comments from interviews of family members and other health professionals, and a tailored nursing care plan which had been vetted by the charge nurse. The strategy was to incorporate both learning and collaboration with other paediatric health workers, bringing the student into the normal routine of the hospital setting. Each student's presentation was then critiqued by their fellow students, the comments becoming more intense as the days passed. In time, the students created ten detailed studies and plans of each age group. By the time the students reached the teenager stage, their skills were razor sharp. At the close of this segment I asked the chief of psychiatry to discuss teenage psychology with the students, as a lead in to their psychiatric training which would follow.

The psychiatrist arrived and presented the usual teenage psychology lecture. The students, as agreed, politely waited with their questions until he finished. Called away, I left the students revving up their question machine. Returning a hour later, I greeted the psychiatrist storming out of the classroom. This doctor was noted for his disparaging remarks on students, so I was anxious about the pilot project and my students. The students, however, were chatting happily, quite pleased they had stumped the psychiatrist on several questions. As the students left for lunch I called my faculty colleague in psychiatry alerting her to the situation.

Her return call after lunch greatly relieved my anxiety. The response was overwhelmingly positive. The psychiatrist had become so engrossed in the discussion with the nursing students he forgot an appointment. He was now going around raving about the calibre of these new nursing students, saying they were even better than his medical students. How the medical students felt about such a comparison I never knew. When the students moved on to psychiatry, this doctor took them under his wing insisting they be present at his medical rounds. As faculty members we couldn't be more pleased with the students' progress, their confidence was increasing with each affiliation as did their reputation. Their psychiatric nursing experience crowned the triple training focus of the pilot project.

While positive comments were welcomed, the ultimate test lay in the registered nursing exams. Because of the project's experimental nature, the Nova Scotia Nurses Association gave us special approval for the students to write the three specialty exams (obstetrics, paediatrics and psychiatric nursing) earlier than their training would normally allow. The exam scores were exceptional. The outcome showed that registered nurses could be trained in a shorter time. So, armed with many positive comments from students, graduate nurses and doctors plus the exam results, we completed our pilot project report and prepared a presentation for a special meeting to be held at the Infirmary. Upbeat, we thought all was going well and future teaching jobs were assured. To add to the positive outcome, I had discovered a possible diagnosis to my handicap.

Reading the latest material on learning problems in children, one description stood out, dyslexia. I easily related to the description of these children and their problems with communications, as well as their emotional frustrations. Recognizing there was a range of severity in such disabilities, I rationalized my situation was likely less severe. Nanny use to say "The devil you know is better than the devil you don't know". Knowing my communication devil was most helpful as I could now keep tabs on the latest medical developments. Not wanting to jeopardize my career I said nothing.

During my year back at the Infirmary as a registered nurse I was mainly in the good graces of Sister Catherine Peter, but she continued to attack other nurses; students and graduates. A pattern to these bouts of rage was still unclear to me. Out of the blue she would strike, the reason often unclear or perhaps on an apparent minor issue. Days and weeks of psychological abuse followed, inevitably reducing or destroying the nurse's confidence. The end result was either the nurse was left crippled, unsure of her abilities, was placed on sick leave or left the hospital. This management style created a siege mentality within the nursing ranks, reduced morale, and stymied any enthusiasm for career advancement. The situation called out for compassion.

No longer class president, I still kept tabs on what was happening through two expert hospital gossips. These individuals rarely get recognized for their abilities. Once alerted to the latest victim, I, and other nurses, moved in to provide moral support and, if the situation warranted, advice on nursing jobs outside the Infirmary (a list I kept updated for such emergencies). Escape was a preferred solution than a wounded nurse. Surprisingly, not all nurses wanted to leave the Infirmary thinking they could weather the storm. One example follows.

For weeks Joan had been the target of sister's attacks, coming to my office on the seventh floor to cry and recover in order to go back on duty. She was determined to stick it out even though I, and other nurses, were seeing the warning signs; fearfulness, increased headaches, lack of sleep, judgment issues, bouts of anger etc.. One Friday afternoon, she arrived in a frightful state seeking help. Within the hour, I telephoned her brother in Montreal, pulled out a resignation form letter which I kept in my desk for such occasions. Once signed, I slipped it under sister's office door (knowing she was away), accompanied Joan to her apartment, helped her pack, took her to the train station, and asked the train conductor to keep an eye on her to Montreal where her brother was waiting. Later I received a note from Joan saying she had a job in Montreal and all was well. I would have sister's wrath to face on Monday morning.

On cue, Monday morning, Sister Catherine Peter barged through my classroom door, Joan's resignation letter flapping in her hand saying, "I know you were the instigator of this. You have also done this for other nurses, the letters are all the same".

Exasperated and willing to admit my action, I replied, "Yes, as long as you insist on destroying good nurses, I will keep trying to help them. Several have found jobs not only in Halifax but elsewhere, and they have gone on to be fine nurses. For the life of me, I cannot fathom why you do this, surely this loss of good nurses cannot benefit the hospital?"

Refusing to discuss the situation, she abruptly turned and, in leaving stated, "I have my reasons!".

Silently I wondered if even she knew what the 'reasons' were, I certainly didn't. By this point in time, I knew sister would not retaliate on me, which was also a conundrum. Joan's resignation would bring a temporary calm. But the repeated stressfulness of such situations was growing tiresome, as nothing I, or anyone else, did brought a permanent resolution nor did it give me any more insight into prevention.

Life continued to evolve on the home front. Sonny and Tinnie's marriage finally ended, each going their separate ways. Rayona, moved to Truro to be with her grandparents, the years in a dysfunctional family leaving their scars. Papa now had legal custody. I would need my child psychology knowledge and skills to help her adjust to her new environment. In time, the wounds healed but there would be lingering after effects. Further links to her parents lessened, they pursuing their own immature paths. In the years that followed, whenever I accompanied Rayona downtown, I would wait to see how she preferred to introduce me to her friends; 'sister' or 'aunt'. It didn't matter, whatever was easier for her.

Back at the Infirmary the big meeting on the pilot project had finally arrived. The audience included students (the pilot project ten plus others), other nursing faculty, general nursing staff, doctors and some hospital executives. This would be my first formal presentation and I was expectedly nervous.

Naively, we thought the positive findings of the pilot project would support the streamlining of nurses' training and still maintain quality. To achieve the positive outcomes of the project, we recommended the learning process needed to be concentrated at the bedside with faculty members serving as mentors. In finishing our presentation, we readied ourselves for the expected questions, but the proceedings shifted in an entirely different direction. Completely ignoring our presentation, the nursing association members launched their own presentation on the future direction of nursing education, advocating a direction completely opposite to our presentation. The bedside learning approach was dismissed, to be replaced by the latest United States trend advocating a nursing degree for registered nurses with students mainly on a university campus. Greater observation of care would take precedent over hands- on training. In conjunction with this thinking they proposed the closure of all hospital based diploma programs. No data was presented to support these decisions. Their dogmatic proclamation left little room for debate. Why they approved the Infirmary pilot project in the first place was never explained. In this somewhat surreal atmosphere two entirely different paths to teaching nurses were being presented, but only one was going to be recognized, a decision that had been made prior to their arrival.

No one was happy. There were loud protests from the audience which were not addressed. Besides ignoring the entire research effort, the association offered no thanks to the hospital, the faculty or the students. We had all been dismissed as irrelevant to the association's planned direction. This would not be my first or last moment of confusion in dealing with a professional association for nurses.

Stunned, the three of us sat over coffee wondering what we might have done differently. Feeling helpless, rejected, and angry we were encountering the cold reality of the aftermath of political decision-making over objective research. We also knew this marked an end of our teaching prospects as there were no faculty openings. For a brief time I filled in for the paediatric supervisor on vacation, a job I now returned to. It was a time of change. After over five years, irrespective of the difficulties, it was hard to say good-bye to a familiar setting and so many colleagues. The question was where.

The pilot project had not been entirely negative. The paediatric teaching position launched me onto a teaching path, one I had dismissed as a career choice in my student days. Irrespective of the meeting outcome, the experience gave me the opportunity to test unique teaching methods, the students did well, and comments by fellow health professionals confirmed we were on the right path.

Within days I learned the Nova Scotia Hospital held some promise as they were looking for faculty. My initial phone call resulted in a job. I'm sure Sister Catherine Peter was relieved to see me go, I surely must have been a thorn in her side. It was time for a different environment, one in which I could fully concentrate on teaching.

Prior to the move, Ron and I took a brief camping trip, in a pup-tent, to Cape Breton, a truly mementous event in torrential rain. Perhaps it was a form of baptism for the next stage of my journey. On a positive note, the rain was an incentive for Ron to build his own mobile trailer during the winter.

Once again I was traveling across the Angus L. MacDonald Bridge to the Dartmouth psychiatric hospital, this time to the educational building. Since my student days, a newly constructed, rectangular, cream-coloured brick building had been erected as a student residence and education facility. The basement and first floor housed faculty offices, classrooms and a magnificent lounge, the upper floors were the student accommodations. For the first time, I not only had my own office but the teaching facilities were superb.

The Nova Scotia Hospital, like other specialty hospitals, had their own three-year, registered nurses program, the students spending considerable time at the Victoria General Hospital for their medical/surgical clinical experience. Already, the nurses association was questioning the feasibility of training programs in specialty hospitals due to the length of time students had to spend in other hospitals and their difficulties in passing the registered nurses examinations. As I arrived, the Nova Scotia Hospital was still admitting about twenty-five students a year, the students coming from similar backgrounds to those at the Infirmary.

Like the Halifax Infirmary, Miss Eleanor Purdy, the Director of Nursing, was also responsible for Nursing Education. Miss Purdy had a striking presence. She was a tall, heavy set woman with a deep voice who had held a senior military position in World War II. For me, she would be a straight, fair, clear and good-humoured leader whom I quickly enjoyed working with.

I was the youngest faculty member, the only one with a nursing degree and the first Roman Catholic, factors which made for an interesting orientation. It became crystal clear that several faculty members did not support my appointment. One faculty member had a strong bias against Roman Catholics. I took the jabs quietly, hoping time would shift her opinion. This eventually happened when one day she described me as 'the most liberal Catholic' she had ever met. Later, this individual sent her own daughter to The Mount, quite a shift in thinking. My age and degree evaporated as issues once we focused on our teaching responsibilities.

As the science instructor for first year students I was responsible for teaching microbiology, pharmacology and anatomy and physiology. My first encounter with government purchasing red tape came when I requested microscope lamps for the lab. Classes began and ended without the lamps. They eventually turned up three months after the course finished. I just improvised. With the latest teaching methods and lots of audio-visual aids the courses went smoothly. I was truly enjoying being a member of a larger faculty, spending lunch breaks in a beautifully appointed nurses lounge, and with my full attention focused on educating student nurses. Yet, there was a darker side to this idealistic setting.

In addition to teaching, I had counselling duties for a number of students, mainly academic issues but some psychological problems. The academic issues could easily be handled through discussion, better study methods, getting help from another faculty member and/or providing extra tutoring. I was less comfortable with certain psychological problems. Perhaps due to my age, I discovered my counselling numbers growing. Out of a class of twenty-five I had about twelve students to council. Of this number, at least seven were suffering from the psychological trauma of family incest. Three were showing severe psychological symptoms, and, I suspected, needed in-depth psychiatric care. While my grandmother hinted at such matters when I was a child, this was my first encounter of such abuse. It took hours of counselling to get the student to acknowledge the mental damage, and what to do when their abuser was often a member of their immediate family. Fighting both guilt and anger, the student was caught between family loyalty and anger at not being protected as a child. No case was identical. Realizing I was out of my depth, especially with the three more critical cases, I sought the mentorship of an older faculty member and a psychiatrist. Their assistance would be critical.

Whenever I counselled the student with the worst problem, the other faculty member and psychiatrist sat in an adjoining office. One afternoon, somehow I must have inadvertently triggered some deep wound. Instantly, the rage in the student exploded as she dove across my desk reaching for my throat. My two advisors leapt to my rescue, the psychiatrist taking immediate charge of the situation. While we had discussed such an occurrence, I had not expected it to be so powerful. The girl was admitted for months of intense psychiatric therapy. I was rattled and unsure if I was really the best candidate for such sessions. Encouraged by my two mentors and prayers for wisdom and verbal skills, I pressed on. The students needed resolution of a terrible injury if they were to progress in their lives. My grandmother's wise words now had more meaning; 'Child, trust no one with your children – family, clergy, teachers etc. – you are responsible for these fragile lives. As a mother, God expects you to care for the next generation'. The whole mess screamed for justice.

By the mid sixties, Papa's Safety Surveys consulting business had become a truck driving school called Commercial Safety School (later a College), using the deserted air force base at Debert. As he set up his classroom lectures, we shared many interesting discussions on curriculum development and dealing with students. Admittedly the type of student was different. To acquire the simulation equipment for truck drivers, my father needed an advanced certificate, only available from a North Carolina post-secondary educational institution. So, at the age of fifty, with a grade ten basic education, he took off for several months with a number of other potential instructors, all younger than himself. Later, these men reported that Papa knew more about transportation than their instructor and outdid them on the exam. With the necessary credentials, and acquisition of the truck driving training simulator the school was started, the green cross I had painted years before on toy trucks becoming the college logo. In no time, the college graduates would lead the truck rodeo competitions, a credit to the talents and commitment of my father and the school faculty.

In the first year at the Nova Scotia Hospital I met my dear friend Margaret (Margie) Pattison. We were instant 'kindred spirits'. We were not only the youngest faculty members but we had also attended private girls schools. Margie had been to Edgehill Girls School in Windsor, Nova Scotia. Margie was petite, and dark-haired with an effervescent personality. She had graduated from the Nova Scotia Hospital and was now teaching nursing arts to first year students. Her family home was directly across the street from the nurses residence, a place to which we would often escape to have a quiet lunch. The Patterson home was a welcoming place with warm and generous parents; her father an engineer at the Dartmouth oil refinery and her mother gifted in crafts. She had an older brother who worked at the Canadian Broadcasting Corporation in Halifax. Our close friendship would last a lifetime however separated by distance and time.

In the spring of 1967, Ron and I prepared for a month-long summer vacation. Like his father, our well-crafted trailer worked with finger-touch control. The wooden box, mounted on four wheels, could easily open to sleep four, and rode smoothly hitched to the back of our Volkswagon. We packed for a long June trip, to include Expo 67 in Montreal, a quick stop in Toronto to visit his parents, and on to see his grandmother, Bertha Schultz, in Pangman, Saskatchewan.

In Montreal we camped at a military base, each day taking a bus to the Expo site. We carefully mapped out the day's exhibits, carrying sandwiches and drinks to minimize our costs. Each evening we returned to camp for a full meal to sustain us for the following day. The exhibits filled our days with delightful sounds, sights and eye-catching wonders giving us a treasure of memories.

After a short stop-over with his parents in Toronto, we headed west taking a United States turnpike, turning north in North Dakota after receiving news of a pending tornado. We arrived in the small town of Pangman on a hot summer's day.

Bertha Schultz was a small woman like Grandma Stull, who warmly welcomed us into her gray weathered shingled homestead, with geese walking proudly in the yard. We were introduced to 'the boys', her male children who ranged in age from their late thirties to their fifties. I marvelled at the expanse of the open fields and the starlit night skies.

Each day, this petite woman rose early in the morning to make twelve loaves of bread. The workers, family and neighbours, ate at least four loaves per sitting. I helped in cleaning the milk churn, ironing and doing the meal cleanup. The meals were so delicious I gained ten pounds in ten days, which would have been disastrous if I had stayed a full year. Having lost so much weight during my illness, the additional weight was welcomed.

Grandma Schultz and I became instant friends. We laughed together as she shared family memories over old photographs stored in a cardboard box in an upstairs bedroom. On one occasion we attended a local tea with other Pangman women. Surprisingly, I felt more akin to grandma Schultz than with her daughter, Lea, my mother-in-law. They were very different women. As we prepared to leave she handed me two feathered pillows and a home-made quilt 'for my first baby' which she made herself. With sadness we waved goodbye. I would never see her again. This introduction to more in-laws gave me a deep feeling of belonging.

On our return trip, we camped in various settings often playing chess under camp light and gazing at the brilliant stars under clear skies. Near Quebec we met two National Geographic magazine photographers whom we invited for supper. They repaid us with tales of their travels across Canada, seeing a UFO dance across the Northern skies, and leaving a big 'thank you' on our car windshield. We were grateful for such a magnificent break, a change to expand our knowledge of the country, and meet family.

My illness, and no menstrual periods, had negated any possibility of a pregnancy. My gynecologist tried a combination of therapies, even fertility drugs, to trigger a normal menstrual period but to no avail. Finally, he agreed to assist me in adopting a child by my 26th birthday, if by then my physical condition showed no change. Ron agreed to adoption as we both wanted children in our lives. My vision of life in the sixties was rather simple. I expected to live in the Maritimes, be married, and have one or more children. I would stay at home until the children were in school, and then return to nursing. Yet, even by 1967 my life was diverting from this path. Little did I realize how far this divergence would be.

I was back teaching the same science courses and, in addition, was asked to design a review of the entire nursing program for senior students to improve their standing in the registered nurses' examinations. The review course would examine most of the science and clinical information relative to patient care in medical, surgical, obstetrical and paediatric nursing. Somehow the graduate nurses in the hospital learned of this review and asked if they could also participate, which I agreed. So, I designed a program of small groups using senior students as leaders. The graduate nurses would become the catalysts stimulating the students with pointed questions. Each week, the groups were given a long list of complex questions to review. As we walked through the different aspects of nursing, system by system, adults and children, everyone was challenging each other. My role was to facilitate group discussions, provide the hand-outs, add additional questions and provide an occasional movie for variation. I had plenty of work just keeping up with the groups. Students and graduates worked exceptionally hard not to lose face in the group discussions. No one was idle. The enthusiasm was electrifying. We greeted each other with jokes and friendliness, the graduates showing a sincere desire to help the students succeed. It was a community of learning.

That fall, troubling signals were too easily dismissed. For the first time in our relationship Ron's behaviour changed. I thought the invitation of his commanding officer to become a Petty Officer was a positive sign, but Ron dismissed it abruptly saying he was getting out of the navy. His love of the navy had suddenly taken a negative turn. When questioned he seemed unwilling to discuss his decision to leave the navy. This was most unusual. Sensing he was determined to make a move I let the matter drift, after all, I thought, we were both young. However, his change in personality became more pronounced when he returned from his next navy exercise in the Caribbean. He appeared troubled, edgy and silent. I sensed something had happened in Haiti, but he again cut me off when I asked for details. Something was wrong and was connected to the navy. In my naiveté, I thought everything would improve once he left the navy. My suggestion to talk to his commanding officer, my father or brother, or even call his own brother was vehemently resisted. Time passed, he seemed to relax, and I made the mistake of thinking there had been some resolution. After leaving the navy and joining an insurance company, he seemed pleased with the change and the money was a definite improvement over his navy salary.

Christmas came and went, and in the spring Ron and I joined several friends on a trip to Montreal for St. Patrick's Day. On our return trip, I attributed my nausea to the train movement. My condition worsened when a conductor asked me to assist a young mother who had given her infant too much baby aspirin. As the train raced through New Brunswick and into Nova Scotia, I worked with the mother sponging the infant and getting the assistance of the train bartender, a father of four, to sterilize several baby bottles filling them with a glucose mixture on my instructions. By the time we reached Halifax, the infant was fine, and the young parents relieved. Unfortunately, I was frightfully ill, having had several bouts of vomiting. As we stepped off the train, the conductor thanked me for my help and suggested that maybe now it was time for the caregiver to get some care.

When the nausea persisted, I made an appointment with Dr. I. Perlin, my gynecologist. I was surprised when he seemed to ignore my symptom, and silently began to examine my face. He remarked that never in his entire career had he seen such a beautiful butterfly marking a pregnant woman's face. As I looked in his mirror I could see the delicate edges of the butterfly, as if my freckles had united in creating a feathery artistic design. Dr. Perlin tried to convince me to come to his next medical class to show my butterfly face. I resisted the offer and compromised in letting his resident doctors see my face on my next appointment. My pregnancy was a surprise, and without a menstrual period the expected delivery date was guesswork. We relied on other pregnancy signs as the months passed. Dr. Perlin's guess was early November, mine was late October. His November date allowed me to continue teaching until late September, enabling me to attend the student graduation.

Instead of the usual three months of morning sickness, I had eight. Every day, I had to work hard to increase my nutritional intake between mid-morning and bedtime. As a result, I gained fourteen pounds in the whole pregnancy. This meant, with wide hips and loose fitting clothing most people did not suspect I was pregnant until my later months. For the nine months, except for morning sickness, I was in robust health.

Ron seemed genuinely delighted with our unexpected miracle calling his family to announce the news. With no maternity leave, I would have to resign my job to have the baby. To cover the extra costs in the first few months, like many colleagues, I started a separate baby's savings account. I toyed with the possibility of returning to part-time teaching in nursing after the delivery but this decision was left to the future. Because of my medical history, Dr. Perlin, kept reminding me of possible complications, but I remained optimistic.

Another important date was also looming. The seniors in my experimental review classes sat their registered nurses examinations. As faculty we waited anxiously for the results as this would be the litmus test for the review program. We were ecstatic when the results were posted. The Nova Scotia Hospital students took first and third place in the provincial standings, and, the crowning achievement, the whole class passed, a first in many years. Even the graduate nurses were thrilled having assisted in the success. It not only reinforced my views on training nurses, but showed that given the right nurturing, all nursing students could succeed. It struck a blow to those who were pushing to close specialty schools.

As my pregnancy progressed, I informed Dr. Perlin of my Grandmother O'Neill's brief labour (i.e. just over an hour) in delivering her nine children. With a wide smile he dismissed such news as wishful thinking, diverting me to the possibility I could just as easily follow my paternal grandmother, which was true. Nevertheless, inwardly I considered the possibility as it could effect my travel to the hospital.

In the summer, Ron and I hitched up the trailer and spent two sun-filled weeks in a Prince Edward Island campsite. An elderly man from Quebec joined Ron for an occasional chess game whenever I took a nap. We returned to Halifax looking forward to the birth of our first child. I planned on resigning early in October, transferring the next senior review to Margie.

The nursing graduation was a joyous event, the students were still celebrating their examination success. There were many hugs and best wishes. One student was off to join the World Health Organization. The world seemed in order as I left the hospital to prepare for parenthood.

The roles had shifted. I was now the maternity patient in the familiar setting of the Infirmary. A Scottish midwife greeted me and assigned a young student nurse to check my vital signs, expecting I would be there for many hours. Labour started with a vengeance at seven-thirty in the morning and by eight-thirty I asked the student to please contact the midwife as, in my own assessment, my labour was moving very rapidly. As the midwife began to check me, she chuckled saying it would be impossible......and not completing the sentence, she raced out the door to call Dr. Perlin. Like my grandmother O'Neill, it would be a short labour. At nine o'clock on October 19th I delivered a beautiful baby boy of seven pounds, seven ounces. Handing me my baby, Dr. Perlin remarked, "If you ever have another pregnancy you'll need to camp on the hospital lawn". With the baby's birth my beautiful facial butterfly disappeared. Like many new mothers, I rejoiced in the miracle of birth. Following the delivery I had anaemia which seemed incidental with the excitement of going home. The apartment glistened to welcome us as I gently placed our baby in his bassinette.

We Christened our first child, Rupert Gregory, to be called Gregory, taking the names of two of my maternal uncles. The following weeks quickly passed as Gregory grew stronger, my weight returned to its pre-pregnancy level, and we slowly adapted to our responsibilities as parents. The anaemia stubbornly resisted treatment. I refused returning to hospital as I had no one to take care of the baby. I knew my mother was beyond caring for an infant. Stoically, I ate foods loaded with iron and prayed my body would eventually make its own correction.

My efforts were in vain as shortly after Christmas, I came down with several bouts of flu, my immune system was under attack. Weeks drifted by as I recovered from one bout of flu to come down with another. Dr. Perlin's concern over my health mounted with each visit as neither the anaemia nor flu were responding to treatment. I kept telling myself this was a minor glitch which would soon pass. All other signs seemed normal. Gregory was blossoming, Ron seemed happy with his job, we regularly talked to parents and friends, friends dropped in to visit, and Miss Purdy called to say a job was waiting whenever I was ready to return to work. Yet, with all this, I could not shake a terrible premonition of foreboding, something was wrong. Since the baby was well, I suspected the intractable anaemia might signal a deeper problem. I was wrong, the problem wasn't me but Ron. That spring a fierce storm blew into my life, without much warning and nearly destroyed me.

In February 1969, on a blustery winter day Ron had a car accident outside of Halifax. The car needed repairs and he obtained a 'loaner' car. I would later discover this accident was far more serious than he reported. Being ill, the incident drifted pass me.

In March, out of the blue, Ron started talking about investing money and moving to a single house. I was not only confused with both suggestions, I wasn't well enough for a move, but Ron seemed adamant. Dr. Perlin kept advising against a move until my health improved. Then for the first time in our marriage, Ron became angry and insisted we 'had' to move. No reason was ever given as to the urgency. Unable to provide much resistance, I gave in. Ron chose the rental house. Slowly I packed the boxes, glad we had few belongings.

With the help of friends, on the April Easter weekend we moved to a lovely house near the Sears Shopping Centre. It was a compact, wooden, bungalow, white with green trim, about fifteen years old. The one and a half storey building contained a master and small bedroom tucked under the eaves, with the other living spaces on the main floor. A naval officer and his family lived on one side and an older couple on the other, the husband a member of the army. My brother, David and his fiancé, Lyle, took over our apartment, repainting it prior to their May wedding.

For the first time in my life I had little energy. By the end of April many boxes were still unopened. I was plagued by an overpowering tiredness and a continuing uneasiness. With a healthy baby and a new home I should have been delightfully happy. At the end of April, I kept having a recurring nightmare. In my dream I found myself turning to introduce my husband only to face a stranger with an entirely different face. I kept waking up crying "No, no, it's all wrong, it's all wrong!" Remembering my grandmother's view of thrice repeated dreams, I phoned David, the only one who would understand my concern. We shared the dream and uneasiness and I was left to wait. The uncertainty seemed to grow worse with each passing day.

On May 7th, Ron left in the morning on a business trip to the Annapolis Valley, intending to mail letters and cards of the baby for relatives. When he failed to attend a scheduled three o'clock bank appointment, I grew concerned as this was not like him. When he did not arrive home by seven o'clock I grew alarmed. I phoned David and, remembering my dream, he came immediately to sit with me through the long night. His initial call to police was dismissed as they assumed Ron was out drinking and would likely return in the morning. Such drinking was totally out of character for Ron. As the hours passed a coldness overwhelmed me with uncontrolled shivering. My ability in handling words rapidly deteriorated. In the distance I could hear crystal breaking, a sound which increased in volume as daylight approached. Confused and bewildered, I knew my life was shattering into pieces. Something was terribly, terribly wrong!

Early the next morning, David called my parents and Dr. Perlin. All three seemed to barge through the door about the same time. As my mother approached me she said "My God Sally, this is your 26th year." While I had forgotten the prophesy of my teens, Mother had not. Dr. Perlin's concern was palpable. With months of poor health this crisis could possibly be the final blow. He prescribed some medication and made sure I had it immediately. Speaking volumes about the calibre of this individual, for weeks he dropped in daily to check on me and the baby. Mother couldn't believe he was the chief obstetrician for the city of Halifax. The hardest phone call was to Ron's parents in Ontario, as we had little information to comfort them.

The days and weeks that followed were a blur. I'm sure if it had not been for Gregory, I would never have survived. The practical needs of a small infant cannot be ignored. The police finally acted providing a missing person's announcement on the radio and later in the newspaper, all to no avail. Family and friends tried to help. David and several friends drove along the route Ron was suppose to have traveled, stopping at the Windsor RCMP detachment to check if there had been any sighting of the car, but nothing. David checked with Ron's insurance company manager who assured him Ron had appeared for the May 7th morning meeting in the Valley, leaving them supposedly to go to Bridgewater to check on his damaged car. The garage in Bridgewater stated Ron never arrived. The truckers at Papa's school conducted their own search of the last sighting of the car, and sent out word through their communication network to other truckers. Papa contacted an old RCMP friend who stayed on the case for months. All activities produced no trace of Ron or anyone who could add any more details.

As the days passed a second shockwave hit. Bills had been unpaid for weeks, a situation which seemed to contradict Ron's push for investments and the sudden need to move. As the debts mounted, the Royal Bank froze our joint bank account leaving me with only the meagre funds in the baby's account. Our credit rating was destroyed. By the time the financial mess ended, I was held accountable for over $10,000 in debt. Our joint bank account was cleaned out to cover debts specifically in Ron's name. Bankrupted, in shock and holding an infant in my arms, I faced a precarious future.

In light of the financial mess, Papa sought the services of a Truro lawyer, Lorne MacDougal, who immediately recommended the sale of all items directly linked to Ron such as his large tool box, trailer, golf clubs etc.. I also began selling whatever I could of my meagre belongings for cash.

Unknown to us, while these tragic events were unfolding in the Maritimes, the Linkerts in Toronto were receiving threatening phone calls from some man asking about Ron. The Linkerts contacted their daughter-in-law's father, then Mississauga's Chief of Police, who placed a police officer on the case. The phone calls ceased for a time. But some weeks later Lea arrived home to find Jacob sobbing uncontrollably mumbling "My son is in the Halifax Harbour". The shock to the family was severe with both Jacob and Ron's older brother dying within the next decade. This left Lea, Ron's mother, and myself to carry the tragic wound of this event. Even with messages transmitted between city police in Toronto and Halifax, no further action was taken due to a lack of evidence. Only Papa's RCMP friend continued to check leads. We had little money for a private investigator.

Papa looked helpless as the crisis unfolded. At one point, looking straight into my face (as if understanding my difficulties with words) he said; " Sally, it's not the lousy cards you have been dealt which matter, life will judge you on how you play your hand". He would repeat these words over and over, trying to get his daughter to understand the decisions which lay ahead. Mother stayed with me for several weeks but finally had to return home. Papa discussed the possibility of me returning to Truro but I begged for a six month trial period to see if I could manage on my own. With over ten years away from my parents home, he understood and reluctantly agreed.

As mother left , Margie, my dear friend, arrived to stay with me. Neither of us were quite prepared for this situation, if anyone could be. It would take some time before my changed marital status fully registered. I was now a single mother with an infant. Margie and I created a semblance of routine, Margie going to work each day and me trying to manage by myself. Talking to Margie was easy, what little talking I was capable of after weeks of this unfolding nightmare. However dark the situation, there were always rays of light. The kindness of people, known and unknown, was amazing. Neighbours cut the grass, did repairs, checked the house, baby-sat Gregory and were there with food and daily reassurances. University and health organization friends arrived at my door with bags of groceries and baby supplies, and others came to help me pack and move. The oil man drained the tank to make sure I had little to pay. There were many others who kindly went out of the way to support Gregory and myself during these dark days.

Yet, I was still unprepared when the Sheriff arrived at my door. Sensing danger I abruptly slammed the door screaming at Margie, "Please, take the baby and run!" Margie without asking why, picked up Gregory and ran to the navy officer's home next door as I fell to the floor sobbing. The officer came and gently asked me to open the door. The Sheriff kept mumbling "Lady, I'm truly, truly sorry, I just need to give you this paper." Shaking I took the paper and never knew what it was. I passed it to David who arrived shortly after. Thinking I was on the verge of a complete breakdown, a decision was made to get me moved and to have all legal matters routed through my lawyer and David. Margie proceeded to look for an apartment in Dartmouth.

Looking for rental accommodations proved extremely difficult in light of the constant reply of 'no dogs and no children'. One day Margie returned home furious at the response of one landlord who asked her if the baby was legitimate. In Halifax/Dartmouth even in 1969 a woman with an infant and no husband was greatly frowned upon. Finally Margie found me a place in a single family home overlooking the Micmac Rotary. The home was owned by a Lebanese family, who also owned the adjacent grocery store. In June, just weeks after my previous move, another group of friends helped me relocate to Dartmouth. Standing alone in my small apartment, I felt shell-shocked and overwhelmed. But the storm was still not over.

In addition to the debt, I was without transportation as the loan car was still missing. I needed a bank loan to cover the debts and get a used car. This is when I discovered that even as a registered nurse, being a woman I could not get a loan, even if my financial situation had been better. My father would have to sign the loan. There was no room for emotions. A loan for twelve thousand dollars [1] (i.e. to cover the debt and car) was finally obtained, Miss Purdy vouching for my employment status. This was quite a financial undertaking as a nurse's annual salary was just fifteen thousand dollars. I was facing years of debt payments. With the loan and Papa's help, I purchased a demonstration navy blue Volkswagon beetle in Truro. At least, I was now mobile and ready to consider getting back to work.

My changed legal status brought further problems. My lawyer informed my father under the law in Nova Scotia I had no legal rights to my child. To alleviate the problem I would have to go to court to obtain legal guardianship over Gregory. I can still see my father pacing up and down furious over the fact that while his daughter brought the child into the world she had no legal status. Fearing someone else might take my child, I went to court and obtained the necessary papers.

The starkness of my living accommodations mirrored my life. The small basement apartment, found by Margie and carefully inspected by her father, was on a quiet street. It was an ordinary white, wooden house with a side entrance, accessed via a paved path from the upper street. It gave me the luxury of my own entrance. Inside, the main feature off the narrow hall was a large kitchen with a picture window, a place where I would spend a great deal of time in the next three years. The other rooms (living room, bed room and bath) were serviceable and small. The bedroom contained a twin bed (a paint can serving as one leg) and a baby's crib. The rooms were sparsely furnished as most items had either been sold or given to relatives, what little there was. An unlisted telephone number gave me peace. Once the place was cleaned, painted, and curtains sewn for the windows, I was settled. My humble surroundings gave me serenity after the storm.

For six weeks, Papa called every evening, depicting his uneasiness with my decision to live alone in the city with an infant. He made no demands for me to change my mind. Occasionally, he popped in unexpectedly for a quick cup of coffee and chat with his daughter or so he said. When it appeared I was managing, he relaxed

Finding child care in the late sixties in Halifax/Dartmouth was a formidable task. There were few child care businesses, and existing ones were either poorly run or too expensive. Most women with babies remained at home or had family members providing child care. Fortunately, with the help of nursing colleagues I found a baby-sitter near the hospital, a young married woman with three children; two boys and a girl. Gregory would spend his days with a loving, middle-class family, growing up with other children. The behaviour of the children depicted a caring household, one that I could relate to.

Slowly adapting to a lifestyle I could never have imagined for myself, I was surprised to receive a letter from Grandma Stull. She was not a letter writer so this was rather special. In the long letter she outlined the loneliness and heavy responsibilities of being a single parent with five children when her husband was killed, many years before. As I read her story and gentle counsel, I realized one person in my family truly understood my circumstances. After that whenever I had a twinge of self pity, I pictured this small lady and thanked God for my blessings. If she could manage with five children, I could certainly do it with one.

Stoically, I was going though the motions of normality, wounded but not dead, and trying to protect myself against further blows in an unstable, unfolding nightmare. Uneasily, I prepared to return to work.

Thus, in the summer of 1969, in my twenty-sixth year , an event did occur which dramatically changed my life. My world in shambles, I stood alone, bankrupted, an infant in my arms, thousands of unanswered questions, increasing legal problems, and a questionable future. Disoriented, confused, lost and severely wounded, I began to restructure my life, however unreal, waiting for someone to explain what had happened and why. My communication ability deteriorated, words arriving like the static of an old radio. On good days I understood bits of the message, and imagined the rest. My responses were blunt and perplexing, thankfully excused by the trauma of the situation. A deadness engulfed my spirit, relieved by the cries and needs of a baby. Instinctively, I knew Gregory and I had to survive.

THOUGHTS & LEARNING

Understanding the politics of professional nursing associations would take years, if I ever fully understood them. An organization created to promote professional nurses, had evolved into a multi-faceted political structure serving many purposes. There was constant infighting among the groups who controlled the three main branches; administration, education and community nursing. Somewhere in the sixties, critical decisions were made which would have major ramifications in the decades ahead. I will comment on three.

First, nursing administration (i.e. nurses in charge of nursing units/programs, supervisors and nursing directors) was downgraded in importance with the emphasis shifting to nursing education and community nursing. Unfortunately, this reduced status occurred as Medicare expanded and executive positions were being filled with individuals with increased financial skills. As nursing administration slipped behind in keeping pace with the changes in the health industry, their leaders were placed in a weakened position to defend themselves as government officials took control of their budgets.

Next, a nursing degree was heralded as the primary goal for all registered nurses, with the education center transferred from the health arena to the university campus. Reducing hands-on patient contact in nurses training was an unfortunate decision which would have lingering ramifications. Our pilot project showed that nurses training could be streamlined but had to remain at the bedside. As degree programs were promoted, diploma nursing programs were downgraded, regarded as outdated and redundant. Sadly, the good qualities of the diploma programs were never grafted onto the campus-based programs. Something was lost in the transition. Why the push for a degreed nurse?

In the sixties, health care planners were thinking of two main levels of care; short-stay, high technology centers where patients would receive specialty, intense surgical or medical care and home care. In the high-tech setting, it was argued, there would be mainly technically trained nurses (i.e. Licensed Practical Nurses or Certified Nursing Assistant with specialty training) and few registered nurses. Even a short-term, step-down facility (i.e. hotels with health care teams and certain specialized equipment) would mainly be staffed with technically trained nurses. Basic care, as the planners envisioned, would be provided in the community (i.e. home care) where the degreed registered nurse would flourish. In this setting there would be mainly registered nurses with degrees because they would function as independent practitioners (i.e. a nurse specialist or a newly created general practitioner), caring for a community of people. While the idea sounded good on paper, the health industry and professional groups resisted the entire idea. Thus, the degreed nurse has ended up being shackled to an out-dated bureaucratic hospital and community structure, and frustrated at being restricted in functioning at her/his maximum potential.

At the same time, essay questions were replaced by multiple choice questions in the professional nurses examinations. The reason given was increased speed and convenience in calibrating examination results. It was evident, not all students did well in such examinations, some capable nurses actually did poorly. Today, the Canadian Registered Nurse Examination (CRNE) has over two hundred and forty multiple choice and short-answer questions in the examinations, which are designed to test the competence of registered nurses in the provinces and territories in Canada except Quebec. The question is whether this method actually achieves the quality outcome intended.

Since the CRNE did not come into effect until the seventies, in the sixties, some nursing associations (i.e. Nova Scotia) were still using the United States nursing examinations. This would prove most beneficial to me when I applied to work in the United States in the seventies.

My often turbulent relationship with Sister Catherine Peter would give me a lifelong interest in the education of health care leaders. I expect my early encounter with the ramifications of her actions on both students and graduates, challenged me to find answers. I knew such behaviour was not unique to one organization. It was my good fortune to meet very fine nursing managers throughout my career, which meant this dysfunctional environment did not have to exist. Yet, as the health industry increased in complexity with the decades, I found the education of its nursing leaders never seemed to receive the attention it vitally needed to keep pace with the changes.

My grandmother told me as a child life offered two guarantees; you would be tested and you would die. I did not expect the testing to be so severe. The event forced me to wonder about predestination and past life karma, with no answers to either. Whatever the reason, the spring of 1969 would leave an indelible mark on my life.

Marriage to me was for life. My life with Ron, up until the spring of 1969, had been a quiet, loving partnership, each of us committed (at least I thought) to building a life together. Perhaps the shock might have been less severe if our life together had been more turbulent. The dramatic finale and financial mess were devastating. We prided ourselves at being conservative, finding special bargains and carefully saving our money. What threads of information we managed to find painted a picture of someone in a panic, desperately positioning his family for safety between two military families. With unending questions and few answers, justice had to be left to a higher power as every ounce of my energy had to be focused on surviving.

The goodness of people shone through the storm as family, friends and strangers reached out to help. To these individuals there will never be enough words of gratitude.

My life had forever changed. Holding the words of my father, 'You will be judged on how you play the cards you are dealt' and my grandmother's, 'Child, this too shall pass..... walk on', caressing my baby I looked stoically ahead.

CHAPTER 5

Survival and Freedom

THE Friday before my Monday return to the Nova Scotia Hospital, Miss Purdy requested silence from the faculty with regard to my problem. This was a powerful request for trained psychiatric nurses skilled at individual and group counseling. I would be eternally grateful for their steadfast abidance to this request. They left such discussions to Margie and me. Like many people from war zones or other traumatic events, I sought solitary healing. Deep down I felt a major discussion might prove fatal.

My faculty colleagues warmly welcomed me back, sticking steadfast to topics of Gregory and updating me on educational programs and student activities. I would have a desk in the education building, my assignments directed by Miss Purdy. Easing back into work, I was asked to do a nursing education review, comparing entrance policies to student performance. Within weeks I produced a report. I concentrated on work during the day and my baby in the evening, pushing personal problems into the background. Yet, life couldn't be so neatly packaged. While my hospital colleagues spared me their analysis of my life, others were less protective.

The mixture of negative comments centered on three points; I was too smart, I wanted a child and Ron didn't, and what man could cope with the stress of a sick wife, a baby and a new job. However hurtful, I tried to analyze the comments. Because of my struggle with words, it never dawned on me I might be smarter than anyone else. Quite the opposite, I thought everyone around me had to be brilliant as they did not have to cope with my handicap. My education push was to confirm to me I had a working brain. As for children, Ron and I talked about this many times before and after we were married. We seemed to be in agreement on this point or at least that was my thinking. However, the stress of a sick wife, a baby and a new job were legitimate points. When I had the courage, I questioned friends and family if they saw any signs of trouble, preceding Ron's disappearance. All conceded there was nothing out of the ordinary. Nevertheless, from my psychiatric nursing I was aware some individuals were capable of hiding a great deal of stress. However, the continuous concentration on the negative began to interfere with my own coping abilities. I needed some resolution.

During the crisis and for many months afterwards I was incapable of crying. Laying in my bed one night struggling with so many negatives and unknowns, mounting legal problems and a financial mess, I remembered the gentle words of my grandmother, "Child, when life gets difficult, as it surely will, be quick to forgive. Forgive yourself, forgive others, carry no baggage, walk on. Leave the details to God." Struggling, I began, each step a frightful effort, "Dear God please forgive me. I offer no excuses. As a trained nurse I was not there to help someone I dearly loved when he was obviously struggling. If he just walked away, then I forgive him and pray he finds a new life after these wounds heal. If he has been killed, then may his soul be at peace. If this is the case, then I leave justice to you, for I do not have the energy or resources to resolve it. Gregory and I must survive." Tears streaming down my face, I found myself on my knees at my bedside. Later I somehow crawled back into bed falling into a deep sleep mumbling, "Do not react...let God deal with this......walk towards the light!"

The next morning I awoke to sunlight streaming through the window with Gregory playing quietly with his toys beside my bed. A huge burden had lifted from my shoulders. Intuitively, I knew the end of my first marriage would forever be shrouded in mystery. For whatever reason, my life needed a major correction. However wounded I had to walk on.

After the education review, my next assignment was supervising three areas in the hospital; medical/surgical clinics, the operating room and two central supply departments (CSD), each located in different wings of the hospital. The psychiatric hospital had regular medical clinics conducted by doctors from the Victoria General Hospital in Halifax. Psychiatric patients were referred to the clinic by the psychiatrists or nursing staff. My task was to manage the clinic rosters and assist the doctors.

In addition, a modern, well-equipped, surgical suite existed for emergencies which periodically occurred. One example was a male patient who severely lacerated his forearms on a broken window in a fit of rage. Heavily sedated, two strong orderlies were needed to restrain the patient while the medical doctor sutured up his wounds. Amazingly, in spite of the bleeding, the patient's blood pressure remained high during the entire surgical procedure, a distinct difference from regular patients. Ward staff and myself checked his postoperative progress, which went smoothly.

The third area of responsibility, was the Central Supply Department (CSD), where individual surgical items and kits were sterilized. In the sixties, this department was busier than normally expected in a psychiatric hospital as sterile supplies were being prepared for the Dartmouth Medical Clinic a few blocks away.

Dartmouth was a growing bedroom community to Halifax. Without its own acute care hospital, its citizens relied on the Dartmouth Medical Clinic for emergency care. The clinic was situated on a main downtown street, in a relatively indistinguishable building. Thousands of people filtered through this facility during the year. To streamline the workload, a triage center, run by nurses, was set up at the main entrance. Once triaged, clients received different coloured tags and were directed to various rooms in the building for care. Individuals with red tags received immediate attention, often being transported across the bridge to one of the large teaching hospitals in Halifax. Ambulances moved in and out on a regular basis. Small teams of health professionals addressed the other categories of care. Fully occupied, clinic staff had delegated the processing of sterile supplies to the Nova Scotia Hospital. The hospital's CSD role intensified in direct relationship to the clinic's workload. The flaw in this service was an outdated autoclave located in the old wing of the hospital. This stainless-steel, barrelled-shaped piece of equipment with a large ship-like wheel for closure, occupied a major portion of the narrow CSD room. It was subject to frequent breakdowns.

One day, sensing danger the moment I entered the CSD room, and unable to formulate words fast enough to alert the older nurse, I grabbed the back of her uniform and abruptly pulled her backwards out of the room. Startled and furious, she turned to yell at me when the autoclave door blew, filling the CSD room with scalding steam. If the blast hadn't killed her, the steam would have given her severe, if not fatal, burns. Realizing the situation, the nurse turned breathlessly saying ; "My God, you saved my life…how did you know?" Equally startled by events, I offered few words saying, "I just knew". The incident, reassured me that in spite of the personal hell I was experiencing, some deeper senses were functioning normally. The autoclave needed immediate repair.

During this same period I met Dr. O. Pudimitis, one of the hospital's medical doctors, a tall, thin, elderly man with a slight German accent who had immigrated to Canada after the second World War. When he asked me about my baby, I broke down in tears. After getting me a huge bottle of multi-vitamins, he asked if we might have lunchtime walks around the hospital campus. This was a healing formula as we walked and chatted about many things (i.e. the weather, music, history, and news, anything but personal matters), all the while I knew he was assessing my physical and mental health.

My single discussion with a psychiatrist was about a series of strange dreams I was having. In my dream Ron, whenever he appeared, had no face. The Psychiatrist concluded this was likely due to shock and would pass, but it never did. Eventually, his image faded away entirely. I did not pursue the matter further because each reference to Ron's disappearance disturbed the slender hold I had on my sanity.

My life continued to focus on work and child care. The day began before six, bundling Gregory and his daily supplies into the Volkswagon, dropping him off at his baby-sitter's, while I drove on to the hospital, the pattern identical from Monday to Friday. Household activities occupied the weekends. With little money, life was indeed simple.

An old pediatrician had impressed me with his views on the damaging effects of commercially prepared baby food preservatives on the immature digestive tract of infants. He was convinced this was one of the main causes of allergic problems in young children. He advocated the personal processing of baby food to bypass the preservatives and ease the child's transition to regular food. This idea now became a necessity. With baby food containers supplied by nursing colleagues, every weekend I cooked a large pot of soup, pureeing a portion for Gregory and leaving the rest for me to have as an evening meal with bread. Large tins of fruit were also pureed. At one point Gregory's pediatrician asked me what I was feeding him, as at three months he had the physical features of a six month old. When I explained, he told me I should bottle and sell the soup, it was a gold mine. As my life had enough complexities, I let this lucrative business venture slip by.

My life had few visitors. However, one warm summer day, a recreational vehicle arrived with relatives from Saskatchewan, members of Ron's family, likely at the bidding of Grandma Shultz. The men appeared with tool boxes and the women with food. While they fixed and tightened every nail and item in the house and stocked my cupboards, they kept asking if there was more they could do for me. Like visiting angels, they appeared and disappeared as if in a dream.

Three months after Ron's disappearance, The RCMP located the loaner car. It had turned up at a Stewiacke garage, delivered one dark, rainy night by a man bearing no resemblance to Ron. The mail Ron had taken with him on the day of his disappearance was still tucked into the visor, and handed back to me by my lawyer. The baby pictures would never be mailed. The incident only increased the mystery. Whatever happened, it was final. My intuition told me I would never see Ron again. What remained was a sickening dread of the police arriving at my door whenever a body was found in the Halifax-Dartmouth area. Each time I prepared myself, only to face the inevitable let down when nothing happened.

In August, Miss Purdy informed me of an upcoming job in Halifax, one, she thought, would fit my skills and give me more money. It was a Nursing Counselor position with the recently created Nova Scotia Hospital Insurance Commission, an organization created as a direct result of Medicare. The Commission was responsible for acute and mental health care in hospitals. Within days, I found myself weaving through the Halifax traffic towards the Lord Nelson Hotel where the Commission offices were located. This would be my first official job interview, one in which I knew little more than the title of the job.

The interview went badly. The middle-aged man seemed uncomfortable with either me and/or the interview. After a brief coverage of my credentials, he informed me that 'they' (it was not clear who 'they' were) never hired a nurse with less than twenty years of experience and certainly never one with 'a child', with a negative emphasis placed on 'child'. The interview was a mistake, and realizing this, I stood up to leave saying, "It is obvious I do not fit your criteria unless I started nursing as a child" thinking to myself, I might qualify if I calculated my grandmother's early training. As I drove home I wondered if a man would have been so badly treated. The biggest question was why Purdy thought I might fit the job. Perplexed, I let it go. I knew her intentions were kind and perhaps it might point to something else.

The following morning when Purdy inquired about the job interview, I told her the sad tale and thanked her for her thoughtfulness. Her only response was a loud "I see!". Unknown to me, she left the hospital with guns firing heading straight to the Commission offices in Halifax where she barged into the Executive Director's office, everyone hearing her loud protestations on how someone she had recommended had been so lousily treated. Her commanding military abilities were to the fore.

Having dismissed the job, I was dumfounded when the same man called to tell me I 'had' the job. Unprepared, I didn't ask many details but requested time to clear my present commitments. He agreed. I arranged my termination remaining a bit concerned about the uncertainties of the road ahead. The job presented both positives and negatives. Certainly there was an economic improvement but in addition I would now have to face difficult questions on my life for which suitable answers had to be prepared. This prospect was frightening.

Just before leaving the hospital I met with the Roman Catholic Chaplain to find out about the newly formed Church Tribunal for troubled marriages. With my marital status in shambles, some future action might be needed. The priest was amazed little of my crisis had filtered through the usual hospital grapevine, a perplexing anomaly to him. While the health community has a rich and efficient gossip grapevine, the silencing of any topic was a powerful statement. Obtaining the necessary information I filed it for the future.

Mid- September, just four months after Ron's disappearance, I embarked on a new path. After delivering Gregory to his baby sitter, I proceeded to catch the Dartmouth ferry to Halifax, a fifteen minute ride, then climb the hill making my way towards the Lord Nelson Hotel office building. The Hospital Insurance Commission office was on the second floor of the hotel office building. It was one huge open office complex, the centrally located boardroom and exterior management offices the only enclosed spaces. The boardroom was surrounded by a number of typical, bureaucratic-gray cubicles, the six foot walls open at the top allowing a steady hum of office noise and little privacy. Executive and senior managers had the luxury of windows. I would occupy an inner cubicle with no window, sharing the space with a senior nursing counselor. For the first time I would be working in a bureaucratic maze, a very different environment than hospitals. While comfortable in dealing with nursing matters, I was never adept at the political side of health care created by Medicare. Fortunately for me, the Commission was in its infancy, a time of growth.

The Commission had a number of counselors (the title often interchanged with 'consultant') responsible for specific hospital specialties; administration, nursing, dietary, laboratory, x-ray, and finance. Each counselor was responsible for reviewing and making recommendations on his/her specialty for over fifty hospital budgets. In addition he/she had to be on top of the latest issues within that specialty, be ready to respond to issues brought to the Commission, and make yearly hospital visits. My responsibilities would focus on nursing administration and nursing education, a formidable agenda. As such, I was astounded to learn my orientation would be brief.

Within weeks of my arrival the senior nursing counselor informed me she was leaving in January to study for her Master's Degree in Nursing. This gave me little time to become fully acquainted with a job that was complex and extensive. Within months I would be alone handling the nursing issues in hospitals and nursing education for the province. Another nursing counselor dealt with psychiatric nursing. Fortunately, I was so green the enormity of the task did not fully register.

Speeding up the orientation, my senior colleague took me to several hospitals to demonstrate our role in reviewing nursing budgets, and discussing issues of importance with Directors' of Nursing. She then guided me through a random number of hospital budgets from the smallest to a large teaching hospital, and swiftly outlined the nursing education formula and issues. Numerous questions went unanswered.

In calculating the nursing budgets (i.e. staffing) I had a variety of formulae. On the general nursing wards (medical, surgical and psychiatric) the formula consisted of so many hours of nursing care per bed per service for three hundred and sixty-five days of the year. Intensive Care Units had a formula with a higher number of nursing hours. Emergency, operating rooms, obstetrics and clinics were calculated on the number of cases per year plus hours of nursing care. Pediatric services had their own formula by service. Such calculations assumed the Commission had the latest data on beds and cases, which I would soon learn was not the case. Any variation from these existing formulae had to be presented to the Commission for approval. Since nursing was a key segment of every hospital, I was expected to make numerous presentations to the Commission.

On a personal basis, even with my new job I was living from one payday to the next, with no savings. By the time the bills and debts were paid, I had about fifteen to twenty dollars, which always went towards the needs of a child. Fortunately Gregory was a baby, as our diet remained relatively the same for three years; healthy, simple and monotonous. Occasionally, when strapped for cash, I was rescued by the government's Family Allowance check to tide me over till payday. My financial circumstances negated noontime lunches with colleagues or after-work bars, something I never missed.

One particularly bad weekend I needed four hundred dollars to pay for my car insurance. I had nothing else to sell and stubbornly did not want to bother my father. That evening after I put Gregory to bed I proceeded loudly talking to God saying, "Are you really listening? Surely you know I am in a desperate situation. If I cannot pay this bill by the first of the week I will lose my car, which is essential to my survival." Struggling I began to beg,

"I know you understand, and my needs are trivial in a vast universe, but please, please I beg of you. I need to hear by nine o-clock otherwise I will have to call Papa like a whimpering child. Please......." The clock ticked on. I don't know what I expected, I was clinging desperately to anything to keep me afloat.

At eight-thirty I was startled by the ringing of the telephone. I cautiously lifted the receiver to hear Aunt Di's voice saying "Dear, I have been thinking about you and wondering how I might help. So, this morning I mailed you a five hundred dollar check. I hope it's of some help". Dumbfounded, I struggled to express my profound thanks. My hand was shaking as I hung up the phone, tears running down my cheek, I dropped to my knees saying, "Oh God, forgive me, you were walking ahead of me all the time". Another crisis passed and I walked on.

Returning on the evening ferry November 6th , my birthday, I was glad to bid farewell to my twenty-sixth year, a very rough segment of my journey. Thinking there would be little celebration, I went though the usual routines with a heavy heart. However, as I was tucking Gregory into bed a knock came to the door. It was David and Lyle with a bottle of wine and a birthday cake. As my brother entered, he declared, "Sis, I pray you never call me again to say you have anything worse in your life. This has been one hell of a year, and I'm glad it's over!" Quiet toasts and positive thoughts filled the evening as we prayed for better times.

Christmas quickly arrived, and for the first time in my adult life, I had no money for gifts. Fortunately, Gregory was a baby and delighted with the glittering lights. It was a sad time for the whole family. It was difficult being 'merry' with a dark shadow hanging over everyone. I was relieved to return to the city to welcome the New Year alone. There would be little time for brooding, a mountain of work awaited me as I returned to the Commission after the holidays.

As my senior colleague stepped off the Commission stage, I faced an avalanche of nursing issues. With the changing of the guard, the nursing emphasis shifted. My senior colleague's strength was in Public Health. I arrived with a background in acute and psychiatric nursing plus nursing education. What this would mean to the Commission and the health industry had yet to materialize.

My initial mistake was thinking the four-drawer filing cabinet in our cubicle held backup nursing information on the hospitals. I quickly discovered the files were practically empty, leaving me with an immediate information demand. While the Commission's central filing system held plenty of general hospital information, I needed specific nursing information to make informed decisions. Since I knew many nurses in the local hospitals, the telephone became my immediate resource along with the Nova Scotia Nurses' Association's library, just blocks from my office. Stacks of files, reports, articles and letters began to pile up on my desk, everyone wanting an immediate reply. Knowing this would continue, I established an office triage system; A- got immediate attention, B-second, C were studies and reports and D was the rest of the reading material. A and B were handled during working hours, C and D got relegated to evening, weekend or travel reading. In time, the file clerk became efficient at sorting the incoming documents even when I was not there.

The rhythm of the Commission followed the weather and Board meetings. In the fall and winter months the counselors concentrated on calculating hospital budgets, dealing with construction or other projects, attending meetings on major issues, participating in government and professional association meetings, traveling to Ottawa, dealing with visiting federal consultants, and being available for Board presentations and questions. From May until October, we visited hospitals to meet with our professional colleagues, review budget matters and identify frontline issues. City hospitals were the exception, as teaching hospitals were more accessible with more issues, visits to them were year round.

My golden key on the Commission Board was Sister Catherine Gerard. She was the former hospital Administrator from my years at the Infirmary, now in her seventies, semi-retired, and the only female of the eight-member board. Sister, just taller than myself, came from a wealthy American family, and had a delightful, intelligent personality. It was a plus we already knew each other. She would not only become my mentor in facing the endless nursing issues at Commission Board meetings, she would also teach me the fine art of board management. I would make frequent trips to the Mount Motherhouse armed with files, reports and construction plans, to be carefully reviewed in preparation for the next board meeting. The Commission Board held monthly meetings except for July and August. Unanticipated, Sister also became my social manager.

Unfortunately, the newness of the job and my personal life left me unguarded for open harassment by an older male Commissioner. One day he corralled me in the hallway, flippantly stating we should spend the afternoon together for the 'good of my career'. I initially laughed off the comment only to realize he was dead serious. He then rephrased his request more forcefully stating we 'would' spend the afternoon together if I valued my job. He left for lunch expecting a positive reply when he returned.

I did not eat lunch that day but walked around the Halifax Public Gardens across from the Lord Nelson Hotel struggling with my desperate need for a job or living with the consequences if I defied this man's request. He had considerable power. I returned to an almost empty Commission office. By this point I had decided 'to hell with it', no job was that important. I would start calling colleagues in the afternoon. As I stepped out of the ladies washroom he blocked my path demanding; "Well, what is your answer?".

I was just about to tell him to get lost when Sister Catherine Gerard stepped through the Commission entrance. I glided towards her, taking her arm saying ; " I believe you should talk to Sister, my social manager, who will be delighted to chat with you about your request."

Without missing a beat, Sister's cold expression focused on the man saying; "Indeed I am!" and, firmly taking his arm, escorted a rather pale-faced man into the boardroom saying; " It appears you and I need to chat".

Sister later appeared at my cubicle asking; "Has this happened before?"

"No" I replied, " and I pray it doesn't happen again. I don't need this hassle". I then thanked her for her quick assistance.

Genuinely concerned, she went on, "Please let me know if this ever happens again. I shall clearly inform the others of my new role which should put a stop to any unnecessary requests". With Sister in charge, no one dared to test the waters again. I was left in peace to focus on the mounting workload in front of me. The aggressive member of the Commission Board never looked my way again. Before me were stacks of issues relative to the provincial nurses association, federal nursing meetings, and nursing education, hospital construction and nursing administration. The political side of my new role would be the most difficult.

At the Registered Nurses Association there were many critical issues. The sixties was a time of great change for nurses. Nursing was evolving from a vocation to a profession. In addition, nurses continued to face a conundrum as to why they lacked power and respect in an industry in which they were responsible for much of the patient care. Struggling for respect within the health industry was not enhanced by the disrespect they encountered through the media. Television and movies continued to place doctors in charge of patient wards with nurses portrayed as stiff cold robots, invisible clerks or sex kittens. Amazingly, neither nursing professional associations and/or women's groups in North America protested such portrayals. At this critical junction, nurses in Nova Scotia , and elsewhere in Canada, made a number of key decisions which would have major ramifications to their lives in the years ahead.

Nurses changed their working hours from eight to ten and even twelve hour shifts on the premise they would have more time with their family. There was little research on the long-term occupational health consequences of such working hours. Next, Chief Executive Officers in hospitals, for financial reasons, began to promote more part-time nursing positions, arguing this would better accommodate the highs and lows of patient admissions. In principle the nurses agreed. At the same time, registered nurses felt that Licensed Practical Nurses (or Certified Nursing Assistants), Nursing Aides and other 'lower' ranking nurses should be removed from hospitals and only be employed in long-term care facilities. The demise of these workers pushed more duties onto registered nurses. In addition, the professional association, quite legitimately, fought to have non-nursing (i.e. housekeeping, laundry, dietary, diagnostic services) tasks removed from registered nurses. It was expected the support services would increase their staff accordingly, but this never happened. For a brief time, with increased salaries, Registered Nurses, likely felt these moves strengthened their position in hospitals, as well it did. Everything was fine until provincial governments began to cut back on run-away health costs in the seventies and eighties. Then, the combination of decreased funding to hospitals and increased salaries began to play out on the nursing wards. Hospitals reduced the number of full-time and further increased the number of part-time nursing positions, and, at the same time, decreased support services. Nurses then found themselves in a much worse state with fewer staff, longer hours, and limited support.

As these events were happening across Canada, these topics were regular agenda items at federal/ provincial nursing consultant meetings in Ottawa.

Nurses would have had greater power in dealing with the provincial government if they could just speak with one voice. This was always a problem, for nursing not only had three major divisions (i.e. administration, education and community), it also had divisions within divisions, each with its own agenda. This lack of unity was often used against them. One example will surmise. After much effort I had convinced the Executive Director of the Commission to support a cross-the-board raise for nurses, arguing this would check-mate a possible provincial strike. Prior to bringing the matter to the Commission board, he requested a meeting of the nursing leaders. The day before the meeting I met with these leaders strongly suggesting they stand united so the raise would be approved. It failed. Dr. Simms knew the exact question to create controversy. The matter was tabled, the moment passed. Similar issues occurred at the provincial/federal meetings.

Prior to 1970, I had no reason to be on an airplane. Now, I was expected to attend nursing meetings, workshops and conferences in both Canada and the United States. Fortunately, limited travel budgets kept such trips to a minimum. On my first trip to Ottawa, I was warmly greeted by the Chief Nursing Officer with "Welcome Sally! I am delighted to ask, how is your baby?" I was both the youngest nursing consultant as well as the first one with a child. My uniqueness would be brief, as I was soon joined by another nursing consultant from the west who had a baby girl.

At these meetings, each province was represented by a nursing consultant for Public Health and one for hospitals. My argument was we would have greater strength if we presented a single report to the federal government on vital nursing issues. After a moment of silence, traditional barriers went up and the matter was dismissed. My efforts at unity were heroic but fruitless. Nevertheless, these national meetings gave me a broader view of nursing from a Canadian and international perspective. I also had access to the knowledge and expertise of federal nursing consultants, as well as a wealth of studies and information to support my arguments for more nursing staff. Returning to the province I faced an unending variety of nursing issues, including nursing education.

I was back in nursing education trying, once again, to promote different teaching methods and modules. Since my earlier experience with the pilot project, not much had changed. The nursing association was still bent on closing hospital nursing schools in favour of university programs, a decision which was being resisted. Continuing to believe nurses could be trained differently, Sister Catherine Gerard and I supported a pilot project at the Yarmouth Regional Hospital. In this instance a self-learning method using video programs was being used with mentors (i.e. faculty). Once again, the results showed promise but the association remained unimpressed. In another instance, to expand clinical teaching areas I proposed the use of regional and smaller hospital if faculty were willing to travel or setting up joint teaching appointments with nursing managers in these hospitals. Both ideas were rejected which resulted in the Halifax/Dartmouth region continuing to have thousands of students seeking clinical experience, with some wards having more students than patients.

Increasing the fluidity between different programs was proposed whereby students could challenge exams and complete the training in a shorter period, examples would be a registered nurse could become a doctor or a nursing assistant a registered nurse in half the time. In the sixties each training program demanded the applicant start at the bottom irrespective of their previous knowledge and experience. No training program was willing to revise their entrance criteria to speed up the training for experienced health workers. Undaunted, I kept trying. My next effort was with continuing education.

With increased expansion of health services, clinical procedures and technology, continuing education was becoming a critical necessity for health workers. The question was how to deliver such education on a regular basis to large numbers across the province. A small working group was willing to take on the challenge. After months of effort a plan was devised whereby the audio-visual department of Dalhousie University would develop educational programs and transmit these via a special Canadian Broadcasting Corporation (CBC) channel to all hospitals. Technical details had to be worked out with CBC and various training departments. The idea was approved by the Commission, but floundered when it reached the legislature where it got entangled in who would dominate such TV coverage. While frustrated by such actions, one hardly had time to be discouraged as there was plenty of issues to absorb my energies. One new area for me was hospital planning.

Every change in hospital facilities had to be reviewed by the Commission. With the expansion of health services, hospital facility plans were arriving for both renovations and new facilities. Since nursing was the largest hospital component, I had the task of reviewing and commenting on most architectural designs. The nursing ramifications were considerable.

I quickly discovered many architects recycled hospital designs from either the United Kingdom or the United States, revamping the plans to accommodate the needs of Canadian communities. Since the United States health industry was similar to Canada's, hospital designs were usually compatible. However, this could not be said for United Kingdom designs as nursing practices differ. Each design, reviewed carefully by myself, and later with Sister Catherine Gerard, was scrutinized taking into account the daily routines of nurses. There were two main problems with most plans. First, by the time the plans reached the Commission, architects had already solidified key decisions relative to walls, ventilation systems, and electrical and service delivery systems, which made the suggestion of changes a very testy topic. Second, nurses, the frontline workers in hospitals, were rarely involved in such planning. Hospital facility planning and design was mainly in the hands of the hospital board, medical staff and the Chief Executive Officer, with comments of the Director of Nursing usually given token acknowledgement. As a result, nurses had to live with poorly designed working spaces which favoured neither patients nor staffing schedules. A typical example was the action of one architect in reducing construction costs for one of the city's larger hospitals. He, with the agreement of the planning parties (i.e. no nurses), reduced the patient rooms on one wing by a foot. This resulted in all semi-private rooms in that wing being too small to effectively negotiate stretchers or other equipment in and out of the room without moving both beds. This singular decision multiplied the nurses' workload and constantly disturbed patients. There were many areas critical to patient care which architects did not adequately address, a prime example were bathrooms which were usually too small and/or ergonomically unsuited for patient equipment and mobility. Trying to get changes introduced, or even support for my ideas, was an uphill battle. While I had Sister Catherine Gerard's support at the board level, more support was always welcomed.

It was during one of these construction meetings that Dr. William Bickerton Clyde Robertson (called 'Bill') stepped into my life. He was a tall, handsome man with dark hair, and a soft Scottish accent. He was introduced as a consultant to the Commission from Dalhousie University. I was immediately impressed with his polite manner, his vast knowledge of the health industry and, of course, his understanding and support of nursing needs in hospital planning. Later when I asked the office gossip who he was, she replied; "He's just arrived from Scotland, was involved with the British National Health System, has three daughters and is 'sort of' married."

I did not ask what 'sort-of' married meant, I had enough personal troubles and felt the problems of others were best left undisturbed. The efficiency of the organizational grapevine was always impressive. I hated to think what they were saying about me. At this time in my life, I was glad to have a medical doctor on the committee who understood and appreciated the nursing role in health care.

In my first inaugural months as a Nursing Counselor I managed to wade through countless budget calculations and survive many meetings. I was running, and being challenged to find answers to improve the working environment of nurses. Not all efforts were successful, but there was progress. With plenty of scope, when blockages occurred, I shifted my energies to another topic. My second Christmas was approaching and I was glad for a break.

My greatest joy came from children. I spent many Saturdays with Gregory playing with the upstairs children (an older boy and a younger girl) while a cake rose in the oven for a 'treat' or, in the summer, we joined their mother in the garden for a barbeque. Sometimes Gregory and I went to the local lake while he quietly built roads and bridges for his dinky cars.

Gregory was growing into a lively, happy child with a mischievous smile and a delight in climbing. My grandmother use to say "it takes little intelligence to get pregnant, but great intelligence and commitment to bring up a child properly". This was certainly proving to be the case as Gregory was an intelligent child demanding an alert parent. Whenever possible we created a game. Our discipline game was 1,2,3 in which 1 meant he had crossed the line, 2 he was getting further into trouble and 3 he was sent to his bedroom. He became so good at the game he often disciplined himself. By two, he would pop his curly head around the kitchen door singing out, "two and a little bit" and run chuckling down the hall and into the bedroom. When I would ask "Well young man what have you been up to" he innocently told me. This game proved helpful when shopping or visiting, as I would whisper into his ear 1, or 2 and he, mostly, would stop what was becoming an annoyance. Another game was creating puppet mitts in the winter whereby we chatted and sang as we drove to his baby-sitters. Like most children he did not like wearing mitts. While my life as a mother had its delightful moments, my social life was non-existent.

With no money for baby-sitters, it was hard to plan for any extras. In the three years I had four male friends; two were going through a divorce, one was Gregory's God father and the other was a legal counselor who also worked at the Commission. There were periodic meals or theatre shows but nothing serious. My main relaxation was enjoying a hot bath, classical music and a good book. Simplicity was the dominant feature of my personal life.

As spring approached, I prepared for my first hospital visits outside of the Halifax-Dartmouth area. Dividing the province into small parcels, I started visiting hospitals on a four-day pattern every second week or so. Each visit entailed a hospital tour. As I walked through the hospital, I memorized facility details along with the pressing needs of the nursing managers. In the evening, I mentally revisited the hospital recording the details into a small tape recorder. As the tapes piled up my nursing files expanded.

The two biggest problems in traveling was my separation from Gregory and traveling as a single young woman. My baby-sitter retained a detailed record of my travels including every possible telephone number she might need. I knew Gregory was happy with this family, but I was constantly plagued with guilt and apprehension. I called every night to check on him. While I justified this time away from my son as necessary, it was never easy.

Traveling as a single woman, for me, presented a number of problems. I continued to wear my marriage ring, as protection against personal questions and unwanted attention. I was ill-prepared for much social interaction outside of work, the wounds were still too fresh. Once I got to know the hotel/motel managers they kindly blocked any unsolicited phone calls except those from Dartmouth, the Commission or the local hospital. They also provided me with valuable travel and community information which further enhanced my data collection.

There was much healing in the beautiful countryside of Nova Scotia as I made my rounds to the various hospitals. The sun rising over the water as I drove into coastal communities in the early morning was breathtaking. I especially loved the small communities with their antique and quaint stores. With little money I became a skilled window shopper. I treasured the freedom and discovery offered to me as I drove my navy blue Volkswagon around the province.

The arrival of Medicare, marked the shift from religious, military and/or nursing administrators in hospitals, to chief executive officers with financial training. Actual power in hospitals was controlled by a triad; the hospital Board, the medical staff and/or the Chief

Executive Officer (CEO). Mostly it was held between the medical staff and the CEO, who controlled the budget. Nursing was excluded from the inner power elite, yet bore the heaviest responsibility for care. Routinely, the Director of Nursing submitted a nursing budget to the CEO who included it with the overall budget presented to the hospital board. Once approved, the hospital's budget was submitted to the Commission. The Commission's approval of hospital budgets rested on the allocation of monies legislated by the provincial government. Usually, the approved budget was less than requested, the hospital receiving written communications on the reasons for the differences. One might expect the Director of Nursing, responsible for the biggest portion of the hospital's budget, would receive a copy of the Commission's letter, but this rarely happened. The Directors were informed what their budget would be and had to trust they were getting the full story.

I first became aware of the problem when working with Florence Gass, the Director of Nursing at the Victoria General Hospital in reconciling her operating budget with what had been approved at the Commission. The figures did not match. Determined to find the answer, I spent days going through numerous scheduling documents and talking to managers. Finally, after many calculations and discussions, I discovered the budget was short about five hundred thousand dollars. In fact, this shortfall had been going on for years. My broad estimate was that the nursing department had been short changed about three million dollars over a five year period, which could have purchased a lot of nursing staff.

The finance director was furious when approached on the matter. He had obviously been rerouting nursing funds to other areas in the hospital, all the while complaining the nurses couldn't manage their own budget. While Miss Gass was pleased with the outcome, I did not endear myself to the accountant, when I further informed him I would henceforth tell Miss Gass precisely what I had approved in her budget.

Suspicious this was occurring in other hospitals, I adopted a similar strategy for all hospitals. With nursing administrators not being told their precise budgets the accountants had a free hand. To offset this imbalance, I told the nursing Directors precisely what the Commission had approved and, in addition, sought their input whenever their hospital's nursing department was on the Commission agenda. Such action was supported by Sister Catherine Gerard. Interestingly, I expected much resistance on these practices but nothing happened.

Being a Director of Nursing was a complex, difficult and lonely job. In the sixties, Directors' of Nursing were women. Once appointed, the Director of Nursing could no longer share her problems with those she managed without undermining her own authority. Thus, one of my unwritten roles was to be a sounding board for the Directors, listening to a variety of issues. Sometimes small matters were handled as we talked, others were more complex. In my travels I heard many tales; health professionals with addiction and/or mental problems, abuse and harassment of nurses, problem personalities (i.e. a doctor demanding that the nurse he was sleeping with be promoted to a Head Nurse position), wars between one group or other within the organization, facility problems (i.e. flies in the operating room), unusual or too many infections, etc.. Confidentiality meant many issues remained strictly between myself and the Director. In certain instances I shared my concerns with my mentor (i.e. Sister Catherine Gerard), without naming the hospital or Director. Sister kindly advised me on a number of strategies. It was evident, these capable health care managers needed backup, someone they could talk to that understood the complexities of their problems and the ramifications of decisions which might involve the entire community. For a moment in time I served that function, supported by my own highly capable advisor.

In the late sixties, small hospitals of ten to fifteen beds were usually large, old, houses donated to the community, with one or more doctors. The longevity of such facilities as acute care hospitals was already under review due to costs and acquiring qualified staff. Nurses in these small facilities had to be more versatile than their counterparts in larger hospitals. They had to be capable of handling emergencies, obstetrics and general nursing care. The size of an emergency could stretch the capabilities of a small nursing staff. An example occurred on a trip I made with my mother and Gregory to a small facility in the Parrsboro area of the province.

Arriving in Truro one Thursday evening, I asked my mother if she would like to accompany me the next day on a short visit to a nearby hospital. She agreed and we took Gregory, then eighteen months, along for an outing. I was certain the visit would be brief and uneventful. Arriving in the village I dropped off mother and Gregory at a park within sight of the hospital.

Arriving at the hospital I discovered there had been a fatal car accident involving a family from the United States. The RCMP were at the hospital and the hospital staff were fully occupied in handling the crisis. I removed my coat to assist the Director of Nursing. Forgetting the time, I suddenly looked at my watch to realize several hours had passed. Alarmed I was about to leave the facility only to be calmed by the Director who informed me my family members were already being cared for at her own home near the park. So, by mid-afternoon I found mother chatting merrily with another lady in the house while Gregory played with his toys on the living room floor. It was quite an exciting day for Mother. After that I considered the unexpected with future visits.

With each hospital visit my files grew along with my understanding of what was troubling hospital nurses. Nothing beats frontline contact. Initially, I thought sharing such information with my boss would be beneficial to both of us, this was a mistake. My first boss, a male, grew steadily irritable with each report stating, "Nurses are always finding problems. They are never satisfied". Being a political appointee, this individual saw every problem through a political prism. His interest in patient care was miniscule. My insistence on action for serious issues was making matters worse. So, I ceased sharing and waited for better days. Eventually, I was rewarded when Bill Robertson took charge of public hospitals and became my boss. My grandmother was right "Everything comes to him (her) who waits!" With Bill's arrival, I was able to flit in and out of the office knowing my reports were not only being read, there was action on items before I submitted the next report.

Much to my amazement, not one Director asked me about my personal life, yet, they all knew. The grapevine was thorough and efficient. I was grateful for their silence and humbled by their generosity. As I finished my visit and started to leave, some of the Directors would place into my hand some baking , knitted item or second-hand children's clothing with the statement "Sally, I though this might help you and the baby." In true Maritime form, they were acknowledging one of their own was struggling. Somehow they were also aware of my financial difficulties. Since I held little power these gifts were accepted as a token of their kindness. However, this proved a bit embarrassing on a trip with the Executive Director.

Out of the blue, Dr. Simms decided to take a two-day tour of a number of hospitals in the eastern end of the province with Bill Robertson, myself and an administrative counselor. Dr. Simms and Bill Robertson sat in the front seat of an old car while the administrative counselor and myself shared the back seat.

It was a whirlwind trip constituting a quick hospital tour and/or a meeting with senior management on a particular issue, and then moving on. My role was to highlight the nursing situation. As we were departing, the Directors' unobtrusively placed a wee parcel into my hands before bidding me adieu. As the parcels built up I struggled to find the right words to explain such actions. Before I had time to speak a chuckle came from Dr. Simms who said: "You will note gentlemen that no one is giving us any gifts. Now it's either a sign the Commission is not paying Sally enough or she has some magic hold over these nurses." When the others joined in the laughter, I relaxed.

With the arrival of winter I was back again in the midst of budget calculations and meetings, but this time I was better armed with more frontline details to strengthen my presentations. Meetings rolled on, and on, sometimes in typical bureaucratic style never reaching a decision. It took lots of patience to avoid being buried in the endless words and documents.

Disguising my dyslexia had become fundamental to my survival. My brain was fully exercised with the mountains of documents I had to read but the endless ministerial letters and nursing reports threatened my security. Whenever possible, I carefully drafted difficult nursing reports at home after Gregory went to bed. I manually wrote and revised pages and pages of material, sticking to brevity and clarity as a defense. Stress and tiredness increased my word difficulties, something I tried to avoid. Constant talking and the need for many written documents left me exhausted at the end of each week.

Just before Christmas, the Psychiatric Nursing Counselor announced she was leaving for her Master's studies in January, transferring her workload to me. After all, the argument went, I had psychiatric nursing experience and a few more facilities would hardly be noticed. Already drowning, I mumbled acceptance, knowing the decision had already been made without my input and at a higher level. I would do what was possible.

By the second Christmas after Ron's disappearance I had enough money for small gifts. Gregory, now two, was almost overwhelmed with the Christmas excitement. Life at my parents home was improving; Papa's truck- driving school was thriving, Rayona was blossoming into a lovely young woman, and David and Lyle had their own beautiful baby girl, Sara. Mother's mental health continued on its ups and downs. She occasionally had difficulties separating the fantasy world of TV shows from reality. I was the only one seeing the steady decline in her mental state.

During the months since his disappearance, my legal problems seemed endless; issues relative to Ron's car accident, unpaid bills and other minor issues. Fortunately, my lawyer handled most of these but episodes did puncture my daily life. One example, during an office meeting with Bill Robertson and two other counselors his secretary entered the room to announce the Sheriff was waiting for me in the guest area. I froze! My meeting colleagues stared at me while Bill quietly asked me to return to the meeting after seeing the Sheriff. I nodded and walked stiff-legged towards the guest area, trying desperately to be brave and expecting the worst. Entering the room I must have appeared frozen and pale.

The Sheriff, apologizing for disturbing me at work, passed me a legal document and left. The abruptness disoriented me. I stumbled back to my cubicle, deposited the document, unread, into my business case and called my lawyer. He apologized for not calling me first and said the matter had already been settled. Shaken, I returned to the meeting, knowing my colleagues had been talking about me in my absence. I mumbled it was a legal matter, trying to appear unruffled, and was grateful when they all turned to the topic of the meeting.

The new year meant more work. Psychiatric nursing issues were added to an already overloaded schedule. My quest for nursing information still unfinished, I decided to focus on the teaching hospitals; the Infirmary, the Victoria General Hospital and the Izaac Walton Killam Children's Hospital. I planned the visits with care.

Once again I found myself face-to-face with Sister Catherine Peter at the Halifax Infirmary, this time in a different role. My first meeting renewed our former relationship, for better or for worse, as I covered the hospital's budget, staffing numbers and her problem of keeping professional nurses. It seemed her time was running out. I knew her management of the nursing department was under review. Our meeting went reasonably well and I managed to get agreement on allowing her Intensive Care nursing staff to meet with the Victoria General Intensive Care nursing staff, a coup in an environment in which such cooperation between hospitals was still resisted. Seizing the opportunity, I took time to rekindle my acquaintanceship with old colleagues. Not much had changed in my absence.

Within weeks of this meeting Sister Catherine Peter was dismissed, and I was informed she would be reassigned to The Mount Motherhouse. Shortly after the announcement, I received a call from her inviting me to lunch in the sisters' dining room, an excluded area for most lay people. I accepted the invitation with some trepidation.

Not surprisingly, Sister seemed subdued when we met. We were practically alone in the dining room giving us plenty of privacy. During the meal we chatted about familiar people and events. Finally, over coffee she asked "I suppose you are wondering why I invited you here today?"

"Yes', I replied, pondering if this was the moment when she was about to tell me what an unmitigated pest I was during my Infirmary years. I braced myself for her reply.

"Well, in all my years at the Infirmary you were the only nurse that stood up to me. Whenever you got angry I knew it was time to listen. Perhaps I did not always respond in the way you expected, but I did listen."

I was dumbfounded!. Unknown to me, I had become the annoying buzzing bee occasionally penetrating her bubble of righteousness. Pressing on I asked; "Surely, Sister, other nurses must have reacted to your decisions and policies over the years, perhaps they did it differently than my rather vocal resistance." I was still not convinced I was the only antagonist.

"No, you were the only one." Then staring past me as if explaining her actions to an invisible court, she continued, "My methods may not have been clear or understood by the nurses but my intention was always to create the best nurses for the Infirmary."

It was my turn to react, "Surely, Sister you must have known your methods were crucifying good nurses. How did it help the Infirmary when some of the most skilled nurses walked away?" She skillfully sidestepped my question. Our conversation went round and round with little resolution. In the end, Sister remained convinced of the righteousness of her methods, and steadfastly resisted any ownership of damage either to individuals or to the organization. Deep down I felt sorry for her because in middle age the views she held sacred were being rejected, a blow to anyone. Perhaps she invited me to lunch hoping I held some magic clue. I didn't. We parted on good terms, for I remembered working beside an excellent nurse. It was her management style that was under question. Our paths would never cross again.

As I walked back to my office I realized that autocrats likely believe their actions are justified, and do not take kindly to being questioned. Fortunately for me Sister belonged to a religious order, under other circumstances antagonists would not have been so kindly regarded. I prayed the new Director of Nursing would bring healing, and open the doors for innovation and growth. As I left my old alma mater, I was already planning my review of the Victoria General (VG) Hospital. Earlier requests had been blocked. Finally, I got approval.

Because of its size and political importance, I planned my review carefully concentrating on key support services (i.e. laundry, general supplies, housekeeping, and the lab), troublesome areas for nurses. If problems exist in these areas nurses compensate using up valuable time which is lost to patient care. I reported daily to Florence Gass but otherwise was left on my own. We trusted each other and I had promised her a copy of my draft report. What lay before me was a two-week window to cover about forty nursing wards. My primary objective was to gather nursing information, a secondary objective was to try and investigate reported support service snags.

Most hospitals have three sets of laundry for every bed; one on the bed, one en route to the laundry and one on the storage shelves. The VG had five sets in circulation, with nurses still complaining there were not enough face cloths, towels and sheets. With so much linen in circulation I suspected thievery. I would quickly learn this was not the case. Slowly I worked my way through the nursing wards and finally down to the basement of the hospital where the bottleneck was found. In a huge room, about thirty by forty feet with a twenty foot ceiling, dirty linen bags were dropping from several ceiling shutes. The room was piled high with laundry bags some several layers deep. A single, long-haired youth was loading the dirty linen bags in carts for delivery to the nearby laundry. When asked, the attendant wearily informed me he had never seen the back wall of the room since he arrived, months previous. I shuddered to think how long some dirty linen had been stagnating in bags.

When I approached the Italian laundry manager asking him about the blockage he exploded " Lady, those idiots up stairs added a two-hundred bed wing to this hospital with no discussion of any expansion in the laundry. Our machines are working overtime and breaking down under the strain. With the current conditions we may never get to the back wall of that room."

I returned to the Commission to see if we might obtain the services of the Technical University engineers to tackle the problem. After much negotiating this finally came to pass. Months later when I revisited the hospital, I realized the resolution of one problem had created another. Now the nurses had too much linen. Some of the extra linen was re-routed to a nearby long-term facility, and old or torn pieces were discarded. My next study area was the delivery of general supplies.

A subtle symptom of internal trouble in large health facilities can be the disruptive delivery of basic supplies. Admittedly, there can be clerical errors but sometimes the errors are too blatant to be ignored. I discovered in my travels, even with constant complaints from the nursing staff, supplies were regularly being delivered to the wrong wards (i.e. urology supplies delivered to gynecology and visa versa). No one could be that incompetent. In addition, nurses told me of vital parts missing on major pieces of equipment, delaying patient services and creating havoc. Fueling the difficulties, was the military-like practices of the supply manager (a former naval officer) who favoured numerous requisition forms, creating delays in ordering and receiving of supplies. In this environment, all I could do was identify the problems and recommend a review of the entire support service, on the premise valuable nursing time, if not patient care, was being jeopardized by such inefficiency. Large health facilities often have bureaucracies within bureaucracies, which can tie up the best systems. My findings created some changes but, as I expected, not enough to streamline the service and reduce waste. My next target was housekeeping.

As I walked through the wards I checked the cleanliness. It quickly became apparent housekeeping deteriorated beyond the fourth floor and halted at the Central Supply Department (CSD) on the top floor of the hospital. CSD was being managed by a strong nursing manager who demanded exact attention to detail. It also reflected the boundaries of the hospital administrators. Nursing complaints of infection had been ignored. I put myself in the bad graces of housekeeping when I issued my report, as they were immediately delegated to the neglected floors for a thorough cleaning. Such action was appreciated by nurses, and gave them courage to demand greater cleanliness in the future. Changing diagnostic services was quite another matter.

Laboratory services, an independent organization to the VG hospital, was in a separate building adjacent to the hospital. This meant, blood supply problems would be more complex as it involved two separate organizations. The problem was that blood specimens were not reaching the lab, resulting in repeated blood tests on patients, both costly and inconvenient for both patients and staff. A quick calculation showed that thousands of blood specimens were going missing each year. I jokingly suggested to Commission colleagues there must be a well fed vampire in the hospital basement. The answer was more mundane. Glass blood tubes were being jammed into poorly designed delivery containers, and transported by under-paid attendants to the lab. Some glass tubes easily broke in transit and others went to the wrong lab (i.e. microbiology instead of hematology). One solution was to move to plastic tubes, styrofoam containers and better trained and paid delivery attendants. Unfortunately, lab authorities were resistant to allocating any additional funds for such changes, so the blood specimen problem continued. This item would reappear later when I returned to Halifax in the eighties.

Nearing the end of my study and trying to save time, late one Friday afternoon I ducked through a short cut between the old and new wings of the hospital, an area used to store equipment. I had barely stepped into the space when my intuition registered 'danger'. Nothing appeared out of order, yet I knew something was wrong and hurried along to the elevator, the hair on the back of my neck curling. Prior to leaving the hospital I stopped off to share my concerns with the security officer who I had become acquainted with in my days at the hospital.

On Monday morning I was shocked to hear the security officer had been found in the same storage area severely beaten and was in the Intensive Care Unit fighting for his life. Devastated, I called Florence Gass. Thankfully, he recovered, and was able to tell the police what had happened. I was never contacted. Security issues were escalating with the growth of the industry. It seemed we were following the Americans a decade later. There was still no discussion of undercover investigators in Canadian hospitals.

Within weeks, I presented Florence Gass with a draft of my review giving her information not previously collected. It was routine administrative work of investigating and clearing bottlenecks. The reason it was not happening was due to the type of skills of health managers, time, money and, in some cases, a lack of understanding of the industry. This administrative flaw would fester for decades creating more and more operational difficulties.

Further hospital reviews were put on the back burner as my workload was escalating beyond my grasp. Recognizing the dilemma, the Commission decided to hire another nurse. The plan was that she would take a portion of the workload.

By my second year, I was facing a personal dilemma that needed resolution. It was time to get my marital status clarified as I needed a legal document to take Gregory out of the province. Since adultery was the only grounds for divorce in Nova Scotia, I would require extra ammunition if I was going to get a civil court to even listen to my case. So, I decided to take my case to the Roman Catholic Tribunal thinking this might give me some sort of letter or legal document to help me. My lawyer, Lorne MacDougal, agreed to assist me in this matter. Mistakenly, I thought this process might be quick. The meetings were held in a high school class room near the Commission office at the end of a working day. The Tribunal route would prove to be foolhardy.

At the first meeting, Lorne and I arrived to face three Roman Catholic priests/lawyers who formed the Tribunal. The proceedings stumbled at the introductions when one of the priest/lawyers stated with a sneer "It appears that Mrs Linkert is being well cared for!" pointing to my fur coat. I was furious and thought of stopping the proceedings at that point as it appeared at least one of the three had a definite bias against women. After my lawyer admonished the individual we pressed on. The legal dialogue dragged on for months, the proceedings flawed by poor administration (i.e. my lawyer's letters not being answered) and continuing negative innuendos towards women. I kept telling myself this torture would eventually get me the freedom I sought. I pressed on.

The second nursing counselor was eventually appointed. After her orientation she scheduled a trip to Cape Breton to get acquainted with her hospitals. The morning she was scheduled to be in Cape Breton, while walking towards the Commission office, I was overcome with a vision, one I had never experienced before. Before me was a television-like image, a running video, in which I was watching my colleague's car teetering on a steep, snowy, embankment with raging water below. I could almost feel the icy mist from the water. The image was so clear I could not imagine everyone passing me that morning couldn't see it as well. The video-like image continued to unfold as I walked steadily towards my office.

When I entered the Commission I desperately needed to talk to someone but feared the revelation of such visions might be detrimental to my job. Finally, ignoring the consequences, I tapped on the door of Dr. Simms, the only person in the office at that early hour. With the vision still running, I nonchalantly inquired; "Is there any possibility you might be contacting the Cape Breton hospitals this morning? I am just wondering if Jane arrived safely?"

Puzzled, Dr. Simms looked up and replied; "No, is there a problem?"

"No" I replied abruptly and retreated, the vision showing the car slipping towards the edge of the bank. I was fearing the worst.

Dr. Simms followed me back to my cubicle asking, " Sally, this is not like you, your upset about something. What's wrong?"

Capitulating, I described my vision and my concern for my colleague's safety. I wondered if we might call without raising an alarm? He left to make the call.

As he left, the vision evaporated. Yet, I did not feel the situation was fatal.

Shortly he returned with news. Yes, the event was as I described. Jane had been rescued by a passing trucker. Her car was lost as it slipped over the embankment into the river. The traumatic event would leave her in hospital for days. (Actually, she would be on sick leave for months) There was no further discussion of relief.

As Dr. Simms turned to leave he said; " My mother had 'that look'. It must be your Celtic inheritance. I never understood what she was seeing but she was rarely wrong. Let me know if you have any more visions".

The vision got me thinking of my grandmother who had regular sightings. This was not a pleasant experience. I was not sure if I was as strong as her unless one got use to such episodes. I was glad of its infrequent occurrence.

With no backup, I played the cards that were dealt. My office triage system continued to priorize the work. To the top of the pile arrived the need for revising the staffing formula for the new Isaac Walton Killam (IWK) Hospital for Children. The old hospital had finally been replaced. More pediatric specialties with increased referrals from the Atlantic region had changed the nursing demands. Somehow I had to convince a mainly male Commission that additional nurses were needed. I spent days talking to the nursing managers getting their views on what were basic staffing numbers. Then, Sister Catherine Gerard and I spent time over my revised calculations as we prepared to ask for a 'reasonable' increase, rather than reaching for the stars. If the request was too extreme, it would be rejected.

On the day of the board meeting I began my presentation by asking each male member of the board how long, in their opinion, it would take to feed a normal six month infant. An hour was the average reply. Next I asked how long it would take in their opinion to feed the same infant if he/she had a cleft lip and cleft palate. The time was greatly extended. Then with a flip chart I showed the number of nurses based on their estimate. Flipping to the next page and said, "But, I am only asking for a portion of that number". The tactic was not intended to belittle the audience. It was intended to find a common platform for dialogue. The method proved helpful as we walked through each nursing ward. The outcome gave the hospital more nurses and the Commission revised formulae. However, not all IWK needs had to do with nursing numbers.

During my trips to the hospital I got to know one of the dietitians. Late one Friday afternoon I received a call from her with an urgent problem. The hospital had a fifteen month old child from Labrador who would not eat regular hospital food as she was use to seal flipper stew. The dietitian had neither access to seal flippers (this being a product of Newfoundland or Labrador) nor an understanding of how to cook the stew. The problem was unless the child began to eat some food her condition would deteriorate. Not familiar with seal flipper stew I nevertheless, reassured her I would try to help. My immediate thought was to find someone from Newfoundland or Labrador to help me. The one name that popped into mind was the Premier, Joey Smallwood. So, I got the phone number and called his office, knowing I would, if lucky, get an assistant. A woman's voice introduced herself as the Premier's secretary. In describing the problem, I asked if there was some way to not only get the seal flippers to the hospital but also a recipe or better still someone who knew how to make the stew. Assured the matter was in capable hands, I left for the weekend.

On Monday, Dr. Simms came to my cubicle the moment I arrived and reported, "I see you were busy on Friday. I just thought you would like to know, Mr. Smallwood's office arranged for a shipment of seal flippers to be delivered to the Children's Hospital by an RCMP constable who, fortunately, also knew how to make seal flipper stew. The baby is eating well, and the dietitian, nurses and doctors are all quite happy."

"Well" said I "that was a great success, don't you think?"

"Well, yes, except for one small factor" said Dr. Simms with a smile. "It is customary for government staff to notify their supervisor before making calls to a Premier's office in another province. Perhaps you could let me know the next time".

Woops, I thought, another blunder. My ability in stumbling over bureaucratic rules was formidable. I knew there were other civil servants who were far better at adhering to the rules. Anyway, I thought, my time as a civil servant was coming to an end. It was not because I didn't like the job, I was being backed into a financial corner.

As the provincial Conservative government patted themselves on the back in holding civil service pay raises to zero for two years, I was edging towards disaster. As the city's costs rose my minute economic cushion was evaporating. My salary bore no resemblance to my responsibilities. As a nursing counselor I received $2,000 less than my male administrative counselors who had less responsibilities. Several attempts to increase my salary proved hopeless. Government pay scales were being rigidly enforced. Deep down I wondered if the Commission felt they had me trapped. Surely I would not leave the province with a young child. I was reduced to gambling on the daily travel allowance (i.e. the Volkwagon being very fuel efficient) and reduced food intake. I traveled with bags of raisins and nuts, praying the Director of Nursing would invite me to lunch so I would have at least one main meal. My weight dropped and I started coming down with several bouts of flu. I needed a change!

In my thirties for the first time I sat down to write a resume. Sitting at my chrome kitchen table, aided by sample resumes, I attempted to describe my skills, creating paragraphs for strangers to read. As the drafts accumulated I could hear my grandmother's disparaging words, 'It's a poor fool who must blow his own horn'. Talking to her, I said, "Well, Nanny, this poor fool needs this resume to find a decent job. Right now I dearly need the word skills of my ancestors". It took days. Then, I started sending out letters for jobs advertised in nursing magazines, focusing on both Canada and the United States. I worked in silence. My 'intention' to move was now registered.

At the same time, Bill Robertson, knowing I needed a break, approved an educational conference in Phoenix, noting I could take a slight detour en route to a Canadian nursing conference in Edmonton. Four days in the sun was the most welcomed therapy I could have imagined.

I stepped off the plane into the welcoming embrace of the desert heat. My aching bones rejoiced. At the conference I joined the Arizona delegation as there were no other Canadians in attendance. There I met a member of the Arizona Hospital Association who asked if I might be interested in working in the United States. "May be" I said and thought little more of it as I winged my way onward to Edmonton.

Returning from Edmonton, I had five job offers in the United States (two in California, two in Arizona and one in Illinois). There were none in Canada. All five offers were in nursing and/or health education. In Peoria, Illinois the job was with a computer company in the early stages of developing software for health care. Secretly I began to make contact with all five parties. Next, a Roland Wilpitz (a contact through the Arizona Hospital Association) arranged for me to fly to Philadelphia for a meeting. In accepting his offer, I called Margie who now resided in Virginia, married to Kenneth Rock. This was a fantastic treat to be able to see my dear friend again.

I flew to Virginia, met with Margie and Ken, who helped me catch the train to Philadelphia for my appointment. Arriving in the city of my great-grandmother, I walked to the hotel, a block from the commuter stop. This being winter, I was wearing my maxi-length fox/muskrat fur coat and muskrat hat, later described by Wilpitz as the attire of the first blond Eskimo he ever met.

The hotel lobby was busy as I waited for Roland Wilpitz to appear. On time, a heavy set, six foot, middle aged man with graying hair, approached me speaking with a loud Texan accent suggesting we chat in his hotel room, an invitation which I hesitantly agreed to. As we entered his room I laid my fur coat and hat on a chair near the entrance and asked if the door could be left ajar. Smiling, he agreed. With little chit chat, he got down to the interview, pulling out my resume from his leather business case. The interview went on for some time, his questions precise and focused on my nursing skills. Finally, he retorted, "How the hell old are you anyway?"

Crushed, I thought 'He thinks I'm too young to be a Director of Education at his hospital'. Quickly gathering my wits I asked " Is there a problem with my age?"

"No", he replied, "I'm just amazed you have done so much at your age. You have certainly been busy. This is fine. Next you need to come to Arizona to see our hospital before making a decision. I'll be in touch about the travel arrangements" The interview was over. Since he was inviting me to Arizona, I took it as a positive.

Returning to the main hotel lobby he insisted I take a yellow cab back to Virginia, passing a wad of bills into my hand to pay the driver. Margie was shocked when I stepped out of the yellow cab at her doorstep. We had much to chat about.

After many months, the church Tribunal finally reached a decision. Because there was a child my marriage could not be annulled. This I understood. For a moment they seemed to agree I needed to get on with my life, even suggesting I might even marry again sometime in the future. Then came the punch line; "However, even if you marry again and your first husband should appear years later, you will have to leave your second husband and return to your first".

Stunned I responded, " This is insane! If I understand you correctly, you are saying that if I am in a second marriage, a marriage which could be longer than my first, and, God forbid, if there were more children, I would just up and leave this family and return to my first husband who I was married to for three years. I'm sorry gentlemen, I am trying to find some resolution to a very difficult situation and this is totally unacceptable". Turning to my lawyer I continued; "Lorne, this is finished" and left the room.

Standing in the darkened corridor waiting for Lorne, I realized the last thread of my former life was being cut. If I proceeded with a legal divorce, as was my plan, I would be excommunicated from the Roman Catholic Church. Deep in thought I was startled to hear a voice behind me saying " God is not in buildings". I turned expecting someone to be standing there, only to find a vacant corridor. At that moment, a gentle peace engulfed me and I knew whatever path lay ahead it would be all right. As Lorne joined me he said "Sally, you have done your duty and more. It's time we proceed to a divorce. This won't be easy but we are going to give it our best try".

In time, my divorce hearing was scheduled with Lorne's partner handling the case. David accompanied me to the hearing. Thankfully, there were few people in court. I had requested the financial mess not be brought into open court and my lawyer concurred.

For the first time I listened to the findings of police reports from Nova Scotia and Ontario plus the RCMP report from the friend of my father who listed Ron's disappearance as 'suspected foul play'. David took the stand and recounted his version of events. The lawyer then carefully summarized the details, making a request for a divorce under exceptional circumstances.

As the judge leaned over his bench I expected some comment on the difficulties of such a case in light of provincial laws. Instead he glared at me and asked, "How do I know she hasn't killed this man and cleverly buried his body?"

David's instant reaction was, "You son of a bitch……" as he climbed over the railing heading right for the judge. My lawyer grabbed his jacket and pulled him back into the seat, while addressing the judge saying, "Your Honour, perhaps we could meet in chambers," and the two walked out of the courtroom.

I felt battered and abused from the legal process. All I could think of was, 'This nightmare is never going to end. Now they think I killed him………Oh, God help me!" David and I sat silently, a deadness hanging in the air.

Eventually, my lawyer returned saying the matter was under review, with a look that said, a divorce is likely impossible in light of the judge's opinion of events. I returned home nursing a severe headache and went to lie down. David described what had happened which infuriated my father. After a brief rest, I bundled Gregory into the car and returned to the city. Panicking for the first time, I felt trapped unable to survive financially and unable to escape. Closing my mind, I prepared to press on praying desperately for a miracle.

As the weeks drifted by with no word, I prepared for the worst. Then Lorne phoned me at the Commission to say the divorce had been approved, the legal documents would be forthcoming. I could barely control my joy and left my office abruptly to walk alone in the park, savouring the beauty of every flower and the strutting duck. Inwardly I was screaming 'I am free! O God, I am free! I am free!' Now I could truly negotiate a job change.

Events were moving fast. I flew to Cottonwood, Arizona in December. A rural community with a small hospital needing a Director of Education because the Arizona State Nursing Association was attaching increased continuing education credits to the annual renewal of nursing licenses. Roland Wilpitz's job offer had several positives; less traveling, independence in running my own education department, and Ron's relatives living in Phoenix, a two hour drive away. I flew home via Toronto, a blizzard practically stranding me in Ontario. I still had four other options to consider with comparable benefits but no relatives in close proximity. I was facing a dilemma. As I mulled over the offers I chatted with my father on the pros and cons of each option. He understood my need for change and kindly left the final decision to me.

Walking to work one morning I began my usual dialogue with God. "OK, I need Your help. This is a major decision. I will be stepping off into the unknown no matter which offer I choose. I am definitely heading to the United States, the question is which route. So, lets agree the first one that contacts me today I will accept as your guidance in making my decision". For someone who had survived three extremely difficult years, this dialogue made perfect sense. I trusted in a power higher than myself.

As I entered the Commission office a clerk came running to say "Someone from Arizona has been trying to get in touch with you for the past hour, he's on the phone."

I reached my telephone and heard Roland Wilpitz's Texan accent asking, "Well, are you coming or not?"

"Yes", I replied. "Can you tell me what I am suppose to do next. In your official employment letter will you kindly spell out what I need to do to get to Arizona". Within the week his letter arrived with all the details. I was on my way!

The Commission was shocked at my resignation. I was not indispensable, they could find other nurses. My father's advice was, 'Your job in life is to make it easier for those walking behind you' and so it would be. There had been many changes during my watch; communications with the Directors' of Nursing had expanded; the nursing files were bulging with back-up information; formulae for calculating nursing staff had increased with more nursing positions in many hospitals; standards had been created for Intensive Care Units; nursing needs in construction planning had been elevated; and a bit of progress had been made in nursing/health education. Circumstances had forced my hand to consider another path. It was a plus my move would be to a warm location. Prior to leaving Canada I had one important mission. Not knowing when I might return to Canada, it was imperative Gregory meet his Linkert grandparents.

Dressed in a camel-coloured, woollen coat and hat, Gregory at four boarded the airplane for Toronto. He had run freely in the airport as Papa and I waited for my flight. Once seated he asked the air stewardess for some juice and a pillow and then went to sleep. Going through my mind was the fear Lea would be greeting a child that looked like her own lost son. The purpose of the trip was to connect Gregory with his genetic inheritance, and the Linkerts needed to meet their only grandson.

As I walked towards the smiling faces of my in-laws at the Toronto airport, I could see the strained expression on their faces. This would be a difficult visit for all of us. Lea's first words as she reached to hug Gregory was "He doesn't look like Ron". Our eyes met knowing as two mothers we were thinking the same thing.

The occasion was both happy and poignant. They were delighted to see Gregory, Lea hugging him at every opportunity, and Jacob holding his small hand as he walked about, tears brimming in his eyes. Carl, Marion and their daughter Cindy were also present the whole weekend. Saying good bye was emotionally draining, fortunately Gregory was too little to understand the difficulties being experienced by the adults. Papa greeted me at the Halifax airport. I was now home to begin packing for Arizona and the challenges which awaited me in the southwest.

THOUGHTS AND LEARNING

My brief time at the Hospital Insurance Commission was when Medicare was in its infancy in Canada. A publicly funded health system was introduced by the federal government to spare Canadian citizens the overwhelming financial burden of health care costs. Its primary focus was on hospitals and medical expenses, not prevention. In addition, the idealistic founding principles did not foresee the need for limitations and accountability. There were minimal utilization limits, no provisions for advances in drugs and technology, or population increases which would have major impacts on health costs. Run-away costs were evident from its inception. In the decades to follow, federal and provincial governments tried to rein in such costs with little effect. Next the federal government moved to offload health to the provinces and territories, a move which is still ongoing. Shifts in funding would have serious implications for patients and health workers, many who continue to be uninformed as to what was really happening.

Why nurses, the largest segment of any health organization, continue to have the least influence in the health industry remains a mystery. One could speculate on various reasons such as it being a female organization or the demotion of nursing administration but no single issue fully explains why this has happened. In the late sixties, from my perspective, nurses needed to speak with one voice, to take a primary leadership role in the health industry, be more involved in the details of health funding, and have greater involvement in facility planning and construction. Areas where I pressed for change. Tinkering with working conditions (i.e. hours of work, full-time or part-time, etc), provided some short-term gains but in the long term crippled nursing in later decades. Nursing should have greater visibility and say in an industry where they carry a major responsibility for care. Unfortunately, their importance will likely only be recognized when the numbers plummet and the industry faces a scarcity of supply.

My efforts in health/nursing education were disappointing. Perhaps it was too early for change. If the industry is ever going to surmount the perpetual shortages of health human resources, then the traditional way of training health workers needs to be redesigned. Learners need an education system that can quickly adapt to the needs of a changing industry and individual learning needs. Perhaps one day there might be a single learning entrance for all health workers, and a format which allows learners to progress along vertical or horizontal paths as their learning needs change. Titles as we know them today maybe irrelevant or changed to reflect a more unified system. It was evident in the sixties the barriers to advancement for many health workers was a tragic waste of valuable talent. Perhaps future leaders in health education will have the courage to streamline the learning process to make it serve the learners.

"It's an ill wind that blows no good" was a common phrase of my grandmother's. If life had not forced me to take greater risks, my journey would likely have been very different. The generosity of Nova Scotians was truly humbling. In addition to the many kindnesses of nurses, others also came to my aid, a few examples; a service station owner near my Dartmouth apartment let me park my car free overnight in his garage on severely cold winter days. The Truro furrier gave me a special deal on a unique muskrat and fox fur coat and hat, which kept me warm on winter trips around the province. My dentist, Dr. I. K. Lubetsky, did dental work for me and checked Gregory for years insisting his bill would come 'later'. My dear lawyer, Lorne MacDougal, who guided me through civil and religious legal courts with grace and kindness, and also kept deferring his bill to 'later'. For so many people, a mere 'thank you' seems so inept for without their help I may not have survived these very difficult years.

Being a single parent was never part of my expectations. The loneliness, immense responsibilities, lack of funds and societal rejection were difficult hurdles. As a single female with a baby I was not welcome at social gatherings, even at church. Social conformity, which meant being married, was firmly in place in the late sixties and deviation was frowned upon. My own mother found it hard to cope with a daughter of questionable marriage status. As a working mother I also endured the stigma of being regarded as the prime reason for juvenile delinquency, a frequent comment in woman's groups. In addition to social rejection, the disparity of salary between myself and males doing the same or similar job was disheartening.

My life functioned on two very diverse levels; stoically simple at a personal level and extremely complex at a professional level. At the end of a busy week I treasured the peace and renewal of weekends spent with children, classical music and books. A life far removed from the daily demands of addressing mounting nursing problems in an expanding health industry. It was no wonder I had difficulties describing my life even to my family.

Without the religious foundation of my youth, however much I resisted certain segments, I would never have had the strength to survive. Irrespective of the denominational trappings which religious organizations possess, I knew God 'was not in buildings' but in my own heart which gave me comfort and guidance to face many difficulties. I knew healing would take a long time and a different working environment would improve my chances.

The trauma of Ron's disappearance would leave me with a deep wound and scarring for life. Whenever a loved one dies it is vital to have closure, the whole purpose of a funeral. Without that, a chapter in my life remained unfinished. I would spend a lifetime trying to find the right words to explain this mysterious segment of my journey. Fortunately, Gregory was too young for this event to have major significance.

With a mixture of excitement and fear I packed for my move to Arizona. I was leaving the comfort of my Maritime roots and my country with a child of four. Before me lay many uncertainties but this one step had improved my finances and found a better environment for Gregory and myself. I was on my way to the southwest.

CHAPTER 6

Sojourn in Arizona

IN the spring of 1973 Gregory and I left Nova Scotia for our southwestern adventure. I was twenty-nine and he was four. My Visa and working documents were waiting for me at the Boston airport, and once checked and cleared, we flew on to Phoenix.

The desert, emerging from its winter siesta, was putting on its hot summer mantle. April was still comfortable. By mid-May, I was told, the temperature would climb to 102-104 °F. To me the heat was welcoming. Phoenix, as 'The Valley of the Sun', exemplified its unique desert status. At an elevation of roughly one thousand feet, it was surrounded by mountains which captured the intense summer heat. [1] My destination, about ninety minutes north of the city, was expected to be cooler.

We were met at the airport by a hospital employee. The chatter was light as we left the airport traveling north out of the Phoenix basin. I quietly soaked in the desert landscape and tall saguaro cactus as we sped towards the Verde Valley, which lay between Phoenix and Flagstaff. As the red rock replaced the dry desert, I was reminded of my Island home. Perhaps instinctively, like a magnet, I was attracted to the same red soil of both lands.

Cottonwood, a small rural community in the Verde Valley had an acute/long term care health facility called The Marcus J. Lawrence Memorial Hospital. This would be my abode for the next three years where I would assume the position of Director of Education. This rural setting of Arizona is best described by Bill Weir. "Below the cream-and red-colored cliffs of the Mogollon Rim, the Verde (Spanish for Green) River brings life to its broad desert valley. The waters come from narrow cannons of the Oak Creek, Wet and Dry Beaver creeks, West Clear Creek , Sycamore Creek, and other streams. Prehistoric Indians made camps in the area, finding a great variety of wild plant foods and game between the 3,000-foot elevation of the lower valley and the Rim country 4,000 feet higher." [2] The valley, a fertile forty mile stretch of land, was surrounded by mountains and mesas, heavily timbered slopes, and colourful red rock formations, second only to the grandeur found in the state's Grand Canyon and Monument Valley. It contained several small communities; Cottonwood, Camp Verde, Clarkdale, Cornville, Jerome, Lake Montezuma, Rimrock, McGuireville and Sedona. A history of the key communities showed that Cottonwood was a ranching community and recognized for its hospital; Camp Verde was the location of the old cavalry fort erected in the 1860s plus the tourist attraction of Montezuma Castle and Well; Clarkdale had been a copper smelting town for the mines in Jerome between 1911-

1950, the mines having closed in the 1950s; and Sedona the magnificent red rock country, was a mecca for artists and seniors seeking a beautiful retirement retreat. For a short period Jerome had been the fifth largest city in Arizona with a population of about fifteen thousand. In it's hey day, it was described as; "Mines closed for brief periods, then rebounded. So many saloons, gambling dens, and brothels thrived in Jerome that a New York newspaper called it the *wickedest town in the West*" [3] This fading frontier would give me a very different environment from my Maritime roots.

My grandmother's phrase 'from whence they come' had meaning when looking at health services of the valley. The original inhabitants were generations of Indian tribes, followed in recent times by the United States cavalry, and later rough and tumble mining communities, cattle ranchers who ruled the open range and ordinary people seeking a desert life. The arid land offered a hard existence for many pioneers. The earliest mention of health services was recorded in the nineteenth century cavalry documents which stated; " At present half of the last built set of quarters for the men is used as a hospital. A very good building is in the process of erection. The ward room being only 20 by 30 feet is too small for the probable want of the sick." [4] The ailments listed for the cavalry were malaria, diarrhea and dysentery plus injuries from clashes with local Indians. Later I discovered a Canadian link. In 1871, following the death of her husband, Elizabeth Young, a Canadian with two sons came to the Verde Valley to be with her brother. She joined the 5th United States cavalry as Hospital Matron. When the cavalry left the valley, 'Grandma Young', as she was familiarly known, became the sole provider of health services for some years. She died in Camp Verde in 1905 [5].

While operative, the mining company built four hospitals in Jerome; one in 1894, one in 1899 called the Hampton House, one in 1917 which had to be abandoned because it was built over an earth fault, and finally one in 1927, a well-equipped modern hospital. This hospital continued operation until 1952 when Phelps-Dodge Company ceased its copper mining operations in the area. At the same time, while the mines operated, a First Aid station existed at the Clarkdale smelter with one nurse along with a nearby medical clinic. When the mines closed, Jerome and Clarkdale were practically ghost towns, their status when I arrived in the southwest.

As for the hospital's name, Marcus J. Lawrence and his mother, Carrie, arrived in the Verde Valley in 1931 from Washington D.C.. When her son was killed in 1938, in his memory Carrie donated funds for the first clinic in Cottonwood. She would continue to be a generous contributor to the clinic, and later hospital, for years. By 1945 the small county clinic became a hospital. When the Jerome hospital closed in 1952, health services for the Verde Valley moved to Cottonwood.

Roland W. Wilpitz became the hospital administrator in 1957. He was born in Texas, served in the Navy Medical Corp and in military intelligence during World War II, received his Bachelor of Arts at the University of Arizona, his Master of Science in Hospital Administration from Northwestern University, and was well known in state professional, Masonic and Elk organizations. In 1960 he began efforts to create a modern hospital facility, his vision being a 'little Mayo of the West'. By 1965 an ultramodern, fifty bed acute care facility became a reality with five local physicians and medical specialists coming from Phoenix to provide weekly or bi-weekly clinics. In 1968 a twenty-bed Skilled Nursing Facility (previously called the Extended Care wing) was added. Four years later the Rehabilitation wing of the hospital was completed to provide physiotherapy, occupational therapy, respiratory therapy and social services. Finally, just before my arrival, a four-bed Coronary Care Unit was opened bringing the bed total to seventy-two [6], with plans for further expansion. While Wilpitz evoked strong reactions in people, loved by some and hated by others, he would still be remembered as a visionary for health services in the valley. My new environment presented many interesting possibilities.

Just as I was getting settled into the community the wild west landed on my doorstep. Within the first week the local sheriff was shot by cattle rustlers and someone peppered the local saloon with bullets over a 'misunderstanding'. Since guns were foreign to my family, I held an abiding uneasiness about them the whole time I worked in Arizona. Since retreat was unthinkable, I pressed on.

The hospital loaned me a small Ford truck until I was able to put a down payment on a standard-shift gold Ford Pinto (which I called 'Betsy'), the cheapest car in the dealership. Most drivers preferred automatic shifts. The Pinto came with a cooling system, not air conditioning. Since rental accommodations were few, I was fortunate in finding a reasonably priced townhouse, in a row of ten, near a ranch. Gregory was delighted to see horses munching on tall grass practically in our back yard. For a few weeks we lived in a partially furnished unit adjacent to the one we would eventually occupy while waiting for my household belongings to arrive from Canada. Nursing colleagues helped me find a baby sitter, a middle-aged, Mexican woman who cared for a number of children. She insisted the children take a daily siesta, even Gregory, which he did. In this transitional stage, Uncle Fred (a younger brother to Bertha Shultz in Saskatchewan) and Aunt Ruth Cords arrived from Phoenix.

As I opened the townhouse door to a gentle knock, Uncle Fred, a five foot eight inch, stocky man in his seventies thrust forth his powerful hand to greet me. His hands and physique depicted his background as the Corn-Husking Champion of Indiana. His pre-retirement occupation was running a successful service station in Star City for many years, arriving in Phoenix in his late sixties along with other family members. He had the same straight, practical, humorous personality of his older sister, Bertha.

Aunt Ruth, a neat woman of five feet five inches was also in her seventies, smiled gently as she stepped across the threshold behind Uncle Fred. She had been an elementary school teacher in Star City. She was a quiet woman with a quick assessment of people. We would become good friends. I would value her practical council in my years in Arizona. As a couple, they were just about to celebrate fifty years of marriage. They had no children.

In greeting me Uncle Fred stated in a matter-a-fact tone said, "Welcome to Arizona, Sally! We know all about your life from Lea (Uncle Fred's niece) and do not understand what happened to Ron. This type of tragedy has never happened in our family before.

Nevertheless, as far as we are concerned, you are family and we are here for you." His abruptness and clarification of our relationship was deeply appreciated. Once the greetings were over, they had a quick tour of my accommodations. Then Uncle Fred pulled out a Phoenix map marking out the directions to their home. The visit was brief but meaningful. After this, I traveled to Phoenix monthly to see these kind people, their presence in my life giving me a vital anchor in a strange land.

I had promised Gregory we would get a dog once we were settled. For a four year old it couldn't happen fast enough. The local veterinarian, from the United Kingdom, hired by the ranchers to look after their livestock, also dealt with small animals in his clinic. I asked if he would keep a look out for a middle-sized dog preferably a collie mix and one compatible with children. Finally, he called to say he had two dogs to look at.

As Gregory and I entered the kennel the black female dog immediately came forward, the white, male dog, drawing away. The veterinarian stated the black dog was a four month old Taylor dog (which meant little to me at the time), a Collie/German Shepherd mix. It took no time for Gregory and the black dog to bond. We called her 'Toby', a name chosen out of the air. The first night I was delighted to find she obeyed basic commands, her wet nose wakening me in the morning to be let out. From the beginning, she assumed a protective stance with Gregory and myself, a welcome benefit for our family. Each morning she accompanied Gregory to his child care watching over the children while they played.

The final step was to go to church, as, irrespective of my prior dealings with the Roman Catholic Church, I felt a child should have some spiritual presence in his /her life. When I introduced myself to the rather irritable priest at the Cottonwood church his first response was, " The bishops of Canada should be excommunicated in light of their stand of ignoring the topic of contraception. They obviously think there is no sin if it's not discussed". With that position I wasn't about to enlighten him on my rather dubious status within the church, so went to the church in Camp Verde. There I found a kinder, gentler priest from Ireland who asked few questions except one. As the months passed I would arrive on Sunday morning with Gregory and/or one to four other boys and Toby, who waited in the car under a shade tree. On one occasion the priest asked, "Sally, are you collecting children? I know one is yours, I suppose the others belong to your neighbours?" This was true. Occasionally, on Sundays as I was about to leave the mobile park, I gathered up a number of neighbourhood boys, with the consent of their parents. It may have been the only church contact these children would ever have. Responding to the priest's comment I said, "Yes Father, and the agreement is if they behave themselves, we go for hamburgers after service as a special treat". The fast food place got so used to us arriving after church, the owner would hand Gregory Toby's hamburger before he took the rest of the orders. Toby was very much a part of the family.

My life once again followed my Canadian format; children at a personal level and a busy professional life at the other. I was still uneasy about social relationships. This feeling was not ameliorated when I asked "What does a single woman do after hours here in the valley?" "They go to the saloon" , was the reply. Since I had ruled out bars (or saloons) long before because of my reaction to cigarette smoke and my inability to read lips in a darkened room, I decided to stay with a familiar pattern. I was likely regarded as eccentric. Yet, Arizona offered many positives. With so many single parents I just blended in, and with more money my debt was diminishing. As I became more acquainted with the lives of other single women, I judged my adaptation to marriage and divorce was far inferior to American women of my age. Some of these women had been married a number of times while I was still trying to put my life in order four years after my first marriage ended. My professional world, however, was on a more stable footing.

After a quick tour of the hospital, I had a chance to assess my teaching facilities. A large common room for education and other activities had recently been added to the hospital, adjacent to the cafeteria. There had been little educational activity prior to my arrival. This was a well equipped room, more than I could have imagined, with a healthy budget to purchase more. There was enough space for thirty desks and plenty of blackboards and flip charts plus a large pull down audio-visual screen. As I inventoried my equipment and supplies, I could only think of my former students in Nova Scotia and the wonders I might have achieved with such a setup. In addition, unique to any educational setting, there was a well-stocked liquor cabinet. This was locked and hidden, opened only for special hospital Board functions. In the early weeks I focused on getting acquainted with the learning needs of the hospital staff. It was apparent I was in a pioneer role with regard to education at this facility.

Realizing, even in small organizations, communication is important, I asked Wilpitz if I might start a newsletter. He agreed, and in July 1973 the first issue of a monthly newsletter *The Marcus Report* began. The initial objective was to introduce staff to each other, provide short bytes of health news, announce upcoming events and birthdays, and, in time, note the educational offerings. Staff contributed articles, poems and other items. In time, a Licensed Practical Nurse on the night shift, an amateur fictional writer, produced a running story of the valley with a number of characters. The staff tried unsuccessfully to identify the mystery writer. Practically everyone in the hospital was considered except the author. It kept staff intrigued for months.

I was slowly getting the educational plan together when I was called to Wilpitz's office, expecting to provide an update on my progress. The discussion started out that way and then took an unexpected turn.

After a brief questioning with regard to how I was doing, Wilpitz relaxed a bit to chit chat saying, "I expect your first language is not English?"

Wow, I thought, it didn't take him long to zero in on my handicap. Not wanting to jeopardize my job I mumbled something like, "Yes, in Canada not everyone's first language is English", being as vague as possible. Whether he thought my original language was French or not the topic never came up again. Satisfied, he pressed on.

" By the way, you were a hard person to get much information on. I sent a former FBI agent under cover to Nova Scotia and he was manhandled and told off when he asked about you".

I was flabbergasted. While I expected Wilpitz would check my references, I never expected a FBI agent would be needed. This was not only novel, I pondered the international ramifications of such action.

He proceeded to tell me that two males in the grocery store adjacent to my apartment in Dartmouth, physically threw the agent out the store entrance stating 'it was none of his damn business' when he asked about me. My professional colleagues were even less forthcoming no matter what he tried. Getting no where, he returned to the United States. I could only smile at the protectiveness of my neighbours and friends. Wilpitz was obviously curious at the reaction. He apparently found other avenues, or I would not have been sitting in Arizona. With no great reaction to this news, he went on.

"I asked you here because I would like you to take a slightly different assignment than your education contract for the hospital." Now it was my turn to be curious, and I let him continue. He began to outline the pending problem for small hospitals in the state if the Arizona Nurses Association proceeded with their intended continuing education plan for license renewal. The association, like many other health professional groups, was recommending a certain number of continuing education credits each year for license renewal, but their plan had a unique proviso. Such education would only be available from post-secondary educational institutions located in either Phoenix or Tucson. This restriction meant small health facilities outside these two cities would face increased operating costs if their registered nurses had to travel to these cities annually to maintain their license. These large educational institutions were creating a policy which, in their eyes, maximized their resources, but did not take into account the needs of either the learners or their employers. I'd prefer to think it was poor planning than an outright money and power grab. As he spoke I kept wondering what he expected me to do, having just arrived from Canada. Wilpitz had a plan, and I sat in wonder as it unfolded.

His plan was for me to unite the registered nurses working outside Phoenix and Tuscon in time for an early September vote on the policy, just three months away. The magnitude of the mission was enormous. First I had to contact and convince nurses whom I had never met, to vote against this proposal assuming they saw it was a problem. Rapidly, I started arguing against the idea; "First", I said, "We are waiting for a change in state legislation before I can even get my own nursing license". I was in Arizona as an educator with the understanding a change in state policy with regard to 'alien' nurses would occur by the fall. " Second, I do not know the nurses, the professional association or even their voting structure," and "thirdly, being new, I expect the nurses would have great reservations at even listening to me" He was ready for all arguments, passing me a number of documents anticipating my arguments. In the end, I realized this was a critical issue and conceded, saying " I will do my best". My confidence of a successful outcome was fairly low in light of my arguments.

Armed with lists of hospitals and nursing names, I proceeded, first contacting those in my immediate vicinity. Meetings in Prescott and Flagstaff strengthened me as the nurses not only agreed the policy had to be stopped, they appointed me to be their spokesperson. Understandably, both Prescott and Flagstaff with fine post-secondary educational institutions wanted their institutions to be a location of such education.

Still focused on small health facilities, I next contacted nurses in the northeast, Navajo and Hopi country, arranging a meeting at the general hospital in Tuba City. Prior to leaving I called the Director of Nursing to see if arrangements might be possible for Gregory and Toby so they could travel with me. This was achieved.

It was a long trip on unfamiliar roads. The magnificent country was very different from anything I had known in Canada. Bill Weir best describes the geographical wonders of this area of Arizona as: "Multihued desert hills, broad mesas, soaring buttes, vast treeless plains, and massive mountains give an impression of boundless space. Northeastern Arizona sits atop the Colorado Plateau, whose elevations range mostly between 4,500 and 7,000 feet. Several pine-forested ranges rise above the desert near Arizona's borders with Utah and New Mexico" [7] .

The day of the meeting I left Gregory with a Mrs. MacDonald, a Navajo woman and her children. She was the wife of the maintenance supervisor at the hospital. After explaining the purpose of my visit to about twenty to thirty nurses, I left them to discuss the next steps, expecting them to choose one of their own for the September meeting. Instead, when I returned to the room, a senior nurse stated with a broad smile, "We have decided you will be our representative. We would rather have a Canuk than a Yankee". Surprised at their decision, I agreed, thinking I had somehow stepped through a time warp into the nineteenth century. It had been a long day.

Picking up Gregory, I thanked Mrs. MacDonald giving her a gift I had purchased for the occasion. As we drove to our motel Gregory chatted about his day with the two 'guys' who's dog played with Toby. Excitedly, he said his friends showed him their sheep, and at lunchtime, 'the lady' fed him and Toby. This truly impressed a four year old who saw nothing but generosity. Toby served guard duty well that night, growling when someone banged against the motel door.

The next morning, I went with Gregory to a local convenience store for some return trip 'munchies'. As we came out an elderly Indian in dark clothing was standing at the open car window, his both hands holding Toby's mouth wide open. The dog seemed undisturbed. Fearing the young pup might react, I gently asked, "Please, could you close the dog's mouth, I am concerned she might bite you". Unperturbed, he beckoned me to look at the black spots on the back of her throat saying "Those marking show she is a very smart dog. I could use her in the hills with the sheep. But" looking at Gregory and me, "I see she has a very important job already" and gently closed her mouth, patting her on the nose. Toby's wagging tale showed she had found a gentle and trusting spirit in this elderly man. He bid us a good day and walked away.

With all my effort, by the time I returned to Cottonwood I was still five votes short and September had arrived. After a meeting with Wilpitz, it was agreed I would press on to the Phoenix meeting, hoping others might provide the critical votes. This was a major gamble but there seemed little alternative.

The evening before heading to Phoenix I received an unexpected call from a representative of the nurses residing in small communities between Phoenix and Tucson who wanted to join our group. This individual, identifying herself as Dorothy, said she would join me at the meeting room entrance in Phoenix. Depicting my neophyte political skills, I hung up the phone without asking how many votes she held.

At the entrance stood two strong-looking Indian women, one stepping forward to shake my hand and quickly reciting the names of the counties she represented and the number of votes. With little time, I immediately asked if they would sit on both sides of me to help me in pronouncing the names of the voting districts. When the resolution was read, the Phoenix and Tuscon representatives were the first to stand up stating their support. Then it was my turn. Standing up, I clearly pronounced the counties I was representing saying "Yavapai, Mohave, Navajo, Coconino…….", and so on, receiving assistance from my companions as I pronounced each one. The list completed, I went on, "This represents fifty-four percent of the votes, and we wish to state we *do not* support this resolution!" Sitting down I watched a flurry of activity as the votes were counted and recounted. Shocked, the chair asked me to repeat the counties I represented, which I did. Then she announced "It would appear the resolution has been defeated". The job done, one of my companions slapped me on the back and began draping several bead chains around my neck. After hugs and congratulations, I headed back to Cottonwood, a two hour drive. I was almost to the Verde Valley before I noticed the beautiful beaded necklaces around my neck, delightful reminders of the day. The nursing association would later revise and expand the continuing education policy to include many more post-secondary educational institutions and even hospital-based programs. This is all the hospitals were seeking.

Weary, I made a brief stop at the hospital to find Wilpitz already with the news, likely a fellow Hospital Association member was sitting in the audience. His greeting was jubilant; "Great work! After this anything you do is bonus." In appreciation, I received a raise. This was definitely a very different world from my years as a civil servant. As an extra bonus, I got a better office location. Wilpitz decided to move me and the social worker out of the main hospital to a white bungalow across the street. With the continuing expansion of the hospital, office space was at a premium.

The next day, I arrived at the white house to meet Bob Sykes, a tall, six foot man with gray hair dressed in jeans and white shirt wearing cowboy boots, with a cowboy hat tilted on the back of his head. He spoke with a soft Missouri accent as he greeted me and showed me around our new 'digs'. The only disturbed segment of the house was one large room set up as an office with two desks. We would use the kitchen for coffee. Much of the rest of the house was rarely used.

Bob was married to Jean, a petite dark-haired woman, also from Missouri, who was the community social worker. They had two girls, Emily and Beth. Their home was in

Cottonwood. In discussions I learned Bob, while serving in the army in Germany after the war, had a severe head injury due to a motor vehicle accident. He had moved to the Verde Valley a few years before my arrival for the climate and a better life for his children. Bob and his family would become my dearest friends during my time in Arizona. As time passed, I would add Darrel and Florence Smith to this list of close friends.

Darrel (called Smitty) worked in housekeeping. He was a stocky man of average height, and already retired, taking the hospital job to augment his pension. In the past he had been in the military, possibly the Marines. He was an astute man with a charming down-to-earth view of life. He was married to Florence, whom I would later discover was an expert craftswoman. She had previously taught such skills at a school in California. They had both retired to the valley from California, Smitty returning to his roots. Smitty and Florence lived in Camp Verde.

By the late summer, hospital colleagues convinced me of the economic value of purchasing a mobile home instead of renting. This was a giant step for someone who had been living from one pay check to another for years. I investigated the possibility and in time became the proud owner of a partially furnished, two bedroom, sixty-four foot, California built, mobile home. The unit came with a stove, fridge and cooling system. Old Canadian furnishings were replaced with colonial furniture, a decided improvement in my living accommodations. The mobile home was parked at a mobile park located below Mount Mingus, giving me the most spectacular view of the San Francisco Peaks from my kitchen table.

All three of us, Gregory, Toby and myself, were adapting well to our new environment. Each morning, Toby ran freely into the hills behind our mobile home, always returning in time to jump into the car as we headed off to child care. Nothing seemed to be wrong until a neighbour pointed out she was surprised Toby hadn't been eaten by the coyotes, a problem with other dogs. This comment fit my growing suspicions that Toby was 'different'. When a colleague informed me Taylor was a recognized breeder of expensive ranch dogs, it didn't fit my fifteen dollar purchase. I also noted while Toby had a gentle Collie face, her rump and tail had much rougher fur. With these mounting mysteries I returned to the veterinarian. He finally admitted, Toby was from the Taylor kennels and a well-trained dog, but, she was also part coyote, a wildness which was recognized by the other coyotes. He said this wild trait would make her a great family dog. This news not only helped me understand her peculiarities but her wildness gave our wee family a special Arizonian character.

By September, Gregory started a half-day of kindergarten, our first contact with Arizona's educational system. His attire for school was a pair of jeans, a coloured cotton shirt, and cowboy boots. The cowboy boot's practical purpose was to protect the child against rattle snake bites. He loved his boots and had no problem with the raised heel.

School had barely begun when I received a call to come to the teacher's office. I arrived to fine three teachers waiting for me, his home room young teacher taking the lead. "Mrs. Linkert would you please tell us your son's full name?"

I replied "Rupert, Gregory Linkert"

"Is there anything else?" his teacher asked a bit puzzled.

"No," I replied, somewhat lost as to what they were expecting. Then seeing Gregory in the playground I excused myself to chat with him. When asked what name he had given his teacher, he replied, "Rupert Gregory Linkert, the bear." I now understood the problem and returned to the teachers. Hoping to clarify the issue I said, "In Canada there is a children's cartoon called 'Rupert the Bear' and 'the bear' is what Gregory sometimes adds to his name. He's done this before". They nodded politely, and I left, thinking the matter was crystal clear.

In relaying the tale to Bob, he chuckled saying," You and that little guy of your's are so different from the rest of the valley crowd that I'm sure they thought Gregory was saying 'the Baron'. They likely think you are aristocrats on the run. I expect they will hold to that version no matter what you say." Strange, I thought I have much to learn.

The fall was also time for me to get on with my educational task, irrespective of the commendation given to me by Wilpitz. It was not difficult to see education was needed on several fronts; doctors and nurses needed ongoing clinical and some management education, more nurses were needed, and different departments needed courses to upgrade their skills. To initiate the educational effort, I started with some general in-service programs suited to all staff. A culture of learning had yet to be established.

Earlier, in discussions with the local high school teachers, I proposed the start up of a nursing aide program as a co-operative educational idea, giving students some marketable skills. By September, a joint agreement between the high school and the hospital gave me the go ahead. Ten students snapped up the opportunity. Dressed in blue uniforms (provided by the hospital), I began the first three-month, nursing aide program. To first assess their observation skills, I gave each student an assignment of spending time with a patient and providing me with a short written account of their observations, a technique used with other nursing students. The best account came from an Indian girl from one of the local bands. I shared this observation with one of the high school teachers who was surprised at the caliber of this student's comments, a level of comprehension not displayed in her other school work. It was obvious this type of learning had not been requested before.

Simplifying my former registered nursing training program, I designed a curriculum which included anatomy and physiology, infection control, nursing arts (i.e. making beds, bathing patients, providing bedpans and urinals to patients, lifting and moving patients, etc), and ethics. The nursing aides were a welcome addition to the hospital staff upon graduation bringing youth and basic skills to the wards. For these graduates, I designed a certificate which included their academic transcript on the back for ease in moving to other hospitals, as I knew nursing aide programs varied and these students had more skills than most.

At the completion of the course I recommended the Indian girl consider nursing as a career, to which she replied, "My parents do not want me to work in a white man's world". Undaunted, I wrote a letter to her parents suggesting that if their daughter ever found an acceptable career in the health world, I would be pleased to give her a reference. Nothing was heard for a year. Then I received a call from a director of a special research center in New Mexico devoted to Indian health services, where this girl was seeking employment. I phoned the director to highly recommend her, followed by a written reference. I hope she had a fine career helping her own people.

By enticing teenagers into the health field from high school, there were both short-term and long-term benefits to the health industry. As expected, students varied in their nursing pursuits; some used their nursing aide training to find work while pursuing other studies, others worked for a time as an aide at the hospital, while a small percentage went on to higher nursing credentials. The nursing aide course benefited both the individual and the industry for years.

My grandmothers' view was to always make an occasion of something important. So, I convinced Wilpitz the students should have an official graduation with flowers, certificates, speeches and refreshments. He agreed and each graduating class had a special graduation. Having anchored the nursing aide program I now looked to the other learning needs.

Whenever possible I worked with professional associations to obtain continuing education credits for hospital courses, thus reducing unnecessary travel and costs for the learners. Continuing education credits for the doctors were approved through the Arizona Medical Association. Because of their schedule, these classes had to be provided in the early evening which meant Gregory often accompanied me to the hospital. While he enjoyed milk and cookies sitting on the knee of one of the doctors, I conducted the program. This pattern had to be revised when, one day I found Gregory trying to do cardiac resuscitation on his little four and five year old playmates. After that I had to screen the program as to what medical knowledge he might be absorbing. Other staff required different options.

Nurses specified the courses they needed whether it was special clinical issues, new equipment and supplies and/or management. Nurses in the operating room and intensive care areas required material specific to their needs. General ongoing programs were provided to all staff (i.e. fire safety, emergency preparation etc.), while housekeeping, maintenance and dietary staff got programs on infection control, safety and skill upgrading. I searched the catalogues and brought in many audio-visual programs to augment the classes. By the first Christmas a learning culture was emerging, with some, as expected, more receptive to the idea than others. But education was not my sole endeavor.

In my rounds of the hospital I noted the chapel door was locked and asked Wilpitz why. He explained that the chapel was closed because of a lack of cooperation among the various religious groups and certain issues such as two religious groups fighting in the corridor over a dying patient. With little cooperation, religious services had been restricted and the chapel closed. I asked if he would reconsider his decision if some organization could be achieved. He hesitantly agreed. Little did I realize how difficult the task would be that I was volunteering for.

After much effort, I finally got a group of religious leaders to meet at the hospital. The group consisted of representatives from traditional and other, mainly Christian, denominations; Catholic and Protestant, and evangelical churches. The lush valley had attracted many religious groups. In addition to those represented at the meeting the valley also had Mormons, Baha'i, a number of independent churches and a few groups residing in the hills which took me some time to understand their spiritual views. My task, as I saw it, was to establish a set of guidelines for everyone to follow, focusing on the religious needs for birth, illness and death. The first meeting of about ten members got off to a bumpy start when an evangelical minister stated "No women should be at this meeting as they are not equal to men in the eyes of God." Being the only woman, I knew who his comments were directed at. The Episcopal Bishop responded saying "Without Sally there will be no meeting, the chapel will remain closed, and we shall continue to be restricted in what we can do in the hospital". To appease the group, a Baptist minister was chosen as co-chair of the committee. Getting agreement on the guidelines was an uphill struggle particularly on the issue of 'no proselytizing on hospital premises'. One member angrily stated I was restricting his God-given right to get souls into heaven. Wilpitz only smiled when I reported my slow progress. Eventually, tenacity paid off, the guidelines were adopted, the beautiful chapel opened with regular services, and corridor battles ceased. Any difficulties were settled by committee members, three being former military chaplains who appeared quickly to resolve any conflicts or problems.

While spiritual care is usually a nursing plan item, few registered nurses at the hospital felt comfortable dealing with the religious needs of patients. Thus, because I was the co-chair of this clerical committee, the nurses would contact me if any clergy needed assistance whether administering a sacrament or praying with a very ill patient. One of the clergy was a Franciscan monk, formerly from Prince Edward Island and in the southwest for over forty years. We became good friends as he ministered to the needs of the Roman Catholic patients. When I told him of my foggy status in the Roman Catholic church he quietly replied, "We'll leave that matter to God, in the meantime I am glad you are here".

Prior to Christmas I took out the J.P. Penny catalogue to see if Gregory would help 'Santa'. Quickly he opened the catalogue to the adult tool boxes. "That one" he said. My efforts at diverting him to a child's toolbox were in vain. "They're no good" he stated and flipped back to the adult version. Gregory's love of working with wood was already apparent. With the acquisition of scrap wood from the local lumber yard, he and his friend Stephen, the same age, had built a small shed with the help of our neighbour. Harvey

Headley was a quiet semi-retired man living across the street who often came to consult with the two small craftsmen. Harvey was born in Saskatchewan, enlisted in the United States Army in the last war, married a girl from Alaska, Clara, and retired to the Verde Valley. He was also my helper on house matters. So it was to Harvey I went with regard to Gregory's Christmas wish. Harvey chuckled, saying, " Sally, Gregory, even at his young age knows a great deal about woodwork. He makes precise corners and knows instinctively what to do with wood. On the other hand you barely know what to do with a hammer and screw driver. So, I expect Gregory's father can be credited with his carpentry skills."

"Yes" I confirmed. "Both of his grandfathers liked wood work but his grandfather Linkert was perhaps the one with the greater skills. I would hate to stifle his interest in woodwork, but I can't get him the adult tools at his young age."

Harvey then brought out a different catalogue with better tools for children and suggested "How about you get him this set. If you remove the saw, you could tell him that I will be glad to saw any of his wood, just like I have been doing this past summer". So, on our first Christmas, Santa delivered a special tool box (minus the saw) and Gregory continued to work with Harvey building his wee 'house'.

As Christmas approached, for the first time, I felt homesick. Gregory, Toby and myself had been invited to celebrate the festive season with Uncle Fred and Aunt Ruth in Phoenix which relieved the ache. On Christmas Eve Aunt Ruth and I went to a church service at the Methodist church, leaving Uncle Fred to child sit. Gregory and I usually attended their parish church whenever we were in Phoenix. On Christmas day I met the rest of the Cords, a diverse group of individuals mostly from the Midwest. This greatly improved my spirits.

As 1973 came to a close I reflected on my life. I had grown stronger in the desert, the dry desert weather was a tonic to my aching bones, my allergies were less (except during sand storms), I had more money (even after debt payments), a new home and lots of challenges. Gregory was growing into a fine young boy, tanned and freckled. Our family had expanded with the arrival of Toby, a body guard and great companion. Old friends from Canada wrote to fill me in on all the happenings since my departure from the Commission. Lorne MacDougal, my lawyer, and Dr. Lubetski , my dentist, finally, after much pleading, sent their bills. The invoices arrived almost within a week of each other. As if they had consulted each other, both invoices read 'this is the total bill for services rendered', $50, with a hand-written note 'hope your enjoying the sunshine'. Such rare gems are hard to find.

In the new year, a second co-operative nursing aide program was underway with twenty students. In this class I had one student who saw herself as a 'dumb blond' a labeling promoted by her parents and classmates. Assessing she was smarter than her label, I confronted her when she kept deliberately acting 'the fool'. Shocked by my comments, she brightened up and, after completing the aide program stated she was going on to become a forest ranger, much to the amazement of those around her. Another student a Vietnam refugee, had fled her homeland and, alone, was trying to connect with relatives in United States. She had entered pre-medical studies in Vietnam prior to the war. So, it did not take her long to grasp the nursing aide material after I helped her realize the human body had not changed, she just had to translate her French training into English. She eventually found relatives in California and wrote to tell me she was using her nursing aide training as a means of getting back into her medical studies.

In addition to the continuation of the other educational programs, a request was made to have a management program for all hospital directors through Arizona State University. After some negotiations the program was provided on a number of weekends, the university faculty flying into Cottonwood by helicopter, as the hospital had its own heliport. With the hospital educational programs humming along, I began to venture into the community with the agreement of Wilpitz. Of course, these 'extra' teaching projects had to be scheduled outside of my regular working day.

In the early seventies, Yavapai College in Prescott, had expanded into the Verde Valley with satellite educational programs. I was asked to teach a general health program to seniors, the invitation saying 'if you can attract ten students the program will be accepted'. On my first day, walking towards the single story building, I kept telling myself that with luck ten seniors might show up. I had miscalculated. When I opened the door there were about thirty seniors all ready for a chat on health. With health care so expensive, these seniors were anxious to learn every means possible to avoid illness. These classes, conducted from four to five-thirty, twice a week, would prove to be the most lively and delightful educational programs anyone could have imagined. Some seniors swore a long life was attributed to daily amounts of garlic, onions, vitamins, or exercise. Stacks of 'free' brochures were gobbled up and any audio-visual material was viewed with fascination. It was hard to know who was teaching whom. As I ventured into the community I found another teaching possibility.

In my short time in the valley, I discovered most women had accepted the premise that surgical intervention was the only means of delivering a baby, an unnecessary risk for a normal pregnancy. With no local prenatal classes, I thought it would be good to establish one. I contacted other health professionals in Phoenix for support to make sure I was following a program approved by the state. At the beginning, Wilpitz showed little interest, and at times seemed uneasy I was pursuing this topic. Then Bob informed me of strange rumors circulating around the valley relative to Jerome, babies, a hippy haven, and an ex-registered nurse identifying herself as a community midwife. I stepped headlong into the fracas unintentionally one evening when attending a Town Hall Meeting in Cottonwood in an attempt to promote prenatal classes. I was doing well, I thought, arguing the need for safe, normal deliveries, when my brain made a quick calculation of an anomaly between the number of pregnant young women in Jerome and the scarcity of children. Everything would have been fine if I kept my thoughts to myself instead of sharing them with the audience. Quickly skipping over my blunder, I summarized my proposal and sat down.

There was little discussion and the meeting quickly ended. Little did I realize my comments would create quite a storm.

The next morning Bob, upon hearing of my comments at the meeting, burst out laughing, referring to me as 'Alice in Wonderland'. Then he pointed out a sleek black car arriving at the hospital, saying "That's likely the FBI here to investigate your off -handed comment. By the way, you do remember my comments about pregnancies and young women. Young healthy girls are being paid for delivering babies for the infertile of this land?"

Shocked, I asked, "Do you think they will come here to ask me questions?"

"Likely not. Good God girl you created the storm. They will have others in their scope besides you". True to his word, others were questioned but no one appeared at my door. I was certain my efforts had hit a blank wall in light of all the commotion, but not so. Within months, I was given the go ahead to start the prenatal classes. A young woman volunteered to gather the state information and teach the prenatal exercises while I covered clinical matters. As word spread of a natural way to deliver babies, the classes increased. I'm not sure the doctors were pleased with the change, but I received no negative comments, the numbers interested in natural childbirth were still quite small.

By the spring of 1974 Canadian relatives and friends decided I had sufficient time to get settled and it was time to visit. For months, in addition to working, I became a mini-tourist center. A former secretary and, later, Lorne Rozovsky, a legal consultant from the Commission both stayed for a short visit, whereas my parents arrived for two months. In their turn, I picked up each party in Phoenix, and they stayed at my mobile home. However long their holiday, we made the rounds of the Tuzigott National Monument, Jerome, Camp Verde and Montezuma Castle National Monument, Sedona-Oak Creek Canyon, Flagstaff, and the Grand Canyon. In my parents case we also went to Tucson and later to Phoenix to visit Uncle Fred and Aunt Ruth. Father arrived with his golf clubs and quickly found other Canadians for a daily game. Mother's mental state had not improved. She was restless and found the southwest too foreign. She was equally unimpressed with a Tijuana Brass band playing at the Mass we attended in the Cottonwood Roman Catholic Church. In the end, I was not sure the holiday helped her very much.

Papa was enchanted with Arizona having been a John Wayne fan for years. He was delighted when a Mexican cowboy arrived at my mobile home one day to ask if Toby could be kept in, as she was chasing the cattle up in the hills. According to Papa, in departing the cowboy suggested, with a decided drawl, "Mister, we could use the dog at round-up", then tipped his hat and walked back into the hills. Each day, Papa had my car after depositing Gregory and I at our usual drop off points. We shared the driving while touring.

During their stay, my parents had my bed while I slept on the sofa. Often mother retired early, leaving Papa and I to sit on my patio under the magnificent canopy of stars chatting about many topics. One evening, somewhat philosophical, he stated; "This is lovely here in the hills, but, knowing you it could all be sold tomorrow".

"Yes, Papa, I have learned these are just things".

"Your right" was his reply, "just remember if you ever have to run all that matters is your family".

Intrigued, I asked if any member of our family ever had to make such a choice. He did not reply but shifted the discussion to another topic. As always, Papa was very reserved in talking about family matters. We sat awhile enjoying the crickets and the twinkling stars. It was good to have a chance to relax and talk after years of difficulties.

I gave my parents a tour of the hospital and my teaching facilities and a chance to talk to some of my friends. During the visit, I was called away to attend to some students leaving my friends to entertain my parents. It was only after my parents returned to Canada that Bob, as well as Aunt Ruth, questioned me about my mother. Out of the blue Bob asked, "By the way, how do you get along with your mother?"

Trying to find the right words I said, "Well, actually I spent most of my youth with my grandmother", saying little else. Curious as to the reason for the question I asked, "Why, did something happen?"

"Well, when you left that day, we proceeded to tell your parents all that you were doing thinking they would be pleased. Your father was. However, your mother said 'I cannot imagine my daughter doing any of these things as she was the dumbest child I had'. Your father gritted his teeth and tried to brush it off. The rest of us were miffed by the comment."

"Oh" I said, "perhaps I best explain". Then I gave him a brief summary of my earlier life avoiding the truly difficult bits and any mention of dyslexia. After that none of my other hospital colleagues asked about my mother's comments, likely Bob provided some explanation.

Aunt Ruth voiced similar comments stating she was surprised my mother and I were so different. Uncle Fred and Papa got along just fine. It was then I realized with a deep sadness my relationship with my mother would likely never improve. I would be her daughter in name only.

By the end of my first full year at the hospital, an analysis of the organizational culture might categorize it as semi-dysfunctional, a view well supported by Bob and Smitty. The visionary-autocratic management style of Wilpitz definitely aroused strong reactions in some staff. This plus his tendency to hire weak assistant administrators, whether by choice or a limitation of candidates willing to work in a small rural hospital, made the environment at times electric with revolutionary activities by certain individuals anxious to overthrow Wilpitz. Members of this revolutionary party kept changing as people came and went, even in my brief time at the hospital. This culture, I learned, had existed for years. The concept of such activities being unobserved in such a small organization against a very intelligent man boggled the mind. So, from the beginning, I informed Wilpitz that if I disagreed with him it would be to his face as I wasn't interested in overthrowing anyone. I also requested the names of some Phoenix contacts should he see his kingdom collapsing. We never talked about the issue again.

Around this time Bob and I developed 'the Marcus J. Lawrence inverse relationship theory'. This theory held that the farewell party for an individual leaving the hospital had an inverse relationship to their contribution. For example, when a valued pharmacist retired the farewell was almost silent. On the other hand, when an inept assistant administrator was leaving after six months, he had a huge party, with one of many gifts being a handgun. Bob, Smitty and myself had to leave the party room as we were laughing so hard, commenting quietly among ourselves as to whether the gun was intended to shoot himself, his revolutionary colleagues or Wilpitz. Personally, the idea of giving a gun as a gift to a health professional was outrageous. The unstable environment pressed me to look for other options. The first move was to find out more about myself. As such, I registered for an executive development program in California, notifying Wilpitz of my plan. I kept him well informed as, in this instance, secrets were not in my best interest.

The executive development program first phase was to complete hours of psychological tests, a large brown envelope arriving at my home in Cottonwood. I was familiar with the objective of such tests and tried to be as objective as possible with my answers. The next phase of the program was a trip to Los Angeles some months later. In the meantime I kept all doors open.

In contact with old Canadian colleagues, I agreed to participate in a number of workshops in Canada. My speaking colleagues were Lorne Rozovsky an old friend and legal author from the Commission and Dr. David Shires of Dalhousie University, who was working on the computerization of medical records. The workshops were on medical records and death and dying, two rather bland but important topics in the health industry. Flying back and forth into Canada was interesting coming in from the United States. On one trip a customs officer scrutinized my slides, obviously checking for pornography, stating, "Lady, this is the most boring material I've seen in a long time". The next trip had a different slant. Being redirected to a customs officer I expected another review of my audio-visual material, but this time I was handed a card with a blunt command, "You are to check one of the items". When I examined the card it had two words; Anglophone or Francophone. I faced an immediate conflict as I reviewed my family history with one side of the family running from the English and the other from the French. Not wishing to offend either side of the family, I took the pen and on an angle wrote in large letters 'Canadian'. The customs officer, evidently unhappy with my action, replied "You and that damn Newfoundlander just want to give me trouble this morning" I looked up to see a middle-aged man quietly watching the proceedings. Angrily, I returned my gaze to the officer saying "When will Canada get beyond the 1600s. This card is an insult to all those Canadians who do not fit your rather narrow parameters. What about the Germans, Eastern Europeans, Asians, Africans and so many others, are they not citizens of this nation?" With that I strode towards the older man asking him, "What foolishness has our tax dollars been going to these days, I've been out of the country." As we walked to retrieve our luggage he filled me in. Little did I realize this Anglo/French issue would reappear later in the seventies.

As my spring guests departed in 1974, the summer heat arrived. On weekends, seeking a cool location for picnics, Gregory, Toby and I would escaped to Jerome (at a higher elevation than Cottonwood) or along the Verde River. Some days we went to Sedona to soak in the arts and crafts, other times we went to a local flee market, where I found a treasure of books. An elderly man sold second-hand books, and once he knew I loved history I got twenty-five cent bargains on excellent books. Once he had ten small volumes of the French Revolution, at ten cents a book. I would load the books into Gregory's wagon and take them to the car before going to the rest of the stalls.

After months of visitors, I was somewhat unwelcoming when I replied to a letter from Bill Robertson who wrote to say he got my address from Lorne Rozovsky and wondered if he might visit while en route to California. I wrote back saying Phoenix was terribly hot in the summer but included my phone number if he wanted to chat. Actually, I was not entirely sure why he was visiting. Undaunted, he phoned to say, "The heat is no problem after all I worked in India". So, in the summer of 1974 Bill came to the Verde Valley. I booked a room for him at the local motel. Little did I realize this would be a turning point in my life.

At the airport I watched his handsome figure stride towards the airport gate, the appearance of a man on a mission. As I drove northward Bill and I chatted about the Commission and the health industry. Toby, for the first time, welcomed a male into our home without a whimper. She had not been as welcoming to either my father or any other male. Gregory and Bill hit it off, Bill using his International scouting skills at building stone forts in the hills where they went for walks. In the days that followed, besides touring the same locations as my other visitors, we talked and talked about life, our careers, Canada and the United States, and finally the future.

At the top of the list was our former marriages. Bill did most of the talking as I was still reluctant to open too many difficult doors. His marriage was finally over, his wife leaving him and the three girls after hearing he had leukemia. The three girls (one set of twins) now teenagers, were also ready to depart, leaving Bill to reevaluate his life. He was in Arizona to see if there might be any future between us. Both older, we now looked at life in more practical terms. While we knew each other professionally, there was a great deal of personal information that was unknown.

For days we talked, over meals and sitting out under the vast starlit skies of the Verde Valley. Bill, at forty five, was a versatile individual, having lived in three continents and reinventing his career many times. He did his post-secondary and medical studies at the finest universities in Scotland, going to India as a Medical Missionary for the Presbyterian

Church of Scotland. This career ended when his first wife deserted him taking the three children back to Scotland. He remained in India alone for two years. Returning to Scotland, he studied to be an orthopedic surgeon only to have this pulled away when the British government cancelled the orthopedic positions. He then shifted to health administration, working for the National Health Service. A few years later, he was invited to Dalhousie University in Halifax to teach preventative medicine and became a consultant to the Nova Scotia Hospital Insurance Commission where we first met. Sometime after I left Canada, he had resigned from his position as Director of Hospitals in Nova Scotia to assume the position of Director, Hospital Insurance with Health and Welfare Canada in Ottawa.

We discovered in those few days that we had a great deal in common; as a doctor and nurse we chose a life of healing and, I learned in working with him, we agreed on many aspects of the health industry. We both loved history, a rare sharing. While we came from different Christian backgrounds, we both accepted a spiritual belief in God with skepticism regarding church organizations. We also liked classical music, art, learning and a simple life. For all the positives I was plagued with reservations. My debts were still not resolved, baggage I did not want to carry into another relationship. While I told Bill of my dyslexia, I realized he would not fully understand the problem until we were together. Then, with his command of words would my handicap divide us? Bill had a diagnosis of leukemia and I knew he did not accept the usual cancer therapies. He had three teenage daughters, all programmed by a different woman. I remembered a nursing colleague who married a doctor with three teenagers and when they ganged up on her she had a mental breakdown. Gregory, now six, had no male giving him orders, and I wasn't sure how this would work. Grown children in a second marriage had their own opinions and they usually did not like change. I also knew for a relationship to work we needed to live in the same place. This meant, in my opinion, I would be returning to the cold of Canada, after just getting adjusted to the warmth of Arizona. It also meant, I would be looking for another job, when I was just getting started with the one I had. However, the deepest barrier was more profound. While I truly wanted someone in my life, I feared my love for any male was a kiss of death, somehow the earth would open and suck him into to some black hole. This irrational terror blocked my ability to make a commitment. I was still struggling with these issues when we said our good-byes with a light 'We must keep in touch'. Could I overcome this terror to take the risk of a different life? In the summer of 1974, I was doubtful. For the first time in years my heart and head were in conflict. However, a Scot with a mission was not easily diverted.

⊷⟐⊷

Later in the summer, I flew to California, arriving at the Los Angeles International Airport the day it was bombed. The airplane I was on was the last one allowed to land. Other planes were being diverted to nearby airports. As we embarked, airport security rushed us towards exits and out of the main terminal. Four people were killed and thirty six injured, from a bomb left in a coin locker. The bus driver was visibly shaken as I boarded.

I arrived at the executive development program office to greet my mentor, a former director of General Electric, and a psychologist who had reviewed my tests. I learned much from this exercise. First my mentor taped a role playing job interview with him as the employer asking me point blank, sometimes difficult, questions about my career and life. When he played back the tape I appeared impatient with his questions. When he asked me to explain my impatience, I replied, "Surely you can read my resume, why ask the obvious?" He smiled, and holding up my resume said; "Well, as the employer I don't know you, all I have is this piece of paper. I use this to focus my questions to see how you communicate. It would help if you could see this from my perspective." This was very good advice which caused me to change my attitude towards interviews. On the conclusion of this exercise I said, "I guess my resume shows that I haven't been a pure nurse in my career even up to this point". He responded, "That's because you have always been a manager or trouble shooter. While trouble shooters are familiar in the corporate world I did not know they existed in the health industry". This was a different perspective.

The psychologist focused on two issues. He first started out by saying " It appears from the test results that you have little regard for your appearance, you seem to be focused on achieving mental goals" Then looking at me he asked bluntly; "Lady, have you ever looked in the mirror?" I was at a loss for words. My mother's childhood comments that I had no looks were still indelibly etched on my brain. Perhaps what I saw in the mirror differed from what others saw. Admittedly, some features had improved; my two-tone hair was now more blended with the help of blond streaks, my glasses were more modern but others remained such as buck teeth and reactive skin. The picture had been ameliorated, that's all. However, his comments alerted me to the odd reaction of some males when I concentrated on their lips. I realized it might be best to shift my gaze when lip reading, not an easy task. Finding little response to his first question, he proceeded.

"As a young blond female you enter a room, and as the person greets you to engage in a conversation, you leap right past the greeting talking about things for which a question hasn't even been formed. Do you know why you do this?" I knew only too well why I was doing it, a bad habit from my youth. As he spoke, I realized my fear of words had inscribed my behaviour. I would have to discipline myself to slow down, let the other person speak and only respond to what was asked. Without going into my family situation nor telling them of my dyslexia, I was now seeing myself through someone else's eyes. On another trip to California I discovered I had skills for non-health type jobs, such as being a detective or broker. I also went for several interviews with large corporations in California, one being the Bechtel Corporation, in San Francisco, the largest engineering company in the United States with thousands of employees and projects in many countries. They were looking for a Director of Health Services. As I walked along the corridor there wasn't one female photograph on the wall, and I wasn't interested in being it's first female 'token' manager. Yet, these experiences told me there were other types of health jobs for which I might be qualified, information which strengthened my confidence.

The summer ended, and Gregory was off to grade one. By this grade the mothers in the Verde Valley were daily instructing their children not to accept candy or anything from upper class children as drugs were a problem on the school grounds. This was a disturbing problem in elementary school.

In this grade Gregory had an older Mormon teacher, a lady who visited the homes of all her students. When she arrived at my place she was impressed with the number of books. Then she began to tell me about Gregory. She said he had a fine selection of friends and was quite protective of his little friend 'Jimmy' who went to school with him each day. She then said "Gregory has a long fuse but he will react if provoked" Without being asked she continued; " We had a bully in the class who kept pushing Jimmy and pulling his book away. Gregory first told the bully to stop bothering Jimmy and put Jimmy's chair next to his. The bully tried something different each day, always against Jimmy. Then, one morning after the bully pushed Jimmy to the ground, Gregory rose from his chair and silently walked up to the bully and socked him in the jaw, knocking him to the ground. Saying not a word, he returned to his chair and continued reading his book. After that the bully left Jimmy alone and stopped much of his actions as he kept eying Gregory not knowing when he would react."

I was shocked as this was not Gregory's usual behaviour, and said so.

His teacher calmed my worries. "Do not be upset, Gregory is usually a quiet and polite young man. He showed great patience in trying to get a reasonable response, and when that didn't happen, he reacted." She then went on to tell me in great detail how Gregory was doing in his school work. This was the finest teacher I ever met in Gregory's education.

At the hospital, *The Marcus Report,* and the regular education programs were progressing well, along with the community projects. Life was busy. Another class of nursing aides began with ten high school students plus ten adults. An advertisement was placed in the local newspaper seeking adults over forty who might be interested in becoming a nursing aide. They had to specify if they physically could work an eight hour shift. I quickly found ten mature women (I never asked their age), several of a Mexican background. There was an instant symbiosis in the partnering of a youth and a mature student. Again it was a three-month program, the blue uniforms now becoming a staple part of the hospital team. Clara Headley, my neighbour, one of these mature students, struggled with anatomy and physiology, requiring many hours of evening tutoring in my home. Later I learned her first language was Russian, having been brought up in Alaska.

As Christmas approached I asked Wilpitz if we might have a party for the young children of hospital staff. By having a full afternoon of movies, singing and treats plus Santa, it might give parents a chance to do some shopping and it would be a gracious gesture from the hospital. It was agreed. I rented the cartoons, an accordion player was found, a Santa was found who needed no padding, and the kitchen staff outdid themselves with superb treats. It was a splendid day ending with Santa passing our Christmas socks of fruit and other goodies to each child. At the completion of the day, Santa agreed to visit the patients taking Gregory by the hand. As the duo entered the room the elderly patients played along with the festivities. Gregory was very impressed when Santa helped me lift an elderly man up in bed. Santa had been a military medic and was quite familiar with the technique. It was a fun-filled day with much joy. We again celebrated our second Christmas with Uncle Fred and Aunt Ruth.

Bill had not been idle. He wrote long letters and we had extensive calls almost every weekend. I was melting under his Scottish charm but still hesitant, which must have been perplexing for him. We agreed to meet in the spring at Disneyland, an adventure which Gregory and I were keenly looking forward to.

At the beginning of 1975, Wilpitz presented the ultimate challenge asking me to train twenty street people from Phoenix as nursing aides. I interviewed sixty candidates to find twenty, those rejected were either too ill, too far gone on drugs or could barely read. In the group of twenty there were some real tough individuals. This round of training bore the trappings of a boot camp, as much as I knew of it. Every day, I had to drill the students on cleanliness, deportment, and relationships with other hospital staff and patients. For some, this seemed to be their first time under such discipline. One morning 'pep talk' was overheard by Wilpitz who informed me I would have made a good Marine drill sergeant. Slowly they began to change. Six had to be dismissed for different reasons, but the fourteen that completed the course were unique. This was exemplified one day in the emergency room.

Short staffed, I agreed to cover the emergency room with one of my students. It had been a quiet day when in the early afternoon a rather sickly looking, derelict male arrived seeking pain medication. The doctor, a middle aged man, examined him, while the man kept moaning and describing symptoms of a possible kidney stone. My student, not present when the man arrived, arrived at the completion of the examination.

She quickly looked at the man and asked the doctor if he had given him any drugs. The doctor replied "no". With that she turned and shouted at the man " You get to hell out of here! This is an act. He is just making the rounds looking for drugs."

The man, cursing at her, jumped off the examination table and scurried out the emergency door with no evidence of any pain, yelling back at us "Where the Hell did she come from?"

The doctor and I looked at each other in amazement. It took this streetwise youth to slice through the act. Some of these students possessed knowledge not found in textbooks. When the time came for references, I wrote to the Good Samaritan Hospital in Phoenix explaining the value of three of the students who were heading back to the city. Perhaps a different nursing group needs to be trained to deal effectively with street people, those with some prior experience who speak the language.

After this, whether as a reward or a legitimate need, Wilpitz asked if I might be interested in attending a video training program in New York State as he was about to purchase more audio-visual equipment. Always interested in acquiring more skills I accepted. So, I flew to the east for a one week program, being one of two women in attendance. The other woman was a middle-aged professor from Tucson. The males were mainly industrial trainers. In a very short period I learned about script writing, lighting, makeup and camera work from two delightful Italian instructors. Like my earlier experience with theatre management, this course gave me increased respect for television production managers. The precise timing and expertise of television programs masks an array of skills that the public never see.

Prior to heading back to Phoenix, I made a quick detour to Nova Scotia to visit my family. While there, Lorne MacDougal called me to his office to inform me of a similar case to mine in which a young woman with two children had just lost her husband. The RCMP had pulled my file and he wanted to alert me to a possible RCMP call in Arizona. Such a call never occurred. As I jetted back to Phoenix I had much to think about.

In the springtime, with Toby at the kennels, Gregory and I flew to California, meeting Bill in Los Angeles for our Disneyland adventure. It was an exhausting, fun-filled weekend enjoying all the magic of this fantasy world. The child in me was enchanted with the rides, characters, entertainment and many treats. It had been a long time since I had truly had a fun weekend. It also took great enterprise to have a romantic interlude with a seven year old in tow. Bill and I were growing closer as the months passed and I knew I would have to come to a decision.

In the fall, Gregory started grade two. Life seemed to be progressing smoothly on all fronts. My education calendar was full with new ideas and topics being suggested by a staff now familiar with a learning culture.

Wilpitz had another challenge. He asked if I could set up a three-month, technician course, advancing the training of some of my nursing aides. A curriculum was designed to teach such procedures as dressings, the administration of basic drugs (i.e. aspirin), enemas, pre-operative preparation and the catherization of female patients , procedures usually associated with Licensed Practical Nurses. Ten individuals registered for the course and all passed. These technicians focused on the small range of procedures, which they mastered with ease and skill. Soon patients began asking for these nursing technicians to do their dressing as they had fewer infections than the registered nurses, a sad commentary on the training of these senior nurses. By this time I had negotiated with Yavapai College nursing program to have both the nursing aide and nursing technician programs credited towards a nursing degree. A few of my aides went on to become Licensed Practical Nurses and one to be a Registered Nurse. The Americans, with a severe shortage of nurses, were more receptive to my idea of credit for hospital-based learning towards higher education. Shortly after this I was invited to become the Director of the Yavapai College nursing program. Realizing I was considering a possible move back to Canada, I let the offer pass.

At Christmas, Bill arrived to propose and I was ready with a positive reply. My debt had finally been paid off. Irrespective of my concerns and fears I had to take another chance at love. I had made it this far with a firm belief in God, I would walk on with the same trust. Seven years as a single parent had been a lonely part of my journey. It was time for a change. We shared our news with Uncle Fred and Aunt Ruth and I phoned my parents, assuring them we would be home for a visit once I returned to Canada. Aunt Ruth helped me select a silvery/green evening dress for my second wedding and a lady in the hospital auxiliary made a long, white lace cap with a hood to go over it. With shoes and simple pearl jewelry my wedding attire was ready.

As the weeks passed, with no immediate replacement, I arranged all the teaching materials so the next person could get off to a running start. I was hoping the break would be brief but that was beyond my control. The seniors and ambulance attendants would be able to continue with the blood pressure clinics. A retired obstetric nurse from Chicago replaced me with the prenatal classes. *The Marcus Report* was transferred to the Occupational Therapist who had helped me prepare other issues.

I notified the school of our move and they had Gregory's school records ready. Since, the public schools in Arizona closed in May, I worked around that date to travel north. Toby required a bit more planning. The veterinarian informed me that because of her wild streak, she would never accept another master. So, there was no choice but to prepare her for a move to Canada. Since she had never been greatly confined, in kindness it was best to tranquilize her for her airplane trip in a dog cage. The dosage was first tested on a trip to Phoenix. Similar to my previous move from Canada, I was amazed how quickly I sold my car and mobile home. To reduce my belongings, I had a garage sale before leaving.

Thinking I might be looking for work in Ontario, I wrote to the Ontario Nurses' Association and received a rather curt reply saying the province did not need any more nurses and there were no jobs. I thought to myself 'welcome home'. Shifting my focus, I discussed with Bill the possibility of doing my master's studies as a means of easing my transition back into Canada. I contacted Ottawa University and eventually received the registration documents. One of the last items was a reference from my current employer. When I informed Bob that I had asked Wilpitz for a reference he looked concerned, "Well, don't be upset. Wilpitz has never given anyone a good reference." I wasn't expecting raves but an average reference would have been nice. Within a few days Wilpitz's secretary gave me a copy of the reference sent to Ottawa University. I opened it anxiously not knowing what to expect. Amazed, I began reading the glowing terms to Bob and I gave him a copy for posterity. Doors were opening again for further study.

The night before we were to depart, Toby went to lay on our patio. At dusk, a family of coyotes came down the mountain and howled their good-byes. A neighbour came by to say, "Now tell us she's not a coyote, however diluted?" Leaving was difficult for all of us but for Toby it would be saying farewell to familiar territory and an 'extended family'.

The most difficult moment was bidding farewell to Uncle Fred and Aunt Ruth, who had become my Arizona family. As I hugged Aunt Ruth, she quietly whispered into my ear, "Sally, don't be surprised if your mother is not pleased with your marriage". This was most unusual for her but her wise council was tucked into my heart as I headed north to Ottawa.

THOUGHTS AND LEARNING

My sojourn in Arizona was a time of healing and growth. It has been said people either love or hate the desert. I was one who fell deeply in love with its stark beauty, the open skies and canopy of nighttime twinkling stars. The desert offers an enchanting beauty and splendor that is hard to rival. I was blessed with many positive memories and the joy of meeting some truly fine people.

Roland Wilpitz opened the door to this southwestern part of my journey. Perhaps he was not the easiest person to work with but, to me, he was both fair and generous, giving me four raises in three years. Six years after I left, in 1982, he died at sixty-one after twenty-two years at the Marcus J. Lawrence Memorial Hospital. One of the speakers at his eulogy said, "He left a big mark on the Verde Valley". In an earlier newspaper article, Mike Medigovich, the hospital's board chair, commented in naming the new $9 million dollar addition to the hospital in Roland's name: "If it hadn't been for Roland (Wilpitz) we wouldn't have the fine facility we have today. It is in appreciation for his years of hard work and expertise that we (the board) decided to name the new addition in his honor........ Most men envision things they would like to do. Only a few have the knowledge, foresight, dedication and energy to build those dreams into a reality that makes life better for others" [8].

By 1979, the hospital had expanded to 112 beds, employed 177 staff and had a budget of $4.7 million. Marcus J. Lawrence Memorial Hospital had grown into one of the finest small-town hospitals in the country. Wilpitz's dream had been realized.

Being the Director of Education with an open mandate gave me the opportunity to test some of my earlier ideas. I was able to provide a great deal of education for hospital employees within their own facility, including programs with continuing education credit approval from professional associations. In addition, the cooperative nursing aide program with the high school gave teenagers an entrance into the health industry along with marketable skills. The Yavapai College credit of the nursing programs (nursing aide and nursing technician) facilitated an easy transition for some in furthering their nursing careers. I worked with three relatively unrecognized human resource populations for the health industry such as the Indians (or First Nations in Canada), mature adults and street people. Training programs should to be tailored to these and other groups. There is no reason why these groups can not proceed to higher nursing levels.

With the growing population of seniors expected in western countries, there is a need to reassess their role in health services. Seniors are quite capable of monitoring and assisting with health prevention. This was my first encounter with seniors in an educational setting and I found them challenging, humorous and supportive.

My efforts at setting up prenatal classes may have made a small change in the dominant philosophy of surgical intervention for normal pregnancies. I would like to think, in time, a natural child birth method might have flourished as an alternate option for mothers seeking a less intrusive delivery method.

My time in Arizona gave me the opportunity to not only work in the American health industry, but also to experience personally the health care services offered to humans and canines. The first incident was with Gregory. Much to my consternation, he awoke one morning complaining of severe pain in his right side. A diagnosis of appendicitis was confirmed following a physical examination and blood work. Having taught pediatrics, my mind jumped to possible complications as the doctor suggested surgery. Bob and Jean sat with me during his surgery which went well. He then became a star patient in one of the wards, having so many stuffed animals on his bed you could hardly see him. The cook also made him special milk shakes once he was well enough to take liquids. This was a positive experience with the entire medical bill covered by my health insurance at the hospital. Health services for me were not so pleasant.

I woke one morning to discover half my face swollen like a balloon due to a gum infection. The young local dentist immediately prescribed penicillin, which helped the infection but left me with a number of side effects. After the swelling receded the dentist made an appointment with a Phoenix orthodontist to clean out the infection. Thank heaven, the day before my appointment, Bob insisted that he and his daughter Emily would accompany me to Phoenix.

In the admission, with no dental insurance, I was asked to make full payment of several hundred dollars. The orthodontist examined my upper gum, injected about six to eight shots of local anesthesia, and proceeded with the surgery. Once the surgery was over, I was bounced out of the chair. The receptionist cheerily placed written post operative instructions in my hand along with a prescription for pain medication and said 'good bye'. She made no effort to ask me about transportation nor if I was driving myself back to the Verde Valley.

Slightly disoriented, the anesthesia holding back the pain, I settled myself into the front seat of Bob's Jeep to head north. I was a bit disconcerted when Emily suggested stopping at McDonalds. Her objective wasn't food but two bags of ice in case we needed it for my face. Within sight of the Verde Valley the freezing evaporated and I found myself in excruciating pain and grateful for the ice. Bob drove to the hospital to get my prescription filled, and insisted Gregory and I stay at his place for a few days. It took days before I was able to return to work. While the surgical intervention was excellent, the postoperative care left much to be desired. Different again, Toby's illness gave me a taste of veterinarian services.

Toby got into a bird's nest and required surgery because the veterinarian feared small bones could perforate her abdomen. The veterinarian was much kinder with regard to payment, giving me an installment plan. Toby was in over night at the clinic, arriving home with a huge scar. Comfortable on her favourite rug, I nursed her quietly or as much as a part-coyote would allow. In summary, generally the American health services seemed to be good except for post-operative dental care. Yet, there were other signs that the general population had reservations regarding their care.

Whenever a friend or acquaintance was admitted to the hospital I would make an effort to daily drop by to check on them, letting the nurses know I wanted to be notified if there were any difficulties. In time, I discovered others, particularly seniors, whom I never met, at admission were stating we were old friends. Often I would go to the admission department or the nursing ward to greet a complete stranger, both of us acting as if we were old friends. How this started I can't remember, but in time Wilpitz, who noticed everything, said, "For someone new to the Verde Valley you certainly know a lot of people". Perhaps it was my senior health classes which triggered this activity as I asked the seniors to help with another outreach program.

Realizing seniors had to pay to get their blood pressure taken, a difficulty for those on fixed incomes, I asked the seniors in my class if they might help me set up a community blood pressure screening clinic in the valley. They were delighted. I also solicited the services of the volunteer ambulance drivers, who needed to keep up their skills. Together, under the auspices of the American Heart Association and the good will of Babbitts grocery store, the first free blood pressure screening clinic was established. The grocery store provided a place, tables and refreshments. The seniors maintained the records and the ambulance drivers took the blood pressures. A grocery store was the best place as everyone needed groceries. The seniors also kept tabs on those with high blood pressure. My role was that of a coordinator. Success in one community eventually led to a similar clinic being established in Sedona. It was at that point one of the doctors stopped me in the hospital corridor saying; "Why don't you take your socialized medicine and go home" . One could not please everyone.

On another occasion when visiting Uncle Fred and Aunt Ruth, they asked me to review the hospital bill of an old friend who had just died. I was shocked at the charges and began to place a red mark beside any I thought out of the norm, which came to about a thousand dollars on a relative short stay. Later they told me the hospital administrator asked, "Has a health professional reviewed this bill?" When they said 'yes', the hospital bill was immediately revised. After that I had a number of bills to review, all having similar strange charges. It spoke volumes of an over ambitious billing process and inadequate monitoring by insurance companies.

The elderly seemed troubled over health care costs which forced many to do a great deal to prevent illness. Their efforts at health prevention stood in contrast to many Canadians who, with the establishment of a publicly funded health system, saw health care as a right with little need for them to practice much prevention. In the end, I could see the positives and negatives of both health systems. Perhaps the best system is some combination of the two with increased personal responsibility and greater accountability by the industry.

While United States offers many opportunities, and its people are likely the most generous in recorded history, there were some aspects of living there which I found troubling. The right to own a gun remained a constant problem for me. Guns were not part of my upbringing, whereas there was an easy acceptance of such weapons by some Americans. One hospital department head revealed at a luncheon that he had six hand guns, ten rifles, and a bazooka in his home. In another case, I was told an artist and his wife, a nurse, living in Jerome, had numbers of guns and ammunition in their basement. Equally, it was regarded as funny when someone shot up the local saloon. Perhaps it could be argued these were lingering trappings of the old west, but still it seemed odd that ordinary citizens needed such weapons in a democratic nation. Equally mystifying was the number of women's bodies found in the vicinity of the Verde Valley during my three years, all between the ages of fifteen to forty. I kept a running count of these as the stories appeared in local newspapers. The numbers were significant, and if it reflected the tip of the iceberg, then it was evidence of something more sinister. When I asked my fellow hospital colleagues, the off-handed reason was drugs and hippies. If these were the reasons, then there should have been an equal number of males. In addition, there was an underlying culture of a heavy use of booze and drugs, with ten and twelve years olds turning up drunk at emergency and teachers giving notice of older children peddling drugs to youngsters at school. While this pattern of booze and drugs would eventually reach Canada in later decades, it was alarming to see as a parent in the seventies.

It took me seven years to recover from the abrupt ending of my first marriage. While I was able to cope on different levels, it took time to risk loving someone again. I required a slow healing process, others are different. It was evident many American women were more resilient and able to respond faster to relationship problems which either said they possessed stronger social skills, which was likely true, or carried unhealed wounds. I would never know. What I did know is there is a time for everything and this was my time to try again. Older, I knew such decisions did not come with guarantees, a change of direction would have its own treasures and learning. For me it was another opportunity to grow.

CHAPTER 7

Ottawa Odyssey

S PRINGTIME, and another relocation. In 1976, Gregory, myself and Toby landed in Ottawa, a far cry from my 1973 desert scene. Spring tulips and crocuses were peeping through the snow welcoming the warm sun after a long winter's rest. Our sun-kissed faces stood out against the winter complexion of others. This Ottawa stay would be brief as Bill and I juggled various living arrangements prior to our fall wedding. Initially, I house-sat for a government official on vacation arranged by my cousin Susan O'Neill who was then in Ottawa. While waiting for the moving van from Arizona, I helped Bill pack what remained of his house following his divorce. Then our combined households were placed in storage as our new home would not be available until August. We prayed everything would come together in September at Bell's Corner, Nepean, a suburb of Ottawa, in time for school opening. Our wedding was set for September 25th , with my master's studies beginning in October. The juggling of so many schedules was fraught with uncertainties and stress.

My grandmother believed events often ran in threes, and this was certainly true for our family in 1976, with three weddings. I had no sooner announced my wedding plans when both Rayona and my cousin Susan indicated they too were to be married, the dates just months apart. I would be one of Rayon's bridesmaids, and she would be my only bridesmaid. Rayona's wedding was to be held in Truro, Nova Scotia while Susan's and my own would be in Ottawa.

Registering Gregory for school involved a French language test, something I argued against considering our prior residency in Arizona. To my amazement he passed, Bill noting he correctly answered the words similar to Spanish. Then I remembered, as the children played in Cottonwood, they interchanged English and Spanish words.

In July, Bill drove us to the Maritimes to meet my family for the first time, which went rather well. Gregory, Toby and myself would stay with my parents for about six weeks while Bill returned to Ottawa. Upon Bill's departure, I became aware my parent's home was in crisis. Aunt Di, recently widowed, had come to live with my parents after a number of small strokes. Slightly disoriented during the day, her condition exacerbated at night leaving her wandering about in a mixed state of confusion and rage. Mother, unable to cope with such stress, retreated. Papa, under siege, was asking for help. Thus, my weeks at home were spent contacting old colleagues in the health industry hoping to find a nursing home for my aunt, a task complicated by the fact she was not a resident of Nova Scotia.

Eventually, a place was found in a facility in Pugwash willing to accept paying residents. I helped my aunt prepare for her move, labelling her clothing, and completing the necessary documentation. Papa and I drove her to Pugwash, where she was placed in a private room overlooking the water. Having cleared away one problem I realized another was confronting me.

Even with medical intervention my mother's mental state was worsening, certainly accelerated with my aunt's arrival. I was uncertain what the future held. So, I had the difficult task of pointing out to my father the symptoms to look for should her condition deteriorate further, praying it would never happen. By now familiar with her mental problems, my father took the advice in stride. It is never easy discussing such matters with family.

Returning to Ottawa, Bill and I hoped for a church wedding, an idea which was somewhat problematic. The Roman Catholic and Anglican churches would have nothing to do with two divorced people, while other churches we attended did not seem to fit our religious views. Finally, Bill suggested St. Andrew's Presbyterian Church, the religious denomination of his family. There we found a kind and generous minister, Dr. Arthur Currie, who openly welcomed us, and fully understood our circumstances. I was aware that once I married in the Presbyterian Church, the Roman Catholic door would be permanently shut. For me, since God was not confined to a building or a denomination, my spiritual anchor was firm. I felt it was my destiny to be a Presbyterian. With our marriage plans on more sure footing, I turned to face the first major test of my upcoming studies.

A pre-math course, required for my master's studies, just about flattened me. I knew additional studies after years in the health field would be both humbling and challenging, but did not expect my first course would be such a problem. Since I had never taken grade twelve, I was unprepared for this level of math. I found it difficult to understand the questions of fellow students let alone know the answers. I was in a panic. To resolve the problem I put in extra hours of personal study reviewing high school math and working with fellow classmates. While I successfully passed, this first academic hurdle left me apprehensive about the road ahead. Stubbornly, I pressed on as life was moving along at a rather fast pace.

Near the end of August we moved into our Bell's Corner home, next door to a Roman Catholic Church, a school playground at the rear, and a park in front. It was a back-split, white, wood frame house, with four bedrooms, one designated as a study. Our favourite spot would be a large family room where we spent many cherished hours. Bill's gardening skills would create an enchanting oasis of flowers, with a vegetable garden and fruit trees in the back.

Gregory started Grade Three at Bell's Corner Elementary School, a block from our home. In no time he had two friends, a boy from Holland and another from Hong Kong. He had no sooner started school when Bill and I were asked to talk to his teacher, a very fine male teacher formerly from Prince Edward Island. In pre-school tests Gregory scored exceptionally high in abstract design, quite unusual for his age. Tests also showed he was very good in math but needed help in English. His teacher agreed to give Gregory extra time with art and design, while Bill started working on his English. I was truly grateful for this added help in Gregory's life.

Having had few medical tests in the past seven years, I went for a complete physical once I was back in Canada. When the physician asked Bill and I for a joint meeting, we were both concerned. Then with some solemnity he informed me I had a positive Lupus test. This was the seventies and doctors were just getting information on a number of immune diseases, this being one. Concerned, he advised no pregnancies and to reduce stress if I wished to avoid complications. Even with this, he stated, I might have six years. Not a positive prognosis before a second marriage. Fortunately, both Bill and I were health professionals and faced this diagnosis stoically.

My grandmothers phrase, 'The devil you know is better than the devil you don't know' applied to this disease as it did to dyslexia. It finally explained a number of symptoms that had lingered after, what might be described, as a Lupus 'crisis' in 1969; sore joints, fatigue, skin breakdown, limited resistance to viruses, etc.. The disease, Systemic Lupus Erythematosus (SLE), is often described as the body becoming allergic to itself. The body overreacts to an unknown stimulus and makes too many antibodies, or protein directed against body tissue.[1]

As Bill and I reviewed the medical books at home we noted the disease had various outcomes, some worse than others. We decided to focus on the positive. I suppose there was some comfort in both of us having an immune disease, we shared a mutual frailty. Over the years our conditions steadily improved without medical intervention. We focused on prevention avoiding any aggressive therapies. Any change in our marriage plans was never contemplated, we would walk on together. That evening we made plans to make sure Gregory's future would be protected.

Just before the wedding my parents and Rayona arrived from the east, and Bill's relative, Peter Vidot, his best man, arrived from Toronto with his wife Peggy. With great joy, I also welcomed my dear friend, Margie (Patterson) Rock from Virginia with her husband, Ken, and their first son, an infant. We had shared difficult times, now she wanted to be part of a happier event.

On my wedding day as Papa and I drove in the taxi to the church, he said "Sally, your mother is not happy with this wedding. Bill reminds her of her brothers who were priests, and, in addition, he's a Presbyterian". I gently took his hand and replied; "I guess, Papa, that will have to be mother's problem. This is my choice" and the matter was closed. Aunt Ruth had judged my mother correctly.

Our wedding plan was for an early evening service, the two large candelabras providing a quiet ambiance to the occasion, accented by white-silk kneeling cushions, both provided by Dr. Currie. It was a small occasion attended by a few family and friends, followed by a reception at a nearby hotel. Neither Bill's daughters nor his mother were in attendance. His oldest daughter, Barbara, was already working in the Maritimes and the twins, Christine and Marjory, were at university. Bill's mother, in her seventies, was to arrive later for a month's visit. We decided to delay our honeymoon until the next summer in light of our rather overbooked lives. As I sat watching our guests celebrate our wedding I realized with boundless delight I had been given a second chance, and prayed this time it would be for life.

With the wedding and other events crowding the earlier months, it was October before I had time to appreciate my surroundings. Over the years, family ties had connected me to St. Catherine's and Toronto, but not until the seventies was there any reason to visit other parts of Ontario, let alone the capital of Canada. An interesting historical sketch of the city shows that "the first inhabitants of the Ottawa area were the Algonquin Indians who called the Ottawa River the "Kichesippi" – the Great River – and called themselves the Kichesippirini (People of the Great River). French fur traders named the Ottawa River after the Outaouais tribe. After the War of 1812 between Canada and the United States the 200-kilometre Rideau Canal was designed to establish a link by waterway between Montreal and Kingston (then Canada's capital) via Ottawa. The thirty years that followed the building of the Rideau Canal saw Ottawa (by then called Bytown).progress mainly because of the thriving forest industry. In 1857, Queen Victoria chose the City of Ottawa as the seat of the new government. [2]

In it's original inception Ottawa was named the Capital of the *'Province'* of Canada, made up of Upper and Lower Canada, today the provinces of Ontario and Quebec. [3] From its beginnings the Maritimes and western/northern parts of Canada seem to have little mention which rather typifies the centralized thinking of Ottawa for the past hundred and fifty years. Regardless of this short-sightedness, Ottawa blossomed over the years, growing along with the escalation of the federal bureaucracy and other government-linked organizations. Two well-recognized post-secondary educational facilities existed in the region; Ottawa University and Carleton University. I would be attending the former institution.

The Master of Health Administration program at Ottawa University admitted about fifteen students each year, mostly males. In 1976, more females registered for the program, this group of older women arriving with many years of clinical experience. The two-year program consisted of course work in the first year, an internship between the first and second year, and course work and a thesis in the second year. There were a number of courses on the health industry, plus accounting, economics, statistics, and epidemiology, with a heavy emphasis on research, an odd focus when most graduates were returning to practical management positions in the health industry. University life hadn't changed much in the intervening years. There were too many papers and expectations of professors, and, for a program on health administration at the master's level, there were surprisingly few professors with much health industry experience. Since our class had a number of older students with much experience in the field, class discussions often took a decidedly different slant than an academic perspective. For the first time I faced computers in learning, huge machines with punch cards, an extremely frustrating exercise. Like Dalhousie University in Halifax, Ottawa University had numbers of programs in old houses located within the vicinity of the main university campus. The health administration program was anchored in a gray, nondescript two- story house where we had most of our lectures.

In the first semester I found the health industry material relatively easy which contrasted considerably with difficulties in mathematical based courses like statistics and accounting. Barely passing the first tests in these two latter courses, I sought help from two classmates, promising my assistance in any health assignments in return for their tutoring. Once again, I relied on my old skills of memorizing to help me through most courses.

Even though Bill had a reasonable salary, money was tight. A divorce, lawyers, mortgage, and three family members attending university (myself and two daughters) stretched the budget. Getting quickly through my studies was imperative. The family, mainly Bill, myself and Gregory, existed on a nourishing but basic diet with few frills, something I was all too familiar with. I preserved as much fruit and baked muffins, fruit loaves, cookies and other items as needed. Any large purchases were tabled for a later date when funds, we hoped, would be more plentiful.

Something which never entered our minds was how our marriage might effect former in-laws. One day a letter with familiar hand writing arrived addressed to Bill. In the letter Lea asked not to be cut off from her grandson once we were married. We immediately reassured her in a phone call that this would never happen. By the mid-seventies Lea and Jacob had moved to Saskatchewan, where Jacob passed away. Understandably, Lea, now widowed, needed reassurance that her ties to her grandchildren were secure. Bill and I simply extended our in-law list.

If a stress meter existed, I'm sure at this point in my life it would have broken the scale. The amount of change in a relatively short time was beginning to register, when Bill's mother and another lady arrived from Scotland for a visit. For me, this first, month-long visit of Bill's mother was somewhat of a blur. The day before her arrival Bill informed me his mother had difficulties with dogs. Since hiding Toby was unthinkable, I prayed their relationship would somehow work out as I would be leaving them together when I went to university. Sometimes miracles occur and this was one. The two became buddies nourished by the endless jars of muffins and cookies provided for their tea breaks. A child in the house seemed to be no problem for his mother. Jennie would later write sending her love to Gregory and pats for Toby.

Jennie Robertson, in her late seventies, was older than my parents and with her Scottish heritage had a different perspective on life than mine. She was a well proportioned five-foot-five woman, who prided herself at being rather attractive in her youth, which her photographs supported. As we became acquainted, I realized she was a woman of deep contrasts, inner turmoil and emotional outbursts within a reserved Victorian frame. She had been reluctant to marry, found marriage restrictive, and was haunted by odd male-female relationship views, the source remaining a mystery. She also preferred an emotional religious experience even though she had been a lifetime Presbyterian. Getting married in her late twenties, she had three pregnancies with two living children, a girl and a boy. Her mother's death weeks before the birth of her first child was a decided blow which resulted in some child-rearing problems with her daughter. Bill's older sister, married with three sons, lived in Australia. His father, a military officer and businessman of Glasgow, had died some years before. While Jennie made no direct comment on our marriage, it was clear she wasn't entirely pleased with her son's divorce and uncomfortable with my presence in his life. She immediately took exception to the use of candles and kneeling cushions in our wedding photographs, letting me know these were un-Presbyterian. In the early days she had difficulties with my Canadian accent, but this soon passed. Somehow, in an environment of so many strong personalities meeting for the first time, we survived, although Jennie, upset over our empty dining room, kept threatening to send her furniture from Scotland. Since we were in no rush to purchase such items, we somehow dissuaded her from taking action. Perhaps much of the newness of her son's life was ameliorated by the fact she recently had successful hip surgery which had restored her independence. She took daily walks, finding a quaint tea room nearby called 'McDonalds', and arriving home one day in an eighteen wheel truck, having hailed the 'lorry' on the main highway when she got tired walking. She was a woman of strong opinion which was not easily diverted. During her visit we made a trip to Toronto to see the twins. There at a family dinner I was delighted for a brief moment to have the appearance of an expanded family, a youthful dream of mine which continued to drift beyond my reach.

During Jennie's visit, Janie Limond, also from Scotland, dropped by en route to California to visit distant relatives. She was a friend of Bill's mother, keeping an eye on her in Ayr. Bill knew the Limond family when he lived in Ayr becoming a close friend to her brother, Tom, the county administrator. Janie, a tall lady of the Lamont clan, was in her sixties and spoke with an Ayr accent. She came from a well-to-do family, her father owning an ironmonger store for many years. Now alone (her parents, brother, and sister, Fay, all having died) she was reaching out for contacts. Perhaps, because of my grandmother, Janie and I became instant friends. She would become an essential part of our family in the years ahead.

As Jennie and Janie departed, I prepared for our first Christmas in Ottawa. I had always loved Christmas and was determined to fill our home with all the color and joy of the season. We had a Christmas tree upstairs and downstairs, with lots of goodies. This would be my first meeting of Bill's three daughters, grown young women. All three had the beautiful dark hair and complexion of Scottish lassies. Barbara at nineteen was the oldest and the twins, Christine and Marjory, were two years younger. Barbara and Christine were taller than Marjory. In personalities they were quite different, the twins, being fraternal, did not even look alike. Barbara clever, quiet and hesitant was already working with the mentally handicapped in the Maritimes, a career path she would maintain. Christine, the most attractive of the three, more emotional and outgoing, was still uncertain of her future but already attending Toronto University. Marjory, the smallest of the three, was the quick, practical one, who had already decided on being a lab technician which she was pursuing in Oshawa. They were close to their mother, and, not surprisingly, dubious of their parents divorce and my role in their lives. The atmosphere was tense as we all walked gingerly, trying our best to find a secure footing. This fledgling beginning marked our relationship, as the girls would take decades to come to terms with their parents divorce, even though their parents had both remarried. This was an all-to-familiar pattern of children of divorced parents. I knew my role would be circumscribed by what they could manage as grown women and decided to adapt to what the setting presented. A more mature relationship with Bill would eventually come from one of the three, and that would take years. Programmed by another woman, my views would seem foreign to them. It was also a time for Gregory to meet his step-sisters, a novel experience for him. Our first Christmas of getting acquainted went cautiously well considering the complexities.

January brought the vengeance of an Ottawa winter, freezing temperatures and mounds of snow. Everyone seemed to be adapting well to the cold except me. Gregory readjusted quickly to the northern climate, even Toby grew extra fur on her paws and rolled with delight in the snow. I added sweaters with each drop in temperature until I looked like a roly-poly snowman. Since I traveled back and forth to university by public transit, extensive waiting for buses in the freezing cold was stressful. It was hard to avoid the physical and mental toll, both, according to the textbooks, detrimental to someone with Lupus. My joints ached and my skin reacted. I kept telling my body it had to adapt and pressed on.

The Master degree students felt stronger as they entered their second semester and were more vocal in challenging some of the course material and opinions of their professors. While I was familiar with statistics in the Nova Scotia Health Insurance Commission in arguing for more nursing staff, by the mid-seventies health statistics had taken on a life of its own. Something had changed in how such data was being used for decision-making. For example, a visiting faculty member, a statistician, confidently stressed that statistical data was now being used by high level government and institutional leaders in planning with little need or validation from frontline administrative or clinical professionals. A whole new professional group had been created. There were numerous examples of how such data was being used, one will suffice. Based on data collected by two young statisticians, health care institutions in Ontario proposed firing numbers of operating room nurses to save money. Since the data had not been checked by operating room nurses, key operational and management details had been ignored particularly with regard to scheduling. The decision created a huge uproar from hospitals and when the error was brought to the attention of senior decision-makers the firing of staff had to be rescinded. Other similar and costly decisions would take years to unfold. It reflected a shift in decision-making with questionable accountability. But this practice wasn't confined to Canada.

In one episode of a British TV comedy show based on the health industry, a statistician held the scene as he eloquently reported on the outstanding statistical performance of a certain hospital. Behind him stood the hospital administrator, anxious and frustrated, desperately trying to interrupt the statistician with "but....but....but...." Finally, when the speaker paused, the administrator loudly interjected," According to your figures this is the best run hospital in the country, but there are no patients." To which the statistician calmly replied,"That is just a formality" and proceeded on with his presentation. Was this a comical depiction of what was happening in publically-funded health institutions not only in Canada but elsewhere? Older students in the class voiced their objections to a practice of insufficient frontline input, but to little avail. The ramifications of this practice coupled with skyrocketing health costs left disturbing questions on what was happening to the health system.

Financial and economic classes showed health costs had been escalating since the inception of the publicly-funded health service, with both federal and provincial governments struggling to introduce cost controls. Even in the seventies, while the Canadian health industry was being heralded throughout the world for its generous philosophy and care to its citizens, behind the scenes the program was already sucking up more and more government monies, and reducing funds for other government services such as education, social services, municipalities etc.. Governments (federal, provincial and territorial) were facing a dilemma. On one hand, politicians and citizens deplored increasing taxes to pay for escalating health costs, while on the other hand there was little incentive to increase the personal responsibility of citizens in preventing illness nor making professionals and institutions more accountable. The outlook looked bleak. In addressing the problem, in 1977 the federal government introduced a transfer agreement with the provinces and territories known as Established Program Financing (EPF) which imposed limits on federal contributions in return for transfer tax points to the provinces. The old fifty/fifty (the federal government matching every cost in the provinces) agreement was scrapped. From this point, increases in federal funding was based on a formula in which transfers increased in relation to growth in the economy rather than on actual expenditures for hospital and physician services. The provinces/territories quickly discovered the federal government could also alter this formula in freezing transfer funds leaving them scrambling to cover more and more health costs our of their provincial/territorial coffers. [4] The federal government had found an exit. For the next three decades federal politicians would cleverly reduce their funding commitment to health care while, at the same time, declare themselves the saviors of the publicly-funded health industry, a key ploy in most elections. As students we were uncovering many questions and concerns about the health care system with few answers. The idealism of the inception of a national health system was already waning.

As the new year got underway, Gregory's teacher informed us he was using different names at school; one day it was Gregory Linkert, the next Gregory Robertson. He was old enough to discuss such matters, so Bill and I asked him if he wanted to change his name. He replied "Yes, I'd like all my names. Then I will have as many as Bill". Bill's full name was William Bickerton Clyde Robertson. So, Gregory's name was legally changed to Rupert Gregory Linkert Robertson. I was unsure how the Linkerts would feel about this so decided to meet with Lea the next time she visited her son in Toronto. As it turned out her visit coincided with an exhibit of King Tut in the spring. Arrangements were made for Bill, myself and Gregory to go to the King Tut exhibit and on to supper with Carl, Marion and their two daughters, Cindy and Tammy. Gregory wanted to tell his Grandmother himself. Once done, she gently hugged him saying, "I am so pleased you kept the Linkert name" and the matter was settled. During this visit I watched as Gregory shared his uncle's delight in wood working, a familial link between the two.

This meeting was fortuitous, for within weeks Lea phoned to tell me the tragic news of Carl's sudden death, the loss palpable in her voice. Within a decade she had lost a husband and two sons. Although a fine athlete, Carl loved bike riding, he had a sudden heart attack. The stress of the disappearance of his brother and family crisis had taken its toll. The sixties aftershocks were still reverberating through the family.

Old memories of these past events could return easily. One evening, Bill, unable to call and stuck at a late meeting, did not arrive home for supper. I put Gregory to bed and waited. As the clock ticked a familiar coldness returned reminding me of the 1969 nightmare. "Oh, my God", I cried, "it is happening again!" By the time Bill arrived home I was sobbing uncontrollably, sick and unable to speak. When he finally understood what had happened, he promised to always phone if delayed, a vow he faithfully kept.

As the first year of master's studies was coming to an end, the university faculty were having difficulties finding me an internship location because I had worked in so many different health organizations. Finally it was decided I would go to the Canadian Nurses Association to do a management study. I regarded this as a positive move one that would give me the opportunity of learning about my professional organization. The internship would cover the four months from the first of May to the end of August. I would report to Dr. Helen Mussallem the Executive Director.

I looked forward to meeting Dr. Helen Mussallem, who was well known to all Canadian nurses, having an international reputation as head of the national nurses' association since 1963. Her career had many facets. She started out as a nurse educator in British Columbia, later serving as a lieutenant in WWII, and her 1957 report on Schools of Nursing in Canada was essential reading for nurse educators. She obtained a baccalaureate degree from McGill University and a Masters and Doctorate at Columbia University in New York. With only two percent of nurses with a bachelor degree in Canada, there were even fewer with a doctorate degree. Actually, Dr. Mussallem was the first Canadian nurse to earn a doctoral degree. She had also received the Order of Canada in 1969. [5]. My initial thoughts were that this would be a marvelous learning experience.

Since there had been few nurses in previous health administration classes, this was the first time the Canadian Nurses Association had an intern from the master's degree program. I was welcomed, given an office, and free access to all the organizational records, including the library, for the management study. After outlining the objectives of the study and my general approach, I was pretty much left on my own as Dr. Mussallem's busy schedule meant she would be traveling most of the summer, touching base with me whenever she was in Ottawa. I was determined to conduct a thorough review, or as much as four months would allow, and set about drawing up detailed plans for the summer. In comparison to previous studies of large acute care hospitals, a review of the management practices of an association was considered a relatively straight forward process or so I thought.

In my investigation I became close friends with the librarian, Margaret Parkin, an older woman approaching retirement. As a professional librarian she seemed to know every book and document and retrieved not only the material I asked for but often provided additional items to enhance my research. I searched the historical records to find out the thinking of the original pioneers of this organization. Interesting material emerged. The intent of the 1908 founders was to have a national nursing license giving nurses greater mobility, especially at a time of few nurses. This idea was soon superseded when provinces saw the lucrative benefit of creating their own licensing procedures which immediately restricted mobility. The original idea of promoting frontline nurses had long succumbed to the premise of honouring nursing leaders, and by the seventies the focus was on nursing educators. My days were spent scrutinizing stacks of minutes, correspondence, reports, books and documents and talking to staff, sometimes being directed by them to look into other issues. All seemed to be going well which was reflected in a letter Dr. Mussallem sent to the Director of the School of Health Administration in July which stated:

> May I assure you that we are delighted to have Mary E. (Sally) Robertson with us, as a student resident from 2 May to 30 August 1977. The staff had enjoyed working with her on the project "An Internal Study of the Organizational and Managerial Effectiveness of the Canadian Nurses Association". All comments regarding Mrs. Robertson's interpersonal relationships and rapport with staff have been positive. This, I believe, is exceptional considering the nature of her study.

> Personally, I have found Sally Robertson to be diligent, methodical worker of unusual perception who has quickly gained an insight into the role of this organization. She is able to analyze objectively and effectively....... In closing, may I say how fortunate I believe you are to have a student of Mrs. Robertson's caliber in your de-

partment. We have certainly enjoyed working with her over the past few months. [6]

This was her opinion of my work prior to reading my final report. Obviously, she was not expecting any serious problems to arise with the review, which was my opinion until I ventured into the finances. A copy of this letter was given to me when I returned to the university in the fall.

While the Board minutes seemed to infer the organization was financially in the black, my investigation discovered the complete opposite. The organization had been tumbling into the red for some time. The reason board members were unaware of the problem was because the Finance Director, the one male in a female organization, had been combining capital (the association's building) and operating budgets, which was contrary to usual accounting practices. This gave the impression the organization had a huge financial surplus when, in reality, it was facing a major deficit. Discussions with association auditors revealed they had tried to get the matter addressed but without much success. Barring this unorthodox accounting practice, I still had to find out why the organization's finances were so far in the red. So, I began to dig deeper.

As with most professional associations, revenue was mainly derived from registration fees in each province, the national nurses association receiving a percentage of the annual fee. However, correspondence revealed this steady revenue flow was about to be interrupted by two of the larger provinces who found they were not receiving enough benefits for their annual contributions. The potential loss of such revenue could further damage the financial stability of the organization, a matter which should have been a key board item but had never appeared. On the expense side there was both mystery and run-away costs.

Besides the usual operating costs of running a national office, there were some anomalies. Two individuals in Toronto were receiving regular payments for unknown services, or at least I couldn't fine any documentation. Other professional services seemed high with no evidence of any bidding for such contracts (I would later discover this was not unusual in Ottawa). In addition, the national nursing magazine was being printed at a racetrack printing shop in Montreal with the nursing association paying for both the paper and printing, an unusual arrangement. Then there were translation costs (i.e. English to French) for every document in the association, costing thousands of dollars with no guideline or monitoring to determine need. Expectedly, since the Board thought there was plenty of money, cost restraints had never been introduced. When I sought answers from the Financial Director he became irritable and then refused to see me. The Assistant Financial Director, a woman who had been in the association for years, informed me her efforts to alert the Board had been blocked by the Financial Director. As my investigation continued I realized I had inadvertently stepped into a hornets nest, a dangerous position for a student which immediately precipitated lengthy discussions with my Academic Advisor. While Dr. Mussallem had been kept up-to-date on the overall progress of my study, efforts in scheduling meetings during the late summer proved difficult, after all I was just a student.

Since accounting was not my strong suit, I brought all the financial material, calculations, and accompanying graphs to my professor, after I had triple checked every detail. We both went through every aspect of the study, especially the finances, he advising me to add more written comment to some segments. There was no disagreement on my findings, the facts spoke for themselves. We were well aware of the political and organizational ramifications of what my report was about to reveal, and for this reason every word was carefully scrutinized. I drafted and redrafted and redrafted the material, trying desperately to make sure the finances and each recommendation were well supported. In light of the financial problems my first recommendation was that the organization needed to strengthen the management/ financial skills of senior staff and board members, a suggestion which I knew ran counter to the current thinking in many nursing associations.

I submitted my report on Friday afternoon prior to a holiday weekend, thinking Dr. Mussallem would have time to read it before my final week of residency. My university Advisor suggested my family and I take a trip outside Ottawa for the holiday weekend while he secured a copy of the report at an unknown location, evidence of our mounting concern over the reaction to its content. On Tuesday morning, I entered the Canadian Nurses Association building convinced my nursing license was likely in jeopardy, if not my hide. I was not to be disappointed.

Within minutes of my arrival the door to my office opened and a whirlwind blew in. Dr. Mussallem aimed her anger at me with an opening salvo, "No one could understand an organization like this in four months!" I thought to myself, no one asked me what I had done before entering my masters studies, this review was familiar territory. There was no point in replying, she wasn't looking for dialogue. She stormed on and on about the report and the findings, yelling and pacing up and down the room making it impossible for me to read her lips or translate her words, although the negative atmosphere left no doubt she was displeased. The unanswered question was whether she was displeased with the report content. When she hesitated to catch her breath I took the opportunity to ask the obvious question, "Is there anything which in not correct? I will be glad to revise the report before I leave on Friday". She snapped back, "That is not the point, I've had the figures checked and rechecked. They are correct". At that point it dawned on me her anger was likely only partially meant for me, perhaps some of it was towards the Finance Director who she trusted to keep her informed. No one likes surprises, especially the chief executive officer of a national organization. For the moment, the messenger was getting all the flack. Preparing to leave, she challenged me with a final question, "By the way, what do you have on the nursing leaders in Nova Scotia?" and, not waiting for a reply, left the room. The wind having been sucked out of my sails, I sat down breathing a deep sigh and eventually phoned my Advisor. We had envisioned various scenarios, none like this. I realized, in a politically charged atmosphere like Ottawa, there would be a rippling effect from such a report, even one done by a student.

Gratefully, Dr. Mussallem would be traveling and unavailable for the rest of the week. After some time, I mustered up my courage to see what the others knew. The Librarian greeted me with a huge smile, "Well, this is the first time we've had an honest report on this place, congratulations! Some of us have read your report and it was certainly carefully crafted. You may have saved this organization but don't expect any thanks or recognition". I was well aware that a messenger with bad news is rarely honoured. The Assistant Financial Director, informed me she was now in charge of the finances, the Financial Director had resigned on the weekend, shredding numerous files before leaving. No mention was made on what action was to be taken on the questionable financial issues. I was pleased to hear the organization would recover.

At home, I called the Nova Scotia Nurses Association to talk to an old colleague. She chuckled and asked, "Sally, what are you up to these days to stir up such a storm from such great heights?" I brought her up-to-date on my internship without revealing precise details only Dr. Mussallem's parting comment. My friend understood and replied, "She certainly tried to get something on you but, as far as I know, the doors were sealed. Those I spoke to this week followed much the same pattern, we talked about your professional record, refusing to add any personal details. She was not pleased". I asked my friend to convey my sincere thanks to those who were contacted. As I hung up the phone I was in awe of such kindness, and grateful my Canadian nursing license was with such generous people on the east coast.

As expected, my final week was quiet as I cleared my desk and spent time in the library doing some pre-coursework reading for the upcoming academic year. On Friday, as the Canadian Nurses Association door closed behind me I expected any further contact with the professional association was over, it had been brief and unexpectedly turbulent. Later I learned my management report, locked away, was available to a select few at the association. As the years passed, I quietly checked off the implementation of my recommendations as they appeared in the Canadian Nurses Association professional magazine. While the messenger wasn't welcomed, I held some hope that maybe my report gave further life to the association. I was feeling foreign in this environment which was frequently confirmed in my role as the wife of a federal civil servant.

Bill's federal job required our attendance at a number of social engagements which gave me contact with other federal civil servants. If the description of their working environment could be taken literally, the best one could say was it was dysfunctional, the worst it was abusive. A mix of ambitious, over-inflated egos, constantly changing direction and objectives, frequent organizational restructuring and an undercurrent of political intrigue was destructive to professionals who thought a federal job would give them a chance to make a difference. The shattering of ideals was etched on many faces. Others were counting the days to retirement while some talked about escaping to jobs outside of Ottawa. The nation was losing some of its finest leaders. There were always those who thrived in such an environment, not necessarily the altruistic or generous of heart. Unless one was interested in the latest promotions or crucifixions in the federal government, such social occasions were difficult. Ottawa possessed the trappings of a company town or perhaps the royal courts of a bygone era. Barring the limitation in conversational topics, such social occasions also presented me with an interesting physical reaction to certain individuals whenever I shook their hand. The moment my hand touched theirs, I became severely nauseated, struggling to avoid throwing up on their shoes. Fortunately, the personality of such individuals made them assume I was simply overwhelmed in their presence. In addition to a highly charged ego and ambition, I sensed that the personality of these individuals contained some powerfully negative energy. The only reference I had was a similar reaction in Arizona to an individual who later turned out to be associated with the mafia. Such negativity has many causes, which I was not interested in finding out. Whatever the reason, all I could do was warn Bill to avoid these individuals, which was not always possible in the federal bureaucracy. Fortunately, Ottawa also offered more positive outlets.

Some part of me felt deeply at home with Presbyterians. Perhaps it was their individualism, their practical approach to life, their humor and their warmth of character. Unlike other groups, if there were four Presbyterians in a room they would have four separate opinions with each person ready to argue his/her position should it be necessary. This was refreshing. As a family we attended weekly services at St. Andrew's Presbyterian Church in downtown Ottawa. Even though Bill had a busy federal job, he found time to be a church elder with a district of people to visit, plus some committee responsibilities. One church activity involved the sponsorship of a Vietnamese refugee family, the Leungs.

The Leungs arrived in Ottawa with five children; three girls and two boys. Bill, Gregory and myself worked with a church group to clean a rented house and to help them get settled. Mr. Leung was surprised to find Bill, a medical doctor, scrubbing the walls of his house. A relative who spoke English assisted communications in those early days. Businesses were generous in helping these new arrivals. Realizing the family was ill-prepared for an Ottawa winter, I got the mother to understand the need for vitamins and took her to Sears to purchase winter clothing for the children, a difficult process when we had no shared language.

When we discovered Mr. Leung was an art instructor, Bill and I purchased some Japanese brushes and paint and went to their home. When he saw the materials he quickly took a brush and expertly created a lovely bamboo picture on the open newspaper. Then he excused himself and momentarily returned with his Chinese brushes in hand. It was then I realized this was truly a master artist, for what other artist, in running for safety, would make sure he/she had their art brushes. Mr. Leung would later have art exhibits in Ottawa and his family would add much strength to our growing country.

Another positive was the magnificence of the outdoors around Ottawa. As a family we went for picnics, hiking and cross-country skiing offering us plenty of fresh air and physical exercise. I shall always cherish springtime in Ottawa with the array of tulips. What a spectacular gift from Holland in tribute to our military and their efforts in the last great war. During this time we also purchased a small sailboat, Bill being an avid sailor. Our sailing days were few because of me. For someone who regularly got seasick on the Prince Edward Island ferry, unexpected winds and abrupt movement of a small sailboat proved overwhelming. Bill would later reroute his joy of sailing into board sailing for which I was eternally grateful. We quickly realized ship cruises were not likely in our destiny, unless they never left the dock.

Gregory was doing well in school, covering grades three to six at the Bell's Corner Elementary school. He was growing into a fine young man, Bill and I working to make sure he had a rounded life and experiences. By ten he had traveled quite a bit, to different parts of Canada, and the United States. In the summer he spent time with a local German family with four children, getting to know how other people lived. It took time for us to blend as a family, the different seasons bringing their treasured memories.

There was little time to dwell on my internship or other feelings as in the second year of my master's studies I was facing both coursework and a thesis. Endless assignments and planning my thesis research occupied my days. My thesis topic was to be on "Women in Health Administration: Survey of the University of Ottawa MHA Graduates". The study was to see what was happening to women in the health industry with a Master of Health Administration (MHA) credential. One hundred and twenty-seven responded to the survey with a response rate of sixty-seven percent. The data, once collected and analyzed, showed that women did poorly in the health industry, as men progressed faster and higher. Most women, except those in religious orders, got locked into assistant administrative roles and continued to earn less than males even though they had similar and/or higher academic credentials. For this reason, a higher percentage of women were unemployed after graduation and/or seeking work in non-hospital settings. In the seventies, the leadership ranks in the health industry were still male dominated,[7] a statistic which was not encouraging. I also discovered many Master of Health Administration students did not receive their degree because they never completed their thesis. Students employed after graduation away from Ottawa got too busy and their research data became out-dated. A somewhat tragic loss of money and effort.

The fall was so busy, a call from the Canadian Nurses Association for a job interview was both unexpected and not entirely welcome. There had been a deathly silence since I left the organization, and a job interview seemed inconceivable. Yet, I was curious. It was a fall day with intermittent showers. Preoccupied as I walked towards the location of my summer internship, I was unsure if further contact was even advisable. Within sight of the building the sky opened and, with no umbrella I got drenched. This I thought was a bad omen. I went immediately to the washroom trying to dry my hair with paper towels, all the while thinking of my Los Angeles mentor's advice, 'First impressions count in an interview'. The image I saw in the mirror looked more like a drowned cat in a rather dowdy outfit of slacks and sweater.

I entered the interview room to a cool reception from Dr. Mussallem and a warm welcome from a man who introduced himself as Dr. Bernard Bourassa of the Canadian Hospital Association. Responding to their numerous questions on my background, I kept wondering what job I was being interviewed for. The call made no mention of the job title or details. Finally, it was my turn to ask questions. I soon discovered the job had to do with the Nursing Unit Administration (NUA) program, a correspondence course for nursing managers across Canada which was jointly administered by the two professional associations. The program was being moved from Toronto to Ottawa and they needed a new Executive Director. I was familiar with the program having taken the course when I was at the Nova Scotia Hospital Insurance Commission. However, traveling home on the bus I expected my chances of getting the job were slim if the nursing association was party to the decision, and therefore said nothing to Bill, convincing myself I was likely one of several potential candidates.

When I received the job offer in the mail two weeks later, I had some explanation to give to Bill. In light of the job market for women with a Master in Health Administration degree, I did not think it prudent to ignore the offer. Yet, to accept such an offer I would be working on two fronts as another semester of studies and a thesis still lay ahead. After discussions with Bill and my professors, I accepted the position well aware of the difficulties of such a decision.

I asked one of my fellow classmates, Dorothy (Farmer) Malcom, from Saskatchewan, another nurse and a fellow master's student, to be my assistant. Dorothy was from the west, had worked in Australia and shared similar views on nursing and management. She was a quiet individual with an unruffled, humorous personality, a professional who gave one hundred percent quality work. I kept telling her we came from the two provinces with the least political influence in Ottawa, which might be an advantage. There were three professionals in the program, a Roman Catholic sister , who had been with the program for years, who worked in the Montreal office plus Dorothy and myself in the Ottawa office. The team would consist of three professionals and two clerical staff. As expected, my workload skyrocketed with little relief on either front.

The Nursing Unit Administration Program, initiated in 1960, was an in-service education program to assist nurse managers and others in middle management in hospitals to improve their administrative skills. By 1962 the program was available in both English and French. The nine-month program consisted of twelve home-study lessons sandwiched between two workshops. Workshops were provided in seven locations across Canada in the fall and spring. By the mid-seventies about four hundred students were being admitted each year, coming from all provinces and territories and most health services. By the late seventies about nine thousand nursing managers had completed the program. International programs were provided in Lebanon, Haiti, Botswana, and Zaire with a total international student enrollment of one hundred and thirty-one. Besides the central Toronto office (now being relocated to the Canadian Hospital Association office building in Ottawa), there was a small office at the University of Montreal. The Nursing Unit Administration

Program had its own Board with members appointed from both the Canadian Nurses and Canadian Hospital Associations.

The office move went reasonably well except for the mountains of storage material accumulated over seventeen years, much outdated and covered in dust. With the cost of storage space in Ottawa running at nine dollars a square foot, I had an immediate task of streamlining this bottleneck. In the interim, Dorothy and I had to manage the current academic year while reviewing the distance education program for possible change. Problems quickly appeared. At the beginning of the program, each student received a stack of journal articles, workshop dates and locations, several pages of assignment questions and the name of their Academic Advisor. The journal articles, while covering nursing management issues, lacked focus or a central management philosophy and did not always connect with the home-study assignment component. Most Academic Advisors lived in Toronto with little appreciation of the nursing problems in rural and remote parts of Canada, a matter which became apparent in an argument between a nurse manager in Labrador and her Advisor in Toronto. The senior nurse, isolated in a remote northern community in midwinter, when asked to submit an organizational chart, obtained one from a friend at the Montreal General Hospital and in the many boxes listed every man, woman and child in her northern community. Her Toronto advisor wrote a large F on the assignment, showing little understanding or humor of the frustration of this nurse manager and her working environment. There were daily issues of similar ilk.

Serious administrative issues soon became evident. Every month each student submitted an assignment, mountains of centrally managed assignments landing daily in our office to be rerouted to Advisors and/or returned to the student, the two clerical staff recording the assignment in and out date, and academic marks. The workload and mailing costs were tremendous considering the number of students. The clerical staff divided their time between being postal clerks and copying endless journal articles. Poorly written mailing codes meant assignment packages were ending up in the United States, Europe and even Saudia Arabia. The central filing system, not in alphabetical order, wasted endless time in trying to locate a student's file. While the clerical staff were being inundated with clerical problems, Dorothy and I were facing numerous adjudication issues between students and advisors, trying to keep up with the latest management material and preparing and conducting workshops across Canada, in addition to our studies. In this mêlée we also found the evaluation process was out of balance.

The student's passing grade rested solely on a single written exam at the last workshop, leaving little or no value to the home-study segment, which occupied considerable time for many months for both the student and Advisor. A problem with the home study segment was the assignments had become mainly theoretical, with little practical management expectations. As such, it was unclear what management skills the graduates held when they completed the program. To complicate the educational process, both students and Advisors were working with few guidelines, which left the door open for personality, communication and academic problems. In summary, this eighteen year old educational program needed a major overhaul. Yet, change had to be introduced carefully to allow a seamless transition from the old to a new format.

As 1979 began, Dorothy and I worked at becoming familiar with the current educational process while slowly unraveling the old and designing a new program. Every change had the potential of upsetting someone. For this reason, I made sure the Nursing Unit Administration Board was fully informed of every change including weekly communications with my Board chair, a hospital administrator and religious sister of St. Ann's from Winnipeg. In the meantime there were other issues, characteristic of Ottawa, like French to deal with.

Every organization has at least one or more office gossip, and the Canadian Hospital Association was no exception. With an open-door policy, a middle-aged woman from the hospital association sector made weekly rounds, easing into the chair just inside the door of my office. While I appreciated access to the latest organizational news, I also had to endure her ritualistic innuendo which went like, 'It's too bad Mrs. Robertson you are not French. It is important that every key position in Ottawa has someone that speaks both languages'. Usually I gave no reply, thinking it best to hold my cards for a more suitable moment. However, one day she arrived when I was tired and I reacted saying, "Surely, as an intelligent person, you do not believe that non-French speaking Canadians are unqualified for any significant Ottawa job? Perhaps, before it is too late, Canada may wake up to the realization if it doesn't stop this parochial and political foolishness we will become a second-rate country because we have not promoted the best leaders for the country". In a huff she left, not to return for a couple of weeks. I kicked myself for losing my temper over this irritation. Undaunted, she eventually returned to continue her weekly French mantra.

In light of this reality, the Nursing Unit Administration Board decided I should take French lessons. For a dyslectic struggling with English, mastering another language was quite a task. Yet, I had learned much in my word battles, and memorizing as much as possible, was able to soon grasp enough of the language to follow a general conversation. Speaking French proved more daunting. My tutor was a French-speaking man from Tunisia who came to my office to conduct weekly classes. But I was not the only one facing such demands.

During our first years in Ottawa, Bill, was immersed in French language studies. For an individual who mastered a number of foreign languages in India, he excelled. In no time he was speaking fluent French and enjoyed communicating in another language. However, it was soon brought to his attention that since French wasn't his first language, his expertise in speaking the language would have little benefit in any advancement in his career. This, to me, spoke volumes about the atmosphere in Ottawa. However, having enough on my plate I decided to just concentrate on the cards in front of me.

Change meant that the Nursing Unit Administration Program had to be broken down into small segments. An initial step was to solicit opinions on the program from nursing managers and chief executive officers in the health industry across Canada. Both groups seemed unhappy with the program, growing impatient with the limitations in management skills of the graduates at a time when the health industry was growing and needing more capable leaders. In these discussions I floated the idea of a decentralized program. This generally appealed to most leaders.

We created new student guidelines shifting the strength of the evaluation (75%) to the home-study assignments, leaving the remainder (25%) to a multiple-choice exam at the final workshop. The assignments were changed to practical management issues, the student asked to introduce change into their own organization with due regard to cost and value. Guidelines were established for the evaluation process for both students and Advisors, clarifying the process to all parties. Such guidelines, outlined in separate booklets for each group, allowed plenty of room for personal judgment.

Then I began recruiting educational advisors, estimating one for every fifteen students, individuals with respected nursing management abilities from every province, a precursor for decentralizing the program. Each one was informed s/he would have to sign a yearly contract, a key component being their responsibility to continue the revision of the program through annual, regional, advisory meetings. Only a third of the old advisors (mainly in Toronto), who never worked with a contract, agreed to continue with the new system. For regular communications, a newsletter was established to keep advisors updated between the face-to-face meetings.

To clarify and focus the management principles of the program, a planning group of nursing leaders was set up to create an outline for a new Nursing Unit Administration textbook, to be written in English and French. The plan was to contract twelve English and twelve French authors to follow the outline for their particular chapter. The author's contract gave me the prerogative of requesting a revision of the material if necessary. Revisions were needed in only a few instances. One author, a university professor in Montreal, angry at me for requesting a second revision, sought the input of his management students. To his amazement, they informed him the revised material was the first time his course made sense. The professor called to thank me for pushing him otherwise he would have continued to assume his students understood the material. Having the material written by English and French authors was cost effective as translating an English text would have been far more expensive.

Once the chapters were completed, I hired two editors, one English and one French, as the two books, while based on the same outline, were slightly different reflecting the differences in the two cultures. The English material tended to be more abrupt while the French material used more descriptive phrases to describe similar items. A textbook outline was used to make sure core management principles were addressed, as the health industry had complex management issues. Unlike university programs, many Nursing Unit Administration students did not have access to libraries with a lot of management material. By providing an additional extensive bibliography, each student, with the help of their Advisor, had the option of accessing additional reading if they wished to explore any specific topic. When the editors cleared the textbook material I went in search of publishing bids. It was in this point I faced another interesting facet of the Ottawa environment.

At four o'clock on a Friday afternoon, I opened the bids and selected the one that best met the contract requirements and offered the best price. I then phoned the printer to let him know of my decision. To my surprise he asked, "Will you be in your office for the next half hour?". Confirming my presence, I waited not knowing what to expect. Entering the room with a congenial smile he said, "Where did you come from? I need to shake your hand. This is the first time in my years in Ottawa that a printing contract has been handled properly." Still a bit confused, I asked," Can you tell me what is the usual pattern?" wondering if there was something I missed. Chuckling, he replied, "Well, by the time it is sifted through the political channels, then who you know and whatever else the person thinks might benefit them or their organization, the contract is announced. It usually has little to do with the best bid or meeting the contract details." I wondered how anyone worked in such an environment, especially small business men like this one. He promised to do an excellent job, which he did. The entire textbook process, including payments to authors, editors and printing two textbooks (one English and one French) came in under budget.

The compact, one hundred and ninety page, textbook replaced the stacks of magazine articles eliminating this task for the clerical staff. At the beginning of the revised program, students received a compact program package of a textbook and a student manual containing information on the workshops, their home study projects, how their assignments were to be evaluated, the expectations of their Advisors, and how their assignments would be handled in each province, including what to do in case of a mail strike. The deluge of assignments landing at the head office ceased, giving us the opportunity of setting up a monitoring program to review random assignments. In the meantime the clerical staff had to be reassured their role would actually be expanding as old tasks ceased.

Remembering working with my father on John Deere equipment in Summerside years before, I contacted an inventory specialist to help me with student records. The older man seemed bewildered as he was more familiar with bolts than students. After chatting for some time we finally came to a mutual understanding. Within weeks he created a single card system, which would contain all the student marks and finances, easily retrievable in an alphabetical system. He then found a portable, locked cabinet on wheels, in which the cards sat in neat rows, colour-coded by province. When the phone rang the Nursing Unit Administration clerk could instantly wheel around the cart (called 'R2D2') and within minutes have all the information on hundreds of students at her fingertips. This preliminary manual system was being tested prior to the eventual introduction of computerized format which we knew was a future reality. The filing system, on the other hand, took dog work to reorganize to coincide with the card system.

After many months of hard work, we were finally seeing results. The process had been streamlined, standards and guidelines established and the management material focused in a new textbook. While hospital leaders were complimenting students and ourselves on the quality of the revised program and skills of the students, the increased program expectations had resulted in about fifty students failing, a first in many years. We anticipated and faced the flack of this outcome.

Assured the educational and administrative details had been tested and were workable, we began to upgrade and strengthen the workshop curriculum. Since Dorothy and I were fresh from a learning environment, we were able to bring updated material to the workshops. We also added a number of audio-visual aides. With revised workshop materials we continued our cross-country mission. In the fall and spring, Dorothy and I altered our travel direction starting either from the east or west for the fall and spring sessions. The French program was being run entirely out of the Montreal office, sister having the students come to her at the university. On one occasion, Dorothy and I encountered a national airline strike just as we were about to finish the workshops. This gave me a deep appreciation of the size of Canada. Dorothy, covering the west, was able to duck into the United States and catch a ride on an American airline flight back to Ottawa. I was stranded in Newfoundland where I had to negotiate a ride on a cargo plane to New Brunswick, then catch the train to Montreal and another to Ottawa. I was certainly getting to know Canada.

Weeks of lectures at these workshops was a definite test for a dyslectic. For me, typed lecture notes were practically useless as the letters danced about and I lost my place. Memorizing days of lectures was an option except I discovered students became uneasy if I never referred to any notes. So I devised a prop in which the workshop material was in a three-ring binder with coloured- coded markers. As the days passed I flipped the pages according to the markers, using a single-paged agenda, and never reading the material during the workshop.

By the second year, Dorothy and I were getting into the rhythm of the system, knowing how the hotels/educational facilities worked, especially with regard to audio-visual aids, and becoming familiar with the country. While our days were spent giving lectures, our evenings often included personal chats with nurse managers who were facing complex or difficult situations in their organizations. At one workshop in the west I had four nurses ready to deliver. Being in Banff, I made special arrangements at the facility 'just in case', and asked obstetric nurses to be available should anything occur. We had no deliveries but great fun in anticipation. For the one who started the Nursing Unit Administration workshops in British Columbia in the spring, they had the good fortune of travelling east with the spring blossoms. As a very hard working small team we had the joy of seeing our plans sprouting and growing and benefiting the nurse managers of Canada.

Dorothy and I were so busy managing the distance education program we had little time for our graduation and decided to have the university mail our master degree documents. We had survived the combined workload of our master's coursework and thesis plus working practically full time. Thus, I took little notice of Dorothy's comments that my name was put forward for the Robert Wood Johnson Award. This award was given to *the graduate most likely to make a noteworthy contribution to the advancement of hospital care.* Voted on by both faculty and students, one award was given in each of the five health administration programs (University of Alberta, University of British Columbia, Universite de Montreal, University of Ottawa and the University of Toronto) in Canada. Knowing the caliber of the students in our class, I did not hold much hope in me being elected, but I was wrong. In June, Bill and I flew to St. John's Newfoundland, where the Canadian Hospital Association was holding it's annual meeting. There at a special banquet I received the award for the University of Ottawa along with fifteen hundred dollars. I was somewhat overwhelmed by the whole affair, and the lovely comments and letters of congratulations.

By the summer of 1979, Bill and I were in need of a break and decided to go to the Muskokas once Gregory was out of school. We were all looking forward to this adventure and set out gleefully enjoying the freedom and break. Toby, as always, was part of the traveling troupe.

We had no sooner arrived at the cottage when I was plagued with an overpowering urge to return to Ottawa. Not wanting to disrupt our holiday I kept dismissing my intuitive feelings. By the next morning, unable to restrain myself, I said to Bill, "Something is terribly wrong (a phrase he was beginning to understand). We need to get home at once". Just outside Ottawa, we were stopped by the RCMP informing Bill of an emergency in Scotland. The phone was ringing as we entered our home, Janie had been trying to get in touch with Bill because of his mother. Jennie had a stroke (practically the very hour of my intuitive feelings) and Bill needed to fly to Scotland. His mother had been unwell on her last visit, so this news was not entirely unexpected. Bill immediately took off with the understanding Gregory and I would follow. He would arrive in time to bid a final farewell to his mother. The unhappy circumstances would be my first trip to Britain.

We stayed at Janie Limond's, a two-story, gray stone, semi-detached house in Ayr. For the first time I meet Bill's sister, Marjory, from Australia, his aunt Pearl who had lived for many years in India, and other family and friends. I was struggling with a number of different accents.

There was no church funeral service, everyone gathered around the gravesite while the Presbyterian Minister said a few prayers. The scene was like something out of Charles Dickens, the rain, pouring in sheets, fell into the open grave and danced off the black umbrellas of the small funeral party. Bill, the only son, stood out in the open getting drenched as the rain soaked his black wool suit. I expected all of us would have pneumonia if the service had been prolonged. Once the last prayer was over everyone dashed to cars, to gather again for a post-funeral reception back at Janie's residence.

The wake was quieter than the usual Irish ones of my youth, but then again, except for Bill, Gregory, myself, his sister and Bill's cousin, those present were mainly seniors. It is hard to know what happened during this rather reserved occasion. Bill's female cousin made some nasty comment about 'The blond from Canada' and the next thing I knew she was abruptly ushered out the door by two hostile Scottish ladies. I rather liked the spunkiness of these Scottish women and certainly appreciated the feeling of belonging. We returned to Canada with some small items for the girls as a memento of their grandmother. It had been a quiet closing of a chapter in our lives. There was little time for rest as Bill and I returned to our busy jobs, and Gregory to school.

Positive comments on the Nursing Unit Administration changes were being received daily, especially from chief executive officers of hospitals who found their nursing managers now able to contribute more to management discussions. Some nurses wrote to say the management lessons were proving to be equally beneficial in their community activities. There were still ongoing adjustments but the new format seemed to be running smoothly. At this point, Dr. Mussallem suggested that she and I should submit an article on the program to 'The Journal of Continuing Education in Nursing', which we did. In addition to the positive comments, the program was becoming the best money-maker of all the educational programs in the Canadian Hospital Association. Yet, while we were enjoying all these positives, my intuition kept telling me something unexpected was about to occur. My problem was not knowing what or why.

Early in December, out of the blue, Dr. Mussallem called to request my presence at a special meeting at the Canadian Nurses Association with regard to a complaint from the sister in the Montreal office. This was unexpected as sister had voiced no problems on the occasions I traveled to the Montreal office, when she went to Haiti, or at the time of our many discussions regarding the program changes. In addition, I could not understand why we were meeting at the nursing association when the Nursing Unit Administration program had its own Board to which such matters should have been addressed. I suspected there was another agenda as sister was a rather passive individual and easily manipulated.

On the morning of the meeting, I was surprised when Jean-Claude Martin, the President of the Canadian Hospital Association, appeared asking to share my cab to the Canadian Nurses Association. Jean-Claude had replaced Dr. Bourassa as the head of the association and had been a very pleasant individual to work with. He was a dapper man with a small moustache, a pharmacy and hospital administration graduate from the University of Montreal, and later the Director of the Hopital du Sacre Coeur in Montreal. For the first time, I found him visibly upset, remaining silent as we drove to the Canadian Nurses Association. Upon arrival, he abruptly left the cab heading straight to Dr. Mussallem's office. As I entered the building, I could hear their loud voices, Jean-Claude's voice in anger at whatever was about to happen. He was still upset as he left coming to me saying, "When this so-called meeting is over, come straight back to the office". Jean-Claude's actions alerted me to the unexpected. The political ramifications of my earlier report on the Canadian Nurses Association and changes to the Nursing Unit Administration program must have upset someone or other in powerful quarters.

As the women gathered around a conference table I noted that everyone seemed more aware of the true nature of the meeting than me. From the opening comments it was evident this would be no meeting. Instead it became a semi-court setting with Gerry O'Neill from the Montreal General Hospital (a member of the Nursing Unit Administration Board) serving as my spokesperson/lawyer. While I was pleased to have a member of the O'Neill clan in my corner, I was uncomfortable with the general atmosphere of the proceedings. Ginette Rogers from the Hopital Notre-Dame in Montreal was the chair. Assuming everyone knew each other, there was little effort at introductions. This left me in the dark as to the name or role of an individual sitting next to Dr. Mussallem at the far end of the table. My conundrum increased when I assessed she was from the Quebec Nurses Association, the reason for her presence never being clarified. For the entire meeting I remained silent, thinking it prudent to let my spokeswoman deal with the matter, and hoping as I listened to possibly grasp the true meaning of the occasion.

As I pondered the situation more questions emerged. If sister was so unhappy with her working conditions she had several options. She could have said something to me in our numerous contacts, written to the Nursing Unit Administration Board chair, another religious sister, whom she may have felt more at home in discussing her problem or sent a letter to the Canadian Nurses Association who in turn could have presented her concerns to the Nursing Unit Administration Board through their representatives. After all, the Nursing Unit Administration Board had existed for years.

The proceedings began in French, everyone fully aware I was not conversant in the language. However, I could follow sister's description of how her life had changed for the worse when I arrived. Expectations and work had suddenly increased. Questions were asked by the members at the table to get sister to clarify her problem. Then, sister, thinking she had a captive and sympathetic audience blurted out, "Madame Robertson, beaucoup, beaucoup travaille! (too much work)" It would have been fine if sister had stopped there but, feeling ebullient, she pressed on, and, switching to English, continued, "Madame Robertson is a cold blooded administrator who expects everyone to work hard". Instantly, I saw a quick glance between Ginette and Gerry, both senior nursing administrators, while out of my side vision I observed the visible uneasiness of Dr. Mussallem and the women next to her. The tide had turned!

Ginette, looking straight at sister replied, "Madam Robertson has not asked her staff to do more than she herself has been willing to do. In an amazing short time she has taken this education program from the horse-and-buggy era to the twenty-first century and the responses to such change have been generally positive". Whatever the underlying objective of the meeting, it had failed. The discussions quickly petered off almost to a whimper with Gerry's parting statement , "As you are aware, this matter will be placed before the Nursing Unit Administration Board this afternoon, and I will get back to you with their decision". Everyone scattered. I quietly walked back to the Canadian Hospital Association office praying I had enough energy for the second round. I filled Dorothy in on what was happening as best as I could translate the events.

John-Claude had been busy. All members of the Nursing Unit Administration Board were present, some flying in from the west. The hospital association representatives voiced their anger when Gerry O'Neill outlined the morning proceedings. The nursing association representatives were clearly uneasy. Once again, I remained silent. The beginning discussions centered on the inappropriateness of this issue being brought to a meeting at the Canadian Nurses Association instead of the proper Board. The Board had been fully kept abreast of the changes in the education program and were aware of the reactions. There was some innuendos on the possible political and/or other reasons for such action, but these were sidestepped gently. The events of the morning had been unexpected, and had undermined the Board's authority. After much deliberation, to my surprise, the Board decided sister was to be fired, requesting I convey their decision to her at the Montreal office in person without delay.

The next day, taking the early morning bus to Montreal, I arrived at the Nursing Unit Administration office at the University of Montreal nursing degree program building about mid-morning. Since, I suspected, sister was used as a pawn in someone else's scheme, I had no intention of dragging out the meeting. I began by asking, "Surely Sister, you must have known there were two possible outcomes; I could get fired or you". It was obvious she had expected only one outcome. She calmly accepted the inevitable. We made arrangements for the necessary closure of the office and I said good bye, feeling somewhat like Scrooge in firing someone so close to Christmas. This, however, was not the end of the day's stressful events.

I made arrangements to meet the head of the University of Montreal nursing program for lunch at the Chateau Laurier Hotel. I did not know this woman but suspected she may have been an active participant in the fiasco. Anyway, I needed to talk to her as to the future of the Nursing Unit Administration office. Arriving early at the hotel, I waited, quietly sipping a cup of coffee while looking out the restaurant window at the magnificent city below. Followed by a quick introduction, the atmosphere exploded as my guest harangued me about sister being fired. In her anger she declared that she was in charge of the Nursing Unit Administration Montreal program, to which I reminded her my appointment clearly included the Montreal office. Unruffled, she continued stating her authority in all nursing matters within the university. When she hesitated, I interjected a request that she find a job for sister since she, and possibly others, had managed to get her fired. This request was met by an immediate nod without admitting to anything. Concluding her list of displeasure about me, in a fit of exasperation, she blurted out, "It is obvious, Madame Robertson, you know nothing about the French culture!"

The time had come. I replied, "Well, my little French grandmother will be most upset to hear that. Her name is Florence Secord, from the same family as Laura Secord. I believe many, if not all the Secords in North America, come from Ambrose Secard who arrived in North America in the sixteen hundreds. My grandmother's family came from New York State and she now resides in Ontario. In my opinion her French ancestry is quite legitimate." Dumbfounded, my luncheon party sat as if her wind had been extinguished. For a few minutes she kept looking at me making no comment. Then, with whatever remaining energy I possessed, I asked if she was staying for lunch (praying she was not). To which she quickly mentioned an unexpected meeting and left.

By this point I was exhausted and glad for silence. Unknown to me two older waiters were standing near by and, coming to my table, bowed graciously saying, almost in unison, "Touche Madam, we have been listening. We know this lady well. May we treat you to lunch? Would you like to have an aperitif?" By this point I welcomed any kindness the fates offered, and accepted their kind gesture. I was royally treated to a simple, delicious lunch. Later they helped me with my coat, and got me a taxi. The taxi driver, likely a family member of the restaurant staff, waved his fee as he gently assisted me onto the bus for my return trip to Ottawa. I was grateful for such unexpected generosity, it had been a rough day.

I relaxed into my fur coat as the bus raced along snow-covered roads. While I enjoyed dissecting complex organizational problems and creating a more smoothly running structure for others to manage, I realized the politically-charged environment of Ottawa was not only soul destroying it was not my cup of tea. Being blindsided by those with other agendas was both stressful and detrimental to my health. That weekend I cherished Bill's wisdom as we discussed the ramifications of the past week. A future in Ottawa was already being questioned.

I had barely unbuttoned my coat on Monday morning when Jean-Claude arrived at my office to ask, "Why didn't you tell me you were part French?" I thought to myself, the telephone lines must have been busy on the weekend. My news and years of silence was likely disconcerting to some. Responding to his question I said, "Jean-Claude, you came to my defense out of a feeling of justice because you cared. This I will always cherish. You are far more at home in this politicized environment, I'm not sure it's for me. I am a generation with a mixture of cultures. I love my dear French Grandmother but even she would not appreciate it if I favoured one culture over another. Perhaps a day will come when the people of all cultures, even those with mixed ancestral roots, will be welcomed in the capital of this nation". As he left my office I could see he was struggling to understand my silence and wondering why I had not used my French ancestry to advance my career. Perhaps my ancestor, John Philpot Curran, had the skills for such political strivings. His descendant did not. It was a climate best suited to others.

Bill's federal job was not panning out much better. By the late seventies, another reorganization eliminated his job as the Director of Hospital Insurance and, through his own efforts, he was redirected to being the Director of Professional and Institutional Standards. In this role he set up many federal/provincial sub-committees bringing in the most capable health professionals (doctors, nurses, social workers, physiotherapists etc.) to establish institutional guidelines for about thirty different care fields, such as: Cardiovascular Services, Addiction Services, Diagnostic Imaging Services, Rehabilitation Medicine, Diabetic Day Care, Burn Unit, Palliative Care, Child and Adolescent Services, Emergency Services, Day Medicine, Day Surgery, Stroke Services etc. These guidelines addressed such topics as inpatient and outpatient case load, bed requirements, administrative policies and procedures, staffing numbers and responsibilities, special design features for the units, and even equipment. As the specialization of health care continued to grow, such guidelines were essential for greater consistency of health services across the country, and imperative in planning new facilities. Bill met with various specialty leaders to establish and revise such guidelines. His ability as a committee chair was well recognized. Because of his federal work he was also appointed the chairman of the Canadian Standards Association (CSA) National Committee on Health Services, where he was involved in the planning, organization and review of health service standards. Once again there were numbers of specialists from many health fields. The combination of both jobs gave him a key position in establishing the direction of health standards as health services were expanding. But, in an environment where politics had a higher priority than quality of work, the inevitable was bound to happen.

Over the years Bill had weathered numerous innuendos that Ottawa was no the place for doctors, especially British doctors, and one who had been a missionary. The fact he spoke fluent French was almost regarded as a negative. By this junction, efforts at getting rid of people had become an art form in the federal civil service. The final straw came when Bill applied for a promotion. Knowing the interview would be stacked against him, I used every trick learned in my Los Angeles executive program. I bombarded him with difficult and even cruel questions, the air static with tension. For each one we rehearsed an unruffled response. The day of his interview I waited to hear the outcome. He finally called saying, "Well, they didn't hit all your questions. Nevertheless, I likely do not have a chance, as they have likely already selected the applicant". The appointment went to a general practitioner from Belgium. His first greeting to Bill was, "Well, Dr. Robertson, I know nothing about the Canadian health service, so you will tell me what to say".

As if God heard our cry, within a week we were contacted by an organization from Toronto hired to plan a thousand bed teaching health facility in Halifax. The party wondered if we might be interested in working with the medical and nursing professionals in Halifax in planning this huge project. With little incentive to stay in Ottawa, we both accepted the offer. I resigned from my Nursing Unit Administration position, recommending Dorothy as my replacement. Bill resigned from the federal government. In returning to the Maritimes, I would be completing a full circle.

‑‑◦✳◦‑‑

In the moving transition, I had to return to Ottawa for two weeks and needed a place to stay. Surprised, I received a call from Dr. Mussallem offering me her penthouse, as she would be away. She insisted I come and see the place. Having few options other than a hotel, I accepted. The warmth of her greeting was certainly contrary to some of our previous encounters. The place was spectacular, luxury accommodations with a grand view of Ottawa. I accepted her offer, and quietly walked back and forth to the Canadian Hospital Association for my final days in Ottawa. On my last day, I left her a gift and note of thanks. It was time to move on.

THOUGHTS AND LEARNING

University life, as always, seemed disconnected from reality. There was too little time, too many, and sometimes conflicting, expectations from professors, and faculty with little or no field experience with strong views on how it should be managed. While I was fortunate in having a very fine internship Advisor, some students felt abandoned, especially the younger ones with little or no health experience. I suppose the best part of such education is the chance to stop and reflect on important topics, get updated on the latest research and studies, and sharing the successes and misery of the experience with other students. We had a great class, special individuals who were willing to help each other get over the educational hurdles.

I entered my study of the Canadian Nurses Association thinking that, at best, I might discover some historical gem or be able to clarify some management issue. I did not expect, nor want, to unravel a financial mess. One wonders if behind the scene there were those who suspected a problem existed and used the university to expose it. Or perhaps events unraveled as ordained. It might be argued the financial issues could have been ignored but this would have negated the whole principle of a management study. To his credit, at no time did my Advisor suggest scrapping the financial details or disguising the truth. We worked with the facts and carefully crafted a report to support the data. In doing so we were both aware of the possible ramifications of my report in such a political milieu. However, irrespective of the comments delivered directly to me, the university made no mention of receiving any negative reaction to my study.

Regrettably, there were a number of issues begging for some further dialogue. What would have happened if a national nurses license had continued? Will registered nurses ever get fed up with the limited benefits they receive for the hundreds of dollars paid annually for their license to practice? Will Canada ever follow the policy of Arizona, where health professional licenses are controlled by government at significantly lower fees (by hundreds of dollars)? In light of the costs of running a number of health professional association offices at the national level, often with a duplication of services, will Canada ever reach the stage of unifying these health groups under one umbrella such as a National Council/College of Health? Since my time at the Canadian Nurses and Canadian Hospital Association was brief, I will leave these fascinating questions to future researchers.

The problem in working in the political climate of Ottawa, and perhaps in other national centres, is that there is too much darkness and not enough light. With so much ambitious energy, political intrigue, the acquisition of immense power and money, and levels of corruption consolidated in one space it is amazing it doesn't implode on itself. With all its negativity, this politicized environment in Canada is unfortunately still stuck in a bygone century with Upper and Lower Canada still fighting it out for supreme power. There is only lip service to the needs of the rest of the country, the Maritimes and Newfoundland regarded as welfare, poor cousins, the west as an upstart child, and the north as a wealthy area to exploit. The sad point is that while Upper and Lower Canada continue to focus on their parochial and political strivings, they are in danger of losing the rest of the country and/or being engulfed by outside events. Frustrated with insufficient input into this centralist governance structure, Canada is more in danger of the west and north separating than Quebec, a view barely elucidated in Ottawa. In addition, concentrating on so much political trivia, and not attracting the best leaders in the country, Canada is also in danger of being toppled by unexpected world events because they do not have the resiliency and innovation to succeed. This central rigidity will eventually crack, the question is when and by what trigger.

My time in Ottawa was brief, filled with both triumph and woe. I successfully achieved the next step in my academic education including receipt of the Johnson and Johnson Award, quite an achievement for a dyslectic. My study of the Canadian Nurses Association gave the organization guidelines for recovery, even if the messenger would never be acknowledged. In addition, I had the opportunity to dissect and redesign a national/international, nurse management, distance education program by streamlining the administration, upgrading the curriculum and creating clearer guidelines for both students and Advisors. Later, the entire Nursing Unit Administration strategy was adopted for all the Canadian Hospital Association management education programs, a true complement to the success of the changes. On the negative side, the political intrigue which permeates every crevice of the working environment in Ottawa was suffocating and detrimental to achieving lasting change. Nevertheless, in a short period of time, I learned a great deal about the Canadian health industry, the Canadian Nurses and Canadian Hospital Associations, distance learning, management education for nurses, Canada and some international countries, the value of true friends and colleagues, and my preference for practical management puzzles and problems.

In time I would learn that my semi-court experience was not unusual in the seventies environment of Ottawa. An underlying power struggle was in force and my actions, however altruistic, obviously upset some carefully laid plans and disturbed a number of turfs. My management study likely created problems for both the management staff and the Board of the Canadian Nurses Association. Changes in the Nursing Unit Administrative program may have upset the originators of the program at McGill University, or members of the University of Toronto who lost their long-standing advisory role, and/or decentralizing the program likely bothered those who favoured centralized control. Beyond these circles, there were likely those who simply disliked change. Fortunately, I had angels watching over me. Perhaps in time, others who worked in this environment will tell their stories. While there will be those who had only positive experiences, unfortunately there will be others who may have far worse tales to tell.

It was not difficult to leave Ottawa as I was not seeking power or gold, and did not need an environment which promoted so much negativity. In a setting where politics reigns supreme, and where a lack of reality is regarded as normal, survival of principles must be difficult. Yet, some people do survive in this atmosphere, the question is at what price. For me, I had learned enough about the political centre of Canada.

For our family, Ottawa was a time for beginnings and endings. The most beautiful feature of Ottawa was my marriage to Bill, a healing and restorative element in my life. As two health professionals we had much to share, and this was enhanced by our mutual interests in many topics. We were lovers and kindred spirits on many levels. Our time in Ottawa gave our blended family time to grow.

An example of Gregory's adaptation to his new life was to tell his teacher he had a new dad, three step-sisters, three grandmothers and two grandfathers. His change of name gave further evidence of his evolving world. It took time for him to appreciate the value of his expanded family, especially having a father that brought a male perspective into his life and who loved him dearly.

My move from Arizona presented me with multiple challenges. In addition to the climate, I was adjusting to another marriage and in-laws, three step-daughters, trying to keep Gregory linked to his heritage, becoming a Presbyterian, returning to university and being dropped into a political environment light years removed from the Nova Scotia scene, my prior government reference point. For someone with dyslexia and Lupus this was a tall order. In the seventies, there were no guide books for blended families and no easy answers for personality clashes. In all, we did remarkably well in light of the permutations and combinations.

Through it all Bill made a remarkable shift to a younger family while retaining his interest in his daughters, who were grown women moving on with their own lives. For him, home life was a peaceful oasis from the turbulent working environment of the federal government. However, it took some time for him to adjust to my extra sensory perception, especially when I would tell him who was on the phone and what they needed before he picked up the receiver. I had to control this tendency as it was too spooky. It would take years for him to fully understand my dyslexia.

The seventies also brought final farewells to three family members; Bill's mother, and Jacob and Carl Linkert, who would always be in our thoughts.

My life seemed to be falling into cycles of threes and sevens. Three years each at the Commission and in Arizona, seven years a single parent and seven years since I left the Maritimes. My life had changed, and I expected life had also moved on in the east. The road ahead would have more learning. I could almost feel the enticing breeze of the salt air as I turned towards the Maritimes once again.

CHAPTER 8

Completing the Loop

O UR decade long return to the Maritimes began in Bedford, Nova Scotia. Once again I was overlooking the Bedford basin, this time from a different angle from my Mount days. We purchased a white, wooden, three-bedroom house on Golf Links Road, just off Shore Drive, an odd design with a huge veranda overlooking the water. There would be little time to appreciate the setting as the next eighteen months Bill and I would be submerged in a huge capital planning project, a thousand bed health science teaching complex, which would sap every ounce of our time and energies. Once settled, we daily commuted to a small white house on the edge of the Camp Hill Hospital, in the heart of Halifax and in close proximity to major hospitals. During this period, Gregory, dressed in gray pants, navy jacket, shirt and tie, boarded a yellow bus near our home to attend classes at the Dartmouth Academy, a private school. We had all embarked on new paths.

Bedford, at the north end of the basin, is a town with deep historical roots. Governor Cornwallis, after establishing the garrison at Halifax, began the construction of a road leading to Minas Bay on the Bay of Fundy using Mi'kmaq footpaths as their guide. To protect the route he erected a defense post at the head of the Bedford Basin, named Fort Sackville. The area around the fort was known as Sackville until the mid-1850s when it became better known as Bedford [1]. In our exploration of the area we discovered lingering traces of the old Indian trails and fort. Bill, Gregory and Toby made regular forays to what they named 'Eagle Ridge' which was the highest point in the area, commanding a panoramic view.

For the first time Bill and I would be working side-by-side. We were joining an established group of about fifteen health facility planners consisting of architects, engineers, and other health systems experts dealing with support systems such as laundry, pharmacy, housekeeping, and supplies. Being the only medical and nursing consultants, our task was twofold; to translate the health industry to the planning professionals and communicate the planning process, expressed in architectural terms, to health professionals. The health professionals represented most medical and nursing specialties in the four main Halifax teaching hospitals, which the new health science complex was supposed to replace. We would also be part of the overall project planning committee. Fortunately, we were greeting many individuals we had previously worked with in our Hospital Insurance Commission days.

We joined the planning process at the 'programming stage', following acceptance of the initial proposal by the Nova Scotia government. The programming stage is intended to describe the operational nature of the project, producing a definitive set of documents setting the purpose and conceptual framework for an architectural solution. It defines the human, technical and financial requirements, and specifies building requirements. In addition, it provides a description and analysis of the functions to be performed by the project, and the physical structure required to accommodate them. It includes a description and analysis of the land requirements needed to accommodate the structure and, using bubble diagrams, shows the relationships of the project's components and/or departments [2]. A vast amount of information would be needed for this stage of the planning. The challenge of the program planning team was to provide all this detail for an ultra- modern health science centre encompassing four care facilities on one site; an acute care unit (replacing the five-hundred bed Halifax Infirmary), a geriatric unit (replacing the Camp Hill Hospital for veterans), a long-term psychiatric unit (replacing the Abbie J. Lane Hospital), and an obstetric unit (replacing the Salvation Army's Grace Maternity Hospital). It was understood these four hospital components would be serviced by a central support structure. All city hospitals, except the Izaac Walton Killam Hospital for children, would be involved in the planning due to the interconnection of health services and support networks.

We would be working for Built Environment Coordinators (BEC), an architectural firm out of Toronto, the owner, Doug Roughley, making periodic visits to Halifax to assess the progress of the project. In charge of the Maritime team was Bill Nycum, an American architect with Vietnam ambulance experience, who guided us through the BEC method of planning, an impressive systematic and detailed process of identifying every space component.

At the beginning, Bill and I decided there would be a single medical/nursing plan. Once a draft document was created, Bill would work with the medical groups to negotiate the overall health services, a complex process involving not only the acute and long-term health services but also diagnostic and support services. My task would be to work with the nurses in identifying the space details for every service area, getting agreement on the size, activities, anticipated changes in technology and care, and determining the most effective support systems (i.e. pharmacy, laundry, supply systems etc). First, the draft document had to be created.

In the early days we assembled stacks of health facility planning documents to identify what standards existed in North America and globally. To our surprise we discovered many inconsistencies, gaps, and missing guidelines in the literature. Health facility planning and design had not been a major endeavour in either architectural or health professional education programs, because up to the incorporation of publicly-funded health systems, such activities catered to a rather limited market. Communities were not in the habit of building or replacing health facilities quickly. In addition, most health professionals had little or no involvement in the planning or designing of their working space, so finding references on their views was practically impossible. In addition to the literature we poured over numerous examples of health facility designs, reviewed material on basic planning and design issues and updated ourselves on the latest health care technology and delivery systems. When there was no available material Bill and I actually paced out spaces from memory as we both had experience in acute, obstetric, geriatric and psychiatric services.

Once the draft document was ready we separated with Bill setting up his medical working groups and me the nursing groups. Bill spent endless hours getting the doctors to agree on what services would move to the new site and what would stay in the old hospital facilities, requiring expert negotiating skills.

With the help of the Directors of Nursing in the various hospitals a central committee and a number of nursing working groups were established. The central committee consisted of Directors of Nursing, while the working groups focused on specific clinical areas (i.e. medical, surgical, obstetric, psychiatric, geriatric, operating room, emergency and intensive care units). My task was to collate the comments of all groups, reviewing and expanding on the draft material, and reporting back to the main Directors group for sign off. These discussions were, on the whole, fascinating and highly productive as we focused on the planning of each nursing service right down to the electrical outlets, while trying to visualize what nursing might look like in the years ahead. Several underlying objectives were agreed upon to facilitate such planning: because of the size of the health centre maximum daylight was needed for patient care and lounge spaces; the institutional nature of patient rooms needed to be ameliorated; nursing work spaces would be reviewed with regard to flow patterns, distance and walking time; and efforts would be made to increase the resiliency of the nursing areas for emergencies and unforeseen shifts in care. While each service had its own pattern and needs, some issues took hours of discussion.

There were numerous unique features considered for this health complex, a few are presented. Four-bed wards would be replaced with private and semi-private rooms. Larger patient bathrooms would be considered to accommodate increased technology and other hospital equipment. Each patient's bed would have finger-touch panels to conceal intravenous poles and examination lights. Delivery rooms would be equipped with a wall panel to hide delivery equipment so the mother would not have to move. The double-corridor design of nursing wards would be replaced by a y-shaped floor plan with supplies delivered by elevator behind the nursing station. Communication systems at the nursing stations would be designed to combine multiple wards for emergencies and/or staff shortages. Educational spaces would be located away from patient wards. Operating rooms would be located on the same level as the emergency entrance, reducing the need for elevators. The operating rooms would have a special delivery cart system and surgical lights, cameras and other technical devices would be attached to the ceiling. Intensive care units would have electrical columns beside each bed to accommodate current and anticipated technologies. A unit-dose medication system would be introduced with pharmacists preparing the medications. Electronic floor beams would facilitate a robotic supply cart system. Computers would handle patient records and interdepartmental communications. A weather-protected interior street would connect all hospital components with restaurants, cafeterias, drug store, bank, crafts, art gallery, library and other stores available for visitors, patients, and long-term residents. The nurses, having a chance to give their input, provided practical incite in making the spaces work better.

One of the main problems with most health facility planning is the lack of representation from two key groups, patients/residents and nurses. Amazingly, while these two groups spend most of their time in health facility bedrooms and bathrooms, they have the least input in designing such spaces. At best, a token nurse may be found on the main planning committee. For this reason, in the past, when cuts were considered for health facility plans to control costs, it was usually the basic accommodations (i.e. bedrooms and bathrooms) which were cut, resulting in unending frustrations for both patients and nurses once the facility was built. This has been going on for decades. Having an individual with a nursing background on the main architectural planning team, as in this project, was indeed rare.

Realizing words were insufficient in explaining the importance of bedroom and bathroom spaces to architects, I pressed for a bathroom mock-up to be set up at the Halifax Infirmary, phoning several old colleagues to help with the experiment. Once ready, I watched as several young architects left the planning office to review the demonstration bathroom. By four in the afternoon there was still no sign of them. At almost closing time they boisterously entered the building stating that they now, for the first time, understood why nurses were so upset with bathrooms. The nurses, primed for the chance at getting their point across, had these architects fitted out with every device they could find (i.e. intravenous poles, casts, walkers, wheelchairs, etc) to illustrate their problem with poorly designed bathrooms. It worked! I would never have to discuss the issue again. For days these architects had their heads together redesigning bathrooms and arguing now from personal experience. While the architects had been convinced, it would take a much higher power to convince the main project committee made up of political, government (mainly Public Works), community representatives and architects, primarily men, to understand the problem.

One day I received, anonymously, a memo that was in circulation from the Deputy Minister of Public Works to his staff. It stated in so many words to 'watch out for Robertson' who has a fetish about bathrooms. She is asking for far too many bathrooms in the health science complex and ones that are far larger than currently available in most hospitals'. At the main committee meetings this Deputy Minister consistently rejected any change in bathrooms, numbers or size, until his wife got ill and was admitted to a hospital room without a bathroom. In considerable pain, she had to use a bathroom down the hall. Armed with this personal experience, my antagonist abruptly shifted gear and began to support my bathroom recommendations. Sadly, it took such personal experience to achieve such a change in thinking.

Home life under such grueling conditions was limited. We cherished our evenings and weekends even though it often entailed reading many documents. There was little time for much else. Gregory was doing well in school, the Dartmouth Academy giving him an academic discipline which would help him in the years ahead. Bill's gardening was reduced to large pots of summer flowers on the veranda, a delightful array of colour to enrich our lives.

When the first summer arrived, Gregory, now older, negotiated with his father to take on a summer project of his own. He wanted to work on the garage interior to create an array of wooden hanging devices for garden and other equipment. Bill and Gregory worked on a plan which left Gregory ordering and receiving the wood, and being personally in charge of his own project. A neighbour came over one evening to ask what hold we had on Gregory as he watched him work steadily each day, taking a small break at lunch time. Little did he realize that Gregory was perfectly delighted working with wood. I'm sure the spirit of his grandfather Linkert was there with him as he measured and fitted each piece of wood.

Janie Limond came to visit for a month in the summer, enabling us to take a much needed break, with weekend forays into various parts of Nova Scotia. She brought news of Scotland for Bill and I would come to value her practical advice. In the early nineteen eighties Janie and I were just getting to know each other.

Sometime during this period we received, unexpectedly in the mail, three beautiful watercolour art pieces from Mr. Han Leung, our Vietnamese refugee now established as an artist in Ottawa. We framed these lovely pieces to hang in our dining room. In the following years we would receive an annual update of his family in their Christmas greetings.

Our darling Toby suddenly aged, her white chin and refusal to take adventurous walks signaling her time was drawing near. One early winter evening she failed to return with Bill on their brief walk. The next day she was found in a neighbour's swimming pool. Chasing some animal she had died of heart failure before entering the water. The Arizona veterinarian had warned me about her early demise but this did little to alleviate our great loss. It took weeks for us to realize she would no longer be physically part of our family. Her spirit would walk on with us for the rest of our journeys.

In the second year of planning, just as Bill and I were getting settled in our new surroundings, life took an unexpected turn. In January 1981, much of the programming planning details had been completed. For a brief period, Bill and I proceeded with an extensive evaluation of the planning details to determine whether the space allocations identified in the planning phase met a set of American health-facility planning guidelines, the only mathematical calculations available at the time. I worked for weeks on the calculations, only to discover the guidelines for rehabilitation (i.e. physiotherapy and occupational therapy) were incorrect. I'm not certain the government representative believed my figures until he personally checked the calculations with the American company. Upon reassessment the American company revised their material. The project was now ready to move to the conceptual design and scale model stage, the step prior to presenting the plans to government.

The general reaction to the conceptual and scale model designs was very positive, with the Hon. Gerald Sheehy, Minister of Health saying: "Efficiency and environment have been the overriding priorities in planning this new medical centre. We want people to feel that this is not only an efficient facility for the dispensing of health services, but also an environment designed for their needs. The built-in efficiency of the design and ease of access to everything, combined with attractive public spaces should create a congenial sense of ease for patients, visitors and hospital workers"[3].

In the hiatus of waiting for further government reaction and identifying the next steps of planning, we began to encounter delays in being paid by the head office in Toronto. This was partially due to the slowness in provincial government payment to consulting firms, a drawback with large government contracts. With both of us in the same company, without a substantial financial cushion, it was necessary to reassess our situation. In addition, the hefty workload was creating physical problems, a cancerous throat scare for Bill and blood in my urine, definite signals for a change.

The project was also in limbo. There were lingering planning issues which would take ages to resolve. Relocating obstetrics to the health science center did not sit well with those who preferred it closer to the children's hospital. After numerous discussions on both options, the children's site was selected for obstetrical services. Another issue was cost. The provincial government had estimated construction costs much lower than the planner's best analysis for such a complex, highly technical, teaching facility. Even with the dismissal of obstetrics, there was little reconciliation of costs, which remained an unresolved sticking point right up to the time we left. Realizing the next planning phase would be mainly architectural, the ongoing uncertainties left us with little alternative but to move on. This hectic and fascinating learning phase was over.

Within weeks Bill had a job offer from the Foot Hills Hospital in Calgary, and a second from Veterans Affairs Canada, which had moved its federal government head office from Ottawa to Charlottetown. He eventually accepted the job as Chief Medical Officer for Veterans Affairs Canada. Once this was anchored, I applied for and got a job as the Director of Nursing for the psychiatric hospital in Charlottetown. After twenty-five years I was returning to my birthplace.

The Halifax health science center would not become a reality for another fifteen years and how much of this early planning exercise and detail ever reached fruition is unknown. All planning documents were left with Bill Nycum and Associates in Halifax. It would be nice to think such effort had some value. Whatever planning was incorporated, by 1997 the Queen Elizabeth II health center would dominate Halifax, the largest adult academic site in Atlantic Canada with over fifteen hundred learners. It would consist of ten buildings on two sites, encompassing adult acute care, psychiatric and geriatric services and support networks.

It was strange returning to my birthplace after so many years. While much was familiar, much had changed. Our residence was a one -storey, three-bedroom, wood-framed
house with a large finished basement, on Queen Elizabeth Drive in Charlottetown, just off
Victoria Park. Queen Elizabeth Drive did not exist in my youth. The house had a lovely
large front lawn and fenced-in back yard, where Bill would create another vegetable garden.
Sadly, we were also facing a twenty percent mortgage rate which would strain our finances
for some years.

Returning to my Island culture was quickly brought home to me one day when an
elderly man stopped me on the street to inquire; " I believe you are John O'Neill's grand-
daughter, and Ray Stull's daughter". I nodded. Then moving on he pointedly asked; "Are
you a Liberal or a Conservative?" To which I replied; "I thought voting was a private matter". Annoyed, he went on; " Your grandparents always voted Conservative but, I suppose
you are like your father, who always insisted on voting for the 'right' person, irrespective
of party". Not waiting for a reply, he grunted and walked on. Strong political and religious views were still present, if only with the older members of society. In addition to my
questionable political views I was returning as a Presbyterian having been brought up a
Roman Catholic. This, I expected would be a touchy issue. It was time for me to reset my
bearings.

Bill's federal office, initially in the Charlottetown Post Office building on Queen Street,
would later move to a newly constructed Daniel J. MacDonald Building on Kent Street.
The federal working environment retained much of its Ottawa characteristics, although
the move to Prince Edward Island had ameliorated some of the severe edges. Being on
the periphery of the Ottawa scene, Veterans Affairs tended to attract a different cadre of
professional, those who preferred the intimacy of a smaller community, or sought a short
stop-over on route to higher ambitions, or needed a haven after some surgical reorganization in Ottawa. Thankfully, there were fewer of those who made me nauseated on a first
hand shake. At social engagements, many wives, familiar with the shopping in Montreal,
Toronto and Ottawa complained openly about the limitations of Charlottetown. I spent
my time talking about the treasures available to the discerning shopper to a somewhat
nonresponsive audience. For me, the federal government environment was easier to handle
wrapped in an Island blanket. In the early years, Bill was spared a degree of the usual dysfunctional foibles because of the fine leadership of one Assistant Deputy Minister whom
he worked under. For this we were grateful.

As the Chief Medical Officer, Bill's national responsibilities required considerable
cross-Canada travel and occasional trips into the United States and Europe. Once his
orientation was over, he faced the daunting task of creating a new and inclusive package of services for veterans eventually called the Veterans Independence Program. Once
approved, this program gave Canadian veterans health and social benefits to extend and
enhance their ability to remain in their own homes as they aged. However extensive, this

home care package of services would be less costly than maintaining huge veteran hospitals. Once implemented, it would see the closure of veterans hospitals and/or beds across Canada with the exception of St. Ann's Hospital in Quebec. His tenure as Chief Medical Officer would not only see the introduction of this innovative program for veterans but also the establishment of other services and standards. Bill's original idea was to test the home care program on veterans as a preliminary move for the rest of Canada, however, this latter step failed to materialize.

Gregory was pleased he could put school buses behind him and walk to school. He was back into street clothes, although, I think, he rather liked the consistency of a school uniform. Coming from Dartmouth Academy he easily adapted to the Prince Edward Island school system. In the early days at school he was surprised when a man introduced himself as his cousin. It was John O'Neill who was responsible for audio-visual aides in the Island education department. This was a signal to update Gregory on his Island family history as we were determined to remain settled until he completed the remaining years of his schooling. For me, my job in the psychiatric hospital would present some unique challenges, a few I anticipated.

The longevity of my psychiatric hospital tenure was evident in the first two weeks. After touring the nursing wards, reviewing available records and documents and seeing what had to be done, I came home and drafted my resignation, to which Bill quietly replied; "It's that good, heh?. How long do you think you have?" I replied; "Maybe six months, at most a year. So much change is needed it is bound to upset a lot of people. Yet, I cannot sit and do nothing. I'll write everything down and leave it to the nursing leaders. My task will be to begin the process. After that I'll take a rest". He did not like me facing another stressful job and insisted on the need for a rest as soon as this job was over, to which I agreed.

Knowing psychiatric care usually receives the 'shakings of the bag' when it comes to provincial health care funding, I was not surprised at what I discovered. The psychiatric hospital's impoverished funding affected every area of the nursing department. In addition to an operating funding shortfall, the Hillsborough Hospital (formerly called Falconwood), unlike other psychiatric institutions, had a number of serious problems. Patients of all types were housed together on some wards; the young and old, mentally retarded and psychiatrically challenged, even those with chronic physical illnesses were in the psychiatric facility because there was no long-term accommodation. In addition, there were some outdated and questionable administrative practices, the number and variety of nursing staff were far below the minimum standards used in Nova Scotia in the seventies, in-service and continuing psychiatric education needed immediate resources and the working environment in an aging facility presented conspicuous safety concerns for both residents and staff. The question was where to begin? At the time of my arrival, the Island had been addressing mental illness for over a hundred years.

The first hospital in Prince Edward Island (called the Hospital for the Insane) was erected at Brighton Shore in 1845, which was immediately confiscated to become an isolation hospital for Typhus patients. A year later it returned to its mental health status. By 1880, a new facility for one hundred and forty patients was opened three miles outside the city overlooking the Hillsborough River, on one hundred and twenty acres called Falconwood. The site was expanded at the turn of the century for another one hundred and twenty-five patients listed as the 'crippled, infirm and indigent'. A fire in 1931 almost destroyed the hospital. Three years later renovations were completed. In 1956 an acute care facility for seventy-four patients was added. A year later, the Falconwood Hospital name was replaced to more effectively reflect the change in care; Hillsborough Hospital for acute care and Riverside Hospital for long-term care [4]. When I arrived the hospital was entering another phase with the establishment of an acute care psychiatric unit at the Queen Elizabeth Hospital, and the need for more modern long-term mental health care facilities at the Hillsborough/Riverside Hospital.

Those who choose to care for the mentally ill are very special people which I wrote about in one of the earliest issues of the Nistonia Notebook newsletter, saying; " Human dignity in a long-term psychiatric environment requires the greatest discipline of all health workers as residents often do not have the communication skills or emotional stability of patients/residents in other health facilities. It takes rather unique, caring health professionals to work in this setting to provide a warm home environment, realistically knowing that limitations of facilities and resources place recognizable restrictions on progress. Nevertheless, devoid of all gadgetry, programs and educational degrees, the key ingredient in the health process remains that of one individual having a genuine caring concern for another with every action and word rooted in respect for the person he/she is serving"[5].

Each Nursing Director sets her/his own signature on a health facility. I began my tenure with regular meetings with the nursing managers asking the usual questions such as: What do you currently do? Why? Is there a different, more streamlined way of doing this work? What are the major issues and problems of importance to nursing? Quickly the issues emerged. A few examples follow.

The age of the facility created problems for nurses, who, on occasion, had to physically carry patients up and down stairs for outings because of a lack of elevators. This activity was contributing to long-term back problems, a costly item in any nursing budget. An immediate solution was to relocate certain patients to reduce this occupational hazard, which was done. However, this opened discussions for the need of more reorganization which would take months to complete.

Reduced funding for nursing staff plagued the facility with severe staffing issues, especially on the evening and night shifts. In one instance, two nurses could be dealing with about twenty to thirty unpredictable and potentially violent patients. When one nurse had to leave for meals or supplies, it left the other nurse in a very precarious situation. As an interim safety measure I had emergency alarm buttons installed between two or more nursing stations. One evening a nurse just managed to reach the buzzer when an angry patient punched his fist through the nursing station door.

In my early nursing rounds I noted bruises on certain patients, particularly on the more difficult wards, which could not be attributed to falls. A memo was circulated that patient abuse would not be tolerated and that any suspicious marks on patients would be investigated. Patient abuse is an ongoing issue in all health facilities, but more so in facilities where patients have, for various reasons, less ability to voice their problems (i.e. children, elderly, comatose, retarded or mentally ill). The main problem was one individual, a male orderly, with long-term tenure at the hospital. As I pushed to either stop his bahaviour or get him dismissed, he threatened me with physical violence. I contacted the local police. Eventually, he resigned.

Following this, I realized this more complex ward needed major restructuring. At that point I was blessed with the arrival of a nurse with a religious background, a Roman Catholic nun, looking for a challenge. The physical and mental care improved as staff began to see the possibilities of a different nursing approach. One day this head nurse came to my office asking for hockey sticks to replace shuffle boards, as the residents found them too difficult to use. After much discussion, the hockey sticks were approved on the proviso that they would be immediately removed if any injury occurred to either residents or staff. During my time there were no safety incidents with the hockey sticks.

Conflicts with the medical staff were inevitable. The first problem was the verbal abuse the nurses were experiencing from two psychiatrists, a husband and wife. They both regularly screamed at the nursing staff, belittling them over minor issues. Once the nursing staff were informed that such behaviour was unacceptable and abusive, they were encouraged to submit incident reports every time it occurred. Fortunately, I was working with a medical director, Dr. Mark Triantifillou, who was a fine administrator. As the incident reports arrived I filed them with him, as we both worked to change the behaviour of these two doctors. The reaction of the male psychiatrist was to stand in the hallway in front of my office screaming; "Why don't you damn Robertsons take your standards and get out of here, you are not wanted!" Years before, he had been on a federal committee with Bill regarding medical psychiatric standards. The steady pressure eventually forced them to change, giving the nursing staff strength to resist future incidents. Another issue was a bit more troubling.

Electroconvulsive therapy (ECT) was still being administered to residents. The nurses, likely to speed up the procedure or to placate the anesthetists, began to prepare the anesthetic syringes. To an outsider it might seem acceptable but the registered nurses' license did not sanction such activity as this is a medical procedure. Approaching the head of anesthesia with the problem, I suggested the matter could be easily resolved if he would sign a document taking full responsibility if anything should go wrong. He refused. His defense was to angrily accuse me of not trusting my nurses and, because of my stand, ECT would henceforth be delayed. The nurses were shocked at the response, realizing they could expect little support from the medical staff if anything happened to a patient due to the anesthetic. The practice stopped. While the nurses put out the necessary supplies, the anesthetists had to arrive early to prepare their own syringes. The anesthetists remained peeved at my interference with, what they regarded, was a convenience. I had little time to dwell on the issue as there were other nursing issues needing attention.

Nursing scheduling, manually done by nursing managers, was a time consuming activity which plagued the daily operations of the wards and left supervisors spending endless hours calling in replacement staff. Eventually, I asked Holland College computer department for help knowing that computers were already in use for such scheduling in Arizona in the early seventies. The nurses eventually saw the possibilities of a computerized scheduling system once they provided the technician with all the complexities of staffing a nursing ward. Another item was the lack of uniforms.

By the eighties, psychiatric nursing staff had chosen to replace their white uniforms with jeans and, in many cases, T-shirts. This resulted in little demarcation between residents and staff. The problem was compounded when nursing staff had to bath and care for messy patients, leaving their street clothes badly marked by the end of a shift. Not only was there a concern about infection, there was a question of appropriateness. The objective was how to achieve flexibility in a dress code. Eventually, we introduced colourful cotton tunics, made by the hospital auxiliary, which could be worn over street clothes and dispatched to the laundry at the end of caring for a difficult patient or at the end of a shift. On occasion, orderlies wore a white cotton uniform when escorting residents to the acute care hospital, a practice which the acute care nursing staff appreciated as they could tell who was the patient. A similar view was voiced by some residents, who stated such uniforms helped them identify hospital staff. This remained an ongoing issue as we tested various measures in achieving some resiliency in hospital dress. Yet, these were small items in comparison to the wider concern over the need for a therapeutic environment for the residents.

Facilities for enabling the mentally ill to enjoy the outdoors were limited to verandas off some of the old nursing units which mostly went unused, a fenced in area at the back of the hospital, and a summer camp in another part of the Island. Access to most outdoor activities varied with the resident's diagnosis. The old days of having a farm attached to a mental hospital had ceased, dismissed by those who regarded such activities as demeaning to patients. All too often, health industry practices follow such trends and fads with little effort at preserving some of the benefits of old practices.

One nurse suggested wooden seat-swings, familiar on many Island farms, to enhance the old verandas. I petitioned the maintenance staff to build a couple on a trial basis. After much wrangling, one was set up on the veranda of one of the more challenging nursing units. It was an immediate success. One resident, who had remained silent for years, asked if he could care for the swing, clearing the snow in winter and spending many hours lost in his own memories swinging on the veranda. With this success, others ideas were contemplated.

Trying to create a more therapeutic environment within the beautiful hospital setting, I began discussions with another provincial government department and sought a federal government grant. The goal was to create a 'therapeutic park' for the residents. Miraculously, Ernie Morello, a member of the provincial Public Works Branch, fascinated with the idea, took up the challenge. In consultation with hospital staff he eventually created a plan and model for a new park which was described in the hospital newsletter as: "The design....is quite unique in that it addresses many of the needs of the adult mentally retarded incorporating a scenic view and play activities. The intent is that this would comprise one segment of a multi-faceted park concept all directed towards expanding the therapeutic value of the on-campus environment" [6].

Next, through a federal Katimavik grant, groups of youth volunteers from across Canada arrived consecutively over a period of many months to assist in the creation of the park. During their work period, the majority of youth lived on the hospital site. As the months passed, the therapeutic park slowly emerged under the skillful guidance of Ernie, members of the hospital staff and the Katimavik youth workers. To enhance the park, I negotiated the transfer of an unused federal government greenhouse to the hospital grounds at no cost, to be heated by steam from a nearby power plant. Once established, and under the guidance of the Occupational Therapy staff, the greenhouse flourished providing flowering and decorative plants for all nursing units as well as the hospital grounds. While the therapeutic park was under construction, the staff were asked to consider a different approach to the usual summer vacation for the residents.

Summertime for the mentally ill is a time to get outside after months of being cooped up in an institution. For many, this often meant traveling to a summer camp, an environment not dissimilar to the hospital. In the summer of 1982, a different idea was introduced whereby a mobile therapy unit (i.e. a small bus) traveled around the Maritimes in June and July, tailoring the vacation for residents to give them a variety of experiences. Nursing and recreation staff traveled with each group as they went to Brudenell, Summerside and Cavendish on the Island, Cape Breton, and Halifax in Nova Scotia and Moncton in New Brunswick. For off-Island trips, I contacted former mental health colleagues on the mainland to provide the necessary backup to the traveling groups. Comments from the mental health team showed the value of the idea: "I feel that the advantage of this type of activity away from the hospital is an excellent learning experience. Normalization, for example, when the trip is 'a vacation'....the joy of relaxing, having fun with exercise and lots of fresh air. Most important was the one-to-one resident/staff ratio for individual attention". Another found that "some of the patients found it quite thrilling to be off the Island, although I don't feel they all understood where they were. It showed how they acted away from the hospital and how well they were able to function which was quite surprising". And finally, "after busy days the patients slept well at night with the usual anticipated early risers. Like all vacationing people each group upon their home arrival enjoyably shared their trip hilites with both residents and staff. This venture proved most beneficial and is recommended as an inclusion in next year's planning". [7]

The loss of a farm attached to mental hospitals was an unfortunate decision for there were many residents who thrived in this setting, particularly those familiar with a rural background. One incident shows the need for some flexibility in such decisions. A Mi'mkaq resident, a strongly built, six foot, male, often dropped into the chair just inside my office door to visit. One day he mumbled; "If they ask me to paint another stupid thing in OT (Occupational Therapy) I'll destroy the place!" I looked into his troubled face and asked; "What would you like to do?" He quickly replied, "I'd like to go haying". I told him I would look into it. In time, I found a local farmer familiar with the mentally ill and needing help with haying. No money was exchanged. I weathered the negative comments of those who resented such activity. The arrangement worked amazingly well, the farmer chuckling one afternoon informing me his helper was eating him out of house and home. When haying was over the farmer, wanting to thank the resident, purchased a small television as a gift, which the resident proudly shared with other residents. The fresh air and physical work was most beneficial to this individual, opening questions on the value of similar activities for other residents.

To facilitate communications, I worked with the staff to create a hospital newsletter. It was not the first, as the nursing and adolescent department had their own newsletter for some time. This one, titled 'The Nistonia Notebook', was for all staff. The title was chosen from a Mi'mkaq legend in which Nistonia, the daughter of the chief, was turned into a magic stone. The reason for the title was described in the newsletter as: " In this legend a beautiful magic stone was created that would, if kissed, cure all manner of ailments. This seemed to be a suitable ingredient to our sincere wish as health workers that a magic cure would allow all those in our care to return to the health and happiness that they seek" [8]. The newsletter, run by the staff, became a vehicle for sharing information, describing the current activities, and reporting on special events such as the 'Open House' where the public was invited to come and understand the care provided to residents. The quality of the production was very impressive.

As change was trickling throughout the hospital, and I was negotiating with colleagues at the Nova Scotia Hospital for extended psychiatric nursing training support, the provincial government, in their infallible wisdom, decided to cut the nursing staff budget. Already below standard, this meant we were entering an unsafe and risky staffing situation. I protested such measures to the great annoyance of the hospital administrator, who preferred compliance in line with his former military background. When the nursing managers, on their own, asked for a meeting with the Minister of Health to support my stand, the hospital administrator threatened to fire me for insubordination. The situation was untenable, and I resigned, hoping it would delay or prevent the proposed cuts, which it did. I was immensely proud of the nursing managers who demonstrated their newly acquired professional strength by taking such a stand. They were well able to proceed without me. I left plenty of written instructions and they would tailor the changes to their circumstances. It was time for a rest.

The greatest compliment I received following this brief tenure at the mental hospital was from an old friend of my parents whose son was on one of the more complex care wards. She stopped me in the grocery store one day saying; "Sally, thank you for giving us back our son. With less medication he is now well groomed when we visit and delighted in telling us about his toys and park. This has been a wonderful gift to us when we thought we had lost him forever." I told her that I was just the facilitator on restructuring the care, her son was now in the hands of capable nursing staff who well understood his needs.

For the first time in my adult life I was freed from punching a clock. For the next six months I dove into reading stacks of books. Like a dried sponge seeking water, I sought out every book title that I had not had time to read. Regular trips were made to the University of Prince Edward Island Robertson Library where I found books on history, archeology, biblical archeology, archaeastronomy, astronomy, astrology, health and healing, alternative therapies, and anything else which caught my eye. When the university shelves were exhausted I scoured book catalogues on similar topics and subscribed to Biblical Archeological Review (BAR) savouring every issue. Like a detective, I followed the scandal over the translation of the Dear Sea Scrolls, tracked the activities of the Knight Templars from the Middle East, to Europe, Scotland and North America, and recorded common threads permeating many ancient civilizations. I asked, and received, a copy of the Mormon books and even found a toy maker, a Mormon, in Murray River (near Aunt Di's old home) who had been in the French Foreign Legion and had traveled throughout South America. He was willing to share his many slides and stories on his travels. During this period, when Bill came home from work, he would ask; " Just tell me what country and time period we are in" as by the end of each day I had marvelous tidbits to chat about. I was relishing my freedom and the wondrous world of books as I knew this hiatus would not last.

My grandmother often said that mystery was good for the soul and the ancient records held many mysteries. While we may think our modern health system is the finest ever created, ancient records show mankind has achieved remarkable advances throughout the centuries, and may still hold secrets we have yet to discover. The most sobering point is that even with their accomplishments these earlier civilizations eventually faded, along with their health knowledge and skills presenting us with a timely warning. This wonderful interlude gave me a treasury of reading and time for family and community activities.

Returning to my birthplace after twenty years was an enlightening experience. Shortly after my return, my Aunt Margaret (O'Neill) noted I now talked and thought like 'people from away'. Irrespective of how much I had changed, for the first time in decades it was good to meet people who knew my family, particularly my father and mother in happier times. Needing to enhance my grandmother's tales of Island life, I sought books on Island history and enjoyed the writings of Lucy M. Montgomery. Walking about the city I relished the easy blend of Victorian and modern architecture, a comfortable Island mix. The city had maintained its small community intimacy, a lost treasure in other places. As I walked along familiar paths in Victoria Park I could once again hear my grandmother's familiar voice saying; "Child, come along, stop dawdling, you must keep up". It was good to be back on my Island in mid-life. I would have almost a decade in this enchanting setting, a time for many changes in my life.

In addition to the demands of his federal job, Bill kept active with Board Sailing (or Wind Surfing), gardening, church work and other social engagements. After a brief instruction in Board Sailing in Bedford, Bill acquired the necessary equipment and enjoyed skipping over the waters in the Charlottetown Harbour and off the north shore, from April to the first fall of snow. With the long summer evenings, he would come home after work and relax on the water before dinner.

With more time, he created a lush vegetable garden in the back yard, experimenting with compost methods, companion planting and different types of vegetables giving us a rich variety of fresh produce during the summer. He even experimented with growing spinach and kale in cold frames, under a foot or more of snow in the winter. The plants were thick and nutritious providing rich greenery for our winter diet. In addition, he had numerous flowering plants in the front garden which expanded when we built a solarium in the front of the house. This oasis of greenery, with brightly coloured flowering plants blew away any drabness of winter.

Soon after our move, we joined the St. James Presbyterian Church. Bill became a church elder with a regular list of members to visit. He was also involved in several committees, and we both took a spell at being Sunday School teachers to a group of teenagers. As a new elder he was asked to give a presentation on his missionary work in India. This was the first time I would see his many slides and have more detail of his medical missionary life in India. I was proud to be his wife and so impressed with his commitment, compassion and depth of care for the poor of India, plus Tibetans and lepers. His hand surgery on lepers enabled them to seek employment once their disease had been treated. It reminded me of a comment made regarding the knights of old: "Armed with love, compassion and knowledge, one can cast off the cumbersome and crippling armor of religious dogma or political and economic dialectics to carve out, with supple and determined strokes, more appropriate social structures and a more rewarding human environment, using equally sharp edges of intellect and heart" [9].

Being from Scotland, Bill was welcomed as a Presbyterian, his missionary work adding to his credentials. My former background as a Roman Catholic presented some unease. For a few, it would take years for acceptance. Old, strongly held barriers take time to dissolve. My approach was to walk gently in another Christian house.

In our Sunday School role with a class of teenagers it soon became clear they had a limited grasp, if any, of the Bible and were visibly bored with the prescribed material we were expected to follow. So, after some thought we decided to restructure the program introducing several ideas such as an ethical card game, movies and attending church services in other Christian churches. The ethical card game was a hit with some youth bringing other school mates, non-Presbyterians, to share in the discussions. Much the same occurred with the movies, arranged in the relaxed setting of a church member's home, where the ethical issues of each movie were discussed. In light of the content of modern movies it took some time to select an appropriate one for a Sunday school class. But the idea of attending services in other Christian churches was not welcomed by all parents. A small core of students participated, and, I believe, learned from the experience. The basic principle was to acquaint these young people with the rich diversity and beauty of Christian worship. The reasons why these methods worked varied. Student participation was lively and encouraged as they were pressed to expand their thinking on ethics and religion and their role in society. It was a learning experience for everyone. However, as Gregory moved on to university, our contact with this age group was waning and it was time to step aside for younger parents. It was also time to see our children move along on their own journeys.

Once Gregory realized we were not on the move every two to three years, life settled down for him. As a teenager he was almost as tall as his father, was doing well in his studies, usually in the top five. He even had a spell at being a co-editor of the high school newsletter with Luke Triantifillou, the son of the Hillsborough Hospital psychiatrist. Bill taught him board sailing on the Charlottetown Harbour once he had mastered a swimming course. Gregory's summers were occupied in attending computer camps provided by Holland College, being a camp counselor for the Presbyterian summer camp in Indian River, and even picking blueberries. He was growing into a quiet, independent-minded individual, with an interest in engineering. Graduating from grade twelve he received prizes in biology and music and a scholarship for the University of New Brunswick (UNB). We were surprised over the music prize as Gregory showed little predilection for music. His explanation was typically Gregory, he enjoyed the mathematical challenge of music, a unique perspective from the musical pursuits of most teenagers.

At the time of Marjory's wedding in 1983, Gregory, at fourteen, flew west ahead of us to spend some time with his grandmother Linkert, the timing coinciding with the gathering of Canadian and American Shultz relatives in Pangman, Saskatchewan. This was a great opportunity for him to meet a number of his relatives. They were delighted to see him and to tell him all about his roots and his natural father. The days culminated in a family dinner at the local Lutheran Church hall. At a certain point in the meal Gregory was asked to speak. As a teenager in the company of strangers this was quite a challenge. He thanked his relatives for sharing their thoughts and information about his natural father and family roots, concluding his remarks with; "However, the only father in my life is Bill", the simple statement firmly clarifying his relationship with his relatives. His grandmother told me later how proud they were of his courage and the significance to them of this important point. After this visit, Gregory joined us at the Calgary airport, as we continued our journey west to Marjory's wedding.

For some mothers, two most difficult times in raising children are when they start school and head off to university. The day finally came when Gregory went off to the

University of New Brunswick, enrolling in the engineering program. Since he would have less funds than the girls, in his final year of high school I taught him cooking, sewing and household finances, to the gasps of some local church women. Such skills, I thought, would give him greater independence. We expected the early days at university would be difficult for him but he said little. What we did not anticipate was a call in his first semester with Gregory announcing he had found his 'true love' and wanted to get married. For a socially shy individual this was an amazing statement. I gasped and begged Bill to intercede. He kindly traveled to UNB for a long fatherly chat with Gregory. Bill gently but firmly pointed out the need for him to establish his career before committing himself to a marriage. His wise counsel was accepted. His grandmother Linkert, upon hearing the news, was adamant that the Shultz/Linkert males were not ready for marriage until their late thirties. The episode, thankfully, passed.

At the end of his first year at university, Gregory announced as he arrived home that he needed to chat about his budget. Bill and I, familiar with the ups and downs of the girl's university finances braced ourselves. With a grin Gregory announced he was twenty-five cents off his estimated budget, to which his father laughed and immediately handed him a quarter. He spent most summers at UNB pushing ahead in his studies, arriving home at Christmas often with another university friend. He marched steadily through his studies as he had done in high school. As he approached his fourth year, we were in close touch with Lea, as she was determined to attend her grandson's graduation.

Over the years I had remained in touch with Lea, sending her photographs of Gregory and keeping her updated on his progress. This was the first time Lea and I would meet since the 1969 crisis, and I knew, now in her seventies, she needed to talk about it however difficult it might be for me. The plan was that she would spend some time with us in Charlottetown prior to us all travelling to UNB for Gregory's graduation. In the days prior to leaving for Fredericton, we chatted about the events of 1969, a deep wound for both of us. With no funeral we found closure impossible as most churches were reluctant to consider a memorial service under such circumstances. The unexpected nature of the event and the remaining mystery left scars and an unquenchable need for answers. The wounds were still sensitive after almost twenty years.

Gregory's graduation was a time of immense joy for all of us with toasts and warm comments on his future. He received a scholarship for biomedical engineering at the University of British Columbia, a surprise to Bill and I as we did not see Gregory in this field but realized four years of university can change an individual. I was not surprised that Gregory was heading west but, like many Maritime mothers, lamented he would be living on the opposite coast, a long way from his family. Bill's three daughters, now in their twenties, were also on the move.

Barbara, Bill's oldest daughter, attended Dalhousie University and received her Bachelor of Psychology degree with honours. We traveled to Halifax for her graduation to share in her accomplishment and pleased with her decision to continue working with the mentally retarded, a path she had chosen from high school. Unfortunately, her venture into further studies was fraught with problems. In light of her initial scholastic success, when she asked us to sign a bank loan for her master's studies, we didn't hesitate. Barbara left her studies and eventually moved to the west coast, where she continued in her chosen career.

Marjory, completed her lab technology studies in Ontario and, upon graduation, found a job at a small hospital in Grand Forks, British Columbia. In 1982, she would travel to the Island with a close female friend and David Phillips, who she introduced as her fiancée. The understanding was her father would accept her choice and, in so doing, pay for her wedding as the girl's mother was refusing to provide any financial support. We accepted our responsibility and prepared to travel west the next summer. Thus, in 1983, Gregory, having travelled ahead to visit his grandmother, joined Bill, myself, and Janie in Calgary, as we all headed west to Marjory's wedding at Christina Lake in British Columbia.

It was a strained affair with all family members present, my first and only occasion in seeing the girl's mother. The twins were still actively trying to unite their parents irrespective of their changed marital status. For the first and last time, the wedding photographs would capture the whole family. For Marjory it was all positive. She had found the security she was seeking. This would be her home for the next few decades, where she would bring up three sons; James, Robert and Alex.

Christine, stepped away from her initial venture into university life to work in a variety of restaurants in different parts of Ontario. She had a busy and full life with a number of boy friends, one relationship in the eighties turning abusive. We invited her to stay with us on the Island after a distress call from Ontario. At the airport, we greeted a rather wounded soul, the symptoms were troubling but I said nothing. It would take some time for her to heal and regain her self confidence. In time, she found work in Charlottetown, armed with a sheet of paper containing my family names as employers wanted to know her Island connections. She came home with three job possibilities, eventually taking part-time work at two restaurants, advancing in one to a managerial level. After months with us, she returned to Ottawa. Later she would obtain her Bachelor of Business degree and, went on to become a successful Certified Financial Planner. Her clairvoyance, far superior to mine, provided fascinating discussions during her stay. Such difficulties would give Christine greater maturity. Her brief time with us on the Island would create a stronger bond. As the children were forging their own careers and lives, coming and going, my relationship with Janie Limond blossomed, giving me the wise council of an older woman.

Each summer, usually in July, Janie arrived from Ayr, Scotland, for a month's visit. Her arrival gave us an excuse to become Island tourists, an annual dose of taking in the delights of the warm summer sunshine, rich red soil, white sandy beaches, and welcoming lush countryside. With each summer's outing I renewed my acquaintance with my beloved Island. As we travelled I included the many tales and stories from my grandmother or other family members, inserting humor and life to dry historical information.

Janie was a tall, regal lady. Faye, the middle sibling, had years of poor health, and, as I understood, worked as a bookkeeper in an Ayr business during her adult years. She died a few years prior to Janie's visit with us in Ottawa in 1976. Tom, her brother, the youngest sibling, became the chief government administrator for Ayr county. He died in 1970. None of them married. Janie's ancestors had resided in the Ayr district of Scotland for generations, her father owning a large ironmonger store. Her mother's family, McGill, had connections to the founders of McGill University in Montreal. Bill had been friends of the Limonds during his brief time in Ayr following his years in India. Later, Janie would be his main contact when his mother lived in Ayr.

I met Janie when she was in her sixties, the thirty years difference in our ages seemed to have little significance, we became instant 'kindred spirits' as Lucy Maud Montgomery would say. Perhaps her visit reminded me of my grandmother and a familiar, gentler Victorian era. She brought a wealth of old-fashion morality and common sense which I deeply appreciated as we chatted over the complexities of life in the eighties. We prided ourselves in finding numerous places for tea. Over many cups of tea we enjoyed lengthy female chats, a true luxury for me. Somewhere in our travels we found a lady who read tea leaves, just like my grandmother. On another occasion, taking a short cut, we stepped onto Kent Street up against the black limousine containing Prince Andrew and Sarah Ferguson, the motorcade obviously taking a different route than the one outlined in the morning Guardian. Startled, Janie yelled out; "It's Fergie!" when she recognized the occupants, a closeness to royalty she had not experienced in Britain. With that the limo sped off. That day we had more to chat about. We also relished the quality found in Island crafts, purchasing handmade capes and coats which we wore for years. Some days we stayed at home, enjoying lunch under the small maple tree in our back yard. Janie loved the small town flavour of Charlottetown especially the hardware stores, a reminder of her youth. While we enjoyed this summertime venue, Janie's life did have other dimensions.

For generations of Ayr children Janie had been their music teacher, the school established in her family home. Some of her pupils went on to renowned careers. In addition, Janie was a long time soprano in the Ayr-Choral Union which put on many fine oratorio performances, and a life-long member in the Presbyterian church choir. For these reasons we sought out and attended a number of theatrical offerings each summer, leaving us with lingering memories and many laughs. While we waited for a concert, we often enjoyed whatever tourist options the area provided. Two occasions stand out. One day we were in a Mi'mkaq community store where I was looking for doeskin boots. It was a quiet mid-week day with just the three of us in the store. While paying for the boots the man asked me who I was. I was pleased to find out he remembered my father with some fondness. In completing the transaction he abruptly left the store and returned with a chief's headdress or at least that is what it looked like to me. The beautiful white feathers flowed to the floor.

He wanted Bill to try it on and I took photographs. This was an unexpected and kindly gesture which I attributed to his respect for my father but nothing was actually said. At another time we had a grand visit to the new Souris Hospital, a facility which we had a hand in designing. More on this later.

As Janie's vacation drew to a close, we made our annual pilgrimage to the Anne of Green Gables musical at Confederation Centre. As the years passed we became experts in knowing every line and song, yet, we never seemed to tire of the show. With some sadness I bad farewell to Janie as she departed for Scotland. Yet, however much I enjoyed her visit, it presented some scheduling problems.

To accommodate her visit once I started consulting work, I had to rise at four in the morning to put in about four hours of work before my social activities began. About three in the afternoon I took a brief nap which recharged my batteries for the rest of the day. This schedule, workable for a month, enabled me to meet my contract obligations and the needs of my very special guest.

After a six month sabbatical of reading it was time to get back to work. This time I chose an independent path, establishing a consulting business, Robertson Associates, in partnership with Bill. I finally found my niche. Now, I was able to choose projects which fit my interest and time. In the early eighties, I purchased my first computer. It was a clunky IBM compatible computer and a dot printer, the models being similar to the one used by Island farmers as computer service options were slim. I embarked on an enormous learning curve, the handbook providing endless frustrations as I struggled to use the right codes in writing any document. To force me to use the equipment, I volunteered to publish a monthly newsletter/magazine for St. James Presbyterian Church, titled 'The Shell'. It consisted of ten to fifteen pages, making it more a magazine than a newsletter. This volunteer activity, lasting nearly eight years, spawned other newsletters.

Working from home gave me the best of two worlds, I was available as Gregory completed his high school education and I could set my own work schedule. The unusual nature of this working arrangement, however, especially for a woman, presented some problems. The local community felt I had nothing to do and continued to make requests for me to volunteer for fund-raising projects or to bake for church events. While baking was feasible, other time-demanding requests had to be curtailed. During these years from 1983 to 1992, my independent status as a nurse puzzled the Prince Edward Island Nurses Association when it came time for my annual license renewal. To them I was an anomaly, not a 'real nurse'. Yet, somehow, I squeaked through the process with enough health projects. As a backup, I also retained my registered nurse's license from Nova Scotia and Arizona.

Because of my Island location it was prudent to diversify my contracts into health and general projects, covering the Maritime provinces, as the Island was a very small market. The type of health contracts covered such areas as facility design, nursing administration and management education. In addition, during this time I was appointed as the female and nursing representative on the Prince Edward Island Occupational Health and Safety Council, created to establish the first Act for the province. Health and safety issues in many working environments were escalating due to the speed of social change and the introduction of new technologies, chemicals and other factors. Women were especially vulnerable facing increased stress due to family and work responsibilities. In addition to health projects, I also diversified into operational reviews, public relations, publications and a sports study. The following is a brief sample of a few projects.

In renewing my contact with Bill Nycum and Associates in Halifax, I returned to planning the nursing components for a number of hospital renovations in Nova Scotia. These were communities in which health services were shifting from acute hospital care to extended care. Nursing planning information was repackaged for extended care facilities in Amherst, Springhill, and Digby. An update was also required of the obstetrical nursing service information created in the early eighties, when the maternity hospital was relocated near the children's hospital. However, the best facility design contract for me was for a new hospital facility for Souris, Prince Edward Island, where the latest standards and design features for nursing would be used. Unlike other planning exercises, the Souris Hospital Board did not make major cuts to the design so the facility would be one in which the bedrooms and bathrooms would actually be built to standard. We were delighted to be part of the opening ceremonies for this new facility on January 14, 1989 as members of the Nycum Associates team (my name never appearing on any documents or plaques).

That summer when Janie arrived, we got permission to tour the facility. It was such a pleasure to walk through what would be classified as a 'one-stop' health facility, uniquely designed for a small rural community in Kings County, a community founded in 1727 as an Acadian fishing centre. The $6 million dollar, white, wooden structure was nestled into a rolling hill overlooking the sea. It contained acute care and extended care beds along with community health service offices. The inclusion of doctors offices near the hospital was discussed as a future option, a means of bringing all health services onto one campus. We enjoyed the bright, large, patient rooms and well-designed, spacious bathrooms, clear visual lines from the nursing station to emergency, pediatric and other key areas, plus the sunny, open and welcoming cafeteria for family members as they visited and/or waited for tests or appointments. This was a facility designed with patients and nurses in mind. The facility would eventually be recognized by health leaders in Canada for its original design and service options for rural and remote communities. It was a fine tribute to the effort of community leaders, architects and builders after years of planning. But health facility planning and design were not my only health contracts.

Conflicts between health workers are common, and there were two mediation projects which required delicate negotiations. One was in Nova Scotia, a battle between the medical staff and the Director of Nursing. In this case Bill's administrative skills were essential in dealing with the medical staff. Another was on Prince Edward Island, a conflict between registered nurses and nursing assistants when a new Director of Nursing decided to eliminate the role of nursing assistants in the hospital, a decision with major ramifications for a small community where jobs were scarce. Both issues were eventually resolved with all parties reasonably satisfied with the outcome. Paramount to such negotiations was to ensure the parties could continue working together after the disagreement. In such conflicts it is beneficial to use outside consultants, individuals familiar with hospital operations, to listen to the parties and help the Board reach a viable solution. Contracts easily shifted from administration to education, with management education a topic of ongoing interest.

Management education was addressed in a number of ways. During these years I became a satellite professor in teaching an introductory 'Nursing Management' course for the Post-RN Nursing Degree program out of the University of New Brunswick. The classes were taught on the University of Prince Edward Island campus. This was the only management material in the Bachelor of Nursing degree curriculum, which, I personally felt, was insufficient. At the time the Island did not have its own nursing degree program. In my approach to management education, I revamped my teaching notes from child psychology to management. In child psychology I stressed love and truth. In management, I stressed respect and truth. In both instances when either principle was damaged relationships deteriorated. Such views seemed idealistic in an environment which held that economics had greater priority than ideas. I was well aware, in an industry with tight budgets, economics could not be ignored, it just needed to be placed in the right priority. My views on leadership were close to those presented by Parker J. Palmer in his pamphlet on 'Leading From Within' which states: "A leader is a person who has an unusual degree of power to create the conditions under which other people must live and move and have their being – conditions that can either be as illuminating as heaven or as shadowy as hell. A leader is a person who must take special responsibility for what's going on inside him or her self, inside his or her consciousness, lest the act of leadership create more harm than good." A key point presented by Palmer, and important in today's health industry, is the tendency to deprive both patients and employees of their identity. In our health facilities, each individual's life story needs be submerged in order to accommodate the organization's objectives. Palmer surmises that this type of culture comes from a profound insecurity on the part of people in power, those we identify as the leaders. Such thoughts as these are rarely discussed in most leadership training programs which continue to promote an organizational culture of power and control. On the economic side, I kept pressing nursing leaders to 'seize the moment' to take control of their budgets and to promote innovation. Nurses needed more skills in arguing their needs within a fiscally restricted working environment, as other groups were becoming far more aggressive in their demands. This was not a receptive idea to many nurses who preferred to focus on care, a perfectly understandable position but not necessarily helpful in gaining more funding.

Similar teaching opportunities occurred as a guest lecturer in the Health Administration program at Dalhousie University in Halifax, and in discussing the establishment of a management training program for long-term care facilities. Reversing the role, I was also a mentor to senior health leaders on the Island who were in the Canadian Hospital Association correspondence course. In the latter case, I was seeing the learning process from a different perspective than in my Ottawa days, and enjoyed the change. While health contracts occupied considerable time, general contracts also emerged as the years passed.

My first contract arranged entirely over the telephone was with a home care corporation in Toronto, the director learning of me through old colleagues. She needed a portable, procedure manual for home care registered nurses. The idea was to design a manual that could easily slip into the nurses' home care bags. At the time, all reference materials resided in large binders at a central office, totally ineffectual for nurses facing increased complexity in the nursing procedures in homes. The challenge of the project registered when two large brown boxes arrived filled with documents on numerous nursing procedures. My daunting task was to somehow restructure this information into a small, portable manual. A nursing committee located in Toronto was created as my contact group. These were home care experts and, they stated, as we began the project, that they would welcome innovation, but their degree of innovation tolerance was unclear. In the end, I met the company's objective by producing a compact, 5 x 8, three-ring binder manual, consisting of twenty, easy reference tabs. Deleting all basic nursing procedures (i.e. bed baths, compasses etc), I concentrated on the critical nursing procedures. These critical procedures were priorized (i.e. the most critical to the front) with each procedure confined to two to four pages. On the first page of each procedure was a 'nursing alert' segment containing critical points which the nurse needed to know. The relationship with the company Director and Nursing Committee flowed reasonably well considering the complexities of creating such a publication with no face-to-face contact. Other than some fine tuning to address the differences in nursing terminology between Ontario and the Maritimes there were few major revisions. My surgical restructuring of the nursing procedure material was well received, and a pleasant surprise. In time, I knew the redesigned material could be easily adapted to computers for future nurses.

This was not my first publication, I had previous experience with the Nursing Unit Administration textbooks. Yet this, plus my experience in publishing a church newsletter/magazine, 'The Shell' eventually led to a number of other writing endeavours. During this decade, newsletters were provided for the PEI Gerontology Association, The PEI Writer's Association, the United Way of PEI, the UPEI Chaplaincy Centre and for university chaplains across Canada. As secretary to the UPEI Chaplaincy Centre I had an occasion to meet a representative from the United Church of Canada visiting from Toronto. He asked if I would be willing to produce a cross-Canada chaplaincy newsletter, a communication tool for chaplains of different Christian denominations in a number of universities. Thus, began a four year arrangement in which the news for chaplains was collated at McGill University, sent on to me where I produced the newsletter, sending the 'master' copy back to McGill for printing and distribution. For this activity I was paid through the United Church office in Toronto. This unique arrangement became a point of humorous discussion at the post office as I made my quarterly mailings. With such increased writing demands I decided one summer to register for a writer's workshop at Dalvay By- the-Sea

Hotel. There I not only received valuable and blunt criticism of my writing but also some essential information in running a small business.

Such general contracts in the latter part of the eighties also found me working with Angus (called 'Gus') MacFarlane, a man in his sixties who had semi-retired from Ottawa to Prince Edward Island. Gus was a former Member of Parliament for the Hamilton region serving in Pierre Elliot Trudeau's government as Whip of the Liberal party. Prior to his parliamentary experience, Gus had been a university coach promoting basketball, football and hockey and was key to the establishment of a Ministry of State for Fitness and Amateur Sport (later called Sports Canada). In World War II he had been a fighter pilot. His interests were many including a number of charitable organizations.

Gus was an extravert, a flamboyant speaker with a musical bent, a motivator of people, an individual with a keen sense of fair play and one who possessed a vast network of contacts. His mother had been an opera singer, a talent inherited by her son. He possessed a great joy in singing and was comfortable in any media. When he first asked me to join him to do public relations for a charitable fund-raising effort, I agreed on the proviso that we never talk about politics. While he agreed, it was too tantalizing for him not to try, at least once, to get my views on some aspect of politics. He chose the Canadian Senate, a hot topic at the time. It would be the only time we shared any such views. I decided to jot down some thoughts. My views were not positive.

I felt the Senate, however important it might have been in past centuries, was an outdated, stodgy body, a dumping ground for party favourites who had little accountability to the people yet were guaranteed a lifetime income, something the majority of citizens could never imagine. The public saw few visible members of this august body. In the past decades with the Liberal party monopolizing federal politics, political appointments to the Senate had practically created a duplicate chamber of government, a rubber-stamp institution which was a waste of tax-payer money. In addition, the political chambers had too many men and lawyers leaving more and more citizens with little voice or interest in an institutions that did not speak for them. Arguing whether Senators should be appointed or elected seemed pointless when there was little intent of changing the general malaise or accountability of the chamber. My humble suggestion included; if this chamber was to continue the numbers representing each political party should be controlled, anyone assuming the role should be required to take advanced education on parliamentary organization and management principles, there should be a tenure limit, and the members should be appointed/elected by the provinces and territories not a federal party. As an off-handed statement I proposed the Senate should be replaced in whole or part by a Council of Grandmothers, as a means of bringing some horse-sense to the Ottawa environment. I assured Gus that he could be comforted in knowing my views were in the minority. After this whenever Gus felt inclined to discuss politics I left him to those who relished the topic. My inner sense told me the political structure of Canada, so sacred to many, would remain unchanged and continue to lack the resiliency needed to survive the storms ahead. Fortunately, Gus and I had plenty of work to keep us busy.

The public relations roles introduced me to a variety of new skills. With the help of a local photographer I learned how to use a rather large, complex camera of Gus's, racing to get photos into the local newspaper in time for the next press run. Dealing with the media (i.e. newspapers, radio and TV), people comfortable with words, was a daunting task for a dyslectic. Press releases became easy after some initial fumbles. Gus and I even produced a series of eighteen TV shows, me writing the scripts and Gus interviewing people from various service organizations. Fund-raising events brought me into contact with many people through committees and public relation events. It was a fascinating and expanding role for me.

Gus and I worked together for almost six years, and during the later years he obtained a federal grant for a study on the feasibility of a major, international, bicycle event for June on the north shore of the Island. Gus, through his contacts in Sports Canada, realized the international community was looking to expand the bicycle racing sites in North America and thought the Island would be a prime location. My task was to review stacks of bicycle racing material, the latest administrative details and standards, attend meetings and create the reports. The race area was planned for the Dalvay By-The-Sea Hotel area, covering the beaches of Dalvay, Brackley and Stanhope. Our task was to interview numbers of local groups on establishing such a race and in the recruiting of a large number of volunteers needed for the event. We found fantastic support for the idea. While cycling had lost some of its earlier status it was still important. Historic records showed it had been a very popular activity at the turn of the century. Race logistics were tested on a blustery, rainy day in June using thirty to forty professional bike riders from across the region who were required to cover nine 14.5 kilometer laps, a distance of 130.5 kilometers in the beaches area. The race was a success. This trial would eventually lead to the "*Tour de PEI*", a world class ladies cycling event. This project would highlight my time with Gus.

Whenever Gus was out-of-town, I would drop in to his apartment to handle his mail and telephone calls relaying information to different people across Canada. One evening as Bill and I were returning home, I decided to stop at his apartment to check his mail. As I reached the front door I realized something was wrong as the music was blaring and his lights were on. He was supposed to have left the Island the evening before. I opened the door with my key to find Gus lying on the living room floor. I knew when I checked for a pulse that he was dead. I raced to get Bill who in turn contacted the necessary authorities. Gus was in his late sixties.

On a cold, overcast March day I attended his funeral at the Presbyterian Church in the role of honorary pallbearer. The church was crowded with local and distant friends and acquaintances from the community, charitable organizations, sports and political arenas. A eulogy to Gus by Paul H. Schurman in the Canadian Paraplegic Association Spring newsletter, the '*Caliper*', best summarized his life: "The game or contest of life is not decided in how long, but in how well it is played. Gus played it intensely – enthusiastically – with optimism – cheerfulness – good sportsmanship – courage and faith. For the life he lived – the character he built – the influences for good that he set in motion – speak now to every heart that knew him ".

Following Gus's funeral I spent days with his sister from London, England and his sister-in-law from Montreal sorting through his belongings. I was pleasantly surprised to find his sister had the same outgoing personality. She had been on the London stage, and travelled throughout Britain and Canada entertaining the troops during the last war. As a memento of her brother, I was pleased to give her a copy of one of our TV shows. Following this sad occasion, it was good to have some small projects.

For a brief spell I was into reorganizing general business organizations, one a provincial charitable office and the other at the Presbyterian church. The provincial charitable office in Charlottetown involved the introduction of computers, a new avenue for me. In this instance I was aided by Gregory and a fellow university student, both in the engineering program with expertise in computers. At the end of the project, I asked Gregory and his friend what they thought of working with me. After a brief glance between them, and with a huge grin, Gregory said; "Awesome, Mom, pure awesome" and the two went out the door laughing, leaving me to translate the word 'awesome'.

Another office reorganization was at St. James' Presbyterian Church. This I volunteered to do thinking it would be similar to other office projects. After a brief review, I again saw computer technology as the answer to membership lists, finances and other routine office procedures. To achieve this a Computer Committee was created with myself as chair along with six other members, some with church tenure and others with computer experience. As we gathered for our first meeting, Dr. John Cameron, our Minister, somewhat hesitantly stated he had a question from the Elders that needed to be addressed. The question was "whether 'she' was leading the committee members astray by getting the church into computers?" Being the only female in the group it was easy to know who 'she' was. Silence fell as the members tried gallantly to give an acceptable reply. Then, a senior member of the group, with a quiet chuckle, stated; "Well, John, I hadn't thought of it before but if I was ever looking for someone to lead me astray I think Sally would be a good choice" This immediately invoked the laughter of the entire group. The meeting proceeded in discussing the viability of computer use and the obvious uneasiness within the congregation over such technology. In the end I proposed a different strategy. We would dissolve the committee and set up several working groups, each with a single mandate. So began the quiet, slow, revolution within the church. The working group members consulted over Sunday coffee, or the telephone and assisted each other when needed. Within a few years the membership, finances, and the main office gradually adopted computers, and once established no one looked back. 'She' did not lead them astray because she had an excellent team.

By the early nineties, Gus's death heralded the closing of a number of doors. My grandmother's prophesy of events occurring in threes was about to repeat itself. Within a short span of years my Aunt Di, and my father and mother would pass away, the older generation stepping aside as the next stepped forward.

Over the years I kept in touch with the nurses at the Pugwash nursing home where my aunt resided. Her high blood pressure eventually resulted in several mild strokes, and finally her death. Her funeral wishes were clearly stated, she wanted to be buried on the Island next to her husband, Neil, and to have a Roman Catholic priest in attendance. It was the latter request which presented some problems.

With the senior members of the family incapacitated, her funeral arrangements were left to my brother David and myself. Since I lived on the Island, it fell to me to make the necessary funeral arrangements while David, working from Nova Scotia, arranged for her body to be transported to the Island funeral home. Her clergy request, which seemed straightforward, would be difficult to achieve.

Since my aunt had been a Presbyterian her entire married life, a funeral home was selected that catered to Protestant funerals. When I first contacted the young Roman Catholic priest I tried to sound rather vague about my aunt's religious history, insisting it was her dying wish to have a priest at her funeral. I understood his hesitation as he gently said he would get back to me with a decision. Aware the request might be impossible to meet, I contacted Dr. Cameron, explaining my dilemma. I'm sure there was some discussion behind the scenes between the two clergy for within days I was informed of an acceptable compromise. Both clergy would be present at the funeral home chapel service, an arrangement which seemed to please all parties as there were still members of the Walker family living in the community.

As my aunt lived away from the Island for many years broken by brief summer residencies, and in a nursing home in Nova Scotia for over ten years, David and I expected few at her wake. Yet, there was a surprising number of local people who turned up, some because of their connections with the O'Neill family. The most fascinating individual, for me, was a spry, rather outspoken elderly lady who pigeon-holed me with an abrupt question; "You certainly don't look very Irish?" She had hit a familiar note. Over the years I learned that I was not Irish enough for the Irish, German enough for the German or French enough for the French. I comforted myself in thinking that I belonged to a new category, the Rainbow People, which someday may have their own recognition. Smiling I turned to face her rather stern gaze and said; "I suppose not. If you are looking for purer members of the Irish clan then perhaps you would like to speak to my two cousins", as I pointed to John and Phillip O'Neill standing across the room.

She quickly glanced in their direction and returned to me saying; " I guess you'll do! What relation are you to Helen O'Neill?" When this information was provided and accepted, she launched into telling me of her connection with my aunt, opening a window into the first World War years on the Island.

She and my aunt had been close school friends for years at St. Joseph's Convent. She then pinpointed a specific day in their lives, their graduation. On a sunny, warm June day, both young women, in their youthful exuberance joined other girls and boys to celebrate their newfound freedom with a picnic at Rocky Point. She described with some detail the ferry ride, walking barefoot in the surf (quite risky for the time), a picnic and singing favourite songs. It had been a joyous event, forever etched on this lady's memory. That day she gave me a rather special gift of seeing my aunt as a young woman with jet-black hair and beautiful pale complexion, happily savouring the delights of youth. Sometimes funerals are a time of such revelations.

The quiet chapel service for my aunt went well, and was further enhanced when both clergy went to the Protestant graveyard for a closing service. I thought, somewhat prematurely, that enlightenment between religious groups had finally arrived. I was mistaken.

The following week as I scurried about the town on a number of errands an elderly lady in great distress confronted me; " Well, you came home long enough to destroy all our traditions".

Startled by her remarks, and naively thinking she had mistaken me for someone else I asked; " I'm sorry, are you talking to me?"

Infuriated, she continued; "It's about your aunt's funeral. You have no respect for Island traditions which your elders held dearly. Having both a Roman Catholic Priest and Protestant Minister at a service in a Protestant funeral home is disgraceful". Trying to ameliorate the situation by saying this was my aunt's dying wish had little effect. Having voiced her frustrations over my social blunder, she angrily stomped off. While future generations may face different problems, in the late eighties remaining echoes of old religious walls still existed especially when it came to funerals. While I respected tradition, times were changing. The second death was far more difficult.

My father's trips to the Island lessened as his eyesight deteriorated due to cataracts. Whenever I asked about his old Island friends his usually response was that they were likely all dead as he had lost contact over the years. By father was now in his seventies.

One day, having run into Johnny Squarebriggs Sr., an old acquaintance of Papa's who lived near the Veterans Affairs building on Kent Street, Bill suggested that it might be a good time to have an open house for him inviting whatever old friends still existed on the Island. Through Johnny, we eventually contacted a small group of old timers to help plan the occasion. Close to the actual date, Island sports writers announced the open house in their regular newspaper columns.

It was a lovely August day as we prepared for an unknown number of guests. Papa started the day sitting regally in our front solarium, the many plants providing a lush green and colourful setting for the occasion. In no time the doors opened and the day was filled with people greeting each other after many years of separation. As the humidity rose the guests moved to the coolness of the backyard. It was Papa's day so Bill and I melted into the background making sure there were plenty of seats and refreshments for everyone. About forty people attended the open house, some popping in for a brief reminiscence while others stayed for some time. A core of seventeen senior men stayed longer, old friends who had once shared special times together, their voices rising with bouts of laughter as they talked about the thrills and sorrows of bygone sporting events or other activities. I was amazed how quickly they could recall old sport scores and minute details of some athletic glory of the thirties and forties. John McNeill, Sports Columnist with the Summerside Journal Pioneer, welcomed Papa back to the Island noting his prior induction into the PEI Softball Hall of Fame, his many hockey achievements and presenting him with a small plaque in honour of the occasion. A younger sports writer, who dropped in for a short spell remarked " Imagine having so many Island sport greats in one place. I thought most of these guys were dead". This special group of elders, some who had not been together in years, spent the afternoon relishing the achievements of their youth and the companionship of old friends. A magical touch seemed to fill the air. The day was captured by Phillip O'Neill, my cousin, who took photographs and presented Papa with a small album to take home to Truro. The event was fortuitous, for life was about to take a different turn.

Within weeks of the open house, David called to tell me Papa had been diagnosed with lung cancer. His days of smoking had finally caught up to him. Bill and I drove to Halifax to see him and chat with the health team. Papa, as with so many events in his life, took the diagnosis stoically. Chemotherapy treatments were scheduled immediately. As his treatments progressed and problems emerged David/Lyle and I agreed to take turns staying with him as he was now alone, mother had been in a nursing home for years.

For the first time in my life I would be nursing my own father. As the winter settled in, I travelled to Nova Scotia to my parents small, two-story, rental home on the main street of Truro. He was up and about but slightly unsteady on his feet. One morning while helping him with his morning wash and shave he turned and bluntly asked; "Sally is this what you did for a living? Did I actually spend good money for you to do this?" I could see the puzzled look on his face and replied; "Yes, Papa, and I truly loved caring for people, it is what I liked the best of being a nurse. Next best would be teaching and lastly solving problems to make the health system work better. As you know, I chose jobs that best fit my family and my health. When lifting and moving patients became too difficult I shifted to teaching and the rest is history. The worst times were in the political arenas where I was never at home. I can assure you your money was well spent. I dearly thank you for opening the door to this wonderful world for me in helping me get to the Mount". "Good" was his only reply as we moved to another topic.

As the days drifted on we talked about many things, family and life in general. One afternoon, we were watching on TV a circus rider clinging to the side of a horse as he circumnavigated one of the main Circus-tent rings, Papa remarked; "When I was a boy, my grandmother taught me to do that". Surprised and hoping I might learn more of my ancestors, I inquired "Which Grandmother, Papa? Was she a circus performer ?" But like the past, the window was closed as quickly as it had been opened. It had always difficult to get Papa to talk about his family. Understandably, other topics had taken precedence with his illness.

Being a non-practicing Anglican and rarely attending church, I understood when Papa announced he would become a Catholic. The day came when the Roman Catholic Priest,

Father O'Neill (no family tie), arrived to baptize Papa with me as the sole witness. When the priest left, Papa turned to me to announce; " Well, now Sally, I'm Catholic and your Protestant". I replied with the following story; "Papa, Nanny once told me that when we die it will be our hearts that will be judged. If we are considered worthy to remain in heaven, we will be directed to a series of doors. If Catholic it will be the Catholic door, if Presbyterian the Presbyterian door, if Jewish the Jewish door, if Muslim the Muslim door etc.. There will be doors for everyone. However, when we open the door, we will discover just one large room. For it is only humans who create these institutional labels not God. A universal God has far more important things to think about than what church, synagogue or temple we attend. Papa, you and I have never been stuck on labels ". With that I proceeded to the kitchen to make supper and heard my father chuckle, saying; "Yes, and your grandmother was a very wise lady".

Christmas came and went as Papa's illness shadowed our thoughts. In January I returned for another round of duty praying he would not develop the usual complications of such an illness. If his cancer progressed to his brain it would mean sending him to a long-term care facility, something my father did not want. But this did not happen. Towards the middle of February, David called to say Papa had died suddenly while in hospital. Even knowing the outcome, I was heartbroken yet relieved that he would not have to face any deterioration of his dignity. It was a very sad funeral for all of us who loved him dearly. Island sports writers kindly eulogized his passing,

My father was a man of honour, perhaps a passing breed, who truly believed 'his word was his bond'. He accepted all people, irrespective of their race, religion or colour. He was notorious for voting for the best person for the job contrary to the party politics of his day. He strode for high standards in his life, in transportation and sports and always sought the best for his family. His democratic nature allowed me the opportunity to go to university and to learn many things. We had much in common, a view noted by his old friend Johnny Squarebriggs Sr who said; "I had no idea Ray had a daughter, let alone one that was so much like him". For me, a special light had flickered out but I would be left with cherished memories including his deep rich laugh drifting over the summer breeze. Mother's final years would be quite different.

By the time I returned to the Maritimes mother's mental health had deteriorated and she was eventually admitted to the Nova Scotia Hospital. I immediately contacted old colleagues to discuss her care. One nurse who had been on the Nova Scotia Hospital faculty with me in the sixties, now a Director, called saying; " Sally, I must say you and your mother are very different people, she was not what I had expected. She must be the best dressed depressed patient I think we have ever had. I'm calling to say that we will take very good care of her and that her psychiatrist will be getting in touch with you in the next few days".

A long series of telephone calls then transpired with my mother's psychiatrist, a female doctor from the United Kingdom. By the time she called I knew she had been well informed of my time at the hospital and my understanding of mental illness. She asked the usual questions about my family and my mother's depression history from my perspective. We agreed my mother's illness was less a depression than what in the past had been classified as *Irish Melancholia* whereby the individual stepped back from reality while appearing normal. For this reason it was agreed she did not need Electric Shock Therapy. Her treatment plan would consist of medications and group therapy. As the years passed I received a steady update of her condition through my family and colleagues as she underwent the usual pattern of inpatient care and spells at home. As her psychiatrist got to know her she called to say; "Whatever is causing your mother's depression it has something to do with you". This was a surprise as I again reiterated my childhood contact with my mother and my instinctive belief she was not too happy in having a daughter. Yet, I also recalled there was some friction between my mother and grandmother about me which neither elaborated upon. The psychiatrist was determined it was this mystery that she would get my mother to talk about. I had my misgivings. My mother was more than capable of resisting any outside pressure to reveal something she had held secret for many years. My basic hope was that her therapy would give her some peace and enable her to function in society. But such hope was futile as her physical health suddenly changed.

Unknown to me, her psychiatrist had to return to Britain due to a family illness. Mother's replacement psychiatrist, with apparent little discussion with the family, prescribed Electric Shock Therapy. It not only terrified my mother but exacerbated an undiagnosed aneurism at the base of her neck. A call from my brother David informed me that mother had been rushed to the Victoria General Hospital for emergency surgery. The surgical outcome left her with what appeared to be the after effects of a major stroke. Unable to care for herself, she was transferred to a nursing home blocks from the hospital.

After numerous telephone calls to old colleagues, I was relieved to discover that two former nursing colleagues and two students from my Halifax Infirmary days were nursing at this facility. For the next fifteen years my mother would receive the finest care possible and would never return to Truro. All psychiatric medication ceased as she slipped into a long-term geriatric care regime. Another communication network was set up with these caregivers. The nursing home Administrator even dropped in to visit me when she traveled to the Island. Once in caring for Papa he asked me; " Sally, how much are you paying for the great care your mother is receiving?" I replied; "Papa, I do contact the home to know what mother needs but there are no financial transactions. We are blessed in having superb nurses, special human beings who truly care for their residents. These are the people in the health system who are rarely heralded and they certainly never receive the salary they deserve. My only regret is that mother is in Halifax which necessitates a long car trip for you."

My last contact with my mother was when I went to see Papa at the Victoria General Hospital at the time of his cancer diagnosis. Leaving the hospital I decided to duck into the nursing home to see her while Bill went on to a nearby friend's place where I would join him later. As I stepped into her private room and sat on the bed mother, immediately recognized me saying; "Sally, what are you doing here so late at night?" I explained about father's illness, but she was no longer interested. This was her home and the nurses her family, a pattern typical of many long-term residents. She looked well under the circumstances. She was able to communicate with some hesitancy and describe the routines of her life. As we chatted I realized it was like talking to a patient I had known for years. There was little emotion between us. When she grew tired, I slipped away to talk to the nursing staff.

As I walked the snowy streets to meet Bill I thought of my mother. Through old time Islanders I had learned that she had been a vivacious, flapper of the twenties full of life and the center of many social gathering. It was good to know there were years of joy for her latter years were filled with much sadness. She did not like getting old, if forty is old, and losing the material wealth she thought would last forever. I arrived when the bubble was about to burst and perhaps this too played into her reaction. She likely did not want a third pregnancy, definitely not a girl and one that was so different. Yet, my grandmother always said there was a reason for everything. So, I quietly thanked my mother for her role in my life, for she not only brought me into the world she became the catalyst to force me to consider other roads where I found a treasure of experiences. I was comforted in knowing she was content and well cared for. My role in her life was to facilitate this process.

Months before Bill and I were heading west, on March 17th, my mother died of respiratory complications. A weakened respiratory system due to years of smoking was an easy target for a springtime viral infection. As I attended her funeral I prayed that she had finally found peace and the joy she once knew as a young woman. Irrespective of what type of relationship exists with parents, a great emptiness occurs following their deaths. For it is the end of an era and the realization that you have now entered the senior ranks of the family.

Like many women in their forties my life was busy and demanding with both ups and downs. The older generation was quietly exiting while the younger ones were gathering their belongings to take their place on the stage of life. Middle age physical problems coupled with Lupus presented a number of difficulties. Like an infected tooth, my wrists and ankles ached constantly, and grew worse with winter weather. I kept dropping dishes and stumbling when walking on frosty streets. My resistance to infections was worse in winter, each bout of flu reducing my energies. Still I resisted any major medical intervention, holding to treating the symptoms and boosting my immune system. Deep down I surmised that strong medications would weaken my immune system and certainly reduce my longevity. Bill followed a similar philosophy. He never took any medications for his leukemia. Each spring for over fifteen years he had his routine blood tests, while I held my breath. Over the years his blood tests steadily improved, his illness being treated only with diet, exercise, meditation and a stable family life. Of course, this was in total contradiction to the accepted medical practice for both conditions where strong medications are the usual prescription. In the end, one wonders if every individual with such conditions really need such strong invasive treatments.

An inverse relationship existed between my physical health and my ability to communicate. Whenever I was ill or extremely tired I tended to cut my sentences short, tending to be somewhat abrupt. Large social engagements were exhausting. There were just too many words to deal with. By my late forties, dyslexia had become an old companion, not necessarily an easy one, but its peculiarities had become second nature.

Times were again changing, signaled not only by the deaths of family and friends but also Bill's approaching retirement and Gregory's decision to step aside from his University of British Columbia scholarship.

Bill's love of gardening rose to the surface whenever he thought of his retirement. He kept saying; "Victoria......Victoria......Victoria" when we chatted about where we might live. It was also abundantly clear I needed an easier climate from the long winters if I was to survive with Lupus. So, when Bill had a federal meeting scheduled in Victoria, we both flew west to assess the possibilities of a move. I was flabbergasted by the house prices. A basic three-bedroom house was nearly $100,000 more on Vancouver Island than an equal-sized home or larger in Prince Edward Island. All our efforts at being mortgage free would be lost with a move. But we were prepared to take the pluses with the minuses as we did in the past. The die was cast once we put a down payment on a house. What was not anticipated was Gregory's decision to leave his master's studies.

We had barely returned home when Gregory called to say he was quitting his studies at the University of British Columbia. When he was asked to put electrodes into the head of a live cat he refused. Being cruel to animals was definitely not in his nature. There were long phone chats to discuss the ramifications of such a decision. While we understood it was better he make a clean break early than waste time and money in a program he detested, we wanted him to realize what the decision meant. Our earlier misgivings about biomedical technology for Gregory were never mentioned as, we knew, this decision was his. Finally, he bundled up his belongings and returned to the Island. Fortunately, he would be there to help me pack for our move to the west. From February to June, Gregory and I cleared every room, sliding boxes of garbage down the long driveway for pickup and arranging for the recycling of books and other items. Bill pitched in whenever he could.

In July of 1992, we had a two-day garage sale selling every item not suited to our new life. There were so many people who turned up for the sale that a police car arrived to check on the activity. Every plant in the solarium was sold along with outdated sports equipment of the children, furniture and household items. It took all the effort of Bill, myself and Gregory to keep up with the sales. We were definitely downsizing.

Near the end of July the movers arrived and once packed, we started our westward journey. Standing on the ferry deck watching the red clay disappear in the ship's wake, I had a lump in my throat as I bid farewell to my dear Island, likely for the last time. At that moment it dawned on me that I had become a wanderer, a far cry from my youthful idea of having deep, permanent Maritime roots. I accepted what lay ahead with the usual mix of apprehension and excitement. Somehow in the gentle sea breeze I heard my grandmother's voice saying; "Child, your journey is not yet over. Walk on. You still have much to learn". Comforted, I turned to join Bill and Gregory.

To avoid the busy summer traffic we awoke at four o'clock in the morning and stopped driving by three in the afternoon. We travelled light, making our own snacks during the day and catching an afternoon meal prior to an early bed. Needing to meet the moving van in Saanich, British Columbia, by a set date dictated our travel schedule. As we motored west we stopped in Ottawa to see Christine, took time to search out a real estate lawyer in Thunder Bay to get papers signed and faxed to British Columbia, was greeted by a huge bear as we entered Manitoba, stayed in Pangman, Saskatchewan a few days with Lea and overnight in Grand Forks, British Columbia with Marjory, David and the boys. After another ferry ride, we finally arrived on Vancouver Island to the sweet sea breezes of the Pacific Ocean. I had traded one island for another. Another beginning with a whole new slate of learning.

THOUGHTS AND LEARNING

It was good to be back in the Maritimes in my middle years, time to renew old ties and be present at some of life's transition points for family members. I was once again indebted to old nursing colleagues who were there to help when the situations became complex. I would regret this loss as I entered another environment, British Columbia, where my health experience was practically unknown.

Returning to my birthplace after twenty years was a fascinating experience. I had changed in my travels and so had the Island, yet there were many traces of the Victorian world of my youth which I cherished. It was healing to walk the streets and byways of this dear Island again for I'm sure it will be forever imprinted on my soul. My understanding of my roots was enhanced in meeting people that remembered my grandparents and parents, and to learn again how my own family reacted to the social pressures of their era. It was also healing to meet people who knew my mother in happier times, as it gave me a better perspective of her life. I never spoke of her opinion of me, nor was I upset that some people never knew there was a girl in the family. Instead I went back to my grandmother's wise council; ' There is reason for everything both good or bad. It is how you deal with the situation that matters. In life, there may even be items that will take years to understand.' There were many reasons for me to return to my Island in my forties, some I understood.

There is joy in planning the environment for patients as it is at this point that innovative ideas and architectural details can be considered. By the time architectural drawings are completed it is too costly to make major changes. For this reason, early nursing input is essential. Nurses, responsible for the twenty-four hour patient/resident care, are best qualified to describe the spaces in any health facility, yet, their input is usually miniscule. The nurses involved in the health science center planning in Halifax enthusiastically participated in the exercise providing valuable incite on details not found in books, identifying current and future care patterns and technology and how to create a more flexible working environment.

If nursing input is weak, patient/resident input is even more dilute. Arguing that members of a planning committee can serve as the voice of patients is impractical as many have limited acute and practically no long-term care experience. Thus, the old method of re-adapting preexisting health facility plans from other countries or parts of Canada continues. There are multiple reasons why this practice should cease.

The quality of health facility design has a major effect on how human resources and support networks work which in turn affects the budget. Greater attention needs to be given to creating a quiet environment for healing, the distance staff travel to carry out daily activities, and the resiliency of the design to adapt to shifting care needs. Greater innovation is needed to examine other design possibilities rather than the boxlike factory structures which dominate our communities. The concept of 'one-stop health services' (i.e. having all services in one location including doctor's offices) creates a setting geared to people. The future will demand health facilities which are not only environmentally friendly, but ones that provide an all- encompassing, convenient service layout for patients and staff, and built at a reasonable cost. The reason health facility planning is so poorly handled is because it is held in such low regard within the health industry.

Such planning is not part of the curriculum of any health professional educational program. While health professionals may complain about their poor working environment, they do not see the point of using valuable time in such planning. Unfortunately, leaving others with little or no health experience to make such decisions, can leave the health worker stuck for decades with a new facility which may be even more inefficient than the old one. The low status of such planning is further exemplified by the neglect of any education program for managers and/or committee members when a project is announced. This results in many facility planners entering the process with few skills hoping to learn on the job. Such projects today are too complex and costly to be left to such thinking. One approach might be to have a Canadian Internet training program available to health care managers which would give them the necessary knowledge and design standards for creating a sophisticated, streamlined health care environments. Greater research is also needed to study innovative service delivery options. While a facility alone will not address all the current problems for health care, a well designed product will go a long way in helping to improve service delivery.

My learning in this area covered two decades. Initially, I realized that the health community had poorly described their working environment to architects and engineers who struggled with their terminology, shifting care service models, escalating technologies and patient and worker expectations. If improved communications with bathrooms created better space designs, then greater communication among the professionals would certainly improve the results.

Mental health always seems to be the poor cousin in the health industry, its funding is always inadequate. Because their political clout is weak, it is easy for politicians to cut such funding with little understanding of the consequences. In addition, mental health has been plagued with fads and trends since the early sixties. Farms attached to long-term mental hospitals closed and large institutions were shut down which resulted in residents being rerouted to group homes while others found themselves dumped onto city streets with limited support. Those on the streets were exposed to attacks for their medications, left in cheap rental accommodations or disoriented and homeless on the streets, begging for handouts on street corners. Many shuffled in and out of acute care mental health facilities where staff had little time or resources to adequately attend to their problems. Some ended up in the legal system admitted to prisons which were equally unprepared to address their needs. After forty years, many cities are facing mounting homeless on their streets while prisons struggle to segregate the mentally ill from criminals. The closure of mental health facilities just rerouted the problem to other arenas leaving the mentally ill, in my estimation, in far worse condition. If large hospitals are not the answer, and shuffling the mentally ill in and out of community programs is not the answer, then innovation is desperately needed. Programs for mental illness and addiction may have to start in school, farms and/or special villages may have to be considered and even some form of employment as public funding for such care is not boundless. The underlying cause of such behaviour definitely needs to be addressed, even if it opens many social wounds. Such individuals need early intervention, a sense of dignity, descent housing and necessary support systems. With the continuous rise of mental illness and addictions, we cannot turn a blind eye to the problem or we will witness the inevitable crumbling of our entire society.

The cause of mental illness is not simple. In my nursing career I witnessed similar behavioural changes due to biochemical imbalances in kidney patients, and one scientist even argued that mental illness might be treated with high doses of vitamins and minerals. He stated many mentally ill patients were malnourished. Whether enough effort is given in mental health to nutritional intake, the effects of exercise and fresh air, and whether the individual needs some purpose in life are all areas for further exploration. My concern was that the old physical restraints had simply been replaced with chemical restraints (i.e. too many drugs) and too often group therapy was being hijacked by the loudest voice. People with mental illness deserve far greater attention than they receive since so much illness has a mental component. A great deal more research is needed, and those who devote their lives to this service deserve far greater support and reward. Mental health workers have been demoted in our health system because we have been blinded by the glitter of surgical and technical achievements. Yet, one would think the soul of a human being has far more value than his/her physical exterior.

Private consulting offered me the diversity of challenges unavailable in the bureaucratic structure of most health facilities. The freedom to choose projects, set my own time schedule and be my own boss were luxuries unavailable to me in previous jobs. In my forties this was, to me, a definite improvement. The diverse contracts forced me to learn many new skills, to travel throughout the Atlantic provinces and to meet people who were not confined to the health industry. It was good to be a novice in a group of writers for it is only when one is pushed that one really learns. I'm unsure if I would have persevered in understanding computers without the stimulus of contracts and deadlines, for the early computers were not user friendly. I spent days and days working with a difficult manual with limited service backup. The west offered new learning opportunities, and I was now approaching fifty.

CHAPTER 9

Pacific Omega

WE arrived on Vancouver Island in July of 1991. Victoria had captured my heart on my first visit the previous spring. Emerging from a cold Prince Edward Island winter, I was enchanted with the lush gardens and cherry blossoms fluttering to the ground like confetti. Nature was welcoming me to my new home. Its July attire was just as bewitching. I was not alone, this land has captured many hearts over the centuries.

People of the First Nations lived on the island for thousands of years, their descendents visible reminders of these ancient roots. While Japanese, Chinese and Russian sailors visited its shores in the past, by the 1700s it was mainly Spanish and English adventurers exploring and mapping its coastline. By the latter part of the eighteenth century the English had taken control, with Captain George Vancouver identifying the place as 'The Island of Quadra and Vancouver'. In time, the Quadra designation was dropped. By the mid-eighteen hundreds The Hudson Bay Company had established Fort Victoria, the site eventually becoming the capital city of a province when the island amalgamated with the mainland. The capital designation held when British Columbia joined the Confederation of Canada in 1871. Saanich, a municipality on Vancouver Island north of the capital city, would be the location of our next home. Saanich, the name chosen from the First Nations people, was incorporated in 1906, making it a young community in comparison to many in the eastern part of Canada.

Our residence on Lohbrunner Road, had a typical west coast presence. It was a brown, one-story wooden house nestled against a large, granite rock under giant pine and cedar trees, the branches hugging the roof and sides of the house. There was an open carport, and rock-hewn stairs leading up to the large, red front door. The rather odd design had been dictated by the grade in the land and surrounding rocks. An open veranda circled the left-hand side of the house, with patio doors opening from the family and living room. The living spaces were bright with a forest atmosphere. We would enjoy many days on the veranda.

Bill's stay would be brief as he had to return to Prince Edward Island to complete several more weeks at Veterans Affairs prior to his retirement. Days after the furniture and boxes were deposited by the movers, I drove him to the airport. For the first time in our marriage we would be separated for almost a month, a situation we did not relish. Gregory and I faced the daunting task of creating a livable environment out of the stacks of cardboard boxes which greeted us in every room. While years of moving had conditioned me to the routines of packing and unpacking, it was never easy uprooting oneself from one part of the country and resettling in another. Moving, always a stressful process, is further complicated by dyslexia especially getting to know another set of historical and geographical details, streets and people and establishing credentials. I often envied the ancient nomads who could pick up their tents and reassemble them in another place. However streamlined the modern moving process, it continues to be cumbersome and stressful. My grandmother had moved a short distance from the country into Charlottetown in Prince Edward Island. My mother had moved within Prince Edward Island and to Nova Scotia. I had wandered from one part of North America to another. I wondered silently if this was progress, the economic realities of my life or some part of my genetic inheritance. The answer would remain a mystery.

By the end of August, our home was mostly settled when Bill, now officially retired from the federal government, arrived by plane. Joyfully, our family was together again. By the fall the three of us had begun our Pacific journeys. Bill started teaching anatomy and physiology at the Traditional Chinese Acupuncture College, volunteered as a supervisor of the woodland gardens in a newly created Government House Garden Society, was busy creating our own home garden, and became an elder in the St. Andrew's Presbyterian Church. I registered Robertson Associates as a British Columbia business and started looking for contracts. In addition, I was appointed the Vice President of the Government House Gardens Society, worked in establishing its first constitution, started a newsletter and dealt with a number of early organizational issues. Gregory contacted the University of Victoria engineering department and registered in the electrical engineering masters program, more suited to his personality. He also assisted me with the statistical analyses for a few contracts.

Prior to arriving in British Columbia old colleagues across Canada had warned me that getting my nursing license and/or finding work would be difficult, if not impossible. After making my initial inquiry with the Registered Nurses Association of British Columbia, I braced myself for a slow and difficult process, initiating a journal just to record my experience. Hundreds of pages of documentation were provided with transcripts, license information from Prince Edward Island, Nova Scotia and Arizona, and references. With over twenty-five years in the health industry I hoped for a positive review, but knew nothing was certain. The idea of a national nursing license was beginning to sound real good for us wandering professionals.

I had few professional colleagues in British Columbia having spent most of my years in the eastern part of Canada. Getting a job, I had been told, would depend on 'who you knew' and I had only two contacts. Fernande Harrison, from Alberta, had been an old colleague since the sixties when we were both young nursing consultants with provincial hospital commissions. Dr. Alan Thomson had been the Director of Hospitals with the Nova Scotia provincial government when we were planning the Halifax health-science complex. In British Columbia, Fernande held the position of Vice President, Patient Care, with the

Greater Victoria Hospital Society (GVHS) and Alan had transferred from one provincial government to another.

Fernande kindly opened the first door for me by accepting my bid on a contract to study the Nursing Committee Structure at the Greater Victoria Health Society (GVHS). Following an amalgamation of several city hospitals and the introduction of a decentralized nursing management structure, the Society felt it was time for a review. This was a complex management study to address a number of significant issues. Individual and group meetings were held with nursing managers. The need for improved communications in their meetings, restructuring committees and decision-making processes were all under consideration. A number of possible options were proposed. It was evident that frequent meetings of large numbers of nursing managers were both costly and cumbersome. To get a handle on the issue each nursing manager was asked to calculate the cost and benefits of a recent meeting. An example came from one manager reported; "In the past month, we have spent about $10,000 and we have not yet made a decision on a critical staffing matter. We are wasting valuable resources on these meetings, funds better spent on other staffing issues". The question was how to streamline the meetings and/or find a different method to connect and process decision-making. Coordinating computers and computer programs between hospitals, a key recommendation, was facing opposition as the Society was unprepared for such a major cost outlay an attitude which would change by the mid-nineties. Decentralized nursing decision-making adopted by the Society, a progressive step, was moving slowly, as pockets of centralized thinking remained and other non-nursing professionals had not been included in the planning. In addition, committee structure and organizational charts did not reflect the decentralized process. My report provided suggestions to ameliorate some of the blockages. What the GVHS nursing managers were encountering was the shift from traditional management structures to systems and relationships. Managing people and processes, especially communications, was becoming a chief priority. The larger the organization the greater the communication problem. These nursing managers were on the threshold of vast changes which would sweep the province in the nineties. My report, accepted by the Department of Nursing, resulted in the GVHS proceeding with the changes.

In the midst of the GVHS nursing study, after months of waiting, I finally was contacted by the Registered Nurses Association of British Columbia notifying me that, irrespective of my years of experience and academic qualifications, I did not qualify for a nursing license. No explanation was provided. Disappointed, but not surprised, I immediately contacted Fernande to inform her of the situation and ask if my health administration credentials would be satisfactory while I continued with the nursing study. Equally surprised at the rejection, she encouraged me to proceed. What I did not know, being new to the province, was that Fernande was then President of the Registered Nurses Association of British Columbia.

Within days I received a second phone call from the nursing association to be informed, by the same individual, that 'somehow' my past nursing experiences had been reexamined and I would be receiving my registration papers in the mail. Amazed at the abrupt turn around, I made inquiries to discover my beneficiary. On my next visit to the Victoria General Hospital I sincerely thanked Fernande. Sadly, I knew of other qualified nursing leaders, without such assistance, who simply gave up trying to get their license in British Columbia.

My contract with the Greater Victoria Hospital Society, led to three others. One was a statistical study of Palliative Care with the Capital Regional District Continuing Care (Nursing) Division, Gregory joining me to do the data analysis from over three hundred questionnaires sent to clients and managers. The nursing managers were very impressed with Gregory's ease in explaining the statistical results and his teaching ability on how to use the computer program. The second contract was a one-week client statistical survey for the Vancouver Island Multiple Sclerosis Society. The third was to write a learning module on 'Marketing Occupational Health Nursing Services' for the British Columbia Institute of Technology (BCIT). Somehow a member of the BCIT faculty heard of me and asked if I would write this module on managing a private business for occupational therapists. However, even with these contracts, I was struggling, and realized a job in a hospital or government might be needed to increase my provincial credentials. I was not anxious to return to a full-time bureaucratic job after almost a decade of independence, but, with Bill retired, another house mortgage, and a need to understand a different health system, it was the most practical step.

While working on the above contracts, I continued to apply for any job suited to my credentials, storing rejection letters in a large three-ring binder. My administrative bent was always intrigued by the statistical number of such letters needed before a positive reply. The number quickly climbed to about seventy. It was by chance that Bill rechecked one from the Ministry of Health to inform me I had a job offer as a Hospital Consultant. So, in 1992, in my late forties, I began a seven year civil service stint with the British Columbia government, a tenure which would see vast changes in the health system.

Shortly after arriving in British Columbia, David called from Nova Scotia to tell me Sonny, my oldest brother, had died. He was in his early sixties and had been unwell for years. I sat quietly on our veranda sadly thinking 'what might have been'. He did not lack intelligence or ability. Years before I met someone in Prince Edward Island who knew him at the Journal Pioneer newspaper. He informed me that Sonny was one of the best advertisement agents they ever had but was too unreliable. In the health industry I talked to many psychiatrists and psychiatric nurses trying to find answers for my parents, and myself. For a short period Sonny attended Alcoholic Anonymous meetings and had a brief hospital stay for his drinking problem. But, like many alcoholics, he refused to take responsibility for his drinking and slipped back into old patterns. After years of drinking and other illnesses his body simply gave up.

Any death is sad, but when the relationship with a sibling never jelled from the beginning, it presents many unanswered questions. My mere presence seemed to exacerbate his belligerence, usually fueled by alcohol. His reaction at times often bordered on the bizarre, highlighting a much deeper psychological cause. He was obviously battling inner ghosts which maybe even he never fully understood. My sadness was that with all my health experience and contacts I could not direct him towards any effective therapy. I could only pray that in death he had found some peace.

My first day at the pale gray, seven-story building on the corner of Blanshard and Pandora, the home of the Ministry of Health, was an awakening. The building, in the red zone of the city, offered a motley milieu. Surrounding its prim exterior was a darker neighbourhood of evident drug trafficking, a needle exchange program near one entrance and mentally ill roaming the streets. The presence of security at the entrance spoke volumes. Support services were straining as the building housed far more workers than it was built to handle. In addition, it did not take long to realize the scampering feet heard in the ceilings after hours and many droppings, suggested the building also housed other tenants besides civil servants. It would take years before there was much action to eradicate the rodent problem, if it ever occurred. The facility presented a unique occupational and safety research site, but no one seemed interested in the topic. Most employees went about their daily jobs serenely oblivious of these environmental factors.

After the usual introductions, I was escorted to a gray cubicle next to a window, one of many, containing an old and badly worn computer and desk. I could hear crystals tinkling every time I turned on the computer, a definite sign of trouble. With no bookcase or place to store files or books, within days I went to the basement where old furniture was stored to get a rather shabby bookcase delivered to my cubicle. There I would store binders of information on the various topics of my responsibility. My dyslexia made me somewhat compulsive in organizing large amounts of information, an increasingly helpful trait in the communication age. In seven years, despite major shifts in my responsibilities, my job description never changed. Attempted revisions never quite kept pace with the reorganizations. My stay at my first cubicle would not last long either as within months the Ministry embarked on a series of reorganizations. In the seven years I would move from one cubicle to another, circling the entire floor, eventually returning to the same cubicle space of my first day. I'm certain the circle had some meaning.

My initial responsibilities were focused on the acute care hospitals in the Thompson/ Okanagan region of the province. The role covered a variety of topics including budgets, planning and construction, addressing critical issues, program and/or service changes, patient complaints and doing surveys when necessary. Many trips were made to the region getting to know the hospitals and resolving problems. As I travelled I was in awe of the miles of forestland and the shear size of the province. Trying to describe the size and complexity of British Columbia in administering health services, a government report described it as: "........three United Kingdoms could fit into its 950,000 square kilometers with room left over for Denmark, Belgium, the Netherlands and twenty Singapores. The province's average population density per square kilometer is just 4.3 people, compared to Germany's 230, the United Kingdom's 242, Japan's 335, and Singapore's 6,500 per square kilometer "[1]. Fortunately, my initial responsibilities would only cover a segment of this vast territory.

In addition to the routine hospital responsibilities, I also composed letters for the Minister of Health on any correspondence relative to my region. From the world of private business where letters could be composed and mailed within days of a telephone call or meeting, I now entered a bureaucratic maze in which letters could take up to two or three months in circulation. Everyone, managers and clerical staff, reviewed the draft letter and made suggestions. By the time the letter returned to my desk for a redraft the composition either made no sense, or the situation had changed or had been resolved. The mind-numbing process had a slave-like quality. An example was one letter, three months in circulation, being returned with the following hand-written instructions; 'This is a Union member, could you redraft the letter so it's more friendly'. I immediately took the letter to our clerical staff saying; " I'm sure you are far more qualified on letter cosmetics than I am". One crisis in the Okanagan resulted in about fifteen letters landing on my desk a day for weeks. Fortunately, generic paragraphs and a computer speeded up the task, but such work was soul-destroying. I was also aware the federal government had a simpler process, but no one wanted to change the system. Sadly, health ministry activities and policies were too often dictated by the media, a reactive management style which wasted countless hours.

My prior study on the Greater Victoria Hospital Society meeting costs and decision-making should have been circulated within the Ministry. For the first time in my professional career I was attending meetings where agendas seemed optional and no one seemed perturbed at taking hours discussing a range of issues with no effort at coming to a decision. I often sat quietly calculating the cost of such activities which was mind-boggling.

By the nineties, the federal funding of 50/50, introduced with the creation of Medicare, had diminished with the provinces and territories shouldering more and more of the health costs. The federal funding contribution to British Columbia had dropped to about twelve percent. The only way the province could adapt to such costs was to cut funding to other services such as education, social services and municipalities. The federal funding shortfall hit the Maritime provinces in the seventies. Its impact did not register in British Columbia until the nineties. So, while federal politicians for decades wrapped themselves in the Canadian flag seeking reelection on the premise they were the guardians of Medicare, they were actually reducing the funding, leaving the provinces to face the steadily rising health bill. As the New Democratic Party (NDP) assumed power in the province in the nineties the need for funding controls was becoming acute, pushing the government to consider a radical idea, 'regionalization' of the entire health system. For several years, confusion reigned as, not content with change on one front, the Ministry of Health also embarked on several internal reorganizations exponentially increasing the stress level for everyone.

Prior to the introduction of regionalization, hospitals in British Columbia were structured in a traditional manner with their own Boards, while community services (Public Health, long-term community nursing care, mental health and addictions) were managed provincially through Ministry of Health departments in Victoria. Service cooperation and integration within the regions was difficult due to the different systems. In just over a decade, this structure would be changed through three waves of health reform. The first wave created fifty-two health authorities; eleven large regional boards (mostly urban), thirty-four community health councils (in rural and remote areas) and seven community health service societies to manage the decentralized community services. Members of the Boards/ Councils were appointed by the government usually from political, union or advocacy groups, many with no previous health industry experience. This first reform step would eventually prove unworkable as small health authorities lacked critical population mass for effective service delivery, and many Board/Council members lacked a clear understanding of their mandate. [2] My task during this phase was to work with the hospital executive and board members in my region, many who were not supportive of such change.

To facilitate the health reform process, teams of civil servants, some from Victoria and others from the region, travelled to the communities to work with the various parties. I was involved with the Thompson/Okanagan team. Everyone was walking a new road with unclear markers. Appointed Board/Council members, all volunteers, were inundated with boxes of information to supposedly help them understand the various aspects and issues of hospital and community health services. Their initiation into this complex world included managing competing demands, age-old conflicts, groups jockeying for power, and, in some cases, outright war between community groups and the local hospital Chief Executive Officer who, they thought, had too much power. Some Board/Council members had to travel hours on secondary roads to attend all-day meetings with no compensation and growing objections from their employer. Complaints came from many directions as the volunteers found themselves overwhelmed in trying to balance an overbooked schedule of health service responsibilities, a regular job and their family. Government employees were equally stretched trying to meet shifting reform policies, unreachable deadlines, being teachers, mentors, facilitators, diplomats, and sometimes referees in the change process as well as making sure services and programs remained on schedule. The expectations for everyone exceeded reality, and may even have awakened a few invisible spirits.

On one occasion, having spent the day and evening at a very contentious meeting, my colleague and I drove wearily back to our lodgings. We had booked into a Bed and Breakfast at Spencers Bridge, a recently renovated old building, which, as we were told, served as an inn at the time of the gold-rush in the eighteen hundreds. It was after eleven as I bid my nursing colleague good night and headed to bed.

Just as my head was about to touch the pillow, I looked up to see a ghostly figure standing at the end of my bed holding a large book. He looked as weary as I felt. He was dressed in what appeared to be worn, leather pants and jacket with a large, somewhat battered hat. I was too tired to be frightened and said to my ghostly roommate; " I pray you are reading the Bible and have no real needs, because I'm too exhausted to chat. Perhaps you would like to spend time with my grandmother" and, with that, I dropped off to sleep. I knew Nanny's spirit would be nearby.

The next morning my nursing colleague commented over breakfast that the place was 'spooky', as she had been awakened by strange noises during the night. When I described my ghostly roommate she, with a rather shocked expression, remarked; "You must be the only human being I know who could drop off to sleep with a ghost in the room". I smiled and thought,' you don't have a grandmother like mine'.

Amidst the confusion and weariness, we also met some truly dedicated people at many levels, who sincerely wanted to improve the health services in the province. Some of those were found in the various planning activities which were also going on in the midst of health reform. My old facility planning skills were once again dusted off and put into service for two small communities; Keremeos in the Okanagan and Lytton in the Thompson. Both communities were wanting to change how health services could be delivered in their communities. I was more than pleased to bring forward the one-stop health centre idea developed in Prince Edward Island. Over the years I learned that it was prudent not to say an idea had previously been developed in some other community. Instead, I brought it out as an original idea tailoring it to a different setting. My role was that of a facilitator, creating the planning documents, setting meeting agendas and making travel arrangements.

A small government jet flew us in and out for these small community planning meetings. For the Keremeos project we landed easily at the Penticton airport but for Lytton the pilot skillfully ducked between the mountains and landed on a minute airstrip in Lillooet. From there we travelled by van over the mountain to Lytton. Poor visibility created exciting landings and take-offs. I was facing a number of travel options in my job; jets, helicopters, boats and cars. I was definitely getting to know the province.

Keremeos, a small community of about five thousand people, is located in the fruit basket of the Okanagan. The name comes from the Similkameen native word *Keremeyeus* meaning 'creek which cuts its way through the flats'. For the first time, many health providers serving this small community came together to plan a single community health center. Getting agreement was more complicated in British Columbia because these health providers had functioned separately for so long, were represented by different unions and resistance to such cooperation was coming from different levels. However, once the Keremeos Health Council calculated the waste of resources in the duplication of services, a single health facility with the pooling of resources was an obvious choice. The planning committee even considered a number of other ideas such as salaried physicians, services designed to smaller cultures in the community (i.e. First Nations and East Indians), day programs for seniors, greater coordination in mental health and addiction programs and a possible transportation system to other Okanagan hospitals. But this planning effort was side-tracked when health reform started to absorb more and more of the Council's time. The community would eventually realize its goal of a new facility, but whether it culminated in a single one-stop health service centre for its citizens would be unclear. In the early nineties the initial steps had been taken. Lytton presented a different challenge and a pioneering effort for First Nations people.

Lytton, with a population of about three hundred, is located at the north end of the Fraser Canyon at the convergence of the Thompson and Fraser Rivers, which was captured by its First Nation's name of *Camchin*, meaning 'the meeting place'. It is one of the oldest continuously occupied villages in North America. It was also a stop-off place for gold prospectors heading north in past decades. Its citizens are mainly First Nations.

In the early nineties, a planning effort was underway to create an innovative centre for the Lytton community, combining western and First Nations healing methods under one roof. Key to the planning was the identification of a seamless blending of western and First Nations healing spaces. The idea was well received, with the title of '*healing*' preferred over 'health' or 'hospital'. This new healing centre was to be built on land already containing a maternal/child centre, a Federally funded program, to amalgamate similar services on one site. Large community meetings were held with representatives from St. Bartholomew's Hospital, the Health Advisory Committee of the Nl'akapmx Nation Tribal Council, youth, elders, service providers, Native bands, Federal and provincial governments, unions and the general public. At times there may have been thirty or more people, the meetings lasting two days, the members gathered in a circle in the local community hall. Discussions centered around current health system problems and needed changes. Ideas for this plan included salaried physicians, doctors making house calls, home care nursing, and a long-term care. These were meaningful and powerful deliberations as this innovative idea had the potential to be a role model for other First Nation communities.

In between the large meetings I spent time with a smaller group clarifying the planning details of a number of ceremonial spaces. We discussed sweat lodges, fire pits, the need for special acoustic filters for the drumming, and smoke filters for the burning of sweet grass. Knowing the Indians in Arizona were effectively managing their own education and healing programs, I had no hesitation in supporting this idea for the Lytton community. I was also aware that Canadian and American Indian groups are in constant communications with each other and a support network would appear whenever a facility was erected. It was time to honour their culture in the healing of their own people. I also needed support in understanding this planning which came from several sources.

Before starting the planning process, I contacted the Aboriginal Health Division in the provincial government requesting the assistance of a First Nations representative and a native healer to be regular members of our planning team for Keremeos and Lytton. A young woman from the Haida nation arrived and a Mohawk healer, originally from Ontario, who resided on Vancouver Island. They both traveled with us and were invaluable in helping us understand the cultural needs of the First Nations. Next, I asked the native healer if I could experience a sweat lodge session so that I might understand its physical structure and healing process. He kindly invited Bill and I to our first sweat lodge experience on the grounds of his Saanich home. The heat of the sweat lodge will be forever imprinted on my psyche. A group of people, of different ages, crawled into the small opening of the sweat lodge and positioned themselves in a circle around the hot embers of a fire, the lodge roof just inches from our heads. Each session was about twenty minutes the native healer gently speaking during the session while the steam, bellowed from the water added to the burning embers. I lasted for one and a half sessions, Bill courageously managed more. The intensity of the heat washed away any trivial thinking, riveting your mind on yourself, life and survival. It's value in healing was impressive. Lastly, Bill and I, attended a week-long, annual community healing gathering at Pahluskwu (Lake) near Lytton. In a typical west coast mist, dressed in rain gear, we listened to speakers tell their healing journey (from illness and experience in religious residential schools), watched videos, joined in healing circles, shared community meals and enjoyed the First Nation performers. One could sense the deep wounds and the growing spirit within these people. However damaged, healing was happening and their spirit would survive. With each encounter my respect and knowledge of the First Nations grew to enrich the written details of the plans.

A combined healing centre is not just for the First Nations, it is a viable option for other cultures as well. For example, Richmond might combine Chinese and western healing methods in one facility while somewhere in the Fraser Valley there might be a combined Ayurvedic and western healing centre. Many cultures have had healing methods far longer than western nations. Why should we think there is only one path to healing. Since many illnesses have a psychosomatic base, it might be more beneficial if some individuals were directed towards less invasive healing methods first than the drugs and surgical emphasis of western medicine. Such an idea will challenge the egos of many individuals, but, thankfully there are already leaders who see the value of such partnerships. Unfortunately, Lytton, like Keremeos, had their facility plans halted as health reform took precedent. To make sure the work already accomplished would not be lost I made a disc of the planning document and mailed it to the community leaders with a comment that they should not give up on their dream. (*In 2008, I was told the idea has been resurrected again. Perhaps their time has come*).

Just as the fifty-two governing bodies and communities were getting familiar with their roles, the provincial government scrapped the plan, dismissed the Board/Council members and created eighteen regional health Boards with another slate of members. The travelling circus began again as a whole new group of Board volunteers had to be educated on the health industry, groups reengaged in jockeying for power and conflicts occurred as health services and programs were amalgamated under these large governance structures. Then in 2001, as these eighteen Boards were getting familiar with the health industry, the provincial government changed gear again, the newly elected Liberal Party scrapped the eighteen regional Boards and introduced six mega-Boards; five regional and one provincial, with another slate of appointments, this time with stronger corporate representation. The corporate focus introduced more non-health professionals into senior management ranks, eventually creating a dichotomy between upper and lower management within the industry. Senior managers, with less health industry expertise, now dictated policy to middle and lower managers who had been promoted through the system. Middle managers quickly discovered their promotional access to upper management had diminished, and support systems which they had relied on for decades had been eliminated. Support system managers, who had provided financial, human resource and other backup to frontline managers, had been seconded to a regional coordination role. With this move, front line managers were expected to handle everything; service delivery, finances, human resources, supply services, etc.. many tasks for which they had little training. The financial bottom line took precedence over service delivery as the regional Boards created another layer of bureaucracy. When the dust settled, the health industry in British Columbia had three bureaucratic layers (i.e. federal, provincial and regional) each setting its own set of policies and directions, not always in unison.

Reaction to health reform varied. To the average citizen, the confusion created by health reform and Ministry reorganization was likely minuscule but those in small communities, when regional health Boards were introduced, felt they had lost input into their own health services. For many health professionals it was a matter of knowing which Board/Council was responsible for their salary and allegiance. Some health workers did get affected when, in 2001, the provincial government reduced the number of health unions and opened the door to non-union contracts. However, there were some health leaders who challenged the need for such a massive change when less drastic measures might have worked equally well. Others complained the reform process lacked consistent vision, and each change in leadership brought a different vision, style and priorities. Also excessive, rapid and often unplanned change undermined the ability of the system to provide quality care. They thought the magnitude of change had been underestimated and there was no evidence of a positive link between health reform and cost containment, supposedly the main reason for the change. By 2001 a provincial government report concluded a decade of health reform had created a constantly shifting organizational structure, eroded the volunteer base of the health industry, and was neither cost-effective nor care-effective. While some positives did occur, such as increased coordination and amalgamation of certain services, the overall health budget showed no sign of decreasing, in fact it grew steadily. Increased accountability and innovative service delivery ideas did not occur other than moving some services to ambulatory care or into the community, ideas which were already in process prior to reform. Some argued the costly, disruptive reform process was more like rearranging the deck chairs on the Titanic. It had been a costly social experiment, focused at the top of the organization for cosmetic and political effect. Decision-making had moved to another bureaucratic layer, with a corporate focus.

By the time the reform process shifted to the eighteen regional boards I had been reassigned from extensive field work to a full-time office role. All the while I was working with health reform in the regions, the Ministry was going through a series of internal reorganizations. Often with scant notice, I had little time to pack by belongings to move from one cubicle to another before heading back to the region. So, as I returned I realized my cubicle location was nearly half way around the circle. Our business cards reflected these internal changes. Professional business cards were finally scrapped as Ministry administration could not keep up with the changes in divisions and titles. Unhappy with professionals travelling with no Ministry identification, one manager got her husband to create business cards on his home computer. He avoided job titles as by the mid-nineties most of us were in some 'transition' role, which was becoming a running joke in the field.

Internally, there was increasing pressure to reduce the number of civil servants with tempting retirement deals. At the same time there was pressure to decrease the number of employees with health experience. The plan, I surmised, was to not only import new blood into the organization but also bring the Ministry in line with the corporate philosophy now permeating the industry. The ranks of medical, nursing and other health professionals diminished as those with general administration, statistics, humanities and other generic backgrounds were hired. The same pattern applied to management positions. Unfortunately, this process introduced individuals with little understanding of the business they were suppose to manage. A typical example was one manager I briefly reported to who greeted me with; "Sally, my entire knowledge of the health industry is sitting with various family members in the emergency department of a hospital. Can you brief me on the Thompson/Okanagan health (no longer just hospitals) issues before I go to a meeting in a half hour?" For a moment I thought of Moses and the Ten Commandments, and was tempted to say 'Thou shalt not...........' but refrained, and began. "Well, in that case the three priorities are........." The many internal reorganizations also introduced a number of inexperienced managers and, sadly, the arrival of an old familiar management style, that of Sister Catherine Peter. As favourites were promoted and later trashed and employees abused, morale dropped. Some poor managers never lasted, but others, amazingly, survived a number of reorganizations.

Reorganization and restructuring were familiar words in the 1990s. Christopher A. Bartlett and Sumantra Ghoshal in their article in the Harvard Business Review perhaps best described the working environment of many managers as they tried to match their organizational structure with the new demands stating: "Top-level managers in many of today's leading corporations are losing control of their companies. The problem is not that they have misjudged the demands created by an increasingly complex environment and an accelerating rate of environmental change, nor even that they have failed to develop strategies appropriate to the new challenges. The problem is that their companies are organizationally incapable of carrying out the sophisticated strategies that have developed. Over the past twenty years, strategic thinking has far outdistanced organizational capabilities [3]."

The favourite organizational structure was a matrix pattern which was unmanageable as it meant employees were reporting to two different people. Such dual reporting, according to Bartlett and Ghoshal, led to conflict and confusion, created informational logjams and overlapping responsibilities produced turf battles and a loss of accountability [4] At a time when organizations needed to minimize and manage complexity, we were going in the opposite direction. One study done by Pamela Ann Azard, in her PhD thesis, presents a picture of the working environment being created by health reform and Ministry restructuring in British Columbia. The data was obtained from one hundred and seven hospitals and fifteen senior Ministry staff with direct responsibility for hospitals. The study presented some interesting findings such as: Board members, board chairs and Chief Executive Officers averaged approximately five years in their positions whereas Ministry of Health officials averaged only 1.1 years. 92% of all individuals interviewed stated that the lack of current experience and/or frequent turnover of Ministry of Health personnel had negatively affected continuity and effective communication between the Ministry and provincial hospitals. 0% of Ministry of Health personnel held degrees in business and only 10% possessed degrees in health care administration. 80% of all hospital respondents felt that Ministry officials in general lacked a realistic understanding of the issues and challenges associated with hospital and financial operations. 73% of hospital respondents felt that the Ministry of Health frequently made decisions which affected their facilities without first consulting them. 57% of hospital participants agreed with the (regionalization) plan in theory and even fewer (46%) supported the plan in practice. 53% of hospital respondents felt that the government had not thoroughly thought through the (regionalization) plan prior to its implementation and suggested that multi-site pilot studies might have been a more logical approach. 68% of board member and board chair populations expressed confusion over the regionalization concept. 89% of all hospital participants expressed concern whether the goal of true community involvement and decision-making would ever be achieved. The frequent turnover of Ministry staff and their preponderance in humanities education presented a sharp contrast between themselves and the general hospital population who possessed substantially more professional experience and educational backgrounds in business and health care.

With the constant restructuring, senior management seemed unable or unwilling to grasp the psychological implications for employees. Many survivors sat amidst the chaos. They had survived the downsizing, the restructuring, the indignity of having their project/job eliminated or removed from their hands and later returned in a revised mess, or asked to guide someone through a task that they were fully able to handle, or sitting helpless as an individual with no health experience insulted regional managers on a complex health issue. It was no surprise to see articles acknowledging that workplace stress had tripled in the past four years, with increasing incidents of rage. In one article, the International Labor Organization in Geneva stated the North American country ranking among the top five nations in the rate of workplace assaults wasn't the United States – it was Canada. In fact the rate of physical and psychological assaults against Canadian women in the workplace was 19% higher than in the United States [5]. While the topic of occupational health and safety seemed important to unions and was highlighted in executive training programs, the psychological damage to individuals from these constant reorganizations was hardly a priority within the Ministry. The general attitude was that employees just had to cope.

With the province reeling from rounds of health reform and numerous Ministry reorganizations, field managers, facing serious service delivery issues, complained they did not know who to call when they needed help. With so much upheaval ministry staff started to coast, not willing to expend a large amount of energy on projects that might be scrapped in six months. This state of chaos reminded me of a quote from the final days of the Roman Empire: "We trained hard……but it seemed every time we were beginning to form up into teams we were reorganized. I was to learn later in life that we tend to meet any situation by reorganizing, and what a wonderful method it can be for creating the illusion of progress while producing confusion, inefficiency and demoralization (Gaius Petronius A.D. 66)". It is not that life does not have change, it is the degree of change and the lack of any appreciation by organizational leaders for the effort expended by so many. As the century came to a close a wave of overwhelming weariness crept through the health industry.

Life on the home front was also changing. Gregory, successfully completed his master's studies and, after graduation, went to Calgary for a couple of years. Then he moved to Burlington, Ontario joining old University of Victoria friends and working as an electrical engineer in a manufacturing company. His grandmother, Lea, was hale and hearty as she entered her nineties, our contact maintained by long telephone calls. She lived in seniors housing in Pangman, near her other siblings. Aunt Ruth, in her late nineties, had her own apartment in a seniors residence in Phoenix. Thinking I might help her at this stage of her life, and still carrying an Arizona Nursing license, I explored the possibility of returning to the southwest but to no avail. There were no openings for a Canadian nurse in her fifties. Papa's advice 'You can never go back………' aptly applied. In the end, Aunt Ruth returned to Indiana to be near other relatives. My Arizonian ties were slipping away with the deaths of old colleagues.

Creativity entered my life through Saturday art classes provided by Ralph Harrison, a neighbour. Ralph, a professional artist formerly from Ontario, kindly agreed to come to our home to teach me the many aspects of art; charcoal drawing, water colour, pastel, mixed media, acrylic and oil painting (including palette work). This creative outlet definitely helped me cope with the stress of my working environment. My childhood love of art never died. While time and other responsibilities had reduced such artistic ventures in earlier years, a door opened for a brief spell in my fifties.

I continued as Vice President of the Government House Gardens Society once I started working but found scheduling impossible once I got involved with health reform. Thus, in 1995, I was pleasantly surprised to be invited to the Government House with the arrival of Queen Elizabeth to officially open the gardens. The volunteers had created a wondrous haven of gardens. Requesting time off for the affair created a momentary raise of eyebrows within the Ministry. It was a lovely sunlit day as Bill and I waited with the other Society officials where the Queen would be speaking and cutting the official ribbon with Lieutenant Governor David Lam.

With Gregory's departure and the constant back-and-forth to downtown Victoria for my job with one car, Bill and I decided to move again, this time to a newly-built condo building on Quebec Street near the provincial Legislature. After another garage sale, we packed and relocated to smaller quarters, our second downsizing. For my final years as a civil servant, I could walk to work and Bill and I enjoyed the many downtown activities and the beauty of a busy, touristy harbour. Sadly, my art supplies had to be placed in storage for a later awakening. For three years I watched Victoria's downtown change with more and more homeless, many with mental health and addiction problems, the aggressive panhandlers making it very uncomfortable for a woman walking along the city streets in the late afternoon.

By the fall of 1995 I was more occupied with a variety of office responsibilities. I worked on whatever landed on my desk. The following are a few of the many projects which occupied my time.

For several years I worked on a Closer to Home Fund (CTHF), a supposed adjunct to the health reform process. The $41.7 million annualized fund was intended to provide quick access to start-up funds for joint hospital/community planning and projects. The focus was on the development of new or enhanced projects to shift more expensive, traditional, inpatient hospital services into the community. By the fall of 1995, a year after the start of the fund, about three hundred and seventy-four projects of various sizes, had been approved. Our division was responsible for reviewing and approving submissions from the Boards and Councils. This entailed talking with the regional representatives, making sure collaboration existed between hospital and community groups, that the project was a new or enhanced service, and the budget calculations met the intended objectives. Many projects actually occurred and achieved the hospital to community shift of services. However, some projects never started because the funds arrived at a time of shifting governance structures, staff changes, unions (hospital and community) refusing to work together, community groups not trusting hospital Chief Executive Officers to manage the project funds, and other reasons. In the midst of my numerous calls to the regions, it was evident that some CTHF funds were sitting in hospital bank accounts collecting interest while others seemed to be lost in a maze of financial figures. With so much money involved, I sensed an internal audit would inevitably be on our doorstep. Thus, in 1996, I pushed the idea that our division preempt the inevitable audit by doing our own evaluation with the aid of two co-op university students. The idea was approved days before our manager received an e-mail from the audit division.

Two health administration master's students from the University of British Columbia arrived and quickly created a computer program to track every project. For months divisional staff contacted the regions gathering data on the projects highlighting whether the project started, the actual budget, and any unspent funds. Since the hospital accounting system was easier to track, we quickly identified over $6 million in unspent funds which the hospitals returned to the Ministry. An equal amount of unspent funds was identified for community services (Public Health, Continuing Nursing Care, Mental Health and Addiction) but because tracking funds was more difficult in this area, it was impossible to determine what had happened to the unspent funds. At a certain point, we were instructed to cease leaving the hospital's refund as our main accomplishment. Once the data was collected, we prepared a detailed report on our evaluation.

If one worked in the corporate world and managed to save the organization $6 million, the accolades would be overwhelming and one might expect a promotion if not a generous bonus. This, however, is not the case in the civil service. Speaking volumes on the management style at the time, the Closer To Home Fund evaluation report required twenty revisions, compared to the usual three of most reports. Numerous comments were added and/or text revised as the weeks passed. This was astounding since the report mainly consisted of project data, comparing approved and actual budgets, noting any unspent funds plus providing some health region tables and graphs. It seemed fairly straight-forward. This number of revisions far surpassed the cumbersome letter correspondence process of Minister's letters. To try and ameliorate the frustration, I suggested a contest, a loonie to the individual who correctly guessed the total number of revisions. No one suggested a number greater than twelve. But this wasn't the end of the madness.

The provincial government had an Employee Recognition Program to supposedly encourage employee involvement, collaboration, initiative and creativity and to recognize individuals for their contribution to the improvement in service, operations and the work environment through suggestions and team-related work process reviews. In a moment of lapsed sanity, with team morale at rock bottom, I thought it would be a good idea to submit the names of our team in recognition for their months of effort, retrieval of $6 million and the evaluation report. At first the suggestion was not only accepted but in the October 1997 Employee Online newsletter it was announced our team was entitled to a cash award of $11,000. Obviously, the mention of money awakened dark forces.

Before we had time to think of the honour, employees from the Ministry's financial division, who filled out the forms for the retrieval of funds, stepped forward and demanded their share. Then the unions got into the act followed by other managers. It was a mess. Months passed as this hot potato was bounced between the various divisions. Finally, as if ashamed of the whole affair, late one afternoon we were ushered into a side room where a sub-sub manager quickly mumbled something about the benefit to the organization and sheepishly handed us a government pen and a cheque, that after the usual deductions was barely more then the cost of an evening meal. It was hard to know whether to laugh or cry. Management had missed the entire point. It wasn't the money. In the midst of so much organizational confusion and low morale, a group of civil servants plus two co-op students, had spent months diligently tracking the funds of over three hundred projects, had $6 million returned to the government for other services, and provided the government with a case of tangible accountability of a very large fund. This evaluation wasn't part of our regular responsibilities. We had made this extra effort as a responsible group of professionals and the organization failed to be gracious. The fiasco soured the two university students against ever working in government. Knowing it was useless to cry over such ineptness, I moved on. My life was still inundated with a constant mound of regional budgets and plans, Minister's letters and other routine tasks, so as the days drifted by I found other interests.

The two UBC co-op students proved their value, even if organizational recognition was feeble. The co-op student program in British Columbia was an arrangement with employers for a student to spent three to four months (sometimes longer) working on an organizational project as part of their learning process. Since I was familiar with students, I volunteered to be the divisional liaison. Within a short time we had about twelve co-op students working on a number of projects, most dealing with computers or the Internet. It was important each student's project was not part of regular Ministry of Health employee's union responsibilities which meant the projects had to be carefully screened prior to approval. The students came from various University of Victoria and Camosun College programs (i.e. business, information science, engineering and computer science). My task was to work with the post-secondary educational advisor, identify and assign the projects, interview and select the students, make sure each student had the necessary working space, computer equipment and payment when they arrived, provide an orientation, coordinated their activities during their stay in the Ministry of Health, and file an evaluation report when they finished. All rather typical of student learning processes.

The students brought a wealth of enthusiasm and computer expertise to the organization and a different mindset. One example was a rangy, shy, and somewhat awkward young man from the engineering department of the University on Victoria who barely managed to get through the interview. I felt his range of computer skills would help in creating an Internet form for the submission of online Capital Project requests, the cumbersome manual submission method being problematic. My idea was practically stillborn when the Ministry of Health web master called to say the student did not have the precise script skills needed to create the form. I began scrambling to find another project. However, two days later the web master called again and, with a chuckle, said the project was back on track. The co-op student learned the entire complex script over the weekend, an accomplishment that amazed him. The form was created. With the number of computer projects rising, to my surprise I found myself dealing with other technology projects, all requiring a quick learning process to update myself on different terminology, programs and processes.

First came the designing of a Ministry division web site. While the Ministry of Health had a general web site, our division, with a number of key programs, was not represented. With the assistance of two clerical staff, who willingly agreed to extra training, we learned to design a web site, write and update information, and understand the glitches and problems of running such a site. The two clerical individuals became expert web site technicians, one going off to California and the other having marketable skills for private enterprise. For me it was an adventure into the exciting world of the Internet where youth seemed at ease. Its appeal was in its creativity and instant communications to vast numbers of people if designed and run properly. Next came the introduction of one hundred and fifty computers.

Finally, the junky cubicle décor and mismatched computers were recognized as barriers to efficient and effective working. The executive decided to change not only the computers but also the working stations for the entire division. A small team was set up with the mandate that there would be no break in operations while the transition occurred, a considerable challenge in light of the many potential problems which could occur. The silvery gray cubicles and metal desks arrived first, installed by contractors over a long weekend. We had a six -week window for changing the computers. My task was to identify the learning needs of every employee, work with the Ministry computer training division to set up specially-designed programs, and provide a detailed guide for everyone to follow with regard to getting rid of the old computers, software and manuals and the steps to follow for the installation of new computers. Focusing on one small segment at a time, a schedule was designed whereby each employee backed up their current files, stepped away from their old computer, attended a day-long computer training program and returned to their workstation and a new computer. Computer technicians were on stand-by to handle any glitches and problems. Even with all the anticipated problems the transition worked amazingly well. What a change! For the first time we were all working with the same computers and software and had generic working stations. In one step our working environment had immensely improved. Whether because of this or simply the luck of the draw, I next found myself managing a teleradiology project in the northwest of British Columbia.

The decision for a northwest teleradiology project was mainly political with no effort made to put the pilot project under the auspices of a university research mandate. Somehow it landed on my desk with a directive that I coordinate a group of Ministry staff to oversee the project.

Teleradiology had been in existence in Canada and globally for years prior to its arrival in British Columbia. The technology enables a high resolution diagnostic image (x-ray) to be sent to another health care facility with a radiologist for interpretation, and providing a more rapid turnaround report for the attending physician. It has various uses, from the transmission of digital images throughout a large hospital complex, to transmission between hospitals, communities and sometimes countries. The purpose of the northwest project, like similar projects, was to give individuals better access to radiologists hundreds of kilometers away, speed up diagnostic reports to physicians to aid treatment, and to save money by reducing patient travel time.

The one million dollar pilot project was designed to connect eleven communities; Queen Charlotte City, Masset, Stewart, Dease Lake, New Aiyansg, Hazelton, Houston, Prince Rupert, Kitimat, Smithers and Terrace. The teleradiology computer system created a virtual radiology department throughout the region. At the time this was one of the largest teleradiology trials in Canada, in the number of hospitals involved and the geographic area covered. The Northwest Region consisted of 253,394 square km (almost 100,000 square miles) with a population of about 83,000. The project started with two radiologists in the region. The radiology department at St. Paul's Hospital in Vancouver was identified as a 'second opinion' or back-up site for emergencies. By November 1996 all sites were operational as some required minimal construction changes to accommodate the equipment.

Needing expert mentoring for such a complex project, I called Dr. Max House in Newfoundland, considered the father of telemedicine in Canada (later to be named the Lieutenant Governor of the province of Newfoundland) who kindly agreed to be my guide. His initial advice was that teleradiology had been tested in other areas with sound evidence of its value. However, I would learn that the main implementation problem would have more to do with the radiologists concerned about their jobs, than the technology. He sent me the Canadian Association of Radiologists National Standards for Teleradiology as a further guide for discussions. Fortunately, I had Dr. House's mentorship, as the project faced problems right from the start. Working with a small Ministry group, we held regular conference calls with representatives in the northwest, from St. Paul's Hospital, and AGFA technical advisors in Montreal.

Technology problems arose due to the sheer size of the region, the remoteness of some communities, and the relative newness of the Ministry of Health, HealthNet, through which the images were to be transmitted. Once these were resolved we encountered a variety of other, sometimes entrenched, problems such as coordination, administrative and service quality issues among the hospitals, difficulties in getting data collected on time, and Radiologists and technicians complaining the system increased their workload. Computer capabilities of users had been miscalculated and were difficult to correct due to a resistance to training. Basically, it came down to a power issue, regional managers and Ministry staff had little authority in forcing radiologists to provide faster service to smaller communities on routine tests. In addition to all these management issues, ongoing health reform disrupted the process when the Community Health Councils were dissolved and a Northwest Regional Health Board created in the midst of the pilot-project schedule. The project also introduced another learning issue for newly- appointed Board members, as well as complex operational and ownership arguments. Holding the project on schedule became a logistical minefield which included a mandated evaluation nine months after its inception. The evaluation was done but the outcome was far from positive.

The evaluation showed a utilization rate of 1959 routine examinations, 46 emergency examinations, and 28 second opinion or consultation examinations. As expected, the system was more beneficial to the most remote communities. Hospitals with a resident or visiting radiologist tended to make minimal use of the technology. Family physicians stated they felt teleradiology improved access to radiological interpretation, especially for emergencies and orthopedic consultation. Reduced time in getting x-ray reports also assisted in treatment decision-making and helped reduce the length of stay for some patients. However, while 95% of emergency examinations were reported in two hours, only 48% of routine exams were reported within the established standard of two working days. Half of the general physicians stated the teleradiology system was subject to equipment failure even though few sites recorded excess down time. In the final analysis, the radiologists, as Dr. House predicted, controlled the project and the outcome. Instead of decreasing costs, diagnostic costs rose at a rate of $115 for every procedure with a 4.5% increase in radiology services. Little data was kept on saved travel time for patients. The outcome was disappointing but not entirely surprising. Yet, I was comforted in knowing a similar teleradiology study involving the Department of Health in Nova Scotia and Dalhousie University faculty had demonstrated that radiologists in a tertiary care centre could provide timely and accurate reporting of examinations from small rural hospitals at relatively low cost and patients were able to save the cost of travelling to regional centres for examinations.

Once the pilot project was completed the teleradiology equipment was signed over to the health region. With other regions wanting the service, we tried to relocate unused equipment for another test but to little avail. In the end, a valuable health service for the citizens of rural and remote communities stopped due to a series of unfortunate factors. Eventually, more of this technology will come to the province regardless of political or other barriers. It is already being implemented globally to enhance health services and there is no reason it cannot work in British Columbia. With this project completed, I moved to a different path.

It is interesting how an inconsequential event often signals something else. Early one morning, quietly reviewing my e-mail, a young woman arrived at my cubical with a rather interesting question; " I've been told you have been married for about twenty years and regularly attend church, is that correct?""Yes" I replied, raising my head to look into the face of a very young woman who was not from our division. I was trying to understand what her question had to do with anything in the Ministry. Perplexed, she stood silently looking at me as if, somehow, I was a foreign specimen under the microscope or perhaps someone out of time. Saying nothing further she walked away with a puzzled look on her face. For the first time in my life I felt old. I wanted to reach out to chat about her question but this was not to be. The encounter, however, was perhaps a bell-ringer to what came next.

A few days later a file arrived, the courier saying; "You have been asked to speak for the Assistant Deputy Ministry at this upcoming conference". There was no discussion on whether I even wanted the assignment. Curious, I wondered what could be so unpleasant that it bounced down the line from such giddy heights, past many capable people, to my cubicle. When I opened the file I discovered it was an invitation to be the opening speaker (the request to the Assistant Deputy Minister) at an upcoming conference on the spiritual care of patients. In a health industry with a political/corporate image to uphold, anything that squeaked of God or a higher spirit needed to be avoided. My obvious age, and eccentricity, made me the likely candidate for the mission. Sadly, in a materialistic world, unable to differentiate between spiritual and religion, such a request presented too many pitfalls for the ambitious. I was delighted and proceeded to compose a brief welcoming speech to the anticipated Canadian and United States delegates. As in all government jobs, the Assistant Deputy Ministry received a copy of my speech well in advance of the conference so he might suggest any changes. None were made.

While health professional training programs talk about the physical, mental and spiritual care of patients, the modern industry pretty well focuses on the physical with an occasional nod to the mental. Spiritual care has been delegated to families, chaplains or clergy, or a small band of health professionals who still believe healing involves a higher dimension. At the conference it was good to meet people who still retained a spiritual healing philosophy. My speech was well received. Later, there was some awkwardness when the American conference speaker sent a congratulatory letter to the Assistant Deputy Ministry on my speech. It likely solidified my oddness.

While physicians in United States were recommending spiritual intervention in patient care plans, and had research data to support the value of such healing, Canadian physicians were mainly silent on the topic. As another century awakened, such spiritual beliefs were being reexamined and supported by physicists who were dealing with energy forms in their ventures into the fine line between mind and spirit. Physicists were providing scientific evidence to support a new and futuristic healing path. Dr. Richard Gerber, the author of two exceptional books on vibrational medicine, presented a working model of this physical-etheric interface, describing the subtle energetic harmonics of the spiritual planes and the interacting multidimensional energy fields of the human organism [6]. Surprisingly, this shift to an Einsteinian, quantum mechanical holistic type of healing may bring us full circle to a form of healing that existed in other cultures and eras. It is/was practiced by some Ayurvedic physicians in India, Taoist healers, American Indian medicine men and women, and by the Essenes of the Middle East. Such views are helping us rediscover the soul of healing which has been smothered by the western political/materialistic health industrial complex. Welcoming this spiritual/ quantum physics approach, Bill and I took a course on Therapeutic Touch. Later we enhanced this training under the capable guidance of Sister Eileen Curteis, at the Queenswood Centre in Victoria, where we became Usui Reiki Masters and Karuna Reiki Masters, spending time helping her in Reiki healing sessions. Reiki healing has been welcomed into the Australia health system, providing care to palliative and cancer patients. As such thinking is accepted globally, Canada may eventually find a place for it in its own health system.

My seven years at the Ministry of Health were drawing to a close. In leaving in 1999, I would cherish the companionship of many of my journey partners, bonds forged under difficult circumstances. I certainly learned a great deal about the health industry of British Columbia and traveled many miles, knowledge which I would recycle for the next phase of my journey. As I stepped away from the Ministry of Health for, what I had imagined, would be my semi-retirement, days spent enjoying art and relaxation, life had a few more hurdles to cross.

—◈—

Our condo building on Quebec Street became one of the 'leaky condo' casualties of British Columbia. In the early days of condo living, I agreed to attend the regular strata meetings. Initially, I thought it prudent when the Strata Board decided to hire an engineer to assess our building in light of the circulating leaky condo rumors. Then I sat in disbelief as he reported that the entire envelope of the building would have to be redone due to mould buildup. The building was less than five years old. Our condo on the third flour of a four story, eighty unit, building was intact but, under strata rules, we were required to foot our portion of the $2.8 million repair bill.

The problem was one of climate and negligence. Federal and provincial government employees responsible for setting building standards had been asleep at their posts. One did not have to be a building engineer to realize the mild climate in the lower part of British Columbia differed greatly from the rest of Canada. That being the case, Canadian building standards were approved which solely addressed the cold regions of the country. Such standards did not allow buildings in the southern part of British Columbia to breathe and, as a result, there was mould built up. Buildings from the early eighties were affected, both residential and public. Soon blue and green building shrouds began to appear in many parts of Vancouver and Victoria.

As this devastating epidemic spread, retirees to British Columbia were faced with an economic disaster. Many faced $20,000 to $50,000 repair costs, lawyer fees, and further loss when they sold their condo. The stress, complicating existing medical problems, caused many to walk away leaving their condo keys with the bank before returning to their former province. Federal and provincial governments moved to distance themselves from any responsibility, even having a high profile provincial study to support their retreating position. Developers were long gone, silently lost in the west coast mist. Real estate agents, knowing there were questions on such properties, went scot free. For all the wailing about every other victimization, the media was conspicuously silent. Senior abuse might be a sensational topic but not this one. Condo owners were left holding the bag with few elected officials having the courage to speak for them.

Bill and I had to scramble as we did not have a huge financial cushion, life had never been that generous. We managed to find an estate sale, patio house up Island while we rented our condo, still a prime location within blocks of many provincial government offices. We packed and moved. By the time our belongings were deposited at our Cowichan Valley residence, Bill came down with Shingles. This was followed a few months later by a gastric hemorrhage. He stayed at home to recover.

When Bill felt better, he decided to return to the gym. Not wanting him to be alone, I went along. Up to this point I had dabbled in some physical exercise. As Bill's health steadily improved, I began using the treadmill and weights and found a steady reduction in joint pain. My physician was surprised at my improved health, and a bit skeptical when I attributed it to weight lifting. Feeling better, I did not hesitate in moving on to field sports, when Bill decided to advance his exercise program. Thus, in my late fifties, I found myself in such track and field sports as throwing a disc, javelin, shot and later a hammer. I was fitter in my late fifties than in my forties. We even competed in senior sports meets, not that I was much interested in competitive contests. I could almost hear by father laughing and saying; "Well, better late than never". Such improved physical health would help me weather not only the condo stress, but additional work and even further studies.

Bill's illness also changed our church affiliation. Not wanting to travel over the Malahat to Victoria, or even the short distance to Duncan, we began attending a small rural Anglican church minutes from our home. Life had enabled me to be a Roman Catholic, a Presbyterian and now an Anglican. Each Christian community offered its own programs and a lovely company of people who shared a common belief.

By the time the dust settled on the leaky condo mess we would lose nearly $100,000, a major financial hit. I sent out an immediate S.O.S. to old colleagues that I needed work. By 2000, I was back into consulting work, this time, for a short spell, with Bill, working with a much younger group of colleagues. The financial crisis forced us to simplify our lifestyle for a few years.

Old colleagues from the Ministry of Health had set up a private consulting firm called Global Tigers Systems Solutions (GTSS) with Robyn Kuropatwa and Paul Sekhon as the principal partners. I would work with this younger group of professionals for about six years. At its peak there were about twenty consultants, some former Ministry of Health employees. We were a mixed group of different ages, cultures, from different parts of Canada, different countries and backgrounds. Within the group there were those with a variety of statistical, administrative, financial and clinical skills, well-versed in the complexities of the health industry. I brought administrative, education and nursing skills to the table. Bill brought administrative, education, medical and Public Health credentials. The initial focus was to provide the newly-created health boards with statistical data for management decision-making. The need for such data was extensive; to know the population of the region requiring health services, the utilization of existing services, how to plan for future services, and how to more effectively argue the regional funding needs with the provincial government. Consultants lived in different locations; Victoria, Cobble Hill, Duncan, Comox, Vancouver, Edmonton and Ottawa. We worked in cyberspace from home computers, linked by the Internet, with weekly conference calls and a monthly face-to-face meeting. While we could set our own time schedule, for the next four years I worked on my computer from early morning until late into the evening, including weekends. These were much longer days than at the Ministry.

Over the years, in addition to tracking projects, I helped to design the company web site, create a statistical training manual for the Ministry of Health, design a computer training program, and prepare business and marketing plans. I became well versed in working with large computer documents and spreadsheets, bouncing substantial files over the Internet, and learning numbers of software programs. However, my abilities paled in comparison to my younger colleagues who were experts in computer technology. When the health authorities shifted from eighteen to six our market shrunk and GTSS moved out of the province pushing eastward in search of other contracts. In a short time the company had contracts in New Brunswick, Ontario, Alberta, and British Columbia plus the federal government.

Knowing the usual longevity of small consulting companies, after a few years I started to look for an additional challenge. By this time Bill and I had pulled ourselves out of the financial crisis and I was toying with the idea of doing my PhD, a dyslectic's Mount Everest. Months of Internet search had been disheartening as one PhD program after another, in the United Kingdom, United States, and Canada stipulated weeks of campus time, something I could not manage because I was still working. Stretching to the farthest spot on the globe, I landed in Perth, Australia, to be rewarded with a positive reply. Curtin University of Technology had a PhD Internet program with no campus requirement. I would be able to work part-time on my studies and part-time at my consulting work. The status of the university was checked with Bill's relatives in Australia, one nephew having been a chaplain there some years before. So, in 2003, my proposal on "Virtual Learning for Health Care Managers" was accepted. I flew to Toronto to attend The Association of Internet Researchers (AOIR) conference and to primarily meet my Curtin Supervisor, Dr. Matthew Allen, who was about Gregory's age. He would prove to be the best supervisor of any of my post-graduate studies. He was punctual with communications and provided invaluable advice and guidance in the next three years. We communicated mainly over the Internet. I would also have a local supervisor, Dr. Samuel Smith, an individual with invaluable distance education experience. My biggest challenge was trying to describe the complexity of the health industry to both supervisors who were not familiar with the topic.

At the completion of the Toronto conference, Bill and I took the opportunity to fly on to Britain for a two week holiday, the first in some years. The first week we stayed in Ayr at a Bed and Breakfast near Janie's home, as she was now ninety. Using Ayr as our base, we spent time with Janie, visited with an old school friend and a cousin of Bill's, and some friends of Janie's. It was great to see Janie again. Age had reduced her long flights to Canada, yet she definitely seemed capable of reaching a century. At ninety she was still driving her own car.

Next we flew to Ireland where Bill was determined I would get to know more about my ancestor, John Philpot Curran. Ireland was booming, the streets were bustling with young people. In Dublin, I stared into the face of my ancestor, a marble bust positioned high on one wall of St. Patrick's Cathedral. I concentrated on his nose, remembering my grandmother pulling at my nose as a child and referring to her own father's pug-nose. Then we travelled by bus to the Glasnevin Cemetery, where we found the grave of John Philpot Curran, a fifteen by six foot marble tomb with 'Curran' etched in large letters on one side. There were no Christian symbols, instead a row of different carved roses embellished two sides, eight feet or more above the ground. Silhouetted like a medieval sarcophagus, the tomb sat high in a place of honour. Considering the time, an immense amount of money had been spent to bring my ancestor's body back from London for internment in this magnificent memorial. It was inspiring. As I stood there I could feel my grandmother's presence and her words; "Now Child, you may understand your grandmother's tears and the family's loss when my father fled to North America. I might have been a fine lady if circumstances had been different, and you would have had a proper marriage dowry". But my journey into the past had more to come.

Later, having anchored ourselves in Cork, we travelled to New Market, the location of John Philpot Curran's residence in the 1700s. Directed to a local baker, the town historian, we made inquiries as to where the house once stood. He seemed reluctant to talk about my ancestor stating that most American visitors wanted to know about their Philpot relatives. When I pressed him further he replied coldly; " We had little to do with the Currans", the comment bouncing me back in time to events I was not party to. Eventually, with diplomatic probing from Bill, we received direction to a farm out of town where the Priory once stood. The site must have been lovely, but we had little time to muse as our presence disturbed a rather large bull which speeded our departure. Driving back through the town we discovered a somewhat neglected cemetery and Sarah Curran's gravesite, a daughter of John Philpot Curran. She is an Irish heroine, who died of a broken heart after her fiancé and illustrious Irish hero, Robert Emmett, was hanged by the British for his involvement in the Irish Cause.

Standing on Irish soil gave me an entirely different perspective of my Irish roots. One could feel the exuberance of a people finally emerging from centuries of British rule, proud of its historic inheritance and embracing the future. A visit to the Cork Gaol (jail) painted a gruesome picture of what might have awaited my great-grandfather if he had returned. He was exiled, his descendants having to make do without their illustrious family ties, an all-to-familiar tale for many political refugees.

On a healing note, I discovered John Philpot Curran and Sarah Creagh had been divorced in the latter part of the eighteenth century. I had not been the first female in the family to be divorced. Regardless of the circumstances, when I received my divorce my mother's reaction was; " You have disgraced the entire family with this divorce. It is far worse for a women than a man (my older brother had also been divorced)". This was a wound I carried for decades. In 2003, it was healed with my visit to Ireland. The trip had also replenished my soul with a deeper appreciation of my Irish roots. In addition, I was able to carry my grandmother's spirit back to Ireland, closing a circle. I headed home to start my PhD.

Over the years I kept returning to a familiar topic, health management education. During the health reform process I watched and listened as health managers were jerked about, particularly middle managers. Each reform step reshuffled management, jobs were lost and managers had to scramble to apply for fewer jobs. To keep abreast of the political and organizational changes managers faced numerous learning difficulties. Not only were they uncertain as to what to learn, the educational options often did not give them programs which understood their complex working environment nor the practical skills needed to improve their stressful conditions. The idea of leaving the industry for months or years to upgrade skills was unthinkable in an environment where their job might be eliminated while they were off studying. Tailored, convenient learning was hard to find. My question was whether it was time to consider virtual learning, after all many other organizations had chosen this route for their managers.

My research data was gathered through an Internet questionnaire working with the e-mail systems in the five regional health Boards. Privacy laws dictated a complicated process in which I had to send the questionnaire through a health authority representative. Detailed negotiations with the regional health authorities took some time. Then, in the spring of 2004, just as I was about to press the button to send out my questionnaire, the health industry had a provincial strike, reassigning most managers to frontline duties. When the strike was resolved after three weeks, I was left with a dilemma. Proceeding was fraught with complications. If I waited for the next window in the Fall, months away, I would likely have to renegotiate all the terms. Proceeding after the strike meant many weary managers would be returning to weeks of neglected e-mail, with little interest in a questionnaire. Nevertheless, after consultation with my regional colleagues I was advised to proceed. Under the circumstances, over five hundred managers replied, providing detailed comments on their working conditions and their learning problems. I had lots of data.

The working environment of many health care managers had changed a great deal in a decade with health reform. The following are a few of their comments on the topic. "The health care environment is in a state of change. Employers are demanding and unreasonable in their expectations of managers. There is a high burnout rate and no real recognition of the needs of managers." "Healthcare management has become tied up in red tape and meetings. We have meetings so that we can set a date for the next meeting and no one wants to make a decision on their own anymore. In the private sector, decisions get made and implemented in the same day. In healthcare it takes three months to do anything. We need to simplify the decision-making process and get on with the job." "The financial constraints are ongoing and more is expected as we try to do more with less. Some see no end in sight and even more cutbacks. There are some managers who are already looking for other options such as early retirement and getting out of the health industry." "Fewer clinical professionals are being promoted into management." and "I think that management positions are less desirable in health care due to many changes and challenges. Because of this managers are leaving and new, inexperienced people are being given these jobs without an adequate educational background" [7]. In addition, this complex working environment had a direct bearing on learning. Managers needed more practical, tailored, learning material provided in a convenient package. Instead, they were offered generic courses mainly in a classroom format. The data gave strength to my argument for a different learning strategy aided by technology.

Like most PhD processes, the university set strict guidelines in the writing of a thesis, criteria much like those found in the United Kingdom. Trying to explain the federal/provincial financial arrangements and health reform to someone in another country not familiar with a health industry, took many revisions. Thankfully, I had Bill's editorial skills to help me through the revisions and the mountain of words. It took well over a year of writing, and rewriting to complete the thesis. There were over thirty pages of references, as in the world of the Internet one is no longer held to one library. My agreement with the health authorities was to provide them with a report of my findings, which I did. I also presented my findings at a number of local health industry and university meetings and at an Association of Internet Researchers conference, this time in Chicago, adding additional comments to my findings.

Since I did not have to defend my thesis in person, the written word alone had to carry the review. Six international doctorate names were provided to the PhD Committee, two were selected, one Australian and one from North America. On the first round, the Australian reviewer, stressing the importance of the thesis topic, felt more data should be presented. In order to accomplish this revision, I worked with a statistical advisor at Curtin and an old GTSS colleague in Vancouver, receiving large electronic files, selecting the appropriate combinations of data and making sure the material jelled. In the end I had numerous Chi Square calculations of significance, the additional effort strengthening my thesis. During this revision period, I was supported with weekly long distance telephone calls with my Curtin Supervisor. The result was an increase in the size of my findings chapter, from thirty to ninety pages, which expanded the entire thesis. I was now ready for a second round of evaluation. Being so convinced another revision was inevitable, I sat in disbelief when the e-mail arrived that I had successfully passed. During this learning effort I never mentioned my dyslexia, although by 2003 the university was more receptive to students with learning problems. I had spent a lifetime wanting to be judged as normal, and saw no reason to change. Like the scarecrow in the Wizard of Oz, I kept trying to prove I had a brain. After years of stumbling over words, getting my PhD was an unfathomable joy. I finally reached the summit of my personal Mount Everest. [8]

I could have received my degree in the mail, but Bill felt such an accomplishment deserved a reward. So, in September of 2007, we flew to Australia, a country we had never seen. We visited Brisbane, Perth and Sydney. Then, on our thirty-first wedding anniversary, at the age of sixty-three, I received my PhD. Dressed in a maroon and black gown with a velvet, black mediaeval hat I attended a very lively graduation in Perth, Australia . There were seven PhD graduates sitting on the stage with the Curtin faculty. Each of us received a beautiful wood- framed degree with the gold logo of Curtin University of Technology. I received an extra handclap for coming such a distance for the ceremony. Next came the five hundred other degrees and diplomas distributed to a youthful parade of scholars, the next generation. While their lives stretched before them, mine was drawing to a close. It was with humility I realized that such an accomplishment is never achieved alone. There are numerous pre-stages and many kind people who guide you through the various levels of study, and one is always indebted to the gifts of past generations. I had been indeed blessed! As my fingers gently caressed the wooden edge of my degree I quietly prayed that my effort in this life would give '*honour to the past, honour to the future and honour to my journey*'. Following my graduation we spent time in Australia visiting with family and friends before flying home to Canada. Another phase of my journey was closing as another door opened.

THOUGHTS AND LEARNING

My father once said that in Canada you became an immigrant just moving from one province to another. It certainly applied when moving from one coast to another. I had to start over again, trying to get my credentials accepted and finding a job in middle age. It was a humbling experience. Nevertheless, I did get some contracts and eventually a government job. While my government experience was stressful, I learned a great deal about the health system in another province, travelled to many communities, and was party to a massive social experiment on regionalizing health care services. With limited research on the reform methods, it will be hard to quantify the effects of such change but many feel it was very costly and accomplished little except perhaps creating another layer of bureaucracy. A massive amount of energy was expended and many lives were disrupted. But such reform was not unique to British Columbia, most western nations, especially those with a publicly funded health system, had been experimenting with such change from the early eighties. While the idea of regionalization, as designed by British Columbia, was different, the outcome of such social experiments were similar. Whether intended or not, the reform process shifted the health industry from a social service to a corporation, with cost control its prime mandate. Contrary to Canada's stand, other countries eventually introduced a dual health system, one public and another private, running in tandem. Since no federal or provincial, politician or political party, has the courage to upset the health industry or its citizens by enforcing stronger accountability and utilization controls, or introduce a dual system, further change is inevitable. Health care will continue to absorb more and more of the provincial budget to the continued detriment of other services. Eventually the imbalance will affect our entire society. Before this stage, perhaps the industry will take a moment to reassess its leadership, and begin promoting individuals with a different vision, those capable of not only reducing the complexity of the industry but focusing more on improved and innovative service delivery.

It is interesting in life how one step builds on the next. By the time I left Prince Edward Island I had about seven years of computer experience, mainly in word documents. By the time I finished with the Ministry of Health in British Columbia I had learned a great deal more about computers and was working with a number of software programs, plus regular Internet use. With the private consulting company, I had the opportunity of working in cyberspace, sending large files over the Internet and working with more communication programs. So, by the time I decided to do my PhD I was well versed in various computer programs and not afraid of spreadsheets or handling large files and sending them over the Internet. Each learning stage had its role.

In my fifties and early sixties, as our family matured and established their own lives, life continued to present many learning opportunities, some more difficult than others. It took decades for me to fully understand my roots, to appreciate the struggles and gifts of my ancestors, and to comprehend my own journey, if it is ever fully understood. I had been blessed with seeing a great deal of North America even getting to Britain and Australia, meeting a wonderful variety of people and stretching myself with each learning opportunity. I grew to love such challenges, however humbling the first steps. As I enter my senior years I will search out new possibilities, as I want to maximize whatever gifts I have received. One lifetime is all too brief. However, at this point, I will close the written narrative of my journey, adding a few general comments in the next chapter.

CHAPTER 10

After Thoughts

Lᴵᴋᴇ many people, my life has consisted of circles and semi-circles, beginnings and end-ings, Biblical threes and sevens and many joys and sorrows. My journey has taken me from the Victorian era to the communication age, from the world of Anne of Green Gables to the cold realities of the twenty-first century. I've wandered across North America, with in-depth meanderings in several Canadian provinces and one American state, plus side trips to Britain and Australia, a very different journey than that of my grandmother or mother.

Having worked in the health industry for over forty years, I have witnessed many changes as I moved back and forth through various roles as registered nurse, teacher, administrator, consultant and civil servant, working in hospitals, government, professional associations and private industry. The health system in Canada has practically completed a full circle, going from private to public and now to public/private. Similar circles have also occurred with herbal remedies, and home deliveries. Health care in Canada has moved from being a privilege to a right, from personal responsibility to surrendering most of care to strangers. Hospitals, previously community structures where people went for minor ailments, emergencies or dying, have become regional, high-tech, all- encompassing health centres. Care has shifted from being an essential part of social services run by health professionals, to a corporation whose leaders now require financial and business skills. Over the decades health professionals moved from having a vocation to having a career. Sadly, as change was occurring on so many fronts, the two essential pillars of healing, love and trust, have been somewhat mangled in the process. Whether such change in the past decades has created chaos may be debatable and is likely dependent on where one happened to be standing, but, for some, it has certainly been a bewildering process.

Is there any chance such change might lead to greater creativity and empowerment in the health industry or has this costly restructuring just intensified an already rigid, bureau-cratic structure. While social scientists may regard health reform as progress, studies show that this expensive exercise has not reduced costs nor improved service, the supposed key objectives of the experiment. There are even those who argue the centralized, industrial health care system may have less to do with health, healing and service than an organiza-tion designed, not for patients, but for health professionals, government and corporations. Whatever the purpose, sickness today has become big business, the golden goose for some, and one of the most costly segments of government budgets. As health care demands more and more of the provincial budget, other services (i.e. education, social services, and municipalities) will continue to suffer. A society, no matter how wealthy, cannot sustain this kind of imbalance for long.

The constantly rising cost of health care, now in the billions, either indicates we are a very sick society, that government is not getting value for money or health has become just another consumer item which will never be satisfied. Unending health demands in the face of ever-tightening budgets have exhausted the spirit of many health workers leaving little energy to be compassionate or prevent people falling through the cracks. As services fail to meet expectations, trust is diminished. The fundamental question is whether current health leaders have the skills to reduce the complexity, increase compassion and trust, and introduce greater resiliency and personalized service.

Changing the health industry has never been easy. Its complexity and layers of power brokers make change difficult. The most recent crisis of health worker and management shortages due to the retirement of many Boomers, is a global issue, with the winning country being the one which is quick to adapt.

The health industry will need to open the doors to new workers (i.e. younger, foreign, different cultures, older individuals) and adopt faster methods of training. Old training ideas coupled with technology may become the norm and the industry may have to entice and hold workers with imaginative incentives as never before. The ranks within the industry may also have to be streamlined as it is plagued with too many titles and too many educational programs, each with entrance restrictions, a lack of fluidity in moving from one level to another and massive duplication.

In addition to the training of more health workers, the industry needs to establish a healing program for its caregivers. It is sad that an organization supposedly designed to care for the sick, pays so little attention to its own workers. Health workers need to be respected, honoured and cared for. In addition, the industry has practically no ability to capture the knowledge and skills of retiring workers, a major concern at this time. Mentoring programs are needed at all levels.

Currently, the delivery of health services remains locked in its traditional pattern of ambulances delivering patients to a central acute care facility with some community services provided once the individual has been discharged. Even with regionalization, it is amazing how many gaps still exist in the service. The idea of a one-stop health site for all services is still in its infancy, and working to establish a convenient transportation network for people getting to appointments, diagnostic tests, or pharmacies is practically non-existent. Back-up care on weekends is poor in many communities. Tailored and convenient services focused on the patient have yet to materialize, a lack of funds given as the prime excuse. The problem is that too much money has been allocated to the loudest demands or to glitzy, and costly, technology and surgeries, at the expense of more practical solutions.

History shows that no matter how sophisticated, a health system can crumble when a society comes under attack. While there are the usual external possibilities (i.e. war, natural disasters, epidemics), change can also come from a different understanding of illness and healing. What would happen if the ideas currently being voiced in quantum physics are true, and healing has more to do with energy balance than our current knowledge of illness would have us believe? As our understanding of life and healing changes, we may find ourselves returning to forgotten healing methods of our ancestors, supported by scientific evidence, theories which may shatter how we look at illness and the need for many aspects of our current health system.

On a personal basis, I believe that every person and event in one's life, positive and negative, has a part to play in the learning journey. My family members each played their part, some more than others, pushing me towards nursing, with a special interest in maternal and child care, mental health, teaching and management. My own experience and encounters with various types of managers stimulated me to find answers to organizational problems and how to educate the next generation of health care workers and leaders. The ending of my first marriage pushed me to seek jobs outside of hospitals, even to leaving my country. While I may not fully understand all the reasons, in viewing my life from my sixties, I understand and accept that everything had a purpose, including my difficulty with words and illness.

Dyslexia was a demanding companion. In a society that did not recognize such a disability it was frustrating and discouraging as a child and often humiliating as an adult. It was unruly when I was upset or ill, and created major stumbling blocks whenever I ventured into academia. Computers provided a valuable tool to help unscramble my thoughts. Yet, with all its problems it was also a gift. Since dyslexia is like working in a foreign language, my heart went out to immigrants, or those struggling with communication; the young, elderly, or confused. My need to organize information made me compulsive in finding innovative solutions in the storage and access of information, valuable skills for the communication age. Love of books, starting from childhood, never ceased. Like an athlete, I needed daily word exercises, for without this discipline my world easily slipped into confusion. For this reason, I spent a lifetime creating word challenges (reports, newsletters, academic studies etc). That way, my companion and I continued to grow with each step.

As the old doctor in Halifax stated, a long-term illness forces one to be disciplined. Lupus, equally demanding, forced me to rearrange my life on numerous occasions. A semi-vegetarian diet, plenty of rest, meditation, exercise, boosting my immune system, and disease prevention, all helped me to survive. By taking up weight training and track and field sports in my late fifties, my fitness improved, something I should have started years before. Since the mid-eighties I have used an electronic acupuncture device for pain which has greatly eliminated the need for most medications and requires little maintenance. Lupus gave me sensors to understand the limits of my physical energy. While I have given both problems due respect, I have mostly tried to ignore them, adjusting my life whenever problems arose and walking on.

In my earlier years I thought the reason I did not react to negative events was because I had difficulties translating words when upset. Perhaps that is so, but, lately in reading Kabbalah I learned that reaction to a situation, not the problem, is the real enemy to human growth. Yehunda Berg states; " When we allow outside forces to influence our feelings, positive or negative, we have surrendered control.........if you react, the situation controls you" [1]. Did I learn this non-reactive approach from one of my ancestors? Maybe. But perhaps I found the principles in my grandmother's wise council when she said; "Child, when things get bad, and they will, be quick to forgive, carry no baggage, and walk on. Time will help you understand the reasons for the storms in your life". Or my father's advice " Play the cards you are dealt. You will be judged on how you react". Whatever the reason, I know with dyslexia and Lupus, if I had spent time dwelling on the negatives, my immune system would have succumbed to some fatal illness. I may not have understood this as a child but it became indelibly etched in my thinking as I grew older. Survival is a great incentive. I was also strengthened by my spiritual beliefs which, while changing over the years, remained steadfast in my acceptance of a higher power.

My grandmother gave me a firm understanding of the need for a spiritual base to one's life and a healthy understanding of the fragile nature of religious organizations. Both my grandmother and father taught me respect for all people, and their right to worship in their own way. The rest of my family, in their own way, nurtured this thinking.

Irrespective of the many changes in my life, I remained a traditionalist, preferring a quiet order to life and seeking people who shared similar beliefs. In life I worshiped in various Christian churches, each providing a unique gift to my understanding of the divine. My views on religious institutions have changed over the years, with a gradual shift away from buildings to the sacred in the entire universe. I believe, the spark of the divine is in every living organism, with each individual having the right to honour that divine spark in his/her own way. While some people may need a building (church, synagogue, temple, mosque, or community building), others may find the divine in nature. For the sacred is not restricted to buildings or specific groups, however rigidly this idea has been ingrained in people over the centuries. As such, intolerance is an insult to the divine.

Over the centuries the human race has been plagued with religious intolerance. While people can wax eloquently on the magnificence of the diversity of nature, the uniqueness of each flower, animal or snowflake, there are still many who cannot conceive of the same wonder and diversity in people. At a time when mankind is starving for spiritual nourishment, it is heartbreaking to find religious leaders devoting so much time to non-spiritual topics. It is no wonder so many people have walked away from traditional religious institutions, shutting the door on all religions and anything spiritual. However, the rejection of traditional religions is not necessarily a rejection of the sacred. The current interest in the environment may signal a move to a natural path to the divine. If we can envision a future of tailored education and health care, why not a tailored spiritual path? Perhaps some day we may have the maturity to respect and learn from the spiritual diversity of mankind and allow each individual the right to choose a number of paths in their quest towards the sacred. My spiritual belief includes a believe in reincarnation, an idea dropped from Christianity in the third century.

Why would each human being have only one chance to reach perfection? Many people, ancient and current, believe that humans have a number of reincarnations (i.e. learning journeys) to reach their ultimate spiritual potential. Such a philosophy extends the life of our soul and no matter how difficult this life may be, it is preparing us for the next spiritual stage of our development. My belief in reincarnation was affirmed when I shared a dream with a North American Indian healer. In the dream I was soaring as an eagle through the Grand Canyon in Arizona. When summoned by an elder female, I landed and quickly changed into a young Indian woman.

In a world which measures lives on material wealth or power, my life will have limited value. However, if weighed on change, resiliency, and learning then it might have greater potential. Irrespective of external judges, I believe my life has been rich in variety and filled with some truly remarkable people. I am grateful for the guidance of so many and the continuous ability to grow. I'm especially grateful for my grandmother's wisdom which guided me through the years, and the pearl of wisdom which was contained in the small white pebble.

CHAPTER 11

Notes & References

Chapter 1: A Victorian Beginning

1. Bolger, Francis W.P. (1973). Canada's smallest island: A history of P.E.I.. John Deyell Company. Prince Edward Island. p.135
2. Ibid p.136.
3. Rogers, Irene L. (1983). Charlottetown: the life in its buildings. The Prince Edward Island Museum and Heritage Foundation. p.51
4. MacLysaght, Edward (1985). Irish families: their names, arms and origins. Irish Academic Press. P.68.
5. Ibid p.135-136.
6. Ibid p.69
7. Schultz, Lorine McGinnis. (n.d.) War of 1812. Retrieved Mar 18, 2001 from http://www.rootsweb.com/~canmil/1812/bios/laura.htm. p.1

Chapter 2: Early Challenges

1. Rogers, Irene L. (1983). Charlottetown: the life in its buildings. The Prince Edward Island Museum and Heritage Foundation. p.287-289

Chapter 3: Health Community Entrance

1. Electro-convulsive Therapy (ECT) was developed in 1938. ECT involves applying a brief electrical pulse (About 120 volts, the amount in ordinary house current)to the scalp while the patient is under anesthesia. This pulse excites the brain cells causing them to fire in unison and produces a seizure. A course of treatment usually lasts two to three weeks, with shocks given perhaps ten to fifteen times. Some doctors give several shocks at a time, one right after the other. Many patients have received over the years several courses of treatment. The use of ECT declined in the 1960s but was re-established in the 1970s. ECT is most commonly used to treat patients with severe depression who fail to respond to medications or who are unable to tolerate the side effects associated with psychiatric medications. ECT may also be the treatment of choice for patients who need a more rapid response than medications can provide. This would include those who are severely agitated, delusional, suicidal, not eating or drinking, as well as those who suffer

from catatonia (a potentially life threatening trance-like state). There remains concerns over whether mental patients are truly free to give their consent for such therapies, the long term damage, and ongoing questions of patient abuse.

Chapter 4: Beginnings and Endings

1. According to the Royal Bank, $12,000 in 1968 would be equivalent to about $40,000 in 2007.

Chapter 6: Sojourn in Arizona

1. Weir, Bill (1992). Arizona Traveler's Handbook. Moon Publications Inc. California p.260.
2. Ibid p.189.
3. Ibid p.200.
4. Linkert, M.E. & Leyel , Martha (1976). The Marcus Report. A Bicentennial Salute to Health Services in the Verde Valley. February . p. 2.
5. Ibid. p.2.
6. Ibid. p.4.
7. Weir, Bill (1992). Arizona Traveler's Handbook. Moon Publications Inc. California p.89.
8. (1979). MJL's addition honors Wilpitz. The Independent. Cottonwood, Arizona. p.15

Chapter 7: Ottawa Odyssey

1. Wallace, Daniel J.. (2005). The lupus book. Oxford University Press, Toronto. p.5.
2. Provost, Michael and Teskey, Julie. (2007) All about the city of Ottawa: the history of Canada's capital. Retrieved June 30, 2007 from http://www.teskey.com/ottawa/index. htm . p.1&2
3. Ibid. p.2.
4. Robertson, Mary E. (2006). Virtual learning for health care managers. Curtin University of Technology, Perth, Australia. P.14.
5. Francis, Daniel (2007). Mussallem, Helen Kathleen. Retrieved July 4, 2007 from http:// thecanadianencyclopedia.com/index.cfm?PgNm=TCE&Params=A1ARTA0005573. p.1
6. Mussallem, Helen K. (1977). (July 27, 1977 communication with Dr. Daniel LeTouze, School of Health Administration, University of Ottawa). Ottawa
7. Robertson, Mary E. (1978). Women in health administration: survey of the University of Ottawa MHA graduates. Ottawa University. Ottawa. P.69-74.

Chapter 8: Completing the Loop

1. Withrow, Alfreda (n.d.) Historical information on Bedford. Retrieved August 19, 2007 from http://www.destinationons.com/common/places.asp?PlaceID=1107 p.1.
2. (1979). Planning process for capital projects. Alberta Department of Hospital Services, Program Planning Branch, Edmonton. Pgs. 37-41.

3. (1981). Minister unveils conceptual design. Camp Hill Medical Centre News. 2(1):1-4. p.1.

4. (1982). The Nistonia Notebook. February. Hillsborough Hospital, Charlottetown p 3 & 4.

5. (1982). The Nistonia Notebook. April. Hillsborough Hospital, Charlottetown. p1.

6. (1982). The Nistonia Notebook. October. Hillsborough Hospital, Charlottetown. p 15.

7. Ibid p.3.

8. (1982). The Nistonia Notebook. February. Hillsborough Hospital, Charlottetown. p.2.

9. Bradley, Michael. (1988). Holy Grail Across the Atlantic. Hounslow Press, Toronto, Ontario. p.358

10. Palmer, Parker J. (1990). Leading From Within: Reflections on Spirituality and Leadership. Indiana Office for Campus Ministries, Indianapolis. p.5.

11. Schurman, Paul H. (1991). Eulogy to Angus "Gus" MacFarlane. Caliper. Sprint. p.1

Chapter 9

1. Robertson, Mary E. (2006). Virtual learning for health care managers. Curtin University of Technology, Perth, Australia p.34.

2. Ibid p 37, 38.

3. Barlett, Christopher A. & Ghoshal, Sumantra. (1990). Matrix management: not a structure, a frame of mind. Harvard Business Review. July-August p.138.

4. Ibid p 139.

5. Cole, Trevor. (1999). All the Rage. Globe & Mail. Toronto. 50-57. p.50.

6. Gerber, Richard. (1988) Vibrational medicine: new choices for healing ourselves. Bear and Company, New Mexico. P.27

7. Robertson, Mary E. (2006). Virtual learning for health care managers. Curtin University of Technology, Perth, Australia

8. Australia universities require their PhD graduates to list their thesis on the Internet so that other scholars can access this material. Thus, if someone should be interested in my thesis, all they have to do is write: Mary E. Robertson, Virtual Learning for Health Care Managers, and the thesis will appear.

Chapter 10

1. Berg, Yehunda. (2004). The power of Kabbalah: technology for the soul. The Kabbalah Centre, Los Angeles. p. 97 & 102

Printed in the United States
by Baker & Taylor Publisher Services